Legalines®

Editorial Advisors:
Gloria A. Aluise
Attorney at Law
Jonathan Neville
Attorney at Law
Robert A. Wyler
Attorney at Law

Authors:
Gloria A. Aluise
Attorney at Law
Daniel O. Bernstine
Attorney at Law
Roy L. Brooks
Professor of Law
Scott M. Burbank
C.P.A.
Charles N. Carnes
Professor of Law
Paul S. Dempsey
Professor of Law
Jerome A. Hoffman
Professor of Law
Mark R. Lee
Professor of Law
Jonathan Neville
Attorney at Law
Laurence C. Nolan
Professor of Law
Arpiar Saunders
Attorney at Law
Robert A. Wyler
Attorney at Law

CONSTITUTIONAL LAW

Adaptable to Sixteenth Edition* of Sullivan Casebook

By Jonathan Neville
Attorney at Law

*If your casebook is a newer edition, go to www.gilbertlaw.com to see if a supplement is available for this title.

THOMSON
WEST™

EDITORIAL OFFICE: 1 N. Dearborn Street, Suite 650, Chicago, IL 60602
REGIONAL OFFICES: Chicago, Dallas, Los Angeles, New York, Washington, D.C.

SERIES EDITOR
Linda C. Schneider, J.D.
Attorney at Law

PRODUCTION MANAGER
Elizabeth G. Duke

FIRST PRINTING—2008

SHORT SUMMARY OF CONTENTS

TABLE OF CONTENTS AND SHORT REVIEW OUTLINE

I. THE SUPREME COURT'S AUTHORITY AND ROLE

A. INTRODUCTION TO THE CONSTITUTION

1. **Basic Document.** The Constitution of the United States currently consists of seven Articles and 27 Amendments. It was created in response to the inadequacies of the Articles of Confederation and was ratified by the nine states necessary in 1788. The Constitution separates the powers of the national government into three branches: executive, legislative, and judicial. Each branch was intended to remain independent yet subject to restraint by the other branches through a system of checks and balances. The Constitution also establishes the federal/state framework of government. The study of constitutional law is essentially an examination of the sources of governmental power and the limitations imposed on its exercise. Through the system of judicial review, the United States Supreme Court has the final say in interpreting the Constitution; hence the heavy reliance on studying decisions of that Court.

2. **Significant Amendments.** The articles of the Constitution contain important protections of individual liberty, including the writ of habeas corpus, prohibition of ex post facto laws, and the Privileges and Immunities Clause. Two groups of amendments, however, provide the majority of the civil liberties enjoyed in the United States today.

   a. **The Bill of Rights.** Many of the states included a Bill of Rights in their constitutions, but none was included in the original Constitution. Adoption of the first 10 amendments, or Bill of Rights, was prompted largely by the concerns expressed during the state ratification conventions. These amendments did not affect state power; they were only limitations on the power of the federal government.

   b. **Civil War Amendments.** The conquest over slavery in the Civil War presented serious social problems. The Thirteenth Amendment, which was ratified in 1865, provided legal support to eradicate slavery, which had been recognized in the original Constitution. In 1866 Congress enacted the Civil Rights Act to prohibit racial discrimination practiced by the states. The President vetoed the Act on grounds that it was unconstitutional, and although Congress overrode the veto, the Fourteenth Amendment was proposed to overcome constitutional objections to the Civil Rights Act. It was ratified largely because Congress made ratification a condition for the rebel states to be represented in Congress. The Fifteenth Amendment prohibited denial of the right to vote for racial reasons.

B. JUDICIAL REVIEW

1. Legitimacy of Judicial Review.

a. **Introduction.** Although there was some debate at the Constitutional Convention about the role of the judiciary in reviewing legislative acts, nothing in the Constitution expressly gives the Supreme Court power to rule on the constitutionality of acts of Congress or state statutes, nor power to review decisions of state courts.

b. **National supremacy.** The division of power between the states and the federal government created the possibility of a conflict for supremacy between them. The Framers of the Constitution resolved the issue with the Supremacy Clause, Article VI, Section 2, which states:

> This Constitution, and the Laws of the United States which shall be made in Pursuance thereof; and all Treaties made, or which shall be made, under the Authority of the United States, shall be the supreme Law of the Land; and the Judges in every State shall be bound thereby, any Thing in the Constitution or Laws of any State to the Contrary notwithstanding.

c. **Judiciary.** Although there is no specific provision for judicial review, the Constitution creates an independent judiciary with power equal to the other two departments. Article III creates the Supreme Court and extends the judicial power to "all Cases, in Law and Equity, arising under this Constitution, the Laws of the United States, and Treaties made . . . under their authority." The judiciary was thus responsible to decide cases, using the Constitution as the supreme law.

d. **Review of acts of Congress--**

Marbury v. Madison, 5 U.S. (1 Cranch) 137 (1803).

Facts. Marbury (P) and others were appointed justices of the peace for the District of Columbia by President Adams and confirmed by the Senate on Adams's last day in office. Their formal commissions were signed but not delivered. Madison (D), as Secretary of State, was directed by the new President (Jefferson) to withhold P's commission. P brought a writ of mandamus directly to the Supreme Court under the Judiciary Act of 1789, which established United States courts and authorized the Supreme Court to issue writs of mandamus to public officers.

Issue. Is the Supreme Court empowered to review acts of Congress (in this case the Judiciary Act) and void those that it finds to be repugnant to the Constitution?

Held. Yes. P's action is discharged because the Court does not have original jurisdiction; the Judiciary Act is unconstitutional.

- The facts demonstrate a plain case for a mandamus action, and under the Judiciary Act this Court could so act.

- P claims that since the original grant of jurisdiction is general and the clause assigning original jurisdiction to the Supreme Court contains no negative or restrictive words, the legislature may assign original jurisdiction in addition to that specified in the Constitution. But P's contention would render the clause ineffectual, an inadmissible construction. The Judiciary Act's grant of unconstitutional jurisdiction is void.

- The grant of judicial power extends to all cases arising under the Constitution and laws of the United States, indicating that the courts must consider the Constitution. Since the Constitution is superior to any ordinary legislative act, it must govern a case to which both apply.

- The Supremacy Clause (Article VI, Section 2) declares that the Constitution and those acts of Congress ***made in pursuance thereof*** shall be the supreme law of the land. Thus, the Court must determine when such acts are actually made in pursuance of the Constitution.

Comment. This opinion has prompted an ongoing debate about whether the Supreme Court is the ultimate voice in constitutional interpretation for the entire government. The Federalist No. 78, written by Alexander Hamilton, argues that the judiciary is the least powerful of the branches in the sense that it controls neither public funds nor the military. The independence of the judiciary allows it to guard the Constitution and the rights of individuals from improper actions of the other branches. Decisions must be governed by the Constitution rather than by any contrary statute.

---

e. **Repercussions of constitutional interpretations.** Thomas Jefferson argued that each branch was responsible to determine for itself the constitutionality of its actions, and that the judges should not be the ultimate arbiters of all constitutional questions, although he recognized that the courts would face constitutional questions more often than the other branches. Abraham Lincoln acknowledged the authority of the courts to decide specific constitutional cases, but argued that such decisions should not constitute government policy. In more recent times, the Court has asserted a broad judicial review power, claiming the responsibility of being the ultimate interpreter of the Constitution. Once a law is declared unconstitutional, the courts simply decline to enforce it. This does not repeal the statute, however. If, as has happened in the past, the Court overrules a prior decision holding a law unconstitutional, then the law becomes valid again.

C. SUPREME COURT AUTHORITY TO REVIEW STATE COURT JUDGMENTS

1. Historical Approach.

a. **Background.** In the Judiciary Act of 1789, the First Congress created lower federal courts as permitted by the Constitution, but did not give them general jurisdiction in civil cases arising under federal law. The state courts were to exercise jurisdiction over such cases, and appellate review was intended to insure compliance with the Supremacy Clause of Article IV. The Supreme Court was authorized by Congress to hear three types of cases on appeal, all of which were to be cases in which state courts rejected claims made under federal law. If a state court upheld such claims, the decision could not be reviewed.

b. **Constitutionality of the Judiciary Act--**

Martin v. Hunter's Lessee, 14 U.S. (1 Wheat.) 304 (1816).

Facts. Martin (D) was heir to the Virginia estates of Lord Fairfax, who died in England in 1781. Virginia claimed title to the estates in 1777 through state legislation confiscating the property of British loyalists; it had conveyed title to Hunter. Hunter's lessee (P) brought an action of ejectment. D defended his title by virtue of two United States-British treaties protecting such British-owned property. The Virginia Court of Appeals sustained P's claim but was reversed by the United States Supreme Court. The Virginia court refused to comply with the reversal, and D again appealed.

Issue. Does the Supreme Court have appellate jurisdiction over the highest state courts on issues involving the federal Constitution, laws, and treaties?

Held. Yes. The Virginia court must obey the United States Supreme Court's rulings.

- The Judiciary Act of 1789, section 25, provided for review by the United States Supreme Court of final state court decisions rejecting claims under the federal Constitution and laws. The outcome of this case depends on the constitutionality of that section.

- Appellate jurisdiction is given by the Constitution to the Supreme Court in all cases where it does not have original jurisdiction, subject to congressional regulations.

- All cases involving the Constitution, laws, and treaties of the United States are included in the judicial power granted by the Constitution to the Supreme Court; hence, all such cases are properly subject to that Court's appellate jurisdiction, and section 25 of the Judiciary Act is valid.

- ♦ Such power is necessary for a uniformity of decisions throughout the whole United States, upon all subjects within the purview of the Constitution.

---

c. **Review of state criminal cases.** In *Cohens v. Virginia*, 19 U.S. (6 Wheat.) 264 (1821), a case involving the illegal sale in Virginia of congressionally authorized D.C. lottery tickets, the Court extended the *Martin* decision to permit United States Supreme Court review of state court criminal judgments. The judicial power extends "to all cases arising under the Constitution or a law of the United States, whoever may be the parties."

2. **Modern Approach.**

a. **Review of state court decisions.** Final judgments or decrees of the highest state court may be reviewed by the Supreme Court by writ of certiorari when (i) the validity of a federal treaty or statute is drawn into question, (ii) the validity of a state statute is drawn into question on the ground of it being repugnant to the Constitution, treaties, or laws of the United States, or (iii) any title, right, privilege, or immunity is specially set up or claimed under the Constitution, treaties, statutes, or commission or authority of the United States. [28 U.S.C. §1257]

b. **Adequate and independent state ground.**

1) **Basic principle.** State courts alone determine state law. The Supreme Court's only power over state judgments is to correct them to the extent that they incorrectly adjudge federal rights. Review is limited to federal issues. If there is an adequate and independent state ground for the state court's decision, the Court will deny review, because a reversal on federal grounds would not change the outcome and would hence be an advisory opinion. Unfortunately, it is not always possible to tell from the state court opinions whether there was an adequate and independent state ground.

2) **Rule for judging existence of adequate and independent state ground.** Until 1983, a brief statement that a state court decision rested on the state constitution made the case immune to federal review, even though the case was essentially decided under the federal Constitution. In response, the Court expanded guidelines for determining reviewability of state decisions. In *Michigan v. Long*, 463 U.S. 1032 (1983), the state court had held that the defendant's search and seizure rights had been violated, essentially based on Fourth Amendment principles, twice mentioning similar state constitutional guarantees, and concluding the opin-

ion with a statement that the ruling rested on both constitutions. The *Long* Court announced a new approach for determination of the existence of adequate and independent state grounds: "If the state court decision indicates clearly and expressly that it is alternatively based on bona fide separate, adequate, and independent grounds," then it is not subject to federal review.

c. **Cases originating in federal district courts.** District court decisions are reviewed by the United States courts of appeals. Supreme Court review of decisions of the courts of appeals is generally discretionary by certiorari or by certification of questions of law. [28 U.S.C. §1254]

d. **Supreme Court practice.** Petitions for certiorari are granted only if at least four Justices vote to do so. Denial of a petition for certiorari is not a ruling on the merits.

e. **Effect of Supreme Court judgments.** When the Supreme Court reverses a state court judgment, it normally remands for "proceedings not inconsistent with this opinion." This allows the state court to review previously undecided issues and reconsider its decisions on matters of state law.

D. JUDICIAL EXCLUSIVITY IN CONSTITUTIONAL INTERPRETATION

1. State Authorities Bound by Supreme Court--

Cooper v. Aaron, 358 U.S. 1 (1958).

Facts. In *Brown v. Board of Education (Brown I)*, *infra*, the Court held that the Fourteenth Amendment prohibited the notion of "separate but equal" in public schools, so that no schools in the nation could be segregated by race. The governor of Arkansas ignored the holding of *Brown* and prevented desegregation in the public schools. One school board's integration plan was suspended by the district court. The Supreme Court granted certiorari.

Issue. Are state authorities bound by the United States Supreme Court's interpretation of the federal Constitution?

Held. Yes. Judgment reversed.

- The Constitution is the supreme law of the land. The judicial department of government has the duty to declare what that law is. Ever since *Marbury v. Madison*, *supra*, the nation has respected the principle of judicial review. Hence, this Court's interpretation of the Fourteenth Amendment is the supreme law of the land. All state officials are bound by oath to support the Constitution.

Comment. To emphasize how strongly the Court felt about this case, all nine of the Justices signed the opinion.

---

2. **Congressional Control Over Jurisdiction of Federal Courts.**

   a. **Introduction.** Under Article III, Section 2, Clause 2, Congress has the power to regulate and limit the appellate jurisdiction of the Supreme Court at any time and at any stage of proceedings. Congress may withdraw particular classes of cases from the Court's appellate review.

   b. **Limits on Congress's authority.** There are two basic theoretical limits on congressional authority over the Court's jurisdiction. First, Congress should not be able to interfere with the essential role of the Court in the constitutional scheme. This would include interference with the Court's independence, as by altering appellate jurisdiction in response to specific Court opinions. Second, Congress should not curtail jurisdiction in a manner that impairs the rights of litigants; *i.e.*, limits on jurisdiction should not violate litigants' due process and equal protection rights.

   c. **Modern attempts to limit the Court's jurisdiction.** In modern times, legislation to limit the Court's jurisdiction has been introduced in response to particularly controversial decisions, *e.g.*, the *Miranda* decision, busing decisions, school prayer decisions, and abortion decisions. To date, these proposals have not succeeded. (Many of these proposals are directed at the lower federal courts as well.)

   d. **Limitation on successive habeus corpus petitions.** In *Felker v. Turpin*, 518 U.S. 651 (1996), the Court considered whether Congress unconstitutionally limited the Court's appellate jurisdiction by enacting legislation that curtailed state prisoners' successive applications for federal habeus corpus relief. The Act precluded Supreme Court review of courts of appeals' decisions granting or denying the right to file a second or successive petition. Since a petitioner could still file an "original" petition (one that is filed for the first time in the Supreme Court), Congress has not deprived the Court of appellate jurisdiction under Article III, Section 2. For constitutional purposes, consideration of these "original" petitions involves exercise of the Court's appellate jurisdiction.

   e. **Original jurisdiction.** Although Congress cannot alter the Court's original jurisdiction, it has restated its scope in 28 U.S.C. section 1251 as follows:

      1) Original and ***exclusive*** jurisdiction of all controversies between two or more states.

2) Original but ***not exclusive*** jurisdiction of:

a) All actions or proceedings to which ambassadors, other public ministers, consuls, or vice consuls of foreign states are parties;

b) All controversies between the United States and a state; and

c) All actions or proceedings by a state against citizens of another state or against aliens.

E. CONSTITUTIONAL AND PRUDENTIAL LIMITS ON CONSTITUTIONAL ADJUDICATION: THE "CASE OR CONTROVERSY" REQUIREMENTS

1. Advisory Opinions.

a. **Introduction.** In addition to the congressional power over Supreme Court jurisdiction, the Court has itself imposed certain limits on the exercise of federal jurisdiction to avoid nonessential interpretation of the Constitution.

1) **Cases and controversies.** Article III, Section 2 limits the jurisdiction of all federal courts to "cases and controversies," requiring federal courts to deal only with real and substantial disputes that affect the legal rights and obligations of parties having adverse interests, and that allow specific relief through a conclusive judicial decree.

2) **Justiciability.** Justiciability is the term of art expressing this limitation placed on federal courts by the case and controversy doctrine. Justiciability is a highly flexible concept, construed narrowly by activist courts, broadly by more conservative courts. The limits of justiciability also preclude rendering advisory opinions (opinions based on assumed or hypothetical facts that are not part of an existing, actual controversy), deciding moot cases (ones already decided) or collusive or friendly suits, or adjudicating purely political questions.

3) **Common scenarios.** Problems of case and controversy and justiciability arise most frequently when a plaintiff seeks an injunction or a declaratory judgment as to the constitutionality of a statute.

b. **Strict necessity.** From its earliest days, the Court has followed a policy of "strict necessity" in disposing of constitutional issues, and has developed certain rules under which it has avoided a decision on many constitutional questions presented to it. These rules go beyond mere jurisdictional requirements. They are intended to preserve the unique judicial function in a constitutional government. In *Rescue Army v. Municipal Court*, 331 U.S. 549 (1947), the Court noted that while the strict necessity rules may delay vindication of rights, the relatively abstract decisions resulting from an alternative policy of accelerated decision would render rights "uncertain and insecure." Even when the Court has jurisdiction, constitutional cases affecting legislation will not be determined:

1) In friendly, nonadversary proceedings;

2) In advance of the necessity of deciding them;

3) In broader terms than are required by the precise facts to which the ruling is to be applied;

4) If the record presents some other ground upon which the case may be disposed of; and

5) At the instance of one who fails to show that he is injured by the statute's operation, or who has availed himself of its benefits.

2. Standing.

a. Introduction. The Supreme Court articulated the standing requirement in constitutional cases as follows: the plaintiff must have alleged such a personal stake in the outcome of the controversy as to assure that concrete adverseness which sharpens the presentation of issues upon which the court so largely depends for illumination of difficult constitutional issues. The personal stake must be a distinct and palpable injury that has a causal connection with the challenged conduct. Standing cannot be predicated upon an injury common to all members of the public. This protects against the courts becoming general policymakers.

b. Public interest not enough--

Lujan v. Defenders of Wildlife, 504 U.S. 555 (1992).

Facts. Section 7(a)(2) of the Endangered Species Act ("ESA") requires federal agencies to insure, in consultation with the Secretary of the Interior, that any action carried out by such agency is not likely to jeopardize the continued existence of any endangered or threatened species. The Fish and Wildlife Service and National Marine Fisheries Service promulgated a joint regulation stating that section 7(a)(2) extended to actions taken in foreign nations, but the regulation was later modified to require consultations only for actions taken in the United States or on the high seas. The ESA also provided that "any person may commence a civil suit on his behalf" to enjoin a government agency who is alleged to be in violation of the Act. The Defenders of Wildlife (P) brought suit against Lujan (D), the Secretary of the Interior, seeking a declaratory judgment that the more recent regulation incorrectly interpreted the ESA. Both parties moved for summary judgment. The district court granted P's motion. The court of appeals affirmed. The Supreme Court granted certiorari.

Issue. May Congress convert the public interest in proper administration of the laws into an individual right such that all citizens may have standing to sue?

Held. No. Judgment reversed.

- A plaintiff must meet three standing requirements: (i) the plaintiff must have suffered an "injury in fact"; (ii) there must be a "causal connection between the injury and the conduct complained of"; and (iii) "it must be 'likely,' as opposed to merely 'speculative,' and the injury will be 'redressed by a favorable decision.'"

- Neither P nor any of its members had any injury in fact (nor was redressability demonstrated, since the funding agencies were not parties to the suit). P's standing, if any, depends on the validity of the "citizen-suit" provision of the ESA. The court of appeals held that this provision created a "procedural right" to interagency consultation in all persons, so that anyone can file suit to challenge D's failure to follow the allegedly correct consultative procedure, even if there is no discrete injury resulting from that failure. In effect, the court held that the injury-in-fact requirement under Article III has been satisfied by congressional conferral upon all persons of an abstract, self-contained "right" to have the executive branch observe the procedures required by law.

- Article III confers jurisdiction on the federal courts only where there is a case or controversy. This requirement is not met by a plaintiff raising only a generally available grievance about government, where the harm is only to the interest of all citizens in proper application of the Constitution and laws. Hence, a taxpayer does not have standing to challenge alleged violations of the Constitution by the executive or legislative branches where the violations would adversely affect only the generalized interest of all citizens in constitutional governance. The federal courts may only decide on the rights of individuals. Vindicating the public interest is the function of Congress and the President.

- If Congress could convert the undifferentiated public interest in an executive that complies with the law into an "individual right" to be vindicated in the courts, Congress could transfer from the President to the courts the Chief Executive's most important constitutional duty, to "take Care that the Laws be faithfully executed."

- The fact that Congress may not eliminate the requirement of a concrete personal injury does not preclude Congress from creating legal rights, the invasion of which creates standing.

Concurrence (Kennedy, Souter, JJ.). Congress may define injuries and articulate chains of causation that give rise to a case or controversy where none existed before, but at a minimum, Congress must identify the injury it seeks to vindicate and relate the injury to the class of persons entitled to bring suit. The citizen-suit provisions of the ESA do not establish that there is an injury to any person by virtue of any violation. The case and controversy requirement assures both that the parties have an actual stake in the outcome and that the legal questions presented will be resolved in a concrete factual context conducive to a realistic appreciation of the consequences of judicial action. The public is entitled to know what persons invoke the judicial power, their reasons, and whether their claims are vindicated or denied.

Concurrence (Stevens, J.). P does not lack standing or redressability, but Congress did not intend section 7(a)(2) to apply to activities in foreign countries.

Dissent (Blackmun, O'Connor, JJ.). Congress granted considerable discretion to the executive branch to determine how best to attain the goals of the ESA, constrained by specific procedural requirements. This does not constitute a violation of the separation of powers. Nor should the separation of powers be deemed violated when Congress requires the federal courts to enforce the procedures. The citizen-suit provisions of the ESA were based on the same understanding that arose from earlier cases in which the Court justified a relaxed review of congressional delegation to the executive branch because Congress provided for judicial review of the exercise of that power. [*See* Immigration and Naturalization Service v. Chadha, 462 U.S. 919 (1983)]

---

c. State with special interest having standing--

Massachusetts v. Environmental Protection Agency, 127 S. Ct. 1438 (2007).

Facts. Respected scientists believe there is a relationship between the rise in global temperatures and an increase in the concentration of atmospheric carbon dioxide—the greenhouse effect. The Environmental Protection Agency (D) determined that it lacked authority to regulate greenhouse gases. A group of states (including Massachusetts), local governments, and private organizations (Ps) petitioned D to begin regulating greenhouse gas emissions. D declined. Ps sought review, alleging that D abdicated its responsibility under the Clean Air Act to regulate greenhouse gas emissions. The court of appeals upheld D's position. The Supreme Court granted certiorari.

Issue. Does a state have standing to contest the regulations of a federal agency?

Held. Yes. Judgment reversed.

- This issue is not a political question, Ps have not asked for an advisory opinion, and the questions are not moot. Ps' dispute is based on the construction of a congressional statute and is properly addressed by the federal courts. Congress specifically authorized this type of challenge to EPA actions.

- D claims that because greenhouse gas emissions inflict widespread harm, the doctrine of standing presents an insuperable jurisdictional obstacle to Ps' claims. When Congress creates a procedural right, such as the right to challenge agency action unlawfully withheld, a litigant can assert the right without meeting all of the normal standing requirements. Pursuant to this procedural right, Ps have standing once they show some possibility that the requested relief will prompt D to reconsider the decision that allegedly harmed Ps.

- Massachusetts has a special position and interest because rising sea levels have already begun to swallow Massachusetts's coastal land. D does not dispute the existence of a causal connection between global warming and man-made greenhouse gas emissions. Thus D's refusal to regulate such emissions contributes to Ps' injuries.

- D claims that there is no realistic possibility that the relief Ps seek would mitigate global climate change, especially since the increase in greenhouse gas emissions from other countries is likely to offset any marginal domestic decrease. But a federal agency's refusal to take an incremental step may be challenged. Reducing emissions from automobiles would be a significant first step. Even if reducing automobile emissions will not reverse global warming, D may be required under the Act to take steps to slow its pace.

- Although the risk of catastrophic harm to Massachusetts from rising sea levels is remote, it is real. The risk would be reduced to some extent if Ps receive their requested relief. Thus, Ps have standing to challenge D's denial of Ps' petition.

Dissent (Roberts, C.J., Scalia, Thomas, Alito, JJ.). The redress of grievances such as Ps' is a function of Congress and the Chief Executive, not the federal courts. To have standing, P must allege an injury that is fairly traceable to D's failure to regulate greenhouse gases. But Ps did not satisfy the basic standing requirements of an injury in fact, causation, and redressability. The redress that Ps seek is global, not specific to Ps. The harm to Massachusetts from rising sea levels is pure conjecture. The connection between automobile emissions in new cars in the United States and the loss of Massachusetts coastland is far too speculative to establish causation. Even if D grants Ps' request, Ps cannot show that it would make any difference, apart from their conclusory declaration that steps taken by the United States could possibly influence other nations to take similar actions.

---

d. **Causation.** The Court denied standing to parents of black public school students in *Allen v. Wright*, 468 U.S. 737 (1984), because of their failure to prove causation. The plaintiffs, whose children attended school in districts that were being desegregated, challenged the failure of the IRS to adopt sufficient standards and procedures to deny tax-exempt status to racially discriminatory private schools in those school districts.

The Court rejected the plaintiffs' injury claim, that as blacks they were stigmatized by the exemption, on the ground that Article III separation of powers prevented courts from enforcing generalized claims that the government act in a certain manner. Finding the plaintiffs' second claim for the diminution of their children's ability to receive an education in a racially integrated background insufficient, the Court stated that the injury was not traceable to the allegedly unlawful governmental conduct, because the plaintiffs did not allege that the withdrawal of the exemption would affect public school integration. The dissent argued that the Court was using the standing determination to review the merits of the action.

e. **Third-party standing.**

1) **Basic rule.** Normally a person does not have standing to assert the rights of third parties who are injured by an allegedly unconstitutional act. There are two reasons for this rule:

a) **Need.** Courts should not adjudicate constitutional rights unnecessarily, and a third party may not want to assert his own rights or may not be able to enjoy them regardless of the outcome of the suit.

b) **Advocacy.** The third parties themselves are usually the best advocates of their own rights and normally would prefer direct involvement because of stare decisis.

2) **Exception.** Third-party standing may be permitted when the plaintiff has himself suffered injury and the third persons in question would find it difficult or impossible to vindicate their own rights, or when the plaintiff's injury adversely affects his relationship with the third parties.

f. **Congressional power to confer standing.** The Court has approved of a statutory trend to permit challenges to federal action (effectively granting standing) on the basis of other than economic harm. However, the requirement of personal injury must still be met. A wide variety of injuries might justify standing under certain federal statutes.

3. **Timing of Adjudication.**

a. **Mootness.** The usual rule in federal cases is that an actual controversy must exist at all stages of appellate or certiorari review, and not simply at the date the action is initiated.

1) **Capable of repetition.** However, issues involving events of short duration (pregnancy, elections, economic strikes) are not neces-

sarily moot if the issues are "capable of repetition, yet evading review."

2) **Criminal cases.** A criminal case is not moot, even though the defendant has served his sentence or paid his fine, if there are any collateral consequences of the conviction, *e.g.*, loss of civil rights or damage to reputation.

b. **Ripeness.** The timing of adjudication is critical; the Court will decide only those issues that are "ripe" for adjudication. It will not anticipate a question of constitutional law prior to the necessity of deciding it or pass upon issues that may or may not arise sometime in the future. These problems generally arise in suits for injunctions and declaratory judgments.

why advisory opinions are not allowed

4. **Political Questions.**

a. **Constitutional decisionmaking by other branches.** The requirement of a justiciable Article III controversy is deemed to carry with it a limitation against the deciding of purely "political questions."

1) **General guidelines.** The Court will leave the resolution of such political questions to the other departments of government. In determining whether there is a political question, the primary criteria are:

a) A "textually demonstrable" constitutional commitment of the issue to the political branches for resolution;

b) The appropriateness of attributing finality to the action of the political branches;

c) The lack of adequate standards for judicial resolution of the issue; and

d) Avoidance of issues that are too controversial or could involve enforcement problems.

b. **Legislative districting.**

1) **Federal review of state apportionment.** In early decisions, the Supreme Court consistently refused to review questions arising from a state's distribution of electoral strength among its political or geographical subdivisions. In *Baker v. Carr*, *infra*, the Court decided that federal courts had jurisdiction over challenges to apportionment plans. The modern approach to ***federal*** elections requires that representation must reflect the total population as

precisely as possible. More flexibility is permitted in apportionment of state legislatures, but grossly disproportionate districts are not allowed. State apportionment may not be used to further discrimination, but numerical deviations resulting from political considerations may be allowed.

2) **Justiciability of apportionment challenges--**

Baker v. Carr, 369 U.S. 186 (1962).

Facts. The state of Tennessee continued to base the apportionment of voting districts on the 1901 census. In the intervening years, the population had grown at different rates in different voting districts. Baker (P) sought to force reapportionment through the courts because the unequal representation was unconstitutional and because the legislature in its present composition would not pass a state constitutional amendment. The lower federal courts denied relief on grounds of nonjusticiability; P appeals.

Issue. Do federal courts possess jurisdiction over a constitutional challenge to a legislative apportionment?

Held. Yes. Judgment reversed and case remanded.

- The mere fact that a plaintiff seeks protection of a political right does not mean a political question is presented. The relationship between the judiciary and the coordinate branches of the federal government gives rise to political questions, not the federal judiciary's relationship to the states. This case involves none of the types of problems normally identified as involving political questions.
- The issue here is whether the state's activity is consistent with the federal Constitution. Case remanded for consideration of that issue.

Dissent (Frankfurter, Harlan, JJ.). The Court improperly hears a hypothetical claim based on abstract assumptions. The Court now permits federal courts to devise what they feel to be the proper composition of state legislatures.

---

c. **Congressional activity.** Since the *Baker* decision, most arguments for nonjusticiability based on the political question concept have failed. In *Powell v. McCormack,* 395 U.S. 486 (1969), the Court considered Adam Clayton Powell Jr.'s challenge to the House of Representatives' refusal to seat him after his valid election, because of a House committee's finding that he had wrongfully diverted House funds and made false reports. The Court rejected Speaker McCormack's claim that there existed a textually demonstrable commitment of determining the qualifications of its members to the House and further, that judicial resolution would result in a "potentially embarrassing confrontation between coordinate branches." In finding that Powell had been wrongfully excluded, the Court noted that the Constitution did grant Congress power to judge its members' qualifications. However, as the "ultimate interpreter of the Constitution," the Court is responsible for determining the scope of that power and concluded that Congress could judge only the qualifications set forth in Article I, Section 2, *i.e.*, age, citizenship, and residence, which Powell had met.

d. **Foreign affairs.** The President has special powers in foreign affairs due to the need for decisive action and a uniform policy with regard to sensitive foreign relations. Congress, however, retains certain powers over foreign affairs, including the power to declare war, appropriate funds, and ratify treaties. The Court set aside lower court decisions on the merits of this issue, holding that the issue was political and should be resolved by the executive and legislative branches.

e. **Justiciability of challenges to impeachment actions.** In *Nixon v. United States,* 506 U.S. 224 (1993), Walter Nixon, a former federal district court judge, was convicted of making false statements before a federal grand jury. He was sentenced to prison, and the United States House of Representatives adopted articles of impeachment and presented them to the Senate. The Senate appointed a committee to hold evidentiary hearings. The committee made a report to the full Senate, which then convicted Nixon on the impeachment articles and removed him from his office. Nixon sued, claiming that the Senate's failure to participate in the evidentiary hearings as a full body violated the Senate's constitutional authority to "try" impeachments. The lower courts held that Nixon's claim was nonjusticiable. The Supreme Court affirmed, holding that the Senate had exclusive authority to try impeachments, the courts had no final reviewing authority, and thus the claim was nonjusticiable. The Court explained that judicial review of the Senate's trying of impeachment would be inconsistent with the system of checks and balances; impeachment is the only check on the judicial branch by the legislature, and it would be inconsistent to give the judicial branch final reviewing authority over the legislature's use of the impeachment process. The Court stated that the need for finality and the difficulty of fashioning relief also demonstrate why judicial review is inappropriate in this case. The Court found that the use of the word "try" does not require a judicial trial; it is not an implied limitation on the Senate's method of trying impeachments.

II. THE NATION AND THE STATES IN THE FEDERAL SYSTEM

A. NATIONAL POWERS AND LOCAL ACTIVITIES

The Constitution grants specific powers to the federal government; the remaining powers are retained by the states. Furthermore, the powers given to the federal government are diffused among three branches: the executive, the legislative, and the judicial. The major issue in this area concerns whether federalism is any longer meaningful; *i.e.*, are there really any limits on the power of the federal government vis-a-vis the states? Are there really limitations on executive power vis-a-vis the legislature? Are these limitations meaningful and valuable in our current context?

1. **The Powers of Congress: The Scope of Granted Powers.**

   a. **Introduction—the legislative power.** Article I, Section 1 lodges all legislative power in Congress. This is the power to make laws and to do all things that are necessary to enact them (such as to conduct investigations and hold hearings, etc.).

   b. **Delegated powers.** The powers of Congress are specifically enumerated. In other words, the federal government is one of delegated powers only, and every federal statute, therefore, must have as its basis one of these enumerated powers.

      1) Article I, Section 8 sets forth many of the powers of Congress, such as the power to lay and collect taxes, to regulate interstate and foreign commerce, to declare war, etc.

      2) In addition, certain other provisions of the Constitution and the amendments thereto grant powers to Congress. For example, see the Fourteenth Amendment (guaranteeing due process and equal protection of the law).

2. **The Necessary and Proper Clause.** The specific powers of Congress may be enlarged by the Necessary and Proper Clause.

   a. **The deciding case--**

McCulloch v. Maryland, 17 U.S. (4 Wheat.) 316 (1819).

Facts. Maryland (P) sought to enforce one of its statutes, which imposed a tax on banks operating within the state but not chartered by the state, against the Bank of the

United States and McCulloch (D), its cashier in Baltimore. The statute in question was similar to others passed in other states during a period of strong state sentiment against the Bank of the United States; the statutes were aimed at excluding the Bank of the United States from operating branches within those states. D had refused to pay the tax. Penalties imposed on D for refusal to pay were affirmed by the Maryland Court of Appeals. D now appeals.

Issues.

(i) Even though the Constitution does not expressly grant Congress the power to incorporate a bank, can it do so under a doctrine of implied powers?

(ii) Is the federal government supreme over the states so that a bank created by it pursuant to its constitutional powers is immune from taxation by the states?

Held. (i) Yes. (ii) Yes. Judgment reversed.

- "Let the end be legitimate, let it be within the scope of the Constitution, . . . [then] all means which are appropriate (*i.e.*, necessary and proper), which are plainly adapted to that end, which are not prohibited, but consistent with the letter and spirit of the Constitution, are Constitutional."

  The government of the United States is a government of enumerated powers, which are found in the Constitution. However, the Constitution cannot contain an accurate detail of all the subdivisions of which the government's powers will admit and of all the means by which they may be carried into execution. Otherwise, the Constitution would become nothing more than a legal code. Therefore, it must be allowed that the government has ample means to execute the powers to which it has been entrusted and that it be allowed to select the best means to achieve the end sought.

  If a means is a direct mode of executing a power enumerated in the Constitution, then those means can be considered incidental to the enumerated power. This is made clear by the Constitution, which gives Congress the power to make "all laws which shall be necessary and proper, for carrying into execution the foregoing powers, and all other powers vested by this Constitution." The word "necessary" does not limit the right to pass laws for the execution of the enumerated powers to those means that are indispensably necessary but rather enlarges the powers vested in government. The national legislature must be allowed discretion, with respect to the means by which the powers conferred upon it are to be carried into execution, which will enable that body to perform the high duties assigned to it, in the manner most beneficial to the people. Therefore, if the end is legitimate and within the Constitution, then the means selected to execute the end is constitutional if it is appropriate to the end and not prohibited by the Constitution.

The creation of a corporation is one of those powers that can be implied as incidental to other powers or used as a means of executing them. The incorporation of the Bank of the United States is a convenient, useful, and essential instrument in the prosecution of the fiscal operations of the federal government. The argument that the federal government is not sovereign and therefore cannot create a corporation because only a sovereign power can do so does not stand. The federal government is sovereign; it is a creation of the people of the United States and not the states. The federal government is not subordinate to the states.

♦ The federal government is supreme under the Constitution, and a tax on the operation of a bank, employed as an instrument to execute the powers of the federal government, is unconstitutional.

The Constitution and the laws made in pursuance thereof are supreme. They control the constitutions and laws of the respective states and cannot be controlled by them. The federal government was created for the benefit of all the people of the United States and can be subject only to all the people. A state, which represents only a part of the people, cannot act to control the government of the whole, which has also been declared to be supreme. The Framers of the Constitution did not design the federal government to be dependent on the states.

The power to tax is the power to destroy. It is also the power to control. The tax that Maryland imposes on the Bank of the United States is an attempt by that state to control an operation of the government of the whole. The tax, therefore, is unconstitutional.

Comment. This case is one of the most important in the history of the Court because it established the doctrine of implied powers as well as stating emphatically the view of the supremacy of the federal government. A strict, literal application of the enumerated powers doctrine—as advocated by Maryland here—would have paralyzed the federal government, since it would have prevented federal exercise of any power not expressly set forth in the Constitution. The United States government under the Constitution would have been no better off than the weak government that had operated under the Articles of Confederation. Unfortunately, the issue of supremacy of the federal government in the American system was not resolved in this case. It took the destruction and bloodshed of the Civil War some 40 years later to close that issue.

---

3. Term Limits on Members of Congress--

U.S. Term Limits, Inc. v. Thornton, 514 U.S. 779 (1995).

Facts. Arkansas adopted a constitutional amendment that prohibits the name of an otherwise-eligible candidate for Congress from appearing on the general election ballot if that candidate had already served three terms in the House of Representatives or two terms in the Senate. The amendment was formulated as a ballot access restriction rather than as an outright disqualification for membership in Congress. A citizen challenged the amendment. The Arkansas Supreme Court held that the amendment violated the federal Constitution. The Supreme Court granted certiorari.

Issue. May a state impose qualifications for membership in Congress in addition to those provided for in the federal Constitution?

Held. No. Judgment affirmed.

- ♦ The constitutionality of state qualifications for members of Congress depends first on whether the Constitution forbids states from creating such qualifications, and second, if so, whether a ballot access restriction is permissible.

- ♦ In *Powell v. McCormack (supra)*, the Court held that each house of Congress could not impose qualifications other than those set forth in the Constitution because the Framers intended the qualifications listed in the Constitution to be exclusive and because the fundamental principle of our representative democracy is that the people should choose whom they please to govern them.

- ♦ The petitioners claim that the Constitution does not expressly prohibit the states from adding qualifications, and that the states have the reserved power under the Tenth Amendment to restrict the choices their own voters may make. However, the Tenth Amendment can only reserve powers the states already had. Prior to the federal Constitution, there was no Congress and the states had no power to set qualifications for service in Congress. The Constitution itself delegates power to the states to specify time, place, and manner of holding federal elections, showing that this was not a power reserved by the states. If the states have any power to set qualifications for membership in Congress, it must be delegated from the federal government.

- ♦ Historical evidence indicates that the Framers intended that states have no role in establishing qualifications for membership in Congress. Besides, if states could formulate diverse qualifications for their members of Congress, the uniformity and national character of Congress would be undermined. The Framers intended a direct link between the federal government and the people of the United States.

- ♦ The petitioners note that the Arkansas amendment does not prohibit anyone from serving in Congress; a write-in candidate disqualified from appearing on the ballot could nevertheless be elected and serve. However, the obvious intent and effect of the amendment is to impose a substantive qualification that renders a class of potential candidates ineligible as an attempt to evade the dictates of the Qualifications Clause.

Concurrence (Kennedy, J.). The Framers discovered federalism as a means to provide citizens with two political capacities, each protected from incursion by the other. The people have a political identity directly with the federal government, not just with the states. The national government is and must be controlled by the people, and the states may not interfere with this federal right of citizenship.

Dissent (Thomas, J., Rehnquist, C.J., O'Connor, Scalia, JJ.).

- Nothing in the Constitution deprives the people of each state of the power to establish eligibility requirements for the candidates who seek to represent them in Congress. It simply does not address the issue, so it cannot act as a bar to state action.

- The people's powers are either delegated to the United States by the Constitution, delegated to the state government, or reserved by the people. Where the Constitution does not speak either expressly or by necessary implication, the federal government lacks that power and the states enjoy it. The Arkansas amendment cannot be invalidated unless something in the federal Constitution deprives the people of Arkansas the power to adopt such an amendment. The Tenth Amendment to the Constitution does not reserve to the states only those powers the states had exercised before the Constitution was adopted, but all powers not delegated to the United States or prohibited to the states.

- The direct link between the House of Representatives and the people that the majority refers to is a link between the representatives of a state and the people of that state and that state alone.

- The Qualifications Clause merely establishes minimum qualifications; it does nothing to prohibit the people of a state from adding further eligibility requirements. Even the requirement of citizenship originally incorporated state laws that varied from state to state.

- The majority's approach also prohibits states from disqualifying congressional candidates who are in prison, have been court-certified as mentally incompetent, or are even ineligible to vote themselves.

III. THE COMMERCE POWER AND ITS FEDERALISM-BASED LIMITS

A. INTRODUCTION

One of the concerns in framing the Constitution was to create a national economy free from the undue restraints imposed by the states. Since that time, the commerce power has become the justification for the expansion of federal powers into many areas other than that which formed the basis for its inclusion in the Constitution. However, the Court has recognized that there are still limits on this power.

B. THE COMMERCE POWER BEFORE THE NEW DEAL

1. Early Developments.

a. **The source of the power.** Federal power with respect to the regulation of commerce is derived from the Commerce Clause (Article I, Section 8, Clause 3), which grants to Congress the power to "regulate Commerce with foreign nations and among the several states, and with the Indian tribes." The Commerce Clause, of course, must be read in conjunction with the Necessary and Proper Clause.

b. **Regulation of foreign commerce.**

1) **Exclusive federal authority.** The regulation of foreign commerce, with very few exceptions, is exclusively within the power of the federal government.

2) **Broad powers.** The scope of what is "foreign commerce" has been held to be extremely broad. For example, it extends to any shipments made on the high seas even though the points of leaving and arriving are both within the United States.

c. **Scope of the Interstate Commerce Clause.**

1) **The early view--**

Gibbons v. Ogden, 22 U.S. (9 Wheat.) 1 (1824).

Facts. Ogden (P) sued to enjoin Gibbons (D) from violating P's monopolistic right to navigate by steamboat between New York City and places in New Jersey. A New York statute had granted these exclusive rights of navigation to Livingston and Fulton, from whom P had obtained his rights. D had two steamboats licensed in the coasting trade under the federal Coasting Act and used them in navigation between New York and New Jersey. The New York court granted P the injunction and D appealed, arguing that the power of Congress to regulate interstate commerce under the Commerce Clause is exclusive. P claimed that the federal power was concurrent with state powers to regulate commerce.

Issue. Does the Commerce Clause give Congress the power to regulate navigation between two states?

Held. Yes. The federal commerce power is a power "complete in itself," includes navigation, and may be exercised within the territorial jurisdiction of a state when the commerce within the state also affects other states.

- The meaning of "commerce" is not limited to interchange of commodities; it is intercourse. "Commerce" includes the commercial intercourse between nations and parts of nations and includes navigation. The power over commerce, including navigation, was one of the primary objects for which the people adopted the Constitution and gave up the Articles of Confederation.

- Congressional power is over commerce "among the several states." This means that Congress has no power over the completely internal commerce of a state but does have power over all interstate commerce. The word "among" means intermingled with. If interstate commerce is introduced into the interior territory of a state, then the power of Congress follows that commerce. The power of Congress to regulate interstate commerce does not stop at the boundary lines of a state but can be exercised within the territorial jurisdiction of the several states. This power of Congress is complete in itself, may be exercised to its utmost extent, and acknowledges no limitations other than those prescribed in the Constitution.

- The regulation of interstate commerce by a state is an exercise of the very power granted to Congress. Regulation of interstate commerce by a state is not akin to a state's power of taxation and inspection because the latter are powers clearly retained by the states and are exercised concurrently with similar, federal powers. Regulation of interstate commerce may or may not be a power shared between the states and federal government. The argument that the federal power is exclusive is very forceful because the word "regulate" implies exclusion of the action of all others that would perform the same operation on the same thing.

- Resolution of the issue of whether there is a concurrent commerce power is not necessary because the New York law clearly collides with an act of Congress. Should a collision exist, it becomes immaterial whether those laws were passed in virtue of a concurrent power, and the state law must yield to the law of Congress. Therefore, the New York law giving P exclusive rights of navigation between two states must fall. The federal Coastal Act will govern.

Comment. Chief Justice Marshall says in this opinion that the only limits on congressional power to regulate interstate commerce are political and not judicial. That is probably the widest interpretation of the Commerce Clause ever given. Marshall's failure to settle initially the issue of whether states hold concurrent power with Congress over interstate commerce left that issue unresolved for many years. It appears from his comments, however, that he leaned toward viewing the federal power as exclusive.

---

2) **Purpose of limiting state regulatory laws.** In broadly interpreting the Commerce Clause, the *Gibbons* Court was attempting to limit the power of the states to enact regulatory laws. However, when interpreting the Commerce Clause, subsequent Courts long vacillated between the broad construction of *Gibbons* and a more restrictive interpretation that emphasized the role of the Tenth Amendment (the power of the states). This resulted in conflicting precedents from which the Supreme Court could later choose to decide Commerce Clause cases. The conflict was finally resolved in favor of a very broad interpretation of the scope of federal Commerce Clause power.

2. **The Beginning of Modern Federal Economic Regulation.** It was not until 1887 and the enactment of the first Interstate Commerce Act that the Commerce Clause was relied on as the basis for the affirmative exercise of federal power. This occurred when Congress attempted to solve certain national economic problems. The Interstate Commerce Act was followed shortly thereafter by the Sherman Antitrust Act (1890) and several other laws.

a. **Manufacturing vs. transportation.** *United States v. E.C. Knight Co.*, 156 U.S. 1 (1895), was a federal antitrust prosecution under the Sherman Act, trying to set aside the merger of sugar companies that controlled 98% of United States sugar refining. The Supreme Court defined federal power by defining the scope of the words "commerce" and "interstate." The Court essentially limited interstate commerce to transportation across state lines (thus narrowing the position taken by the Court in *Gibbons*), holding that "manufacturing" and "production" were not interstate commerce. This holding did not halt antitrust enforcement; in *Addyston Pipe & Steel Co. v. United States*, 175 U.S. 211 (1899), the Court upheld the prosecution of a business combination that acted to increase prices, because this constituted a direct restraint on interstate commerce. The *Knight* approach was used to block New Deal legislation in the 1930s, however.

b. **The direct and immediate effect theory.** In *Houston E. & W. Texas Railway Co. v. United States (The Shreveport Rate Case)*, 234 U.S. 342

(1914), the Court ruled that the congressional interstate commerce power necessarily embraces the right to control the operation of all matters having a close and substantial relation and effect on interstate traffic and commerce; this power includes regulation of the intrastate rates of an interstate carrier that discriminated against interstate railroad traffic. In that action, because the railroad was charging higher rates for interstate distances than for equal distances within the state, the intrastate trade benefited. The Court stated that whenever the interstate and intrastate transactions of carriers are so related that the government of one involves the control of the other, Congress, and not the state, must regulate the transactions. This focus on the practical impact of state regulation differs from the *Knight* emphasis on logical nexus, and the *Shreveport* analysis allowed the Court to reverse direction in 1937 when it was deciding the New Deal cases.

c. **Stream of commerce theory.** The regulation of local stockyards was upheld on the theory that they were a throat through which the stream of beef production flowed from one part of the country to another. [*See* Stafford v. Wallace, 258 U.S. 495 (1922)]

3. **Prohibition of Interstate Commerce as a "Police" Tool.** Congress began to use national legislation to deal with "police" problems; *i.e.*, national legislation was directed at "bad" local activities such as gambling, prostitution, theft, etc.

a. **Regulatory power includes prohibition of commerce.** In *Champion v. Ames* (*The Lottery Case*), 188 U.S. 321 (1903), the Court relied on the Commerce Clause in holding that "lottery tickets are subjects of traffic and therefore are subjects of commerce" in prohibiting interstate shipment of tickets in violation of federal law. The Court reasoned that just as a state may protect its residents by forbidding all lottery ticket sales, so may Congress protect United States citizens from the "widespread pestilence of lotteries" by legislating state-to-state traffic.

b. **Exclusion of "harmful" goods.** *The Lottery Case* served as precedent to support enforcement of the Pure Food and Drugs Act of 1906 against adulterated food that had already completed its interstate transport. [Hipolite Egg Co. v. United States, 220 U.S. 45 (1911)] The Court also upheld the Mann Act (outlawing interstate transportation of women for prostitution) by relying on *The Lottery Case*. [Hoke v. United States, 227 U.S. 308 (1913)]

c. **Limit on police power--**

Hammer v. Dagenhart (The Child Labor Case), 247 U.S. 251 (1918).

Facts. The father of two children employed in a cotton mill brought an action to enjoin the enforcement of an act that prohibited the shipment in interstate commerce of goods manufactured at factories using child labor.

Issue. May Congress prohibit the transportation in interstate commerce of goods manufactured by child labor?

Held. No.

- ♦ Congress does not have general police power. Unlike *The Lottery Case*, *supra*, this case involves goods that are themselves harmless. Congress does not have power to prohibit movement of ordinary commodities.
- ♦ Manufacturing is purely a local activity, not subject to the congressional commerce power. Only the states may regulate purely local matters.
- ♦ Even though this result leaves those states without their own child labor laws with an advantage in interstate competition, Congress simply has no power to force states to exercise their police power or to equalize conditions among the states.

Dissent (Holmes, McKenna, Brandeis, Clarke, JJ.). The Child Labor Act does not meddle with state rights. When products are sent across state lines, the states are no longer within their rights. Under the Constitution, control of such commerce belongs to Congress and not the states. Congress may carry out its views of public policy, whatever the indirect effect on the states.

Comment. This case was the first of many that frustrated attempts by Congress to deal with the many social and economic problems created by the industrialization of America. The conflict between the legislative's and executive's broad view of congressional commerce power and the Court's narrow view of that power came to a peak during President Franklin D. Roosevelt's first term.

C. THE COMMERCE POWER AND THE NEW DEAL

1. **The Court Threatens the New Deal.** Soon after President Roosevelt took office, a flood of new legislation was passed, which attempted to deal with the Depression, a national economic disaster. Much of this legislation was based on the Commerce Clause.

    a. **Relationship or nexus to interstate commerce.** In the first test of New Deal Commerce Clause legislation, the Supreme Court invalidated the Railroad Retirement Act of 1934. [*See* Railroad Retirement Board v.

Alton Railroad Co., 295 U.S. 330 (1935)] The Act established a compulsory retirement and pension plan for all carriers subject to the Interstate Commerce Act. The argument was that such a plan was necessary to the morale of the workers, and that this morale affected efficiency, which in turn affected interstate commerce. The Court held that the relationship of such legislation to interstate commerce was too remote.

b. **The "indirect effect" theory.** In *Schechter Poultry Corp. v. United States*, 295 U.S. 495 (1935), the Court ruled that Congress does not have power to extend the regulation of interstate commerce to intrastate activities that have only an "indirect effect" on interstate commerce. The plaintiffs in *Schechter* attacked the National Industrial Recovery Act of 1933, which promulgated codes of fair competition for trade and industry, the violation of which were misdemeanors. The Court held the Act unconstitutional because the plaintiffs' activity, the sale of poultry only to local retailers, was not in the stream of commerce and because the wages and hours of the plaintiffs' employees would only indirectly affect the price structure of the industry. (The Act was due to expire by its own terms about a month after the opinion was issued.)

c. **Federal power over production of goods.** A year after *Schechter*, the Court invalidated the Bituminous Coal Conservation Act, which attempted to regulate hours and wages of coal miners, by assessing a "penalty" tax on noncomplying companies. [Carter v. Carter Coal Co., 298 U.S. 238 (1936)] In *Carter*, the Court once again relied on the "indirect effect" theory—although nearly all production has some indirect effect on interstate commerce, regulations affecting employees' working conditions relate, not to commerce, but to production, which is a purely local affair. Congress can regulate only activities having a direct effect on interstate commerce.

1) **Due process violation.** The Court also found that the Bituminous Coal Conservation Act was unconstitutional for another reason—it contained a delegation of legislative power to private persons in violation of the Due Process Clause of the Fifth Amendment.

2) **Direct/indirect test.** *Carter* shows the Court's trend just prior to 1936 to move from its geographic definition of interstate commerce to the direct/indirect analysis of interstate commerce used here. Under this analysis, an activity that takes place entirely within a single state may be regulated by Congress if its effect is a direct one. The use of the "direct effect" and "indirect effect" tests allowed the Court to be subjective in its choice of whether to uphold the legislation. Interestingly, this direct/indirect effect test had first been used to prevent state encroachment on federal powers where state regulation was found to burden or affect interstate commerce

"directly." [*See, e.g.,* Houston E. & W. Texas Railway Co. v. United States, *supra*] After 1936, this analysis fell into disuse when the Court began to broaden its view of the scope of congressional power over commerce.

d. **The court-packing plan.** President Roosevelt felt that the Court was judging the public policy of the New Deal, rather than its constitutionality. He proposed legislation to allow him to appoint an extra justice for every justice over 70 years old who did not resign. The legislation never passed, but some observers felt it prompted a change in the Court's analysis of New Deal legislation.

D. THE COMMERCE POWER AFTER THE NEW DEAL

1. **The "Affectation Doctrine."** In 1937, the Court abandoned the "geographical" (*e.g.*, manufacturing is local) and "direct vs. indirect" concepts. The Court's position became that Congress has the power to regulate any activity, whether it be interstate or intrastate in nature, as long as it has any appreciable effect whatever on interstate commerce. This is called the "affectation doctrine."

2. **Labor Relations Affecting Commerce--**

NLRB v. Jones & Laughlin Steel Corp., 301 U.S. 1 (1937).

Facts. The National Labor Relations Act of 1935 provided for union-employer collective bargaining in all industries affecting interstate commerce. Jones & Laughlin Steel Corp. (D), a steel manufacturer, claimed that Congress had no power to regulate its industry. D was an integrated company, owning subsidiaries all over the United States; 75% of the product of the plant in question was shipped out of state, and it got its raw materials from out of state. The NLRB (P) ordered D to comply with the Act's provisions, but the court of appeals refused to grant judicial enforcement of P's order because it exceeded federal power. The Supreme Court granted certiorari.

Issue. May Congress regulate a manufacturer if the manufacturer's activity significantly affects interstate commerce?

Held. Yes. Judgment reversed.

- The term "affecting commerce" means burdening or obstructing commerce or the free flow of commerce, or leading or tending to lead to a labor dispute burdening or obstructing commerce or the free flow of commerce. Labor strife at this plant could conceivably cripple the entire interstate operation of the company; thus, interstate commerce was affected, and Congress may regulate D's activity.

Dissent (McReynolds, Van Devanter, Sutherland, Butler, JJ.). This case arose from the discharge of 10 men for union activity out of 10,000 men who work at D's factory. Any effect this discharge has on interstate commerce is highly indirect and remote.

---

3. Regulating by Prohibiting Commerce--

United States v. Darby, 312 U.S. 100 (1941).

Facts. The Fair Labor Standards Act of 1938 prescribed maximum and minimum wages for workers who manufactured goods for interstate commerce and prohibited interstate shipment of goods made by workers not employed in compliance with the Act. Darby (D), a lumber manufacturer, was charged with violating the Act. The district court quashed the indictment, finding the Act inapplicable to D's employees, who were involved in manufacturing, not interstate commerce. The United States appeals.

Issue. May Congress establish and enforce wage and hour standards for the manufacture of goods for interstate commerce?

Held. Yes. Judgment reversed.

- The interstate shipment of manufactured goods is clearly subject to congressional regulation. Congress has in the past prohibited interstate shipment of various articles pursuant to public policy, and the Court has no control over legislative judgment of public policy. Prohibition of interstate shipment of goods covered by the Act is constitutional as long as the labor standards involved are properly within the scope of federal power.

- Congress has adopted the policy of excluding from interstate commerce all goods produced for that commerce that do not conform to the specified labor standards, and Congress may choose appropriate means of accomplishing that policy. Federal power extends to intrastate activities directly affecting interstate commerce. The means here adopted so affect interstate commerce and thus are within Congress's power to regulate.

- The Act is directed at the suppression of "unfair" competition in interstate commerce, a valid purpose. Therefore, the Act is constitutional.

- This opinion overrules *Hammer v. Dagenhart* (*supra*).

---

4. Judicial Deference Toward Exercise of the Commerce Power.

a. **"Substantially affecting commerce."** In *Wickard v. Filburn,* 317 U.S. 111 (1942), the Court held that Congress may regulate individual home production and use of wheat based on the substantial effect on interstate commerce of the aggregate of such local activity. The purpose of the Agricultural Adjustment Act of 1938 was to restrict the supply of wheat in order to maintain the price, and the power to regulate commerce includes the power to regulate the prices at which commodities are sold. Commerce among the states in wheat was large and important, so the subject was within Congress's power. Even if the activity is local and not regarded as commerce, it may be reached by Congress if it exerts a "substantial economic effect on interstate commerce, and this irrespective of whether such effect is what might at some earlier time have been defined as 'direct' or 'indirect.'"

b. **The commerce power and civil rights.**

1) **Motels.** In *Heart of Atlanta Motel v. United States,* 379 U.S. 241 (1964), the Court held that Congress may prohibit racial discrimination by private motels that accept out-of-town state business. The legislative history of the Civil Rights Act contains numerous examples of how racial discrimination placed burdens upon interstate commerce, which covers the movement of persons through more than one state. Congress may act under the Commerce Clause if the activity regulated is commerce that concerns more than one state and has a real and substantial relation to the national interest.

2) **Restaurants.** In *Katzenbach v. McClung,* 379 U.S. 294 (1964), the Court held that Congress could use its commerce power to forbid racial discrimination by a restaurant on the ground that slightly under one-half of the food it served originated from outside the state. The Court noted that "[a] comparison of per capita spending by Negroes in restaurants, theaters, and like establishments indicated less spending, after discounting income differences, in areas where discrimination is widely practiced. . . . This diminutive spending springing from a refusal to serve Negroes and their total loss as customers has, regardless of the absence of direct evidence, a close connection to interstate commerce." The Court added that there was testimony that discrimination in restaurants had a direct and restrictive effect upon interstate travel.

c. **The commerce power and crime.**

1) **Introduction.** Congress has relied on the commerce power to enact criminal laws and generally the Court has upheld this use of the Commerce Clause. Even though the criminal transaction might be purely intrastate, it might affect interstate commerce if it provides revenue for, *e.g.*, organized crime.

2) **Organized crime.** In *Perez v. United States,* 402 U.S. 146 (1971), after Perez was convicted of loan sharking, the Court held that even when such activities are purely intrastate in character, they directly affect interstate commerce. Congress was supported by adequate findings that loan sharking provides organized crime substantial revenue with which to affect interstate commerce in many forms.

E. THE REHNQUIST COURT'S REVIVAL OF INTERNAL LIMITS ON THE COMMERCE POWER

When Justice Rehnquist became the Chief Justice, the Court began emphasizing the importance of the states in the federal system by finding limitations to congressional power. In 1995, in *United States v. Lopez*, below, the Court placed limits on the congressional commerce power.

1. **Gun-Free School Zones Act--**

United States v. Lopez, 514 U.S. 549 (1995).

Facts. In the Gun-Free School Zones Act, Congress made it illegal for any person knowingly to possess a firearm in a school zone. Lopez (D), a twelfth-grade student, carried a concealed gun to his high school. D was ultimately convicted under the Act. The court of appeals reversed on the ground that Congress did not have power under the Commerce Clause to regulate this type of activity. The Supreme Court granted certiorari.

Issue. May Congress prohibit the possession of firearms within a school zone?

Held. No. Judgment affirmed.

- As business enterprises expanded beyond local and regional territories and became national in scope, the scope of the Commerce Clause as interpreted by the Court also expanded. In cases such as *NLRB v. Jones & Laughlin Steel Corp. (supra)* and *Maryland v. Wirtz*, 392 U.S. 183 (1968), we noted that while the power to regulate commerce is broad, it does have limits.

- There are three broad categories of activity that come within Congress's commerce power:

  Congress may regulate the use of the channels of interstate commerce;

  Congress may regulate the instrumentalities of interstate commerce, as well as persons or things in interstate commerce; and

Congress may regulate activities that have a substantial relation to interstate commerce, meaning those that substantially affect interstate commerce.

- ♦ The Act in this case is a criminal statute that has nothing to do with commerce. Possessing a gun in a school zone does not arise out of a commercial transaction that substantially affects interstate commerce. Nor does the Act contain a requirement that the possession be connected in any way to interstate commerce.

- ♦ The government claims that possession of a firearm in a local school zone substantially affects interstate commerce because it might result in violent crime. This in turn imposes costs on society, which are borne throughout the country through insurance rates. The government also claims that guns disrupt the educational process, which leads to a less productive society, which ultimately affects interstate commerce. If either of these propositions were adopted, there would be no limitation on federal power. The only way to find an effect on interstate commerce in this case is to pile inference upon inference, and the result would be to uphold a general police power for Congress.

Concurrence (Kennedy, O'Connor, JJ.). In a sense, any conduct in the interdependent world has an ultimate commercial origin or consequence. However, the Court must still determine whether the exercise of national power intrudes upon an area of traditional state concerns. Education in particular is a traditional concern of the states.

Concurrence (Thomas, J.). The term "commerce" as used in the Constitution is much more limited than the Court's opinions have recognized. The term referred to buying, selling, and transporting goods, as distinguished from agriculture and manufacturing. Furthermore, the Constitution does not give Congress authority over all activities that "substantially affect" interstate commerce. If it did, there would be no need for specific constitutional provisions giving Congress power to enact bankruptcy laws, to establish post offices and post roads, to grant patents and copyrights, etc.

Dissent (Breyer, Stevens, Souter, Ginsburg, JJ.). Case law recognizes that Congress can regulate even local activity if it significantly affects interstate commerce. In determining whether a local activity will have such an effect, the court must consider the cumulative effect of all instances similar to the one in the specific case. The courts are required to defer to congressional determinations about the factual basis for making this determination. In this case, Congress could rationally find that violent crime in school areas affects the quality of education and thereby interstate commerce.

Dissent (Souter, J.). The Court seeks to draw fine distinctions between what is patently commercial and what is not, which is basically the same distinction between what directly affects commerce and what affects it only indirectly. The Court should not be placed in a position to make these fine distinctions; Congress should have to make them. The majority approach of the last 60 years should prevail.

Dissent (Stevens, J.). Congress clearly has power to regulate the possession of guns to some degree. This power should include the ability to prohibit possession of guns at any location. The market for possession of handguns by persons covered by the Act is sufficiently substantial to justify congressional action.

Comment. Despite the limitations set forth in *Lopez,* the Court gives broad latitude to federal regulation once the commerce power is properly invoked. For example, Congress may:

> Advance interstate commerce (*e.g.,* build highways, license radio and television stations, charter a private railroad corporation such as Amtrak);
>
> Protect instrumentalities or shipments in interstate commerce (*e.g.,* outlaw theft from interstate shipments, destruction of aircraft in interstate flights); and
>
> Prevent misuse of channels of interstate commerce—in effect, develop a federal police power (*e.g.,* prohibition of interstate transport of stolen goods or motor vehicles, shipment of misbranded goods).

---

2. Violence Against Women Act--

United States v. Morrison, 529 U.S. 598 (2000).

Facts. Morrison (D) was a member of a varsity football team at Virginia Tech who raped Brzonkala (P), a female student, and made vulgar remarks about women. P sued D under 42 U.S.C. section 13981, the Violence Against Women Act, which provided a damages remedy for a victim of gender-motivated violence. D claimed that section 13981's civil remedy was unconstitutional. The United States (P) intervened to defend the Act under the Commerce Clause or section 5 of the Fourteenth Amendment. The lower courts held that Congress lacked constitutional authority to enact this civil remedy. The Supreme Court granted certiorari.

Issue. May Congress provide a federal civil remedy for a violent crime on the ground that the aggregate effect of such crimes substantially affected interstate commerce?

Held. No. Judgment affirmed.

- In *United States v. Lopez (supra)*, the Court held that Congress could not prohibit the possession of firearms within a school zone. The rationale was that possessing a firearm is a criminal act, not an economic one. Congress has authority to regulate interstate commerce, but it must show a substantial impact on interstate commerce of actions it seeks to regulate or proscribe.

- In adopting the Act, Congress made findings regarding the serious impact of gender-motivated violence on victims and their families, but used a but-for causal chain to show an impact on interstate commerce from these crimes. The Court has rejected this type of reasoning, since it would allow Congress to regulate any crime if the aggregated impact has substantial effects on any aspect of interstate commerce. This type of reasoning could as easily be applied to family law as well.

- The Constitution distinguishes between national and local issues, and the police power is one that was clearly left to the states and denied to the federal government. Congress has no authority to regulate noneconomic, violent criminal conduct based solely on the conduct's aggregate effect in interstate commerce.

- Section 5 of the Fourteenth Amendment does allow Congress to enforce the guarantee that no state shall deprive any person of life, liberty, or property without due process or deny any person equal protection of the laws. But this applies only to state action, not private conduct. Even if there had been gender-based disparate treatment by the state in this case, it would not have permitted P's suit against D as a private party.

Concurrence (Thomas, J.). The very notion of a "substantial effects" test under the Commerce Clause is inconsistent with the Constitution. This test has led Congress to act as though there are virtually no limits to the Commerce Clause. The Court should adopt an approach more consistent with the original understanding.

Dissent (Souter, Stevens, Ginsburg, Breyer, JJ.). One difference between this case and *Lopez* is that here, Congress assembled considerable data showing the effects of violence against women on interstate commerce. This Act would have been constitutional at any time between *Wickard* and *Lopez*. The majority has revived a distinction between commercial and noncommercial conduct, which had been rejected in *Wickard*. The relative powers of the federal and state systems have changed substantially since the framing of the constitution. The Seventeenth Amendment was a major factor in this change, and the modern integrated national economy is a fact not reflected in the majority's notion of federalism.

Dissent (Breyer, Stevens, Souter, Ginsburg, JJ.). The distinction between economic and noneconomic is not easy to apply. Congress could have approached the same problem with legislation that focused on acts of violence perpetrated at public accommodations or by those who have moved in interstate commerce. The majority's approach could lead to complex rules creating fine distinctions that achieve random results.

Comment. The Court often relies on statutory interpretation to avoid constitutional issues. In *Jones v. United States*, 529 U.S. 848 (2000), the Court avoided a Commerce Clause issue by holding that the federal arson statute, which applied to buildings used in any activity affecting interstate or foreign commerce, did not apply to an owner-occupied residence not used for commercial purposes. In *Solid Waste Agency of North-*

ern Cook County v. United States Army Corps of Engineers, 531 U.S. 159 (2001), the Court held that the Clean Water Act does not cover nonnavigable, isolated intrastate waters used as habitat for migratory birds. The dissent in that case considered the economic aspects of birdwatching and hunting, as well as the migration of birds over state lines, to conclude that Congress's commerce power would extend to cover these waters.

---

3. The Limits of *Lopez* and *Morrison*--

Gonzales v. Raich, 545 U.S. 1 (2005).

Facts. California created a statutory exemption for criminal prosecution for physicians, patients, and primary caregivers who possess or cultivate marijuana for medicinal purposes with the recommendation or approval of a physician. Angel Raich and Diane Monson (Ps) sought to use medical marijuana under the California statute. Ps sought injunctive and declaratory relief to prohibit the federal Controlled Substances Act ("CSA") to the extent that it prevented them from possessing, obtaining, or manufacturing cannabis for their personal medical use. The court of appeals granted an injunction. The Supreme Court granted certiorari.

Issue. Does the federal commerce power include the power to prohibit local cultivation and use of marijuana in compliance with state law?

Held. Yes. Judgment reversed.

- Ps claim that applying the CSA to the intrastate manufacture and possession of marijuana exceeds the federal commerce power. However, *Wickard*, *supra*, and other cases establish that Congress can regulate purely local activities that are part of an economic "class of activities" that have a substantial effect on interstate commerce, even intrastate activity that is not itself commercial.

- A primary purpose of the CSA is to control the supply and demand of controlled substances in both legal and illegal drug markets. Just as the wheat in *Wickard* was part of the regulatory scheme even when it never left the state, marijuana grown within a state affects the interstate market. Congress has a rational basis for concluding that home-consumed marijuana can affect price and market conditions in the national market. Quantities intended for use under the California statute might be diverted into illegal uses.

- *Lopez, supra,* and *Morrison, supra,* are distinguishable on the grounds that those cases fell outside Congress's commerce power in its entirety. The statutes in those cases did not regulate economic activity. In contrast, the CSA directly involves economic activity, including the production, distribution, and consumption of commodities for which there is an established interstate market.

Concurrence (Scalia, J.). Under the Necessary and Proper Clause, Congress can regulate intrastate activities that do not themselves substantially affect interstate commerce, where it is necessary to make a regulation of interstate commerce effective. Congress could prohibit intrastate controlled-substance activities to achieve the legitimate end of eradicating illegal substances from interstate commerce.

Dissent (O'Connor, J., Rehnquist, C.J., Thomas, J.). The federal system promotes innovation by letting the states experiment without risk to the rest of the country. States' core police powers include the authority to define criminal law and protect the health, safety, and welfare of their citizens. California exercised these powers to address serious problems. Allowing the CSA to extinguish the experiment without proof that Ps' activity has a substantial effect on interstate commerce makes federal regulation of local activity immune to Commerce Clause challenge. Congress should not regulate noncommercial activity simply because it may have an effect on the demand for commercial goods or because it may be substituted for commercial activity. Most commercial goods or services have some sort of privately producible equivalent. The marijuana at issue in this case was never in the stream of commerce; possession is not itself a commercial activity. There is a significant difference between this case and *Wickard*, which dealt with a federal statute that exempted small local plantings.

Dissent (Thomas, J.). Ps use marijuana that has never been bought or sold, has never crossed state lines, and has no demonstrable effect on the national market for marijuana. If Congress can regulate this activity, it can regulate anything. The CSA encroaches on the states' traditional police powers.

F. EXTERNAL LIMITS ON THE COMMERCE POWER: FEDERALISM AND THE TENTH AND ELEVENTH AMENDMENTS

1. State Autonomy and the Tenth Amendment.

a. **Recognition of state autonomy.** In *National League of Cities v. Usery*, 426 U.S. 833 (1976), the Court struck down amendments to the Fair Labor Standards Act that would have extended minimum wage and maximum hour protections to state employees. The Court held that Congress, in exercising its powers under the Commerce Clause, had impermissibly interfered with the integral government functions of the states because the amendments would have displaced state policies regarding the manner in which states chose to deliver the services their citizens required. This was seen as not comporting with the federal system. Four justices dissented. *National League of Cities* was overruled by *Garcia, infra*, a mere nine years later.

b. **Renewed supremacy of federal government—*National League of Cities* overruled.** In *Garcia v. San Antonio Metropolitan Transit Authority,* 469 U.S. 528 (1985), the Court held that Congress may enforce minimum wage and overtime requirements against a local government's mass transit authority. The Court found that the term, "traditional governmental functions," used in decisions following *National League of Cities, supra,* produced confusion and a variety of interpretations. The Court stated that the fundamental problem was that no distinction that purports to separate out important governmental functions can be faithful to the role of federalism in a democratic society. The Court rejected a rule of state immunity from federal regulation that turns on an unelected judiciary's decision as to whether a particular governmental function is "integral" or "traditional." The Court reasoned that the political process ensures that laws that unduly burden the states will not be promulgated; the states have political influence in Congress, especially in the Senate where each state is equally represented. The Court said that the effectiveness of the procedural limit is evident by the fact that the states are exempt from the operation of many federal statutes and receive significant federal aid for their own programs.

c. **Limit on congressional regulatory authority--**

New York v. United States, 505 U.S. 144 (1992).

Facts. Low level radioactive waste is generated in substantial quantities by various industries including the medical and research industries, but in 1979 the only three United States disposal sites for radioactive waste were in Nevada, Washington, and South Carolina. Each of these states objected to accepting wastes from other states, and in 1980, Congress enacted the Low-Level Radioactive Waste Policy Amendments Act. The Act authorized states to enter into regional compacts that, once ratified by Congress, could after 1985 restrict the use of their disposal facilities to waste generated within member states. By 1985, only three approved regional compacts had operational disposal facilities—the ones existing in 1979. Thirty-one states (the unsited states) were not members of these compacts. Congress amended the Act in 1985, based on a proposal submitted by the National Governors' Association, whereby sited states agreed to accept waste for seven more years, collecting a graduated surcharge for waste from unsited states, and unsited states agreed not to rely on sited states after 1992. A portion of the surcharges would be collected by the Secretary of Energy, who in turn would pay them to unsited states that comply with a series of deadlines for joining a regional compact or creating their own disposal site. States that failed to meet the deadlines could lose access to disposal sites. Finally, any state or regional compact that was unable to dispose of all waste generated within its borders by 1996 would, upon the request of the waste generator, take title to the waste and be liable for all damages incurred by such generator as a consequence of the state's failure to take possession of the waste once notified that it is available. New York (P) did not join a regional compact, but did enact legislation providing for the siting and financing of a disposal facility. The two target counties objected and joined P in suing the United States (D), seeking a declaratory judgment that the Act violates the Tenth Amendment. The district court dismissed the complaint. The court of appeals affirmed. The Supreme Court granted certiorari.

Issue. May Congress direct the states to regulate in a particular field or a particular way, using them as implements of regulation?

Held. No. Judgment reversed in part.

- The power of Congress to legislate so as to impact state autonomy has been analyzed both by inquiring whether Congress has the power under Article I to so act, and by determining whether Congress has invaded the province of state sovereignty reserved by the Tenth Amendment. But these inquiries may be mirror images, because where a power is delegated to Congress, the Tenth Amendment expressly disclaims any reservation of power to the states, and if a power is an attribute of state sovereignty reserved by the Tenth Amendment, it is necessarily one not conferred on Congress. The Tenth Amendment merely states the truism that all is retained by the states which has not been surrendered to the federal government; yet it requires the courts to determine whether an incident of state sovereignty is protected by a limitation on an Article I power.

- P claims that Congress exceeded its powers not by regulating radioactive waste, which is interstate in character and thus falls within the Commerce Clause, but by directing the states to regulate in this field in a particular way. The Court has long recognized that Congress cannot directly compel the states to enact and enforce a federal regulatory program. A key difference between the Constitution and the Articles of Confederation is that under the Constitution, the federal government can exercise its legislative authority directly over individuals rather than over states.

- Congress may create incentives for states to adopt a legislative program consistent with federal interests, however. Congress has done so by attaching conditions on the receipt of federal funds and by offering states the option of regulating private activity in interstate commerce according to federal standards or having state law preempted by federal regulation. Such incentives do not compel state action. This preserves the accountability of both federal and state officials to their respective constituencies.

- The Act in this case creates three sets of incentives. First, the surcharge provisions provide for imposition by sited states of surcharges that are partially remitted to the federal government and paid out to states that meet specified milestones. The burden on interstate commerce is within Congress's Commerce Clause authority, and the payments are within its Spending Clause authority.

- The second set of incentives allows states with disposal sites to gradually increase the cost of access to the sites and then deny access altogether to waste generated in states that do not meet federal guidelines. This gives nonsited states the choice of complying with federal standards for self-sufficiency or becoming subject to federal regulation that allows sited states to deny access to their disposal sites. The affected states are not thereby compelled by Congress to regulate; the incentives are a conditional exercise of Congress's commerce power, which is permissible.

- The third set of incentives requires states that do not regulate according to federal standards to take title to and possession of the waste generated within their borders and to assume liability for all damages waste generators suffer as a result of the states' failure to do so promptly. But the Constitution would not permit Congress to simply transfer radioactive waste from generators to state governments, or force states to become liable for generators' damages, either of which would "commandeer" state governments into the service of federal regulatory purposes. And Congress cannot require state governments to implement federal legislation. Since neither "option" is constitutional, a choice between them is not permissible either. This take-title provision is severable from the rest of the Act, however.

- No matter how great the federal interest, the Constitution does not give Congress authority to require the states to regulate. Congress must legislate directly, not by conscripting state governments. State officials cannot give Congress this authority by consenting to the federal statute.

- P claims that the first two incentives violate the Guarantee Clause, but neither incentive denied any state a republican form of government.

Concurrence and dissent (White, Blackmun, Stevens, JJ.). The Act is a result of the efforts of state governments seeking to achieve a state-based remedy for the waste problem. It is essentially a congressional sanction of interstate compromises, not federal preemption or intervention. New York in particular should be estopped from asserting the unconstitutionality of the Act after the state has derived substantial benefits under the Act. The Court's opinion that the take-title provision is unconstitutional does not preclude Congress from adopting a similar measure through its powers under the Spending or Commerce Clauses. Ironically, the Court gives Congress fewer incentives to defer to the wishes of state officials in achieving local solutions to local problems, all in the name of promoting federalism.

Concurrence and dissent (Stevens, J.). The Constitution enhanced the power of the federal government, and there is no history to suggest that the federal government may not impose its will upon the states as it did under the Articles of Confederation.

---

d. **Limit on congressional power to use state officers directly.** *Printz v. United States,* 521 U.S. 898 (1997), involved the federal Brady Handgun Violence Precaution Act ("the Brady Act"), which required the state law enforcement officers to conduct the background checks of prospective handgun purchasers. The Court held that Congress may not compel state officers directly to enforce a federal regulatory program. The Court stated that the enactments of the early Congresses contain no evidence of an assumption that the federal government may impose responsibilities on the states' executive power without constitutional authorization. The Court further stated that portions of The Federalist suggest the ability of the federal government to use state officers to execute federal laws, but they do not imply that this can be done without the consent of the states. The Constitution established a system of dual sovereignty. The separation of the federal and state governments is one of the Constitution's structural protections of liberty. The power of the federal government would be augmented immeasurably if it could impress into its service state police officers. Under *New York* (*supra*), Congress cannot compel the states to enact or enforce a federal regulatory program. Congress cannot circumvent that prohibition by conscripting the states' officers directly. Such a practice would be fundamentally incompatible with the constitutional system of dual sovereignty.

e. **States as objects of federal regulation.** In *Reno v. Condon*, 528 U.S. 141 (2000), the Court held that drivers' personal information gathered by state motor vehicle departments is a "thing in interstate commerce," because it is used by insurers, manufacturers, marketers, and others engaged in interstate commerce to contact drivers with customized solicitations. The Court unanimously held that Congress had authority to limit disclosure of this information by state authorities.

2. **State Sovereign Immunity and the Eleventh Amendment.**

a. **Eleventh Amendment principles.** Under the Eleventh Amendment, the federal judicial power does not extend to a suit against a state brought by citizens of another state or by subjects of a foreign state. The amendment reflects the principles that each state is a sovereign entity and that a sovereignty is not amenable to the suit of an individual without its consent.

b. **The Rehnquist Court's revival of state sovereign immunity.** *Seminole Tribe of Florida v. Florida,* 517 U.S. 44 (1996), involved the Indian Gaming Regulatory Act, which allowed certain gambling activities only in conformance with a valid compact between the tribe and the state where the gaming activities were located. The Act also required states to negotiate in good faith with an Indian tribe toward forming such a compact and authorized a tribe to sue a state in federal court to compel negotiations. The Court held that the Eleventh Amendment prevents Congress from authorizing suits by Indian tribes against states for prospective injunctive relief to enforce legislation enacted pursuant to the Indian Commerce Clause. The Court stated that it had traditionally found only one provision that gives Congress power to abrogate state immunity—the Fourteenth Amendment. In *Pennsylvania v. Union Gas Co.*, 491 U.S. 1 (1989), the Court held that Congress could abrogate state sovereign immunity under the Commerce Clause because otherwise Congress could not effectively regulate interstate commerce. However, in *Seminole Tribe of Florida*, the Court found that the rationale of *Pennsylvania v. Union Gas Co.* deviated sharply from precedent and overruled it.

IV. OTHER NATIONAL POWERS: TAXING, SPENDING, WAR, TREATIES, AND FOREIGN AFFAIRS

A. THE TAXING POWER AS A REGULATORY DEVICE

The major issue concerns the extent to which the national taxing power can be used as a means of regulation.

1. **Indirect Taxes.** Article I, Section 8 provides that "Congress shall have power to lay and collect taxes, duties, imposts, and excises . . . [and that] all duties, imposts, and excises shall be uniform throughout the United States." An indirect tax is one imposed for the privilege of doing business (*e.g.*, a license tax) or performing some act (*e.g.*, sales taxes) and is generally exacted from a person other than the one who is ultimately to bear the tax burden (*i.e.*, it is collected from someone other than the ultimate consumer).

2. **Direct Taxes.** Article I, Section 9 provides that "no capitation or other direct tax shall be laid unless in proportion to the census . . ." And Article I, Section 2 provides that "direct taxes shall be apportioned among the several states."

   a. **Definition.** A direct tax is one imposed directly against the property (as a real property tax) or against the person ultimately responsible for payment.

   b. **Population apportionment.** The apportionment requirement means that direct taxes require that the largest states, relatively speaking, pay a greater amount, regardless of the wealth of their citizens, than the smaller states. Because of this unfeasible requirement, the Supreme Court has construed almost every tax (except property taxes) as indirect taxes.

3. **Export Taxes.** Article I, Section 9, Clause 5 provides: "No tax or duty shall be laid on articles exported from any state." "Export" means goods going to a foreign country.

4. **Taxation Where Congress Has No Other Power to Legislate.**

   a. **The primary purpose of tax measures.** When a tax is not supportable under some other specific constitutional power, then its validity depends on whether it is intended as a revenue-raising measure. However, since every tax also has a regulatory effect, the test for validity is whether the tax is primarily "fiscal" (valid) or "regulatory" (invalid).

b. **The child labor tax case--**

Bailey v. Drexel Furniture Co., 259 U.S. 20 (1922).

Facts. A few months after the *Hammer v. Dagenhart* decision (*supra*), Congress imposed a federal excise tax on employers of child labor, covering essentially the same businesses as were involved in *Dagenhart*. Drexel Furniture (P) paid the tax and won a refund case in the lower courts. Bailey (D), the Tax Commissioner, appeals.

Issue. May Congress use its taxing power to accomplish objectives that it cannot reach under any of its other powers?

Held. No. Judgment affirmed.

- Congress may properly impose excise taxes on commodities or other things of value, even where there results an incidental restraint or regulation. Here, however, the excise burdens only the departure from a detailed and specified course of conduct in business.

- The Court must presume the validity of congressional statutes, but this tax is invalid on its face. It taxes only knowing departures from the prescribed business activity and is clearly regulatory in purpose and effect. Its revenue-raising effects are merely incidental.

Comment. In *Bailey*, the Supreme Court indicated that the important thing is the motive of Congress. This means that the Court looks at the taxing statute to see its purpose, its intended effect, and its effect in normal operation (*i.e.*, the Court examines the statute on its face). If the purpose is for revenue, then the tax is valid. If the tax is used to discriminate between "good guys" and "bad guys" (*i.e.*, is used to regulate), then it is unconstitutional. The question is: what is the tax's dominant purpose?

c. **Taxation of gambling.** *United States v. Kahriger,* 345 U.S. 22 (1953), involved a challenge to a federal tax that was levied on each wager made and on gambling employees. The tax also required registration for those gambling. The Court held that a federal tax that discourages specific activity and produces little revenue may be valid. The Court noted that, although the legislative history showed an intent to suppress wagering, it also showed an intent to tax. The Court stated that the penalty on wagering was merely an indirect effect and that, unless there are penalty provisions extraneous to any tax need, courts are without authority to limit the exercise of the taxing power. Because the tax did in reality raise revenue, it was presumptively valid. In a dissent joined in large part by Justice Douglas, Justice Frankfurter contended that the

Court shut its eyes to the true nature of the tax, which he claimed was an attempt to regulate conduct in spite of a lack of a constitutional grant of the necessary power to Congress.

B. THE SPENDING POWER AS A REGULATORY DEVICE

1. **Introduction.** Article I, Section 8 provides that Congress has the power to spend money in order to pay the debts and provide for the common defense and general welfare of the United States.

2. **The Scope of the Power to Spend.**

    a. The General Welfare Clause of Article I, Section 8 is connected to the taxing and spending power. It is a limitation on that power (*i.e.*, Congress may spend only for the general welfare) and is not an independent source of power for Congress. Thus, for example, Congress could not pass a law under the General Welfare Clause requiring seat belts in all cars. The rule is: Congress must tax for revenue and not merely regulatory purposes, and then it must spend for the general welfare.

    b. The spending must be for a "national concern" as opposed to a "local" one. However, the Supreme Court gives great deference to the determinations of Congress in deciding what is for the "common benefit."

3. **Local vs. General Welfare--**

United States v. Butler, 297 U.S. 1 (1936).

Facts. The 1933 Agriculture Adjustment Act authorized the Secretary of Agriculture to extend benefit payments to farmers who agreed to reduce their planted acreage in an attempt to stabilize farm prices. Processors of the covered crops were to be taxed to provide a fund for the benefit payments. Butler (P) was receiver for a processor who paid the tax and brought suit to recover it on grounds that it was part of an unconstitutional program to control agricultural production. The court of appeals held the tax unconstitutional; the government appealed.

Issue. May Congress use its taxing and spending powers to operate a self-contained program regulating agricultural production?

Held. No. Judgment affirmed.

- ♦ The power of Congress to authorize expenditures of public moneys for public purposes is not limited by the direct grants of legislative power found in the Constitution, but it does have limits. Appropriations cannot be made as means to an unconstitutional end.

- ♦ Regulation of agricultural production is not a power granted to Congress; therefore it is left to the states. Attainment of such a prohibited end may not be accomplished through the use of granted powers, here the taxing powers.
- ♦ This scheme, purportedly voluntary, in reality involves purchasing, with federal funds, submission to federal regulation of a subject reserved to the states. Because the end is invalid, it may not be accomplished indirectly through the taxing and spending power.

Dissent (Stone, Brandeis, Cardoza, JJ.). Courts are concerned only with the power to enact statutes, not their wisdom. The depressed state of agriculture is nationwide; therefore, the Act does provide for the "general welfare." There is no coercion involved, since threat of loss, not hope of gain, which is involved here, is the essence of economic coercion. Conditioning the receipt of federal funds on certain activity does not infringe state power.

Comment. Subsequent Commerce Clause cases indicate that the area involved in *Butler* would not now be held to be one of purely "local" concern. Note also that the Court apparently approached the question of the scope of the spending power from the wrong angle. It said that the area (agricultural production) was a "local" one, and therefore the spending power could not be used to affect it. The proper inquiry would first seem to be the determination of what the scope of the spending power really is, since Congress was given this power by the Constitution. Finally, in arguing that the expenditure in *Butler* was invalid, the Court stated that this was not a conditional appropriation of money, but the amounts appropriated were to be expended only in payment under contracts whereby the parties bound themselves to the regulation by the federal government (implying that this was somehow "coercive" and thus invalid).

---

4. **No Coercion of the States by Congress.** The Social Security Act taxed employers of eight or more persons a certain percent of the salaries of their employees; the funds were to go to the Treasury. If an employer contributed to a state unemployment plan, it received a 90% credit toward the contribution of its federal responsibility. Steward Machine Company paid the tax and then sought a refund of taxes paid to the federal government. In *Steward Machine Co. v. Davis,* 301 U.S. 548 (1937), the Court held that the tax was valid. It found that there was no showing that the tax and credit in combination were weapons of coercion, destroying or impairing the autonomy of the states. The Court reasoned that the states were unable to give the requisite relief to the problem of unemployment and needed help from the federal government. The Court pointed out that every tax rebate that is conditioned upon conduct is in some measure a temptation but that motive or temptation is not the same thing as coercion.

5. **Federal Grants to States.** Congress has long promoted federal policy by attaching conditions to the use of funds given to the states. A state autonomy

limitation on such conditions has been suggested but is only conjectural at this point (especially after the overruling of *National League of Cities*, *supra*). The Court has held that Congress may condition such grants on cooperation with federal objectives.

6. **Deference to Congressional Purpose.** Congress is pretty much the arbiter of what is for the "general welfare." Therefore, it is now questionable whether this spending power can be used to enact legislation in almost any field.

   a. **Reasonableness.** The spending program must be reasonably adapted to the attainment of an end that will justify the expenditure.

   b. **Federal influence over state regulation through the spending power--**

South Dakota v. Dole, 483 U.S. 203 (1987).

Facts. South Dakota (P) permitted anyone 19 years old or older to purchase beer. Congress adopted a statute requiring the Secretary of Transportation (D) to withhold 5% of federal highway funds from any state that permitted persons younger than 21 to purchase alcoholic beverages. P sought a declaratory judgment that the statute violated the Twenty-First Amendment and the limits on the congressional spending power. The district court found for D and the court of appeals affirmed. The Supreme Court granted certiorari.

Issue. May Congress refuse to provide federal highway funds to states that do not adopt federal age standards for the sale of alcoholic beverages?

Held. Yes. Judgment affirmed.

♦ It is not necessary to decide whether Congress could enact a national minimum drinking age, because the statute in this case relied on the spending power to encourage uniformity in state drinking ages without actually imposing a national drinking age. Consideration of the Twenty-First Amendment is therefore unnecessary since the legislation only indirectly affects the drinking age.

♦ Congress clearly has authority to impose conditions on the receipt of federal funds, even to attain objectives it might not be able to attain directly. This authority is incident to the spending power.

♦ The spending power itself is limited in four ways: (i) it must be used in the pursuit of "the general welfare"; (ii) any conditions imposed must be unambiguous, so the states may make knowing choices; (iii) the conditions must be related to the federal interest in particular national programs; and (iv) the conditions must not be barred by other independent constitutional provisions.

♦ In this case, the statute is consistent with the first three limitations as it is intended to promote safe interstate travel. P claims the statute is impermissible because it violates the fourth limitation; *i.e.*, it is barred by the Tenth Amendment. However, the independent constitutional bar limitation does not mean Congress may not indirectly achieve objectives it could not achieve directly. The bar prevents Congress from inducing states to engage in otherwise unconstitutional behavior. Because a state may constitutionally raise its drinking age, Congress is not barred from imposing such a condition on the expenditure of federal funds.

Dissent (O'Connor, J.). This condition established by this statute is not reasonably related to the expenditure of federal funds for highway purposes. The minimum drinking age is at best tangentially related to highway safety. If Congress can impose a condition that is so minimally related to its spending objectives, then Congress can interfere in virtually all aspects of state government, merely by citing some effect on interstate travel.

C. THE WAR AND TREATY POWERS AND IMPLIED POWER OVER FOREIGN AFFAIRS

1. **The War Power.** The war power can have tremendous domestic impact.

   a. **Constitutional provisions.**

      1) **Congress.** By Article I, Section 8, Congress has the power to declare war, to raise and support armies, to maintain a navy, to make rules for the regulation of the land and naval forces, and to provide for organizing, arming, disciplining, and calling forth the militia.

      2) **The President.** Article II, Section 2 provides that the President shall be the commander in chief of the Army, Navy, and the state militias when they are called into the service of the United States.

   b. **Regulations under the war power.** Congress and the President, under the Necessary and Proper Clause, have wide powers to prepare for and wage war, and to control the after-effects of war.

      1) **Preparation for war.** Congress has the power to maintain armies, draft civilians, engage in weapons research, etc.

      2) **Wartime regulation.** During war, Congress has wide powers to wage war effectively. For example, Congress has the power to enact comprehensive legislation controlling the national economy. [Bowles v. Willingham, 321 U.S. 414 (1944)—rent controls] And Congress in aid of its powers to make rules for the government of the armed forces may provide for military tribunals to punish of-

fenses against the armed forces. The guarantees of the Fifth and Sixth Amendments (jury trials, etc.) do not apply to military personnel prosecuted in such military proceedings.

3) **Postwar economic controls--**

Woods v. Cloyd W. Miller Co., 333 U.S. 138 (1948).

Facts. Woods (P), United States Housing Expediter, sought to enjoin Cloyd W. Miller Co.'s (D's) violations of rent controls imposed by the Housing and Rent Act of 1947. The Act was passed under the war power to assist adjustment to the housing shortage caused by World War II. D claimed that the Act was unconstitutional. The district court agreed, finding that inauguration of "peace-in-fact" by presidential proclamation precluded further congressional action based on the war powers.

Issue. May Congress continue to regulate the economy under its war powers following cessation of hostilities?

Held. Yes. Judgment reversed.

- ♦ The war power includes the power to remedy the evils that arise from war, and does not necessarily end with the cessation of hostilities. The critical housing shortage directly caused by the war continued after cessation of hostilities, and application of the Necessary and Proper Clause to the war power permits congressional action to deal with war-related problems as it sees fit.

- ♦ Although a potential for abuse from attenuated interpretations of war-caused economic effects is possible, there is no such abuse here. Congress cannot be assumed to ignore constitutional responsibilities in the future, and judicial review would be available should such abuse arise.

Concurrence (Jackson, J.). War powers do not last as long as the effects and consequences of war, nor do they exist merely because of a purely legal or technical state of war. They exist only as long as there is in actuality a state of war, with armies abroad exercising our war powers, as in present circumstances.

2. **The Treaty Power and Foreign Affairs.**

   a. **Constitutional provision.** Article II, Section 2 grants the President the power to make treaties with foreign nations, provided "two-thirds of the Senators present concur."

   b. **The supreme law of the land.** As stated above, the federal government's powers in domestic affairs are limited to those delegated by the Constitution. In external affairs, however, the federal government has all the powers that are the necessary concomitants of nationality and sovereignty. There is no distribution of the power between the federal government and the states, but the federal government power is exercised without regard to state law or policies.

1) Additionally, the Supremacy Clause states that treaties shall be the supreme law of the land, "anything in the Constitution or laws of any state to the contrary notwithstanding."

2) So, for example, in *Hauenstein v. Lynham*, 100 U.S. 483 (1880), a citizen of Switzerland owned land in Virginia and died intestate. Under Swiss law, the decedent's heirs had the right to the property even though they lived in Switzerland. Under Virginia law, the property would have escheated to the state. The Supreme Court held a treaty between the United States and Switzerland took precedence over the state law.

c. **Treaty power as a source of legislative power.**

1) **No limitation by Tenth Amendment.** The Tenth Amendment (the federal government has delegated powers; all others are reserved to the states) is not a limitation on the treaty power. That is, pursuant to a treaty, under the Necessary and Proper Clause, Congress may legislate on matters over which it otherwise would have no power to do so.

2) **Power to implement treaty--**

Missouri v. Holland, 252 U.S. 416 (1920).

Facts. The Migratory Bird Treaty Act of 1918 implemented a treaty between the United States and Canada and prohibited killing or interference with migratory birds except as permitted by regulations made by the Secretary of Agriculture. Missouri (P) brought suit in equity to enjoin Holland (D), a United States game warden, from enforcing the Act. P claims the Act unconstitutionally interferes with state rights and that an earlier similar act of Congress, not in pursuance to a treaty, was held invalid. The district court dismissed the action; P appeals.

Issue. May an Act of Congress implementing a United States treaty create regulations that would be unconstitutional if the Act stood alone?

Held. Yes. Judgment affirmed.

♦ The Tenth Amendment is irrelevant since the power to make treaties is delegated expressly. Furthermore, if the treaty is valid, the statute is equally so, being necessary and proper. The treaty does not contravene any prohibitory words found in the Constitution and is presumed valid.

- The important national interest here can be protected only by national action in concert with that of another nation. Such a joint effort is possible only through a treaty. Since there is no specific constitutional restriction and the national interest requires it, the treaty, and therefore its implementing statute, are valid.

- The state's interest, while sufficient to justify regulation in the absence of federal regulation, is too transitory to preempt specific national regulation, especially when the national action arises from exercise of the treaty power.

Comments.

- The case implies that a treaty can confer upon Congress powers in addition to those granted in Article I, subject to specific constitutional prohibitions. An earlier case, *DeGeofroy v. Riggs*, 133 U.S. 258 (1890), noted that the treaty power may extend only to "proper subjects of negotiation between our government and the governments of other nations."

- For a case where a treaty was not upheld as the supreme law of the land due to inconsistency with a specific constitutional provision, see *Reid v. Covert*, 354 U.S. 1 (1957).

V. FEDERAL LIMITS ON STATE REGULATION OF INTERSTATE COMMERCE

A. THE DORMANT COMMERCE CLAUSE

1. Introduction.

a. **The Tenth Amendment—the power of the states.** The powers of the federal government are, for the most part, specifically mentioned in the Constitution; they are delegated powers. The power of the states is residual; *i.e.*, under the Tenth Amendment the states have all power not specifically given to the federal government.

b. **Division of federal power.**

1) **Exclusive power in the federal government.** The Constitution grants some powers exclusively to the federal government. For example, Article I, Section 8 grants the federal government exclusive power to control federal lands. Any regulation by the states in these areas is prohibited.

2) **Concurrent powers.** The Constitution delegates many other powers to the federal government. At one time it was argued that pursuant to the Supremacy Clause the federal government had exclusive power in these areas. However, this view has not prevailed. The Supreme Court has held that the states may exercise some of these powers concurrently with the federal government, although the Court has held that in certain areas the very presence of the federal government power inhibits, to some extent, the exercise by the states of this same power. Of course, where concurrent power exists, if the exercise of that power by a state conflicts with the exercise of the power by the federal government, the federal government controls.

2. Early Approach.

a. **Federal and state laws in conflict--**

Gibbons v. Ogden, 22 U.S. (9 Wheat.) 1 (1824). (*See supra* for brief of first part of case.)

Facts. Ogden (P) held an assignment of the exclusive right to run a steamboat between Elizabethtown, New Jersey and New York City. The exclusive right to operate steamships in New York waters had been granted by the New York legislature. Gibbons (D) operated boats along P's route, claiming that his boats were duly enrolled and licensed under United States law for carrying on the coasting trade. P sought and obtained a state court injunction prohibiting D's operation. The injunction was sustained by the highest state court, and D appeals.

Issue. Is state regulation of commercial navigation that excludes federally licensed operators constitutional?

Held. No. Judgment reversed. The New York statute is void.

- P admits that Congress has the power to regulate commerce with foreign nations, and among the several states, but would limit the meaning of "commerce" to traffic, buying and selling, or the interchange of commodities, and would exclude navigation. But one of the primary objects of the creation of the federal government was to grant the power over commerce, including navigation.

- The commerce power of Congress must be exercised within the territorial jurisdiction of the states, even though it cannot reach solely intrastate commerce.

- P attempts to analogize between the taxing power and the commerce power, claiming that since the taxing power is concurrent, the commerce power should be. But regulation of interstate commerce is an exclusive federal power. When a state regulates commerce with foreign nations or among the several states, it exercises the very power granted to Congress, and the analogy fails.

- State inspection laws are recognized in the Constitution, but do not derive from a power to regulate commerce. They act upon the subject before it becomes an article of foreign commerce.

- D has been granted, through a federal license, the privilege of employment in the coasting trade. P would restrict such trade to property transport, excluding passengers. Such narrow interpretation would eventually "explain away the Constitution"; instead, safe and fundamental principles must be followed, and coasting trade includes transport of both property and persons for hire.

- For these reasons, the federal license must be recognized, and state laws prohibiting exercise of such licenses are void.

Concurrence (Johnson, J.). The Court need not decide whether to construe constitutional provisions liberally or strictly, but must simply discover the intent and meaning and then execute the will of those who made it. The states, upon obtaining independence, created disruptive commercial regulation, which was the immediate cause that led to the forming of a convention. No states repealed the former statutes, but they fell "lifeless from the statute books, for want of the sustaining power relinquished to Congress." The fact that D based his defense on a license is irrelevant, for only Congress can regulate commerce; any state regulation is automatically void.

Comment. Just five years after this case was decided, the Court decided *Willson v. Black Bird Creek Marsh Co.*, 27 U.S. (2 Pet.) 244 (1829). The state had permitted a private party to build a dam across a navigable creek, and Willson, whose vessel was licensed under federal law, broke the dam. The Court upheld the state law against Willson's challenge, emphasizing that the state regulation affected only a small, navigable creek concerning which Congress had not acted. The law was intended to preserve property values and protect the public health and was, therefore, a permissible exercise of state police power.

---

b. "National" vs. "local" issues--

Cooley v. Board of Wardens, 53 U.S. (12 How.) 299 (1851).

Facts. Pennsylvania passed a statute requiring vessels entering or leaving the Port of Philadelphia (represented by the Board of Wardens (P)) to accept local pilots while in the Delaware River. The penalty for disobedience was one-half the pilotage fees. Cooley (D), consignee of two violating vessels, was sued under the Act. P relied on a 1789 congressional statute that incorporated all then-existing state laws regulating pilots and that mandated conformity with subsequently enacted state regulation, such as the law in this case. D contends that Congress cannot delegate its powers in this manner. D appeals state court judgments for P.

Issue. May Congress permit the states to regulate aspects of commerce that are primarily local in nature?

Held. Yes. Judgment affirmed.

- Regulation of pilots is clearly a regulation of commerce. If Congress's power to regulate commerce is exclusive, the Act of 1789 could not confer upon the states the power to regulate pilots.

- The correct approach looks to the nature of the subjects of the power, rather than the nature of the power itself. Many subjects are national in nature, but some are local, like the one involved here. When a subject is national it is best governed by one uniform system, and therefore requires exclusive legislation by Congress. But a local subject is best handled by the states, which can adapt regulation to the local peculiarities.

- The Act of 1789 manifests the understanding of Congress that the nature of this subject (pilotage of local ports) does not require its exclusive legislation. That understanding must be upheld, and the statute is constitutional.

Comment. Congress has absolute power to regulate interstate commerce. Congress may permit a state to exercise this power, or, in its sole discretion, prohibit a state from doing so. Where Congress has acted to prohibit state regulation, Congress is said to have "preempted the field." Even where Congress has not preempted the field, the very existence of the Commerce Clause forbids state regulation that places an "unreasonable burden" on interstate commerce. The determinative factor is the subject of the regulation; "local" subjects may be more freely regulated by the states than "national" subjects.

---

c. **Direct-indirect distinction.** In addition to the national-local standard used in *Cooley*, the Court in the late 1800s increasingly used a direct-indirect distinction regarding state regulations. [*See, e.g.*, Di Santo v. Pennsylvania, 273 U.S. 34 (1927)—state law imposing license fee on travel agents selling tickets for foreign travel was invalid as a direct burden on commerce] Shortly after *Di Santo*, the Court began employing the balancing test enunciated by the dissent in *Di Santo*.

d. **Licensing cases.** Balance of interests favors the state. The state interest underlying the regulation must not be outweighed by the burden on interstate commerce—*i.e.*, the "balance of interests" favors the state as opposed to the national interests.

1) **Controlling competition.** While state interests in protecting public health and welfare are given considerable weight, a state's interest in controlling competition is not. In *Buck v. Kuykendall*, 267 U.S. 307 (1925), a state statute required interstate carriers to obtain a certificate of public convenience in order to use state highways. The state denied the plaintiff such a certificate on the basis that the territory was already adequately served. The Supreme Court said that this state regulation was unconstitutional, since its purpose was to prohibit interstate competition.

2) **Public safety and welfare.** A state's interest in the public safety and welfare (where it is the predominant purpose of the statute) may justify obstruction of interstate commerce. In *Bradley v. Public Utilities Commission*, 289 U.S. 92 (1933), Ohio had denied a permit to an interstate trucker to operate from Michigan into Ohio, on the ground that the highway was already so badly congested by established traffic that the proposed service would create excessive traffic hazards. The Supreme Court upheld the regulation.

3. **The Modern Approach to State Regulation Affecting Interstate Commerce.**

a. **Introduction.** The Commerce Clause was intended to insure a common market among the states. The Court has been quick to disapprove of state laws that discriminate against interstate commerce or that act to protect local industries against competition. Even if the state gives plausible, legitimate reasons for the barriers, the Court may emphasize the discriminatory effect of the law and hold it unconstitutional. Where Congress has not acted, the states have power to regulate any phase of local business (production, marketing, sales, etc.), even though such regulations may have some effect on interstate commerce, as long as they neither discriminate against, nor impose any unreasonable burden upon, interstate commerce.

1) **Regulation of incoming commerce.** One way to develop a state's economy is to require businesses to operate within the state. The Commerce Clause prohibits such legislation if it burdens interstate commerce and is not necessary to promote a valid state purpose. Protecting local business against out-of-state competition is not a valid state purpose per se, but there may be valid reasons for excluding out-of-state products.

   a) **Protection of health and safety.** Quarantine and inspection laws enacted to protect public health are upheld as long as they do not discriminate against or unreasonably burden interstate commerce. [Hannibal & St. Joseph Railroad v. Husen, 95 U.S. 465 (1877)]

      (1) **Permissible regulation.** A local statute requiring that cattle or meat imported from other states be certified as free from disease by the state of origin has been upheld. The burden on interstate commerce caused by supplying such a certificate was outweighed by the public health objectives of the state law. [Mintz v. Baldwin, 289 U.S. 346 (1933)]

      (2) **Impermissible regulation.** Although having a valid "public health" purpose, a state law requiring local inspection of slaughterhouses prior to slaughter of livestock destined for local consumption has been held unconstitutional because it discriminates against out-of-state slaughterhouses (*i.e.*, it prevents importation of sound meats from animals slaughtered in other states). [Minnesota v. Barber, 136 U.S. 313 (1890)]

   b) **Protection of reputation.** State laws enacted to protect local, publicly owned natural resources are traditionally a proper exercise of the state's "police power," and will usually be upheld by the court—*i.e.*, the court tends to "balance the interests" in favor of such regulations. [Pike v. Bruce Church, Inc., *infra*]

2) **Regulation of outgoing commerce.** *Dean Milk*, *infra*, involved a requirement that imported goods be partially processed within the state. States have also occasionally required that their products be processed within the state before being exported. Such requirements have not fared well despite assertions of valid state interests.

3) **Discriminatory categories.** Modern cases involving discrimination against interstate commerce fall into three categories:

a) State laws that facially discriminate against out-of-state commerce;

b) State laws that favor local economic interests at the expense of out-of-state competitors; and

c) Facially neutral state laws that unduly burden, *i.e.*, "balancing of interests" cases.

b. **Environmental protection--**

Philadelphia v. New Jersey, 437 U.S. 617 (1978).

Facts. New Jersey (D) passed a law prohibiting importation into the state of solid or liquid wastes, in order to protect the public health, safety, and welfare from the consequences of excessive landfill developments. Philadelphia (P) and other cities, as well as New Jersey landfill operators, challenged the law under the Commerce Clause. The New Jersey Supreme Court upheld the law. P appeals.

Issue. May a state prohibit importation of environmentally destructive substances solely because of their source of origin?

Held. No. Judgment reversed.

♦ D's reason for passing the law may be legitimate, but the evils of protectionism can reside in the legislative means used as well as legislative ends sought. D's ultimate purpose may not be achieved by discriminating against out-of-state items solely because of their origin. D has failed to show any other valid reason for its discrimination.

♦ D's facially discriminatory statute requires out-of-state commercial interests to carry the burden of conserving D's remaining landfill space in an attempt to isolate itself from a problem shared by all. Protection against such trade barriers serves the interest of all states, and may even work to the advantage of New Jersey in the future.

- D claims this statute resembles quarantine laws, which are exceptions to the general Commerce Clause rules. But quarantine laws merely prevent traffic in noxious articles, regardless of their origin. D claims no harm from the mere movement of waste into its borders and concedes that when the harm is felt (upon disposal) there is no basis to distinguish out-of-state wastes from domestic waste.

Dissent (Rehnquist, J., Burger, C.J.). D's law essentially prohibits importation of items that could endanger its population, and should be upheld. The Court implies that the challenged laws must be invalidated because domestic waste may be used in the state's landfills. This fact ought not require D to exacerbate its problems by accepting out-of-state waste.

---

c. **Limits on state-imposed embargoes of natural resources.** Early cases upholding restraints on exports of natural resources often relied on state property interests. For example, the Court in *Geer v. Connecticut*, 161 U.S. 519 (1896), upheld a ban on the killing of game birds destined for shipment out of the state because the birds were collectively owned by the state citizenry. *Geer* was overruled in *Hughes v. Oklahoma*, 441 U.S. 322 (1979), which invalidated a state law prohibiting the transport for sale out of state of any minnows caught within state waters, because regulation of natural resources should be scrutinized with modern commerce standards. The *Hughes* Court found the law facially discriminatory and, while it may have served a legitimate purpose, nondiscriminatory alternatives were not considered by the state.

d. **Facially discriminatory fees.** Facially discriminatory fees (and taxes) levied on out-of-state hazardous waste but not on in-state waste violate the dormant Commerce Clause. [Chemical Waste Management, Inc. v. Hunt, 504 U.S. 334 (1992)] Similarly, disposal fees that differentiate between in-state and out-of-state waste are facially discriminatory and thus invalid. [Oregon Waste Systems, Inc. v. Dept. of Environmental Quality, 511 U.S. 93 (1994)]

e. **Subsidies instead of regulation.** *West Lynn Creamery, Inc. v. Healy,* 512 U.S. 186 (1994), involved a Massachusetts law that subjected milk sold to Massachusetts retailers to an assessment, with the entire assessment distributed to Massachusetts dairy farmers. The Court held that the pricing order was unconstitutional. The Court found that the purpose for the milk order was to allow higher-cost in-state dairy farmers to compete with lower-cost producers in other states. The effect of the milk pricing order was to make milk produced out of state more expensive. Even though the pricing order was imposed on milk produced in state as well as milk produced out of state, its effect on Massachusetts producers was more than offset by the subsidy. Consequently, it functions like a protective tariff.

f. **Home processing requirements.** Home processing requirements are generally held invalid. For example, a state may not require that all shrimp taken from its waters be shelled before shipment out of state when it permits the byproducts to be shipped out of state. Such a rule does not reflect a valid state interest in conservation. [Foster-Fountain Packing Co. v. Haydel, 278 U.S. 1 (1928); *see also*, C & A Carbone, Inc. v. Clarkstown, *infra*—summary of processing cases]

g. **Facial discrimination by localities--**

Dean Milk Co. v. Madison, 340 U.S. 349 (1951).

Facts. An ordinance of the city of Madison, Wisconsin (D), prohibited (i) the sale of pasteurized milk unless processed at an approved plant within a five-mile radius of downtown Madison, and (ii) the sale, importation, receipt, or storage of milk for sale in Madison unless originating at a farm inspected by Madison officials, who were not required to inspect any farms farther than five miles from the city center. Dean Milk Co. (P), an interstate milk processor and dealer, was denied a license to sell its products in Madison solely because P's plants were more than five miles away. The state courts upheld the ordinance, and P appeals.

Issue. May a local statute that has a valid purpose but discriminates against interstate commerce be upheld if there are nondiscriminatory yet effective alternatives?

Held. No. Judgment vacated and remanded.

- ♦ The ordinance has a valid purpose and is within the scope of local power. No federal regulation exists on the issue.
- ♦ However, the regulation has a discriminatory effect on interstate commerce. Local statutes cannot erect such barriers to interstate commerce even to further valid health and welfare objectives if reasonable nondiscriminatory alternatives are available to protect these local interests.
- ♦ The record discloses at least two such alternatives: United States Public Health Service inspections and out-of-town ratings and inspections. Permitting D to enforce a nonessential and discriminatory regulation would invite a multiplication of preferential trade areas contrary to the Commerce Clause.

Dissent (Black, Douglas, Minton, JJ.). There is no showing that P was unable to process its milk within the five-mile radius. Local determination of the best method of sanitary control should not be overruled by the Court. To do so elevates the right to traffic in commerce for profit above the power of the people to guard the purity of their daily diet of milk.

Comment. The Court consistently rejects state requirements that products be processed in the state before being shipped out of state. For example, in *Dean Milk*, the Court relied in part on *Minnesota v. Barber, supra*. In that case, Minnesota had prohibited the sale of meat that had not been inspected by a local official within 24 hours of slaughtering. The law necessarily discriminated against meat shipped from other states, and, if copied by other states, would have destroyed commerce among the states. *Dean Milk* is often cited for requiring judicial inquiry into "reasonable nondiscriminatory alternatives."

---

h. Limits on local government control with interstate economic effects--

---

C & A Carbone, Inc. v. Clarkstown, 511 U.S. 383 (1994).

Facts. To finance construction of a waste transfer station, Clarkstown (D) had to guarantee a minimum flow of waste to the station. D enacted a flow control ordinance, which required that all solid waste in the town be deposited at the station. C & A Carbone (P) was a private recycler with a sorting facility in D. D's ordinance increased P's costs, because P could obtain the necessary services out of state at a lower cost than D's station charged. P challenged D's ordinance. The lower courts upheld the ordinance. P appeals.

Issue. May a local government require that all solid waste within its boundaries be processed by a specific local processor?

Held. No. Judgment reversed.

- Although the ordinance has the effect of directing local waste to a local facility, the economic effects reach interstate commerce. P's facility received waste from out of state. D's ordinance required P to send the nonrecyclable portion of the waste to D's local facility, which increased P's costs and hence the costs to the out-of-state sources of solid waste. The ordinance also deprives out-of-state businesses access to D's local market.

- D claims that its ordinance does not discriminate against interstate commerce because it applies to all solid waste, regardless of origin, before it leaves the town. However, the ordinance does discriminate because it allows only the favored processor to process waste within D's town limits. It is an example of local processing requirements that have been held invalid, such as the local milk pasteurizing requirement in *Dean Milk* (*supra*).

- In *Dean Milk*, the city of Madison had required that all milk sold in the city be pasteurized within five miles of the city lines. Although the ordinance had a valid purpose and was within the scope of local power, it had a discriminatory effect on interstate commerce and reasonable nondiscriminatory alternatives were available to protect the local interests. In this case, D's ordinance is even more restrictive than the one in *Dean Milk* because it leaves no room for outside investment.

- Discrimination against interstate commerce in favor of local business or investment is per se invalid, unless the municipality has no other means to advance a legitimate local interest. D has a variety of nondiscriminatory means to address its local waste disposal problems. The objective of fundraising is not adequate to justify discrimination against out-of-state businesses.

Concurrence (O'Connor, J.). D's ordinance is different than the ordinances the Court has previously held invalid because it does not give more favorable treatment to local interests as a group as compared to out-of-state economic interests. Thus, it does not discriminate against interstate commerce. However, the ordinance does impose an excessive burden on interstate commerce when compared with the local benefits it confers.

Dissent (Souter, J., Rehnquist, C.J., Blackmun, J.). There is no evidence in this case that any out-of-state trash processor has been harmed. The ordinance treats all out-of-town investors and facilities to the same constraints as local ones, so there is no economic protectionism. The only right to compete that the Commerce Clause protects is the right to compete on terms independent of one's location. The ordinance merely imposes a burden on the local citizens who adopted it, and local burdens are not the focus of the Commerce Clause.

Comment. The Court has upheld express discrimination against interstate commerce where the statute serves a legitimate local purpose that cannot be served as well by an available nondiscriminatory means. For example, in *Maine v. Taylor*, 477 U.S. 131 (1986), the Court upheld a Maine statute prohibiting the importation of live baitfish because of the adverse biological consequences of nonnative species and parasites.

---

i. Favoring government facilities--

United Haulers Association v. Oneida-Herkimer Solid Waste Management Authority, 127 S. Ct. 1786 (2007).

Facts. United Haulers Association (P) challenged flow control ordinances that required trash haulers to deliver solid waste to facilities owned and operated by a state-created public benefit corporation. P claimed that the flow control ordinances discriminated against interstate commerce in violation of the Commerce Clause. The Supreme Court granted certiorari.

Issue. Does the Commerce Clause prevent states from favoring government facilities if in-state private businesses are treated the same as out-of-state businesses?

Held. No. Judgment affirmed.

- ♦ The difference between the flow control ordinances in this case and the ordinance rejected in *C & A Carbone, supra*, is that in this case the ordinances require P to bring waste to a state-created public benefit corporation. The difference is constitutionally significant.

- ♦ Trash disposal is a traditional government activity. States may favor the government in this area. The ordinances in this case benefit a public facility and disfavor all private companies the same.

- ♦ If states could not treat public and private entities differently under the Dormant Commerce Clause, courts would have to continually interfere with state and local government actions.

Concurrence (Thomas, J.). The entire Dormant Commerce Clause jurisprudence should be overturned.

Dissent (Alito, Stevens, Kennedy, JJ.). There is no meaningful distinction between this case and *Carbone*. In *Carbone*, the facility was owned by a private contractor, but he built it for the town and agreed to sell it back after five years for $1 on the town's guarantee that for those five years he would receive at least 120,000 tons of waste per year. In *Carbone*, the title had not yet formally passed to the municipality, but it was really more of a government facility over the long term. Never before has the Court recognized an exception for discrimination in favor of a state-owned entity in this type of case. Respondents are doing what the market-participant doctrine says they cannot—regulating an existing interstate market while acting as participants in that market. The flow control ordinance should be subject to strict scrutiny.

---

j. The market participant exception--

South-Central Timber Development v. Wunnicke, 467 U.S. 82 (1984).

Facts. The state of Alaska (D) offered to sell its timber, but only with a contractual requirement that it be processed within the state before being exported. In return, the price for the timber was significantly reduced from what it otherwise would have been. South-Central Timber Development (P) normally sold unprocessed logs to Japan. P sought an injunction in federal court, claiming that the requirement violated the negative implications of the Commerce Clause. D responded that its restriction was exempt under the market participant doctrine. The district court granted the injunction, but the court of appeals reversed, concluding that a similar federal policy for timber taken from federal land in Alaska constituted implicit congressional authorization of the state plan. The Supreme Court granted certiorari.

Issue. When a state sells its own natural resources, may it impose post-sale obligations on the purchaser?

Held. No. Judgment reversed.

- The Commerce Clause limits the power of the states to impose substantial burdens on interstate commerce, although Congress may authorize state regulation of such commerce. Here, there was no indication that Congress intended to give such power to Alaska. Congressional consent "must be unmistakably clear." The existence of a federal program similar to the state's is insufficient evidence to support an inference that the state's action was authorized by Congress.

- This case involves three elements not present in *Reeves Inc. v. Stake*, 447 U.S. 429 (1980): foreign commerce is restrained, the state is selling a natural resource, and the state imposes restrictions on resale. Commerce Clause scrutiny must be more rigorous because of these factors.

- The fact that the state acted through a contract is not enough. The market-participant doctrine must be limited to allowing a state to impose burdens on commerce within the market in which it participates. Here, Alaska has gone too far by imposing conditions that have a substantial regulatory effect outside of the market it has entered. This program does not fall within the market-participant exception.

- The protectionist nature of Alaska's program results in interference with interstate and foreign commerce. Thus it violates the Commerce Clause.

Concurrence (Powell, J., Burger, C.J.). The case should be remanded to determine whether the plan substantially burdened interstate commerce.

Dissent (Rehnquist, O'Connor, JJ.). The plurality's decision seems to draw on antitrust law. But antitrust laws apply to a state only when it is acting as a market participant. The plurality thus concludes that Alaska is acting as a market regulator by relying on cases that are relevant only if Alaska is a market participant. The state is merely paying timber purchasers to hire Alaska residents to process the timber, a result it could accomplish in a variety of ways. It is unduly formalistic to hold that this method violates the Commerce Clause.

k. **Protectionist barriers against out-of-state sellers.** There may be attractive benefits for localities to protect local businesses against out-of-state competition. Such regulation may be valid, depending on how much of an impact it has on interstate commerce.

1) **Preserving local price structure impermissible--**

Baldwin v. G.A.F. Seelig, Inc., 294 U.S. 511 (1935).

Facts. G.A.F. Seelig, Inc. (P), a New York milk dealer, purchased milk in Vermont at less than the minimum price set by New York law. New York denied P a license to deal in New York. The New York statute permitted price differentials based on transportation costs and applied special regulation to sales of imported milk. The purpose of the statute was said to be (i) to stabilize the supply of milk; (ii) to keep small farmers on the farms by not allowing cutthroat competition; and (iii) to keep the quality of milk up. P sued to enjoin enforcement of the statute, and the lower courts granted relief. Baldwin (D), a state official, appeals.

Issue. May a state protect intrastate producers against low-cost, out-of-state competition to assure an adequate and safe supply of an essential commodity?

Held. No. Judgment affirmed.

- Distinctions between direct and indirect burdens on commerce are irrelevant when the purpose of a statute is to suppress competition between the states.
- The state may properly impose regulations to assure the health of its citizens, but not to assure their wealth. To uphold this statute as a valid exercise of police power with only incidental effects on commerce would "eat up the rule under the guise of an exception," and would lead to total emasculation of the law against state-levied import tariffs.

Comment. The statute in this case was an economic tool used to ultimately affect the health, safety, and welfare of the state's citizens. Did the Supreme Court rule against the use of economic tools to effect a safety measure indirectly? The Court did not seriously balance the interests here; it simply seemed to say that this type of regulation could not be used. The implication seems to be that direct regulation with a safety measure would be all right; *e.g.*, a requirement that everyone selling milk pasteurize it within five miles of the city. [*But see* Dean Milk Co. v. Madison, *supra*]

2) **Protecting health and safety--**

H.P. Hood & Sons v. Du Mond, 336 U.S. 525 (1949).

Facts. New York law required milk handlers to obtain a license prior to opening any new receiving depot. H.P. Hood & Sons (P), interstate milk handlers, were denied such a license by Du Mond (D), a state official, who found that the requested license would "tend to aid destructive competition in a market already adequately served," thus violating New York law. P challenged the law.

Issue. May a state suppress interstate competition as a means of protecting the health and safety of its people?

Held. No. Judgment reversed.

- Although states may impose even burdensome regulations in the interests of local health and safety, their attempts to advance their own purely commercial interests by curtailing the movement of articles of interstate commerce are impermissible. Therefore, a state may not use its admitted powers to protect the health and safety of its people as a basis for suppressing competition. Because this statute has the prohibited effect, it is void.

Dissent (Black, Murphy, JJ.). The language of the act is not discriminatory, it was not intended to be discriminatory, and it has not been administered in a discriminatory manner. The real issue here is whether all phases of interstate business are judicially immunized from state laws against destructive competitive business practices. This regulation may not be wise, but it is not up to this Court to revise a state's economic judgment.

Dissent (Frankfurter, Rutledge, JJ.). This case should be remanded; we should balance the state's interest in the prevention of destructive competition with the effect that act would have on interstate commerce. Instead the Court treats this as an exercise in absolutes—no matter how important the state's interest is or how unimportant the interstate commerce affected, the state cannot deny an applicant access to the market if that applicant happens to intend the out-of-state shipment of the product that he buys.

Comment—statutes fixing minimum prices. State laws imposing minimum prices on the sale of local natural resources have been upheld as proper "conservation" regulations. [*See* Cities Service Gas Co. v. Peerless Oil & Gas Co., 340 U.S. 179 (1950)—state law fixing minimum price on all gas taken from local fields was upheld as a proper measure for conservation of a local natural resource, even though most of the gas was shipped in interstate commerce]

---

3) **Identifying protectionist purposes and effects.**

a) **Eliminating confusion.** In *Hunt v. Washington State Apple Advertising Commission,* 432 U.S. 333 (1977), the Court considered a North Carolina statute that required that all closed containers of apples sold, offered for sale, or shipped into the state bear "no grade other than the applicable United States grade or standard." A related regulation required the USDA grade or none at all. The statute was purportedly intended to eliminate confusion resulting from a multiplicity of inconsistent state grades. The Washington State Apple Advertising Commission had developed its own grades, widely recognized as superior to the USDA grades, and on which the reputation of its apples depended. The Court held that when discrimination against interstate commerce is shown, the burden falls on the state to justify its regulation both in terms of the local benefits flowing from the statute and the unavailability of nondiscriminatory alternative ways to accomplish the same objectives. The North Carolina statute was clearly discriminatory, because it covered only closed containers of apples, the very means by which apples are transported in commerce. Feasible, effective, and less discriminatory alternatives were available.

b) **Promoting a struggling local industry.** In *Bacchus Imports, Ltd. v. Dias,* 468 U.S. 263 (1984), the Court held invalid a tax provision that exempted liquor distilled from an indigenous plant. Even though the statute was nondiscriminatory on its face, it constituted de facto discrimination.

c) **Permissible state barrier to incoming trade.** In *Exxon Corp. v. Governor of Maryland*, 437 U.S. 117 (1978), the Court upheld a law prohibiting producers or refiners of petroleum products from operating retail service stations in the state because of past preferential treatment from suppliers. Since all petroleum suppliers came from outside the state, there was no discrimination against interstate goods. Nor did the law discriminate against interstate retailers per se, but only against a certain type of retailer. The Commerce Clause "protects the interstate market, not particular interstate firms."

d) **Environmental protection favoring local industry allowed.** Minnesota banned the retail sale of milk packaged in plastic nonreturnable containers but allowed sales in other nonreturnable containers. The permissible containers were composed mainly of pulpwood, which was a major in-state product. The Court, in *Minnesota v. Clover Leaf Creamery Co.*, 449 U.S. 456 (1981), upheld the ban as it was rationally related to the state's conservation interests and the burden on interstate commerce was slight compared to the benefits to the state. There was no discrimination against interstate commerce because the ban applied to all plastic container manufacturers. The Court also rejected an equal protection challenge.

l. **Facially neutral laws and the modern balancing test.** The Court, in *Pike v. Bruce Church, Inc.*, 397 U.S. 137 (1970), set forth the modern balancing test: If a state has a legitimate local purpose for regulating and the effects on interstate commerce are merely incidental, the regulation will be upheld unless the burden clearly exceeds the local benefits.

m. **State regulation of transportation.**

1) **Basic principles.** Where Congress has not enacted legislation regarding the subject matter of commerce, the states may regulate local transactions even though they affect interstate commerce—subject, however, to certain limitations. To be constitutional, state regulation must satisfy these criteria:

a) **Uniform national regulation not required.** The subject matter must not be one that inherently requires uniform, national regulation. [*See* Wabash, St. Louis & Pacific Railway v. Illinois, 118 U.S. 557 (1886)—holding that states could not regulate interstate railroad shipments]

b) **Nondiscriminatory.** The state regulation must not discriminate against interstate commerce so as to "substantially impede" the free flow of commerce across state lines. [*See* Seaboard Air Line Railway v. Blackwell, 244 U.S. 310 (1917)—overturning a state law requiring trains to slow down at crossings because it would have increased the length of the trip involved from 4½ to over 10 hours]

2) **Burden of proof when interstate commerce is burdened.** When the challenged regulation significantly burdens interstate commerce, the state must meet a heavy burden of justification based on its interests.

3) **Further refinement of the balancing test--**

Kassel v. Consolidated Freightways Corp., 450 U.S. 662 (1981).

Facts. Consolidated Freightways Corp. (P) challenged an Iowa statute that, like Wisconsin's law in *Raymond Motor Transportation, Inc. v. Rice*, 434 U.S. 429 (1978), prohibited the use of 65-foot double trailers on Iowa highways (with certain exceptions). Kassel (D), an Iowa official, defended the law as a reasonable safety measure in light of the *Raymond* case. The lower courts held the law unconstitutional, as it seriously impeded interstate commerce while providing only slight, if any, safety. D appeals.

Issue. May the courts examine evidence to determine whether a state's purported interest in safety is real and substantial enough to justify applying its police power to burden interstate commerce?

Held. Yes. Judgment affirmed.

- ♦ A state cannot avoid a Commerce Clause attack merely by invoking public health or safety. The courts are required to balance the state's safety interest against the federal interest in free interstate commerce.

- ♦ Despite the "special deference" usually accorded to state highway safety regulations, and D's serious effort to support the safety rationale, the record here is no more favorable to D than was Wisconsin's evidence in *Raymond*. P has demonstrated that D's law substantially burdens interstate commerce. Therefore, D's law is unconstitutional.

Concurrence (Brennan, Marshall, JJ.). D's law is unconstitutional under *Raymond* since it is protectionist. The plurality and the dissent insist on considering the legislative purposes advanced by D's lawyers. Separation of powers, however, requires that we defer to the elected lawmakers' judgment, not that we defer to the arguments of lawyers. D's statute exists because the governor of Iowa vetoed legislation that would have permitted 65-foot doubles, giving an essentially protectionist rationale for his action. This is an improper purpose. Safety became a purpose for the law only in retrospect, to defeat P's challenge.

Dissent (Rehnquist, J., Burger, C.J., Stewart, J.). Both the plurality and concurring opinions have intruded upon the fundamental right of the states to pass laws to secure the safety of their citizens. D's law is rationally related to its safety objectives. We are essentially reweighing the state legislature's policy choice and are forcing D to lower its safety standards merely because its sister states' standards are lower.

Comment. This case may be viewed as merely an application of the *Raymond* decision to different facts, or as an announcement of a new standard of review. At any rate, the precise issue of this case has become moot because Congress has prescribed federal standards, including authorization of 65-foot double-trailer trucks. [*See* 96 U.S.C. §§1765, 2097]

---

4) **Deference to traditionally local concerns.** Prior to adoption of the *Pike* balancing test, *supra*, the Court in *South Carolina State Highway Dept. v. Barnwell Brothers*, 303 U.S. 177 (1938), up-

held a state statute regulating the width and weight of interstate carriers on its highways. Since Congress had not acted in this area, a state may impose a nondiscriminatory restriction and it will be upheld if it has a rational basis (here, safety and highway preservation).

5) **Challenged regulation must clearly promote valid state interest.** In *Southern Pacific Co. v. Arizona,* 325 U.S. 761 (1945), the Court held that in balancing the effect of a state regulation on interstate commerce against the state's safety and welfare interests, a court may consider the efficacy of the regulation in furthering the state's interest. The Arizona Train Limit Law imposed restrictions on the number of cars permitted on any train operating within the state (14 passenger cars or 70 freight cars). Although Congress had not passed national legislation regulating train lengths, a state law could violate the Commerce Clause if it unreasonably burdens interstate commerce without an offsetting state safety benefit. Additionally, state regulation is precluded in those phases of national commerce that, because of the need for national uniformity, demand that their regulation, if any, be prescribed by a single authority. The serious impediment of state car limitations on interstate commerce indicates the need for uniform national legislation on the subject.

6) **Trucking regulations burdening interstate commerce.** When the challenged regulation significantly burdens interstate commerce, the state must meet a heavy burden of justification based on its interests. In *Bibb v. Navajo Freight Lines,* 359 U.S. 520 (1959), the Court held that a state may not impose even nondiscriminatory safety regulations that conflict with the regulations of most other states where the asserted safety advantages are at best negligible. That case involved mudguards; 45 states permitted the conventional straight mudguards, but Illinois required the use of contour mudguards. The substantial burden on interstate commerce could not be justified by any compelling state safety consideration.

7) **State barriers to business entry.**

   a) **Restrictions on entry of business into state.** The Court in *Lewis v. BT Investment Managers, Inc.*, 447 U.S. 27 (1980), used the *Pike* balancing formula (*supra*) in striking down a state law prohibiting ownership of local investment and trust businesses by out-of-state banks, bank holding companies, and trust companies. A law that distinguishes between out-of-state and local businesses is economic favoritism and constitutes an impermissible burden on interstate commerce.

b) **Balancing approach to corporate anti-takeover statute.** In *Edgar v. MITE Corp.*, 457 U.S. 624 (1982), the Court overturned an anti-takeover statute on the ground that the substantial burden it imposed on interstate commerce outweighed the putative local benefits of the statute. The statute required a 20-day preregistration of takeover offers, during which period the target company, but not the offeror, could communicate with shareholders. There was no indication that the statute had a protectionist purpose or effect.

c) **Neutral corporate anti-takeover statute.** *CTS Corp. v. Dynamics Corp. of America*, 481 U.S. 69 (1987), involved an Indiana anti-takeover statute that applied to all Indiana public corporations. Under the statute, a purchaser that acquired control shares in a public corporation would not acquire voting rights unless the shareholders approved. The Court found that the Indiana statute did not discriminate against interstate commerce, because it applied equally to domiciliaries of Indiana who made tender offers as well as to nondomiciliaries. The Court also found that, although the Commerce Clause is concerned with statutes that subject interstate commerce to inconsistent activities, the Indiana statute did not present such a problem, because it only applied to corporations the state created, and no other state could regulate the voting rights of an Indiana corporation. The Court recognized that Indiana's statute did not prevent purchasers from acquiring control, but did impose regulatory procedures to protect shareholders of Indiana corporations by letting them decide whether a change in management would be desirable. The Court viewed this as a response to the threat of coercive tender offers, a threat Indiana could deem serious. Although Indiana has no legitimate interest in protecting out-of-state shareholders, it has an interest in protecting shareholders of Indiana corporations, whether they are Indiana residents or not. Unlike the *MITE* statute, this act applies only to corporations with a substantial number of shareholders in Indiana, persons whom Indiana has a legitimate interest in protecting.

B. THE INTERSTATE PRIVILEGES AND IMMUNITIES CLAUSE OF ARTICLE IV

1. **Basic Rule.** The Privileges and Immunities Clause states that "The Citizens of each State shall be entitled to all Privileges and Immunities of Citizens in the several states." This prohibits discrimination by a state against noncitizens (or nonresidents) of the state with respect to "essential activities" or "basic rights," unless justified by a substantial reason. To justify an excep-

tion, the state must show that the nonresidents are a peculiar source of the evil sought to be avoided, and that the discrimination bears a substantial relation to the problem. Thus there is a two-part test for assessing possible violations of this clause.

2. **Protection of Basic Activities.** The clause protects activities such as pursuit of a livelihood, the transfer of property, access to the state's courts, etc. [*See* Toomer v. Witsell, 334 U.S. 385 (1948)] The Court has held that sport hunting is not an essential activity, so a state may discriminate against nonresidents in this area. [Baldwin v. Montana Fish & Game Commission, 436 U.S. 371 (1976)]

3. **Justification.** If the state's discriminatory scheme is overbroad, it will not withstand scrutiny under this clause. In *Hicklin v. Orbeck*, 437 U.S. 518 (1978), the Court determined that a state hiring preference for residents was an overbroad solution to the problem of unemployment, because the preference extended to highly skilled state residents who did not have the problem of unemployment.

4. **Discrimination Based on Municipal Residence--**

United Building & Construction Trades Council v. Mayor of Camden, 465 U.S. 208 (1984).

Facts. The city of Camden (D) adopted an ordinance that required that at least 40% of the employees of contractors and subcontractors working on city construction projects be Camden residents. The United Building & Construction Trades Council of Camden County and Vicinity (P) challenged the ordinance as violating the Privileges and Immunities Clause. After the state treasurer approved the ordinance in administrative proceedings, the state supreme court upheld it, holding that the clause does not apply to discrimination on the basis of municipal residency. P appeals.

Issue. Does the Privileges and Immunities Clause apply to municipalities that require contractors to hire the municipality's own residents to work on the municipality's construction projects?

Held. Yes. Judgment reversed and remanded for further fact findings.

♦ A municipality derives its authority from the state. If the state cannot discriminate in this manner, neither can a political subdivision of the state. Nor is the ordinance immune from attack because it discriminates against some in-state residents as well as out-of-state citizens. The former have the opportunity to directly change state law through the state legislature; the latter do not.

♦ P must first show that the ordinance burdens a privilege or immunity protected by the clause. The opportunity to seek employment is a fundamental privilege protected by the clause.

- ♦ The Privileges and Immunities Clause does not preclude discrimination against out-of-state residents if there is a substantial reason for the difference in treatment. Although D alleges several such reasons—including increasing unemployment in the city, declining population, and a depleted tax base—no trial has been held and no findings of fact have been made. The case must be remanded.

Dissent (Blackmun, J.). With no historical or textual support, the Court has expanded the scope of the clause to prohibit laws that discriminate among state residents on the basis of municipal residence. This is substantially different from discrimination on the basis of state citizenship. The protection afforded by the disadvantaged state residents' power to change state law also protects the interests of nonresidents, so the political impotency of nonresidents that the clause was designed to cure does not exist here.

Comment. At some length the Court distinguished *White v. Massachusetts Council of Construction Employees,* 460 U.S. 204 (1983), by describing the different purposes of the Commerce Clause and the Privileges and Immunities Clause. The former acts as an implied restraint on state power to regulate interstate commerce, so when a state acts as a market participant, no Commerce Clause problem arises. The latter clause directly restrains state action so as to promote interstate harmony. Even if a state acts as a market participant, its actions must not violate the restraints of the Privileges and Immunities Clause; hence the analysis applied to this case. The lower court in *White* did not reach the Privileges and Immunities Clause issue, so the Supreme Court did not address it.

---

5. **Practice of Law by Nonresident.** In *Supreme Court of New Hampshire v. Piper*, 470 U.S. 274 (1985), the Court held that a state violates the Privileges and Immunities Clause when it limits bar admission to state residents. In its ruling, the Court concluded that discrimination against nonresidents is not precluded where (i) there is a substantial reason for the discrimination, and (ii) the conduct bears a substantial relationship to the state's objective. The availability of less restrictive means was also examined.

6. **Personal Mobility.** The Supreme Court has long recognized a right to interstate travel but the constitutional sources of the right are not clear. Limitations on personal mobility have been examined mainly under the Equal Protection Clause, but the Court has also drawn on both the Commerce Clause and the Privileges and Immunities Clause. In *Edwards v. California*, 314 U.S. 160 (1941), the Court relied on the Commerce Clause's prohibition of attempts on the part of any single state to isolate itself from difficulties common to all states, and invalidated the "anti-Okie" law that made it a misdemeanor to knowingly bring into California any indigent person who was not a resident of the state.

C. CONGRESSIONAL ORDERING OF FEDERAL-STATE RELATIONSHIPS BY PREEMPTION AND CONSENT

1. **Introduction.** The last section considered situations where limitations on the exercise of state power were derived from the very existence of the Commerce Clause itself. In this section, situations are considered where Congress has actually exercised its power under the Commerce Clause. (*See* the discussion of the preemption doctrine, *supra*.)

2. **Preemption of State Authority.**

   a. **Introduction.** As a general rule federal law is interstitial; that is, it rarely occupies a legal field completely. Rather, federal legislation is drafted on an ad hoc basis to accomplish limited objectives; it normally builds on legal relations established by the states, altering or supplanting them only where necessary to accomplish a particular purpose.

   b. **Legislative intent.** The Supreme Court has often stated that the question of preemption is primarily one of the intent of Congress. This poses difficulties—whose intent is relevant? Did Congress really consider the preemption question and make a conscious decision thereon? Behind this mask of language, the Court really seems to be deciding the issue by determining whether the continued existence of the state law is consistent with the general purpose and application of the federal law. At other times, even where there is no conflict, the Court may use the preemption doctrine to invalidate a state law to avoid having to invalidate it on other constitutional grounds (such as the fact that it imposes an unreasonable burden on interstate commerce, etc.). In addition, in deciding the preemption question the Court also uses the balancing of interests test, *i.e.*, if the state law promotes a valid state interest that outweighs the restrictive effects on interstate commerce, it generally is upheld. The principal case, *Pacific Gas & Electric Co. v. State Energy Commission*, will be considered after the note cases.

      1) **Three types of preemption.** Congress may preempt state power by (i) express statement; (ii) implied occupation of a regulatory field; or (iii) implied preclusion of conflicting state regulations. The only issue in express preemption is whether the state statute falls within the preempted area.

         a) **Field preemption—indicators of congressional intent.** In *Rice v. Santa Fe Elevator Corp.*, 331 U.S. 218 (1947), the Court noted that the traditional police powers of the states are not superseded unless Congress clearly indicates its intent to do so. Such a purpose may be shown by (i) a pervasive scheme of regulation, (ii) the dominance of the federal interest, (iii) the character of the obligations imposed, or (iv) an inconsistency between the objective of the federal statute and the result produced by the state policy.

b) **Conflict preemption.**

(1) **Need for uniform national policy.** In *Hines v. Davidowitz*, 312 U.S. 52 (1941), the Supreme Court invalidated the Pennsylvania Alien Registration Act of 1939, holding that it was preempted by the federal Alien Registration Act of 1940 (although the two did not seem to conflict in any way). The Court cited the broad national power over aliens, and the fact that the Constitution permitted only one uniform system (the federal one).

(2) **Health and safety issue.** In *Florida Lime and Avocado Growers, Inc. v. Paul*, 373 U.S. 132 (1963), the Court upheld a California regulation barring avocados that did not meet the state's minimum oil content standard, even though avocados that could not meet the standard might meet the federal standard. The Court said that this did not seem a likely area for exclusive federal regulation; hence, federal law was simply setting "minimum" standards. Note that this is a "health and safety" issue case.

(3) **Duplicative regulation.** In *Gade v. National Solid Wastes Management Association*, 505 U.S. 88 (1992), several state licensing provisions for hazardous waste workers were struck down, even though the relevant OSHA regulations concerned only worker safety and the state regulations were aimed at both worker safety and public health. Conflict preemption was found present since the federal scheme was interpreted to forbid duplicative regulation. A strong dissent objected to the Court's approval of supersession of historic state powers absent clear congressional intent.

c. **Significance of state's purpose for regulating--**

Pacific Gas & Electric Co. v. State Energy Commission, 461 U.S. 190 (1983).

Facts. The California legislature prohibited certification of nuclear power plants until the State Energy Commission (D) made a finding that a demonstrated technology for permanent disposal of high-level nuclear waste had been approved by the federal government. Pacific Gas & Electric Co. (P) brought suit for a declaratory judgment that the state law was invalid under the Supremacy Clause because the Nuclear Regulatory

Commission ("NRC") had federal authority to regulate use of nuclear energy. The district court found for P but the court of appeals reversed. The Supreme Court granted certiorari.

Issue. May a state impose restrictions on an industry even when the federal government also regulates that industry, as long as the state acts for a purpose not preempted by Congress?

Held. Yes. Judgment affirmed.

- The nuclear waste issue presents both safety and economic problems. As long as wastes are stored temporarily, a danger of leakage exists; until a permanent disposal technique is available, lack of storage space may force premature closings of power plants. The legislation in this case was motivated by both considerations.

- The NRC has control over the safety aspects of nuclear energy generation, but no authority over the economic question of whether a particular plant should be built. Thus, a state moratorium on nuclear power plants is preempted if based on safety concerns, but not if based on economic concerns. Because there was a valid economic rationale, not safety-related, for D's moratorium, the state is not preempted.

- Although the NRC has determined it is safe to proceed with nuclear power plants despite the existing unavailability of permanent storage facilities, the NRC does not compel a utility to build a nuclear plant. Rather than enter this area, the state statute recognizes the federal responsibility to develop and license disposal technology.

- The state law does not frustrate the purposes and objectives of Congress. Congress clearly intended to promote nuclear power plants, but it has allowed the states to determine, as a matter of economics, what types of power plants should be built. Congress, not the courts, must take action if a moratorium for economic reasons undercuts a federal objective.

Concurrence (Blackmun, Stevens, JJ.). States should be allowed to prohibit nuclear power plants for safety reasons.

---

3. **Consent to State Regulation.** Congress may validate state laws regulating commerce that, in the absence of such consent, would violate the Commerce Clause.

    a. **The Wilson Act.** In *Leisy v. Hardin*, 135 U.S. 100 (1890), the Court invalidated an Iowa law prohibiting the sale of liquors as applied to Illinois-brewed beer that was sold in the original package in Iowa. In response, Congress passed the Wilson Act, which permitted states to regulate intoxicating liquors imported into the state as though they had been produced in the state. Thereafter the Court, in *Wilkerson v. Rahrer*, 140 U.S. 545 (1891), held that Congress had exempted certain products from interstate commerce through passage of the Wilson Act, in essence approving congressional reversal of a Court decision (*Leisy*).

b. **The insurance business and the McCarran Act.** After passage of the McCarran Act of 1945, which deferred and limited the applicability of antitrust laws to the insurance business, the Court held that the Act validated taxes that were discriminatory and invalid under Commerce Clause decisions. In *Prudential Insurance Co. v. Benjamin*, 328 U.S. 408 (1946), the plaintiff New Jersey company had objected to the continued collection of a tax of 3% of the premiums received from business done in South Carolina when South Carolina corporations were not similarly taxed.

D. OTHER ASPECTS OF FEDERAL-STATE RELATIONSHIPS

1. **State Taxation of Interstate Commerce.** Recognizing that states need tax revenues and that interstate business must pay its way, the Court has permitted the states to impose taxes on interstate commerce. The risk of double taxation has prompted the Court to forbid discriminatory or "unduly burdensome" taxes, but the rules in this area are far from clear. The Court evaluates such taxes on a case-by-case basis. To date, Congress has been unable to enact legislation to settle the matter.

2. **Intergovernmental Tax Immunity.**

a. **States may not directly tax the federal government or its property.** A state tax levied directly against the property or operations of the federal government (or one of its instrumentalities) without the consent of Congress is invalid. This tax immunity is an implied prohibition stemming from the Supremacy Clause. [*See* McCulloch v. Maryland, *supra*] "The power to tax is the power to destroy," but states cannot be permitted to destroy or even impede the federal government or its agencies.

b. **State immunity from federal taxation—early cases.** Activities of the states were granted immunity from federal taxation, and the doctrine of intergovernmental immunity broadened its scope until immunity was granted to third persons (employees, patentees, lessees, etc.) who were in some way connected with the federal or state governments. In *Collector v. Day*, 78 U.S. (11 Wall.) 113 (1871), the Court held that a state judge's salary was immune from federal income tax. Other older cases attempted to make a distinction between state functions that were "governmental," and hence immune, and those that were "proprietary," and thus subject to taxation.

3. **Regulation of the Federal Government by the States.** Absent express authorization by Congress, the instrumentalities and agents of the federal government are immune from state regulation insofar as the regulation might interfere with their efficiency in performing their functions for the federal government. This immunity is based on the Supremacy Clause.

   a. **Modern narrowing of immunity.** The Court steadily expanded governmental immunities to include, *e.g.*, employees, lessees, and patentees. However in the late 1930s, the Court began to limit immunities. [*See*, *e.g.*, Helvering v. Gerhardt, 304 U.S. 405 (1938)—government employee salaries are taxable by other governments] Today, the scope of federal immunities increasingly rests on congressional statements recognizing or waiving them. Tax immunity is only appropriate when it is levied against the United States or an agency "so closely related to the Government that the two cannot realistically be viewed as separate entities." [United States v. New Mexico, 455 U.S. 720 (1982)]

   b. **Balancing test.** Wherever Congress has indicated its intent, that intent will be followed under the Supremacy Clause. But where Congress is silent, the Court will balance the interests involved (state interests vs. those of the federal government). Where the interests of both favor application of the state regulation, it will be upheld. Where the dominant interest is in the federal government's freedom from restrictions of state regulation (*i.e.*, where there is an interference with functions serving an essential federal government purpose), then immunity will be granted.

4. **Interstate Rendition.** Although Article IV, Section 2 speaks in mandatory terms (a "fugitive shall . . . be delivered up"), the rule until recently was that the duty was not enforceable against a governor. [*See* Kentucky v. Dennison, 65 U.S. (24 How.) 66 (1861); *overruled by* Puerto Rico v. Branstad, 483 U.S. 219 (1987)]

5. **Interstate Collaboration—Interstate Compacts.** Article I, Section 10 (Compact Clause) permits creation of compacts between states with the consent of Congress. Such devices are especially useful in dealing with regional problems of crime, pollution, conservation, and transportation, and are a favored means of settling disputes. Some compacts may be valid even without congressional consent. [*See* U.S. Steel Corp. v. Multistate Tax Commission, 434 U.S. 452 (1978)]

VI. SEPARATION OF POWERS

A. THE POLICYMAKING CONFLICT BETWEEN LEGISLATIVE POWERS AND EXECUTIVE AUTHORITY

1. **Introduction.** The Constitution provides for separation of powers, but there are many gray areas in which responsibilities are shared to some extent. For example, the President may establish the national agenda and propose legislation, but only Congress can enact law. Yet the executive power may also include some legislative authority.

2. **Domestic Affairs.**

   a. **The executive power.** The Constitution, in Article II, Section 1, vests the whole executive power of the United States in the President.

   b. **The President's legislative powers.** The separation of powers doctrine requires that the legislative power be vested in Congress. Nevertheless, the Constitution grants the President limited legislative powers.

      1) **The power to propose legislation.** Article II, Section 3 grants the President power to report to Congress on the state of the union and to propose legislation he deems necessary and expedient.

      2) **Delegation by Congress.** In addition, Congress may delegate some of its legislative power to the President (as well as to other government agencies, such as the Securities and Exchange Commission, etc.) as long as the delegation is pursuant to reasonably definite standards.

      3) **The veto power.** Article I, Section 7 gives the President the power to veto any act of Congress. However, Congress may override a presidential veto by a two-thirds vote of both houses.

B. EXECUTIVE VIOLATION OF THE SEPARATION OF POWERS

1. **Limit on the President's Legislative Power--**

Youngstown Sheet & Tube Co. v. Sawyer (The Steel Seizure Case), 343 U.S. 579 (1952).

Facts. The steelworkers, after prolonged negotiations, went on a nationwide strike during the Korean War. Citing the serious national interest in steel production, President Truman ordered Sawyer (D), Commerce Secretary, to seize the steel mills and keep them running. Youngstown Sheet & Tube Co. (P) challenged the seizure as unconstitutional and unauthorized by Congress. Congress had earlier passed the Taft-Hartley Act, giving the President authority to seek an injunction against such strikes, but had rejected an amendment to permit government seizures to avoid serious shutdowns. The district court issued a preliminary injunction against D, which was stayed by the court of appeals. The Supreme Court granted certiorari.

Issue. May the President, acting under the aggregate of his constitutional powers, exercise a lawmaking power independent of Congress in order to protect serious national interests?

Held. No. Judgment of the district court is affirmed.

- The President's power to issue the order must stem either from an act of Congress or from the Constitution itself. Congress clearly gave no such power; in fact, it specifically rejected the means used by D. The President's authority as commander in chief does not warrant the seizure, as it is too far removed from the "theater of war." His general executive powers are inapplicable since there is no relevant law to execute. The order does not direct that a congressional policy be executed in a manner prescribed by Congress but that a presidential policy be executed in a manner prescribed by the President. Such presidential usurpation of the lawmaking power is unauthorized and invalid.

Concurrence (Frankfurter, J.). Congress specifically expressed its will on the subject, which is that the President ought not have the powers he has here attempted to exercise.

Concurrence (Jackson, J.). A President's actions may fall into a category where Congress has authorized him to act, where Congress has neither granted nor denied him authority, or where his actions are incompatible with the will of Congress. In the last case, the President must rely on his constitutional powers minus the powers of Congress, and his claim to power in such circumstances must be scrutinized with caution. The President's actions in seizing the steel mills fall into this last category. None of the arguments advanced by the solicitor general in support of a power of seizure survives the requisite scrutiny.

Concurrence (Clark, J.). The President must follow the procedures laid down by Congress, namely the Taft-Hartley Act.

Dissent (Vinson, C.J., Reed, Minton, JJ.). The President has a duty to execute legislative programs supporting the armed forces in Korea. The President's action was an effective means of performing his duty, and was clearly temporary and subject to congressional direction.

Comment. Two of the majority justices were willing to agree with the dissent that the President did have inherent legislative powers to act in preserving the nation, but only when there was an absence of any provision passed by Congress purporting to deal with the situation. Here these justices pointed to the fact that Congress had passed the National Labor Relations Act, which set forth specific provisions to be followed by the President in case of strikes that threatened the national security.

2. Foreign Relations and Executive Agreements--

Dames & Moore v. Regan, 453 U.S. 654 (1981).

Facts. On November 4, 1979, American diplomatic personnel in Iran were captured and held hostage. On November 14, President Carter declared a national emergency and froze all Iranian assets in the United States. The next day, the Treasury Department issued regulations requiring licensing of any judicial process against Iranian interests and specifying that any such licenses could be revoked at any time. Dames & Moore (P) sued Iranian defendants for $3.5 million and attached Iranian assets pending the outcome of the litigation. On January 19, 1981, the United States, through Algeria, agreed to terminate all legal proceedings in United States courts against Iran, to nullify all attachments and judgments obtained therein, and to terminate such claims through binding arbitration. This agreement was implemented through executive order. On January 27, P obtained a judgment against the Iranian defendants and attempted to execute the judgment on the attached property. The district court nullified the prejudgment attachments and stayed all further proceedings against the Iranian defendants in light of the executive order. P then sued Regan (D), the Treasury Secretary, for declaratory and injunctive relief against enforcement of the executive orders and regulations on grounds that they were unconstitutional and that the President had exceeded his authority in implementing the agreement with Iran. The district court denied P's claim. P appeals.

Issue. May the President, in response to a national emergency, suspend outstanding claims in American courts by executive order?

Held. Yes. Judgment affirmed.

- The questions presented by this case touch fundamentally upon the manner in which our republic is to be governed. Although little authority exists that is relevant to concrete problems of executive power, much relevant analysis is contained in *Youngstown Sheet & Tube Co., supra.* There the Court observed that exercise of executive power is closely related to congressional action; executive power is greatest when exercised pursuant to congressional authorization and weakest when exercised in contravention of the will of Congress.

- The International Emergency Economic Powers Act ("IEEPA"), by its terms, permits the President to "regulate [and] . . . nullify . . . any acquisition . . . of . . . any right . . . to . . . any property in which any foreign country or a national thereof has any interest." In essence, IEEPA was intended to permit freezing of assets to serve as "bargaining chips." P's attachment and judgment were obtained after the President had acted pursuant to this specific statutory authority. We conclude that IEEPA authorized the nullification of the attachments.

- IEEPA does not directly authorize the suspension of in personam lawsuits, which merely establish liability and fix damages and do not in themselves involve Iranian property. Nor does the Hostage Act of 1868 authorize such action. However, the general tenor of these enactments, combined with the International Claims Settlement Act of 1949, which created the International Claims Commission, indicates congressional approval of, or at least acquiescence in, executive agreements settling the claims of United States nationals against foreign countries.

- P can resort to the International Claims Commission as an alternative forum.

- This holding is limited to the narrow facts at hand where the settlement is a necessary element of a resolution of a major foreign policy dispute between our country and another and where Congress has acquiesced in the President's action.

C. EXECUTIVE DISCRETION IN TIMES OF WAR OR TERRORISM

1. The President, Congress, and War Powers.

a. Constitutional provisions.

1) **Congress.** By Article I, Section 8, Congress has the power to declare war, to raise and support armies, to maintain a navy, to make rules for the regulation of the land and naval forces, and to provide for organizing, arming, disciplining, and calling forth the militia.

2) **The President.** Article II, Section 2 provides that the President shall be the commander in chief to the Army, Navy, and the state militias when they are called into the service of the United States.

b. **The use of armed forces.** Although the Constitution specifies that the President is the commander in chief of the Army and Navy, only Congress has the power to initiate or declare war. The interplay of these powers was not made clear in the Constitution. However, in the event of insurrection or invasion, the President may deploy our military forces against any enemy, foreign or domestic, without waiting for congressional declaration of war.

1) **The Vietnam War.** The Vietnam War called into question this whole matter of the relationship of Congress and the President in the conduct of war. It appears that the President has acquired more power in this area than perhaps was originally intended by the Constitution. This has happened over the years since both the Congress and the President have been unmindful of constitutional requirements at times when action seemed more important than the means of its initiation. The basic question seems to be whether the President has the power to use armed forces against a foreign nation without the authorization of Congress.

a) **National Commitments Report.** During the Vietnam War, the Senate Committee on Foreign Relations examined and reported on the 20th century expansions of executive power, noting that all recent presidents had committed armed forces without congressional consent, "and Congress, for the most part, has acquiesced in the transfer of war power to the [executive branch]." The Committee strongly recommended that Congress reassert its constitutional authority over the use of armed forces.

2) **War Powers Resolution.** In 1973, overriding a presidential veto, Congress adopted a joint resolution called the War Powers Resolution, which spells out the President's authority to use the armed forces. If the President uses the armed forces in foreign nations under specified conditions, without a congressional declaration of war, he must formally report to Congress. In the absence of any subsequent congressional action, the forces generally must be removed within 60 days.

a) **Practical effect.** It is generally held that the Resolution has not effectively restrained executive action (*e.g.*, President Reagan's use of troops in Lebanon, 1982-1984). Presidents have ignored the Resolution, claiming that it is inapplicable or unconstitutional, and Congress has never taken any formal action under the Resolution.

2. **Executive Detention and Trial of "Enemy Combatants."** The Constitution does not contain any general "state of emergency" exception to its provisions that would suspend constitutional rights in the event of a national emergency. The Fifth Amendment does relax the requirement for a grand jury indictment for military cases in actual service in time of war or public danger. The United States Supreme Court has held that the constitutional protections apply even in time of war, such as in *Youngstown Sheet & Tube Co. v. Sawyer, supra*. In *Ex Parte Milligan*, 71 U.S. 2 (1866), the court held that President Lincoln could not suspend the writ of habeas corpus during the Civil War and could not try civilians in military tribunals. In 1948, Con-

gress enacted the Non-Detention Act, 18 U.S.C. section 4001(a), which provides that no citizen shall be imprisoned or otherwise detained by the United States except pursuant to an Act of Congress.

a. **Enemy combatants in military tribunals--**

Ex Parte **Quirin**, 317 U.S. 1 (1942).

Facts. Quirin and others (Ps) were born in Germany and lived in the United States before returning to Germany before World War II. Ps trained in sabotage in Germany, then traveled to the United States in a German submarine to destroy United States war industries. Ps were apprehended by the F.B.I. The President appointed a military commission to try Ps for offenses against the law of war. The President also declared that any person who was a citizen of any nation at war with the United States and was charged with committing warlike acts would be tried by military tribunal. Ps claimed they were entitled to be tried by jury in the civil courts with all the constitutional safeguards. They petitioned for habeas corpus. The district court denied the petition, and Ps petitioned the Supreme Court.

Issue. May enemy combatants be tried in United States military tribunals without the right to a jury?

Held. Yes. Petition denied.

- The Constitution gives the President the power to wage war once Congress declares it. Congress has declared war and has provided that military tribunals have jurisdiction to try offenders against the law of war.

- The law of war distinguishes between armed forces and unlawful combatants. Lawful combatants are subject to capture and detention as prisoners of war, but unlawful combatants are not entitled to status as prisoners of war. They may be subject to trial and punishment by military tribunals. It does not matter whether an enemy belligerent is a United States citizen.

- The Constitution does not extend the right to trial by jury to the cases of alien or citizen offenders against the law of war otherwise triable by military tribunals.

3. **Executive Detention and Trial of "Enemy Combatants" After 9/11.**

a. **Joint resolution authorizing the use of military force.** In response to the attack on September 11, 2001, Congress passed a joint resolution, Authorization for Use of Military Force ("AUMF"), that gave the President broad authority to use force against nations, organizations, or persons that the President determines aided the terrorist attacks. No particular enemy was defined. President Bush committed the United States military to combat in Afghanistan and Iraq and detained alleged enemy combatants inside the United States and at Guantanamo Bay, Cuba.

b. **Detention of enemy combatants at Guantanamo Bay.** The United States military captured several hundred foreign fighters in Afghanistan and held them as "enemy combatants" at Guantanamo Bay, a territory leased by the United States from Cuba since 1903. Under the lease, the territory remains under the "ultimate sovereignty" of Cuba. Some of the prisoners sought writs of habeas corpus in the federal district court for the District of Columbia. In *Rasul v. Bush*, 542 U.S. 466 (2004), the United States Supreme Court held that federal judges do have jurisdiction to consider such habeas petitions from Guantanamo detainees. The Court reasoned that although technically Cuba has sovereignty over the territory under the lease, the United States exercises "complete jurisdiction and control" over the base and may continue to exercise such control permanently if it chooses. As such, Guantanamo Bay is in every practical respect a territory of the United States. Another consideration is the indefinite status of the detention and the lack of any legal procedure to determine the detainees' status. The dissenters argued that the decision extends the habeas statute to aliens beyond the sovereign territory of the United States to anywhere in the world, and that Congress could have changed the habeas jurisdiction of federal judges if it wanted to.

c. **Detention of United States citizens--**

Hamdi v. Rumsfeld, 542 U.S. 507 (2004).

Facts. Hamdi (P), a Lousiana-born Saudi-American, was captured in an active combat zone abroad, detained by the United States military as an "enemy combatant," and held in naval brigs in Virginia and South Carolina. P sought habeas corpus relief against Rumsfeld (D), Secretary of Defense, in federal court in Virginia, claiming that the Non-Detention Act of 1948 barred indefinite detention. The Fourth Circuit held that P was not entitled to habeas relief, despite being a United States citizen, because of military needs. The court held that the joint resolution, Authorization for Use of Military Force ("AUMF"), satisfied the requirement in the Non-Detention Act for an Act of Congress authorizing detention. P appeals.

Issue. Does the President have the authority to detain citizens who qualify as "enemy combatants" for an indefinite period of time with no opportunity for an impartial hearing?

Held. No. Judgment reversed.

- D claims that the Executive has plenary authority to detain pursuant to Article II, but that question need not be addressed because Congress authorized detention through the AUMF. The detention of individuals falling into the limited category of combatants, for the duration of the particular conflict in which they were captured, is a fundamental incident to war and falls within the AUMF.

- There is no reason that the government cannot hold one of its own citizens as an enemy combatant. *Quirin (supra)* held that citizenship does not preclude detention for the duration of hostilities.

- P claims that Congress did not authorize indefinite detention. He also claims that he faces the prospect of perpetual detention, because the "war on terror" is an unconventional war that does not fit within normal law-of-war principles. While indefinite detention is not authorized by Congress, there are active combat operations in Afghanistan against Taliban combatants, and the United States may lawfully detain Taliban combatants during these hostilities.

- Although the AUMF did authorize the detention of combatants such as P in the narrow circumstances of this case, the writ of habeas corpus remains available to every person detained within the United States. The writ has not been suspended. P may properly seek a habeas determination on the issue of whether P falls within the category of hostile forces subject to detention. Due process demands that a citizen held in the United States as an enemy combatant be given a meaningful opportunity to contest the factual basis for that detention before a neutral decisionmaker.

- To satisfy the minimum requirements for such a hearing, the citizen-detainee must receive notice of the factual basis for his classification and a fair opportunity to rebut the government's factual assertions before a neutral decisionmaker. Evidentiary standards may be relaxed so that the government may use hearsay to support the classification. There may be a rebuttable presumption in favor of the government's evidence.

Dissent (Scalia, Stevens, JJ.). A citizen who wages war against the United States may be prosecuted for treason, but unless Congress suspends the usual protections under the Suspension Clause, a citizen cannot be detained without charge. The lower court decision should be reversed. The traditional treatment of enemy aliens that includes detention until the cessation of hostilities does not apply to American citizens. The criminal law process is the only means for punishing and incapacitating traitors. Unless the writ of habeas corpus is suspended, a citizen is entitled either to a criminal trial or a judicial decree requiring his release. The AUMF is not a suspension of the writ. The Court's opinion establishes a procedure that makes P's detention legal, but that is an incorrect application of the writ.

Dissent (Thomas, J.). The detention of P falls within the government's war powers, and the courts have no expertise or capacity to second guess the decision to detain P. The President has constitutional authority to protect the national security and has broad discretion to exercise that authority. The courts should not interfere in these matters. Due process requires only a good-faith executive determination.

Concurrence and dissent (Souter, Ginsburg, JJ.). To the extent that the plurality rejects the government's proposed limit on the exercise of habeas jurisdiction, it is correct. However, the plurality goes too far when it agrees that P can be detained if his designation as an enemy combatant is correct. The AUMF does not refer to detention, so it cannot provide a basis for P's detention. The government has failed to justify holding P in the absence of an Act of Congress, criminal charges, a showing that P's detention conforms to the law of war, or a showing that section 4001(a) is unconstitutional.

Comment. In *Rumsfeld v. Padilla*, 542 U.S. 426 (2004), Padilla, a United States citizen, was arrested in Chicago for participating in a plot to detonate a dirty bomb. He was declared an "enemy combatant" by the President and was turned over to the Department of Defense for detention. Padilla challenged his detention. The Second Circuit held that the President did not have authority to detain Padilla under section 4001(a). The Supreme Court reversed on jurisdictional grounds because Padilla should have filed his habeas petition against the commander of the brig he was incarcerated in. The four Justices in the minority opinion would have found Padilla's detention to be unauthorized under section 4001(a).

---

d. Military commission lacking authority--

Hamdan v. Rumsfeld, 548 U.S. 557 (2006).

Facts. In November 2001, during hostilities between the United States and the Taliban, Hamdan (P), a Yemeni national, was captured by militia forces and turned over to the United States military. P was transported to an American prison in Guantanamo Bay, Cuba, in 2002. Over a year later, the President deemed P eligible for trial by military commission for then-unspecified crimes. After another year, he was charged with conspiracy to commit "offenses triable by military commission." He petitioned for a writ of habeas corpus. The court of appeals denied P relief. The Supreme Court granted certiorari.

Issue. Did the military commission have authority to try P?

Held. No. Judgment reversed.

- The military commission, which was neither mentioned in the Constitution nor created by statute, was born of military necessity. Exigency alone will not justify the establishment and use of penal tribunals not contemplated by Article I, Section 8 and Article III, Section 1 of the Constitution. If such authority exists, it is through the powers granted jointly to the President and Congress in time of war.

- Neither Congress's Authorization for Use of Military Force ("AUMF") nor the Detainee Treatment Act ("DTA") expands the President's authority to convene military commissions. Nothing in the text or legislative history of the AUMF suggests that Congress intended to expand or alter the authorization set forth in Article 21 of the Uniform Code of Military Justice ("UCMJ"). Although the DTA was enacted after the President had convened P's commission, it contains no language authorizing that tribunal or any other at Guantanamo Bay. Together, the UCMJ, the AUMF, and the DTA at most acknowledge a general presidential authority to convene military commissions in circumstances where justified under the "Constitution and laws," including the law of war.

- The charge against P alleges a conspiracy extending over a number of years, from 1996 to November 2001. The crime of "conspiracy" has rarely if ever been tried in this country by any law-of-war military commission not exercising some other form of jurisdiction, and it does not appear in either the Geneva Conventions or the Hague Conventions, which are the major treaties on the law of war. Also, international sources confirm that the crime charged here is not a recognized violation of the law of war. Because the charge does not support the military commission's jurisdiction, the commission lacks authority to try P. P is charged with an agreement, the inception of which long predated the attacks of September 11, 2001 and the AUMF. Although that may well be a crime prosecutable by court-martial or in federal court, it is not an offense that, by the law of war, may be tried by a military commission.

- Article 36 of the UCMJ provides that the rules applied to military commissions must be the same as those applied to courts-martial unless this proves impracticable. Nothing in the record before us demonstrates that it would be impracticable to apply court-martial rules in this case. The only reason offered is the danger posed by international terrorism. However, in the case of P's trial, this does not require any variance from the rules that govern courts-martial. One of the most fundamental protections afforded by the Manual for Courts-Martial and by the UCMJ itself is the right to be present at trial. In this case, the rules applicable in courts-martial must apply.

- Although al Qaeda is not a signatory of the Geneva Conventions, Article 3 provides that in a "conflict not of an international character occurring in the territory of one of the signatories, each Party to the conflict shall be bound to apply, as a minimum," certain provisions, including one that prohibits "the passing of sentences and the carrying out of executions upon detainees without previous judgment pronounced by a regularly constituted court" that provides all of the judicial guarantees that are recognized as indispensable. The procedures adopted to try P violate the Geneva Conventions. Article 3 applies here and requires that P be tried by a "regularly constituted court." "The regular military courts in our system are the courts-martial established by congressional statutes." One of the indispensable judicial guarantees is the right to be tried in one's presence.

- P does not challenge, and we do not today address, the government's power to detain him for the duration of active hostilities in order to prevent such harm.

Concurrence (Breyer, Kennedy, Souter, Ginsburg, JJ.). Congress has not issued the President a "blank check," and there is no emergency here that would prevent the President from consulting with Congress and seeking the authority he believes necessary.

Concurrence in part (Kennedy, Souter, Ginsburg, Breyer, JJ.). Trial by military commission raises important separation-of-powers concerns. Congress has set forth governing principles for military courts in the UCMJ and has set limits on the President's authority to convene military courts. If Congress decides that it is appropriate to change the controlling statutes, it has the power to do so.

Dissent (Thomas, Scalia, Alito, JJ.).

- The President's exercise of his authority is entitled to substantial deference. Under the AUMF, the President is authorized "to use all necessary and appropriate force against those nations, organizations, or persons he determines planned, authorized, committed, or aided the terrorist attacks that occurred on September 11, 2001 . . . in order to prevent any future acts of international terrorism against the United States by such nations, organizations or persons." As noted in *Hamdi*, the "capture, detention, and trial of unlawful combatants" are important incidents of war.

- Congressional authorization for military commissions derives from Article 21 of the UCMJ and also from the AUMF. A law-of-war military commission may only assume jurisdiction of "offences committed within the field of the command of the convening commander," and such offenses "must have been committed within the period of the war." Even before September 11, 2001, al Qaeda was involved in bombings such as the bombing of the World Trade Center in New York City in 1993. Thus, the present conflict substantially predates the AUMF, extending at least as far back as al Qaeda's 1996 declaration of war on our country.

- Law-of-war military commissions have jurisdiction over "individuals of the enemy's army who have been guilty of illegitimate warfare or other offences in violation of the laws of war." It is a violation of the law of war to join an organization, such as al Qaeda, whose principal purpose is the "killing [and] disabling . . . of peaceable citizens or soldiers." P is an unlawful combatant charged with conduct constituting two distinct violations of the law of war cognizable before a military commission—membership in a war-criminal enterprise and conspiracy to commit war crimes.

- Article 36 does not represent an unprecedented congressional effort to change the nature of military commissions from common-law war courts to tribunals that must presumptively function like courts-martial. Instead, Article 36 recognizes that the President may depart from the procedures applicable in criminal cases whenever he alone does not deem such procedures "practicable."

The nature of military commission trials against unlawful combatants in the war on terrorism necessitates that certain information is kept secret in the interest of preventing future attacks on our nation.

Dissent (Alito, Scalia, Thomas, JJ.). Because the military commission is "a regularly constituted court," I disagree with this holding.

Comment. In response to *Hamdan*, Congress enacted the Military Commissions Act of 2006, which authorizes military commissions and denies habeas claims by aliens detained as enemy combatants. It applies to all cases pending on or after the date of its enactment.

D. CONGRESSIONAL VIOLATION OF THE SEPARATION OF POWERS

1. Legislative Veto--

INS v. Chadha, 462 U.S. 919 (1983).

Facts. Chadha (P) was an East Indian who lawfully entered the United States on a nonimmigrant student visa. After his visa expired, the Immigration and Naturalization Service (D) held a deportation hearing. The immigration judge suspended P's deportation and sent a report to Congress as required by section 244(c)(1) of the Immigration and Naturalization Act. Section 244(c)(2) provided that either house of Congress could veto a suspension of deportation. The House of Representatives adopted a unilateral resolution opposing P's permanent residence, and P was ordered deported. P sought review in the Ninth Circuit, which held section 244(c)(2) unconstitutional. The Supreme Court granted certiorari.

Issue. May Congress employ the legislative veto device to oversee delegations of its constitutional authority to the executive branch?

Held. No. Judgment affirmed.

- Although this case has political ramifications, it is primarily a constitutional challenge that presents a bona fide controversy, properly subject to judicial action.

- Article I of the Constitution vests all legislative powers in both houses of Congress. Every bill or resolution must be passed by both houses and approved by the President (or his veto overridden) before it takes effect. These provisions are intended to secure liberty through separation of powers. The bicameral nature of Congress similarly ensures careful consideration of all legislation.

- The action taken by the House in this case was essentially legislative in purpose and effect. The legislative veto replaced the constitutional procedure of enacting legislation requiring P's deportation (a private bill). Yet the Constitution enumerates only four instances in which either house may act alone—impeachment, trial after impeachment, ratification of treaties, and confirmation of presidential appointments. The legislative veto is not enumerated.

- Although the legislative veto may be efficient, efficiency is not the overriding value behind the Constitution. Separation of powers, as set up by the Constitution, may not be eroded for convenience. Therefore, the legislative veto is unconstitutional. Once Congress delegates authority, it must abide by that delegation until it legislatively alters or revokes it.

Concurrence (Powell, J.). There is no need to invalidate all legislative vetoes. This one is an unconstitutional exercise of the judicial function by the House because it decided the specific rights of P.

Dissent (White, J.). The legislative veto is a valid response to the dilemma of choosing between no delegation (and hence no lawmaking because of the vast amount of regulation necessary under our system) and abdication of the lawmaking function to the executive branch and administrative agencies. The legislative veto has been included in nearly 200 statutes and accepted by presidents for 50 years. It allows resolution of major constitutional and policy differences between Congress and the President. Because the underlying legislation is properly enacted, and because the Constitution does not prohibit it, the legislative veto is constitutional.

Dissent (Rehnquist, White, JJ.). Section 244(c)(2) is not severable from the rest of the Act, so the judgment below should be reversed.

---

2. **Line Item Veto.**

   a. **Introduction.** Article I, Section 7 provides that "Every Bill which shall have passed the House of Representatives and the Senate, shall, before it become a Law, be presented to the President of the United States; If he approves he shall sign it, but if not he shall return it, with his Objections to the House in which it shall have originated, who shall . . . proceed to reconsider it. If after such Reconsideration two thirds of that House shall agree to pass the Bill . . . and if approved by two thirds of [the other] House, it shall become a Law." This clause requires the President to approve or disapprove a complete law. For years, Presidents have requested a line item veto that would allow them to veto portions of statutes, leaving the balance intact. When Congress did enact a line item veto, the constitutionality of the statute was immediately challenged.

b. Line item veto unconstitutional--

Clinton v. New York, 524 U.S. 417 (1998).

Facts. In *Raines v. Byrd*, 521 U.S. 811 (1997), the Court held that members of Congress do not have standing to challenge the Line Item Veto Act because they lacked a sufficiently concrete injury. The Act allowed the President, after making specific determinations, to cancel three types of provisions that have already been signed into law, including any item of new direct spending or any limited tax benefit. The cancellation becomes effective when Congress receives notice from the President, but Congress may render the cancellation void by passing a disapproval bill. Shortly after the *Raines* decision, President Clinton (D) applied the Act to cancel sections of two separate statutes, one that waived the federal government's right to recoupment of up to $2.6 billion in taxes from the city of New York and another that gave tax preferences to certain food refiners and processors. These provisions fell within the criteria set forth in the Act, and Congress did not pass a disapproval bill. New York City and several other organizations (Ps) sued, claiming the cancellations were unconstitutional. The district court consolidated the suits, found that Ps had standing, and held that the Act was unconstitutional. D appeals.

Issue. May Congress grant the President a line item veto that allows the President to cancel legislation after it is duly enacted and signed?

Held. No. Judgment affirmed.

- Article I, Section 7 allows the President to return a bill to Congress. This action takes place before a bill becomes law. By contrast, the cancellation provision in the Act occurs after the bill becomes law. A constitutional return applies to the entire bill, but a cancellation under the Act applies only to a part of a bill. These are constitutionally significant differences.

- The Constitution expressly permits the return of a bill, but it is silent regarding unilateral presidential action that either repeals or amends parts of a duly enacted statute. Constitutional silence on a matter as important as presidential action regarding statutes must be construed as an express prohibition of such actions. Presidents may either approve all parts of a bill or reject it completely.

- D claims that a cancellation is not actually an amendment or a repeal. In *Field v. Clark*, 143 U.S. 649 (1892), the Court allowed the Tariff Act, which gave the President authority to suspend certain products' exemptions from import duties upon making certain findings. Such a suspension power differs from a cancellation power because exercise of the suspension power depended on conditions that did not exist when the Tariff Act was passed, because the President had a duty to suspend under specified circumstances, and because when the President did suspend the duties, he was executing congressional policy. A cancellation under the Act has none of these factors that justified upholding the suspension power. For example, the President can cancel a portion of a statute for his own policy reasons, independent of Congress. Congress cannot so alter the constitutional provisions without a constitutional amendment.

- The President has a traditional power to decline to spend appropriated funds. But never before this Act has Congress given the President the unilateral power to change the text of duly enacted statutes. The line item veto procedures are simply not allowed under Article I, Section 7.

Concurrence (Kennedy, J.). The Act threatens the liberties of individual citizens because liberty is always at stake when one or more branches of government seeks to transgress the separation of powers.

Concurrence and dissent (Scalia, O'Connor, Breyer, JJ.). Not all of the plaintiffs in this case have standing. On the merits, the Court fails to observe that the Act applies only after the requirements of the Presentment Clause have been satisfied. This means that the Court's problem focuses on the President's power to prevent certain parts of duly enacted statutes to have full force and effect. Yet there is no difference between Congress allowing the President to cancel a spending item and allowing money to be spent on a particular item at the President's discretion. The latter approach has been allowed throughout history. If the Act had allowed the President to decline to spend any item of spending in the budget bills, it would have been constitutional. The Act uses a technically different approach, but it does not violate Article I, Section 7, and the doctrine of unconstitutional delegation is not a doctrine of technicalities.

Dissent (Breyer, O'Connor, Scalia, JJ.). The Court appears to conclude that a cancellation is the equivalent of a repeal or amendment of a law, but it is not. A cancellation under the Act leaves the statutes as they were literally written, intact. In canceling a law under the Act, the President follows the law. He neither repeals nor amends anything. Congress has granted a contingent power to deny effect to certain statutory language in many other statutes. Finally, the Act does not violate the separation of powers because Congress retains the power both to disapprove a cancellation and to include in any bill a provision that says the Act will not apply.

---

3. Delegation of Spending Power--

Bowsher v. Synar, 478 U.S. 714 (1986).

Facts. The Balanced Budget and Emergency Deficit Control Act of 1985 (Gramm-Rudman-Hollings Act) was enacted to reduce the federal budget deficit to zero over a period of years. Automatic reductions in federal spending were to take place in any fiscal year for which the deficit exceeded the statutory target. The reductions would take effect after the directors of the Office of Management and Budget and the Congressional Budget Office independently calculated the necessary budget reductions. These directors would then report their findings to the Comptroller General, who would make conclusions as to the necessary spending reductions. The President was then required to issue a "sequestration" order mandating the Comptroller General's conclusions. This order would become effective unless Congress reduced spending by legislation. An alternative procedure was also established in case the primary procedure was invalidated. The alternative procedure provided for an expedited congressional joint resolution that would become a sequestration order when the President signed it. Congressman Synar and others (Ps) challenged the statute. The district court held the reporting provisions unconstitutional. Comptroller General Bowsher (D) appeals.

Issue. May Congress assign to the Comptroller General the function of determining which accounts of the federal budget must be cut to meet deficit targets?

Held. No. Judgment affirmed.

- ♦ Standing in this case lies in one plaintiff, an employees' union whose members would not receive a scheduled increase in benefits if the Act is sustained.

- ♦ Although the Constitution gives Congress a role in appointment of executive officers, it does not give Congress an active role in supervising such officers. It has the power of removal only upon impeachment. Although Congress may limit the President's powers of removal, it cannot reserve for itself the removal power. Otherwise, Congress would have control over the execution of the laws in violation of the separation of powers.

- ♦ Because Congress may not execute the laws, it cannot grant to an officer under its control the power to execute the laws. D argues that the Comptroller General performs his duties independently of Congress, but in fact Congress is the sole removal authority for the Comptroller General. Accordingly, the Comptroller General may not possess executive powers.

- ♦ Under the Act, the Comptroller General prepares a report by exercising his independent judgment. This is more than a mechanical function. It requires interpretation of the Act and application of judgment concerning a set of facts; this constitutes execution of the law. In fact, the President is required to comply with the report in ordering the reductions.

- ♦ Because the reporting procedures are unconstitutional, the fallback provisions are effective.

Concurrence (Stevens, Marshall, JJ.). Labeling the Comptroller General's functions "executive powers" is uninformative. Under the fallback provisions, the congressional report based on the Comptroller General's report has the same legal consequences and could not be considered "executive." In fact, the infirmity of this Act is that Congress has delegated its exclusive power to make policy that will bind the nation to an individual agent of Congress, bypassing the constitutional processes.

Dissent (White, J.). Whether Congress or the Comptroller General determines the level of funding available to the President to carry out its duties, the effect on the President is the same. The President has no authority to establish spending levels. Congress has not granted policymaking discretion; it has specified a detailed procedure based on specific criteria. The Act is an effective response to a serious national crisis, and presents no real threat to separation of powers.

Dissent (Blackmun, J.). The better approach would be to invalidate the congressional removal statute, which in any case has never been invoked in its 65-year history.

---

4. **The Appointment and Removal Powers.** Article II, Section 2 indicates that the President, with the consent of the Senate, may appoint ambassadors, consuls, justices of the Supreme Court, and all other officers of the United States whose appointments are not otherwise provided for. In addition, Congress may vest the power to appoint "inferior officers" in the President alone, in the courts of law, or in the heads of departments, "as they think proper." With the increasing complexity of political problems, Congress has begun using the Appointments Clause to create unique offices having characteristics of more than one branch.

   a. **Limit on appointment power.** In *Buckley v. Valeo*, 424 U.S. 1 (1976), the Court relied upon this provision in holding that the composition of the Federal Election Commission established by the Federal Election Campaign Act was unconstitutional. Because of the enforcement powers of the commissioners, who were appointed by Congress, the Court held that they exercised executive powers, thus making them officers of the United States whose appointment was subject to the Appointments Clause.

   b. **The removal power.**

      1) **Judges.** The President cannot remove either Supreme Court or lower court judges. Article III, Section 1 provides that they shall remain in office "during good behavior," and can be removed only by the impeachment process.

      2) **Executive officers.** In *Myers v. United States*, 272 U.S. 52 (1926), the Supreme Court held invalid a statute that said that the President could not remove postmasters without Senate approval. The Court stated that the President could remove all executive appointees at will even though the appointments originally required the "advice and consent" of the Senate.

a) **Limitation on *Myers*.**

(1) **Removal for cause.** *Humphrey's Executor v. United States*, 295 U.S. 602 (1935), limited *Myers* in that it said that officers of administrative bodies created by Congress, where the statute specifies the term and causes for removal, may be removed by the President only for those causes that have been specified.

(2) **Officers performing judicial functions.** *Weiner v. United States*, 357 U.S. 349 (1958), further limited the President's removal power. The War Claims Commission, established by act of Congress, mentioned nothing about causes for removal. The Supreme Court differentiated between officials who were part of the "executive establishment" and those who should be independent of the President's removal power. The Court held that it was unconstitutional to remove a member of the commission without cause, as the commission exercised a "judicial function."

c. **Creation of independent counsel--**

Morrison v. Olson, 487 U.S. 654 (1988).

Facts. The Ethics in Government Act of 1978 [28 U.S.C. §§591 *et seq.*] provided for the appointment of an "independent counsel" to investigate and prosecute specified government officials for violations of federal criminal law. Under the Act, the Attorney General conducts a preliminary investigation of possible violations, and then reports to the Special Division, a court created by the Act. If the Attorney General determines that there are reasonable grounds to believe further investigation or a prosecution is warranted, she applies for appointment of independent counsel. The Special Division then appoints such counsel and defines the counsel's prosecutorial jurisdiction. The independent prosecutor is required to comply with Department of Justice policies to the extent possible. The Attorney General may remove an independent prosecutor for cause; otherwise, the counsel's tenure expires upon completion of the specified investigations or prosecutions. The counsel notifies the Attorney General of the completion; alternatively, the Special Division may find the task completed. Certain congressional committees have oversight jurisdiction regarding the independent counsel's conduct. Pursuant to this Act, the Special Division appointed Morrison (D) to investigate allegations that Olson (P), an assistant attorney general, had lied in testimony to Congress. D obtained a grand jury subpoena against P. P moved to quash the subpoena, claiming that D had no authority to proceed because the Act was unconstitutional. The trial court upheld the Act, but the court of appeals reversed. D appeals.

Issue. May Congress provide for the judicial appointment of independent counsel for purposes of investigating and prosecuting federal criminal offenses?

Held. Yes. Judgment reversed.

- Under the Appointments Clause, there are two classes of officers: (i) principal officers, who are selected by the President with the advice and consent of the Senate; and (ii) inferior officers whom Congress may allow to be appointed by the President alone, by the heads of departments, or by the judiciary. Thus, if D is a principal officer, the Act violates the Constitution.

- The difference between principal and inferior officers is not always clear. It requires consideration of several factors.

  D may be removed by a higher executive branch official, despite having independent powers.

  D's authority is limited to performing specified, limited duties. D has no policymaking authority and must comply to Department of Justice policies.

  D's office is limited in jurisdiction to the terms of the appointment. It is also limited in tenure; it does not extend beyond the completion of the specific task given.

  Evaluation of these factors leads to the conclusion that an independent counsel is an inferior officer. However, P claims that Congress may not provide that an officer of one branch be appointed by officers of another branch.

- The Clause itself does not forbid interbranch appointments, but instead gives Congress discretion to determine the propriety of vesting the appointment of executive officials in the courts. The limitation on this power is where it implicates the separation of powers or impairs the constitutional functions assigned to one of the branches. The very reason for the Act was to remove the appointment power from the executive branch, and the judicial branch is the most logical alternative. By making members of the Special Division ineligible to participate in any matters relating to an independent counsel they have appointed, Congress has protected the separation of powers.

- Article III limits the judicial power to cases and controversies. However, if the Appointments Clause gives Congress the power to authorize the courts to appoint officials such as an independent counsel, which it does, the appointment power is a source of authority independent of Article III. The additional powers granted to the Special Division, such as defining the counsel's authority and tenure of office, are incidental to the exercise of the appointment power itself.

- The Special Division also has power to terminate an independent counsel's office, which is an administrative power. This power must be narrowly construed to avoid constitutional problems. It is thus limited to removing an independent counsel who has served her purpose, but does not acknowledge that fact and remains on the payroll.

- ♦ P also asserts a separation of powers problem because the Attorney General can remove an independent counsel only by showing "good cause." In *Bowsher, supra*, for example, Congress could not involve itself in the removal of an executive officer. Under the Act in this case, however, Congress did not acquire a removal power over executive officials beyond its power of impeachment and conviction.

- ♦ The Attorney General retains the removal power, subject to the good cause requirement. But the Constitution does not give the President unbridled discretion to remove officials of independent agencies. Prior cases have distinguished purely executive officials from quasi-legislative and quasi-judicial officials, but this is an inappropriate distinction for analyzing removal powers. The proper question is whether the removal restrictions impede the President's ability to perform his constitutional duty. Because the independent counsel has a limited function, and because the Attorney General has removal authority for good cause, the good cause restriction does not unconstitutionally impede the President.

- ♦ The second separation of powers issue is based on interference with the role of the executive branch. However, the Act does not permit either congressional or judicial usurpation of executive functions. It also leaves the executive branch with the ability to supervise the counsel's prosecutorial powers.

Dissent (Scalia, J.). The power to conduct a criminal prosecution is a purely executive power, and the Act deprives the President of the exclusive control over the exercise of that power. It does not matter to what extent the Act reduces presidential control; the Act violates the separation of powers doctrine. In addition, D's appointment could be constitutional only if she is an "inferior" officer, but she is not inferior because she is not subordinate to another officer. The final infirmity of the Act is that it improperly imposes restrictions upon the removal of the independent counsel.

---

5. Delegation of Legislative Powers.

a. **Nondelegation doctrine and interbranch appointments.** The nondelegation doctrine provides that Congress may not constitutionally delegate its legislative power to another government branch. In reality, the doctrine "does not prevent Congress from seeking assistance, within proper limits, from the coordinate branches." [Touby v. United States, 500 U.S. 160 (1991)] However, Congress must establish intelligible principles to guide the delegatee body. The Court has only twice found a violation of the doctrine. [*See* A.L.A. Schecter Poultry Corp. v. United States, 295 U.S. 495 (1935); Panama Refining Co. v. Ryan, 293 U.S. 388 (1935)]

b. **Creation of sentencing commission--**

Mistretta v. United States, 488 U.S. 361 (1989).

Facts. In the Sentencing Reform Act of 1984, Congress established the United States Sentencing Commission to devise guidelines to be used for sentencing in criminal cases. The Act replaced the existing indeterminate sentencing process with determinate sentencing, with the Commission's guidelines binding on the courts so that judicial discretion is limited only to cases in which the judge finds specific aggravating or mitigating factors not considered by the Commission. The Act described the Commission as an independent commission in the judicial branch of the United States. All seven members are appointed by the President with the advice and consent of the Senate, and at least three of the members must be federal judges. The Commission must provide an annual report to Congress regarding the operation of the guidelines. Mistretta (D) was indicted on federal drug offenses. He challenged the constitutionality of the guidelines. The district court rejected D's challenge. The Supreme Court granted certiorari.

Issue. May Congress create an independent judicial commission to establish sentencing guidelines that are binding on the federal courts?

Held. Yes. Judgment affirmed.

- Congress may delegate its legislative power as long as the person or body receiving the delegated power is directed to conform to an "intelligible principle" set forth by Congress. The delegation of authority to the Commission is sufficiently specific and detailed to meet this standard. The Act includes three specific goals for the Commission to strive for, with four specific purposes of sentencing to pursue. Although the Commission has significant discretion in formulating the guidelines, developing proportionate penalties for hundreds of different crimes is an intricate, labor-intensive task that may appropriately be delegated by Congress. The Act does not give the Commission excessive legislative discretion.

- D also claims that the Act violates the constitutional principle of separation of powers. The Commission is located within the judicial branch, but it does not exercise judicial power. The novelty of the Commission does not necessarily make it unconstitutional, however, as long as Congress has not vested in the Commission powers that are (i) more appropriately performed by the other branches or (ii) that undermine the integrity of the judiciary.

- Despite the basic principle of three separate branches of government, there is a "twilight area" in which the activities of the separate branches merge. Judicial rulemaking tends to fall within this twilight area. Congress has previously conferred rulemaking authority on the judiciary, such as to create the Federal Rules of Civil Procedure and to establish rules for the conduct of the courts' business. Thus, Congress may delegate to the judicial branch nonadjudicatory functions that do not trench upon the prerogatives of another branch and that are appropriate to the central mission of the judiciary. These delegations, while not involving the judicial power to decide cases and controversies, share the common purpose of providing for the fair and efficient fulfillment of responsibilities that are properly the province of the judiciary.

- The judiciary has a major role in sentencing, and the establishment of sentencing guidelines is not clearly more appropriately performed by one of the other branches. Although the Commission has a political nature, the practical consequences of placing the Commission within the judicial branch does not undermine the integrity of that branch. The Commission is independent of the members of the judicial branch and does not act as a court. Its inclusion in the judicial branch does not expand the power of that branch, which has long been responsible for sentencing.

- The inclusion of federal judges is troublesome, but the Constitution does not specifically prohibit judges from serving on independent commissions. Participation on the Commission involves the exercise of administrative, not judicial power. Because the Commission will only develop rules to be used by the judicial branch, participation by federal judges does not violate the Constitution. The power of the President to appoint and remove Commission members does not affect a federal judge's status as a judge and therefore presents no risk of compromising the impartiality of such judges.

Dissent (Scalia, J.). In effect, the Commission's guidelines are laws, since a judge who disregards them will be reversed. Congress cannot create an agency that has no governmental power other than to make laws, because only Congress can make laws under the Constitution. The Court, by upholding a pure delegation of legislative power, has encouraged Congress to delegate its lawmaking powers more frequently in the future, particularly over "no-win" political issues. The Commission represents a new branch of government, a "junior-varsity" Congress.

---

c. **Delegation of legislative power in foreign affairs.** In *United States v. Curtis-Wright Export Corp.*, 229 U.S. 304 (1936), the Court considered a joint resolution of Congress authorizing the President to prohibit sales of arms and munitions to Bolivia and Paraguay, which were in armed conflict. The President immediately proclaimed an embargo. Curtis-Wright, indicted for conspiracy to violate the embargo, challenged the delegation as unconstitutional. The Court found that Congress may delegate much broader powers to the President in foreign affairs than in domestic affairs, and that it would be unwise for Congress to establish narrow and definite standards for the President's exercise of governmental foreign powers.

d. **The interplay between Congress and the President in foreign affairs.** The President has special powers in foreign affairs due to the need for decisive action and a uniform policy with regard to sensitive foreign relations. Congress, however, retains certain powers over foreign affairs, including the power to declare war, appropriate funds, and ratify treaties. The question has arisen whether the President has unilateral authority to abrogate treaties. [*See* Goldwater v. Carter, 444 U.S. 996 (1979)]

e. **International executive agreements and compacts.** The ever-growing complexity of foreign relationships has led to the adoption of executive agreements and compacts covering minor, everyday matters (such as sales of American products to foreign nations) that would not justify a formal treaty.

1) These executive agreements and compacts are the sole responsibilities of the President and do not require the "advice and consent" of the Senate.

2) These agreements have a status and dignity similar to treaties, and prevail over any state law inconsistent therewith. In *United States v. Belmont*, 301 U.S. 324 (1937), the Court held that an agreement that arose over the diplomatic recognition of the Soviet Union and a later assignment to the United States of all Soviet claims against Americans were part of one exercise of the executive power. Consequently, that power is supreme and can be exercised without regard to the state law policy against confiscation by revocation.

3) Presidential actions taken in accordance with executive agreements are likely to be upheld, at least when not resisted by Congress. In *Dames & Moore v. Regan, supra*, the Court upheld executive action that nullified prejudgment attachments of Iranian assets and suspended pending claims against Iran in American courts. The Court based its approval on specific and implied congressional authorization.

E. EXECUTIVE PRIVILEGES AND IMMUNITIES

1. **Legislative Immunity Not Identical.** Article I, Section 6 states that senators and representatives "shall not be questioned in any other place" for "any Speech or Debate in either House." In *United States v. Brewster*, 408 U.S. 501 (1972), the Court held that this clause did not bar prosecution of a former

senator for accepting a bribe relating to his actions on postage rate legislation. The Clause does not protect all conduct relating to the legislative process, only inquiry into acts that occur in the regular course of the legislative process and the motivation for those acts.

2. **Executive Immunity.** Executive officials are not given any express immunity in the Constitution. And past cases seem to reject an implied immunity under the separation of powers doctrine.

   a. **Judicial-executive relations.**

      1) **Mandamus.** Refer to *Marbury v. Madison, supra.*

      2) **Sovereign immunity.** It is often very difficult to assert claims against members of the executive branch; in many instances the doctrine of sovereign immunity stands in the way.

      3) **Impeachment before criminal trial.** Article I, Section 3 states that any party convicted of impeachment "shall . . . be liable and subject to Indictment, Trial, Judgment, and Punishment according to law." Thus, there is an issue as to whether impeachment must occur before the President or Vice President, etc., could be tried for a crime.

3. **The President and Executive Privilege.** The President has no express immunity, but several Presidents have claimed implied immunity, and some cases have inferred that such an immunity exists. Recent cases seem to indicate that a limited privilege exists, the boundaries of which must be determined by balancing the interests at stake on both sides.

   a. **Clashes between the President and Congress.** The President and Congress have clashed, often over the efforts of one to intervene in the internal activities of the other.

      1) For example, there have been frequent conflicts between legislative demands for information and executive officials' refusal to comply, on instructions from the President, on grounds of interference with privileged deliberations.

      2) In *Committee on Presidential Campaign Activities v. Nixon*, 370 F. Supp. 521 (D.D.C. 1974), the court held that a balancing test would be used, and that here the interests of Congress did not outweigh the President's interest in confidentiality. (However, the information had already been given to a grand jury and there was risk of prejudice to the criminal process through disclosure.)

      3) Finally, there is the issue in the special instances of an impeachment trial, of whether the interests of Congress weigh heavier than

usual. President Nixon refused to respond to subpoenas from the House Judiciary Committee; this was the basis of its third article of impeachment.

b. **Absolute presidential immunity from civil damages.** In *Nixon v. Fitzgerald*, 457 U.S. 731 (1982), the Court held that absent explicit affirmative action by Congress, the President is absolutely, rather than qualifiedly, immune from civil liability for his official acts. In this action brought by a whistleblower who charged violation of his First Amendment and statutory rights when he lost his job with the Defense Department, the Court stated that absolute presidential immunity is a functionally mandated incident of the President's office that is rooted in the doctrine of separation of powers.

c. **Limitations on executive privilege in relationship to the courts--**

United States v. Nixon, 418 U.S. 683 (1974).

Facts. The Special Prosecutor, acting for the United States (P) in the Watergate investigation, sought and received a subpoena ordering President Nixon (D) to produce various tapes and other records relating to presidential conversations and meetings, despite D's motion to quash and motions to expunge and for protective orders. The Supreme Court granted certiorari.

Issue. Does executive immunity give the President an absolute, unqualified general privilege of immunity from judicial process under all circumstances?

Held. No. Judgment affirmed.

♦ D contends that the case is merely an intrabranch dispute between officers of the executive branch and thus lacks the requisite justiciability. However, the Special Prosecutor has been given special authority to pursue the criminal prosecution and has standing to bring this action in the courts.

♦ The doctrine of separation of powers does not preclude judicial review of a President's claim of privilege, because it is the duty of the courts to say what the law is with respect to that claim of privilege, even if the judicial interpretation varies from the President's.

♦ The President's need for and the public interest in the confidentiality of communications is accorded great deference. But absent a need to protect military, diplomatic, or sensitive national security secrets, in camera inspection of presidential communications will not significantly diminish the interest in confidentiality. Legitimate judicial needs may therefore outweigh a blanket presidential privilege.

- Application of a balancing test to the interests involved results in affirmation of the district court's order. P sought the subpoena to assure fair and complete presentation of evidence in a criminal proceeding, pursuant to the fundamental demands of due process. The generalized assertion of privilege must yield to the demonstrated, specific need for evidence in a pending criminal trial.

---

4. No Presidential Immunity for Unofficial Conduct--

Clinton v. Jones, 520 U.S. 681 (1997).

Facts. Jones (P), a private citizen, claimed that when she was an employee of the state of Arkansas, Clinton (D), who at the time was governor of Arkansas, made sexual advances toward her. By the time P filed suit for deprivation of her civil rights and for tort damages, D was serving as President. The trial court ordered the trial stayed until the end of D's presidency on the ground that the public interest in avoiding litigation that might hamper the President outweighed any demonstrated need for an immediate trial. The court of appeals reversed the postponement of the trial, which it considered to be the functional equivalent of a grant of temporary immunity. The Supreme Court granted certiorari.

Issue. Must a claim by a private citizen against the President of the United States, based on actions allegedly taken before his term began, be deferred until the expiration of the President's term of office?

Held. No. Judgment affirmed.

- Certain public servants, including prosecutors, legislators and judges, have immunity from suits for money damages arising out of their official acts because this serves the public interest in allowing such officials to perform their designated functions effectively, without fear of personal liability for a particular decision. This rationale does not support immunity for unofficial conduct, however.

- There is no precedent to support D's position that he should have immunity for unofficial acts purely because of the identity of his office. The President is not above the laws, but is amenable to them in his private character as a citizen, and in his public character by impeachment.

- Despite the importance of the office of the President, whatever the outcome of this case, it will not curtail the scope of the official powers of the Executive Branch. The fact that a federal court's actions in this case may significantly burden the President's time and attention does not establish a constitutional violation. Courts have the authority to determine whether a President's official actions are within the law. Presidents are subject to judicial process in other areas, such as in complying with a subpoena. The separation of powers doctrine does not require federal courts to stay all private actions against the President until he leaves office.

- ♦ The district court did not grant immunity, but it did grant a stay until after D leaves office. This was an abuse of discretion because it did not take into account P's interest in bringing the case to trial. Such a long delay would increase the risk of prejudice to P resulting from the loss of evidence, impaired memory, or perhaps even the death of a party. If greater protection of the President becomes necessary, Congress can provide appropriate legislation.

Concurrence (Breyer, J.). While there should be no automatic temporary immunity, the courts cannot unduly interfere with the President's performance of his duties. The trial court must schedule proceedings so as to avoid significant interference with the President's ongoing discharge of his official responsibilities.

---

5. **The Power to Grant Pardons.** Article II, Section 2 indicates that the President has the power to "grant reprieves and pardons for offenses against the United States, except in cases of Impeachment."

6. **Impeaching the President.**

   a. **Introduction.** Two Presidents, Andrew Johnson in 1868 and William Clinton in 1999, have been impeached and tried by the Senate. In both cases, the Senate voted to acquit. In addition, articles of impeachment against Richard Nixon were adopted by the House Committee, but were abandoned when he resigned from office in 1974.

   b. **Relevant provisions.** Article II, Section 4 states "The President [or] Vice President . . . shall be removed from office on Impeachment for, and Conviction of, Treason, Bribery, or other high Crimes and Misdemeanors."

   c. **Impeachable offenses.** There is substantial question as to what constitutes an impeachable offense. For example, must it be a criminal offense?

      1) One view has been that the offenses must be of a serious crime.

      2) Another view is that the offense need not be an actual crime; it is sufficient if there has been a serious breach of trust or confidence in the integrity of the office, an abuse of government process or use of power, etc.—*i.e.*, a demonstrated "unfitness" for office.

3) The Supreme Court has held that matters regarding congressional impeachments involve nonjusticiable political questions. Thus, whether the definition of impeachable offenses includes conduct besides statutory criminal offenses, or includes every criminal offense, is left to the judgment of Congress. The roles of the House and Senate, beyond the basic principle that the House may vote to impeach and the Senate holds a trial of the charges, are left to the discretion of the respective houses. Even the question of the appropriate sanction in the event of conviction is left to Congress.

VII. THE BILL OF RIGHTS AND THE POST-CIVIL WAR AMENDMENTS: "FUNDAMENTAL" RIGHTS AND THE "INCORPORATION" DISPUTE

A. INDIVIDUAL RIGHTS BEFORE THE CIVIL WAR

1. **Introduction.** The Bill of Rights was added to the federal Constitution to provide additional protection of both individual and states' rights. Originally, the Bill of Rights limited only the power of the federal government; most state constitutions contained their own version of a bill of rights. Through the Fourteenth Amendment, however, the Bill of Rights has been applied to state action.

2. **Pre-Civil War Approach.**

   a. **Limits on governmental power.** The basic Constitution mainly establishes the structure of government, but it also prohibited state and federal ex post facto laws and bills of attainder. [Art. I, §§9, 10] The Privileges and Immunities Clause also provided protection for state citizens. As mentioned above, the addition of the Bill of Rights added no further protection against state action.

   b. **Bill of Rights applied only to the federal government--**

Barron v. Mayor and City Council of Baltimore, 32 U.S. (7 Pet.) 243 (1833).

Facts. Barron (P) sued the Mayor and City Council of Baltimore (Ds) for permitting street construction that had the effect of depositing silt in front of his wharf, making it inaccessible. P obtained a verdict for $45,000 that was reversed by the state court. P appeals on grounds that his property was not granted proper protection under the Fifth Amendment (*i.e.*, there was a "taking" without compensation).

Issue. Does the Bill of Rights accord citizens of the United States protection from ***state*** government acts?

Held. No. Case dismissed.

♦ The limitations on government power expressed in the federal Constitution are applicable only to the government created by that instrument. Had the framers intended them to be limitations on the powers of the state governments, they would have expressed that intention.

- ♦ Any limits on state powers can be found only in the respective state constitutions. For this reason, the Court has no jurisdiction and must dismiss the case.

Comment. Although the Court readily presumed that the Bill of Rights did not apply to the states, it could have inferred otherwise from the fact that all of the Bill of Rights' provisions are cast in general terms except the first, which specifically applies only to Congress.

B. THE POST-CIVIL WAR AMENDMENTS

After the Civil War, the Thirteenth, Fourteenth, and Fifteenth Amendments were added to the Constitution. Each gave Congress power to enforce its provisions through legislation.

1. The Amendments.

a. **Thirteenth Amendment.** The Thirteenth Amendment, adopted in 1865, forbids slavery and involuntary servitude and provided a constitutional basis for President Lincoln's Emancipation Proclamation.

b. **Fourteenth Amendment.** Congress enacted the Civil Rights Act of 1866 to prevent continuing oppression of ex-slaves. The Fourteenth Amendment, adopted in 1868, provided a constitutional basis for the Civil Rights Act but, by its terms, went much further than the problems of slavery and race.

c. **Fifteenth Amendment.** Enacted in 1870, the Fifteenth Amendment prohibited restrictions on the right to vote based on racial grounds.

2. Narrow Interpretation of the Amendments--

The Slaughter-House Cases, 83 U.S. (16 Wall.) 36 (1873).

Facts. A group of New Orleans butchers (Ps) challenged a state law granting a state corporation the exclusive right to operate facilities in New Orleans for the landing, keeping, and slaughter of livestock. Ps' only means of practicing their trade was to pay fees to the state corporation and work at the corporation's plant. The state courts upheld the statute. Ps appeal, based on the following constitutional objections: (i) The statute creates an involuntary servitude forbidden by the Thirteenth Amendment; (ii) it abridges the privileges and immunities of citizens of the United States; (iii) it denies Ps the equal protection of the laws; and (iv) it deprives them of their property without due process of law, all in violation of the Fourteenth Amendment.

Issue. Do the Civil War amendments grant United States citizens broad protection from the actions of state governments?

Held. No. Judgment affirmed.

- Interpretation of the meaning of the Civil War amendments must reflect their historical setting. Therefore, the meaning of "involuntary servitude" in the Thirteenth Amendment is restricted to personal servitude, not a servitude attached to property as Ps' claim.

- The Fourteenth Amendment clearly distinguishes between citizenship of the states and citizenship of the United States. Only those privileges and immunities of ***United States citizens*** are protected by the Fourteenth Amendment; privileges and immunities of state citizens upon which Ps rely here are unaffected, and rest for their security and protection in the power of the several states as recognized in Article IV. The Constitution does not control the power of the state governments over the rights of their own citizens except to require that a state grant equal rights to its own citizens and citizens of other states within its jurisdiction. Therefore, Ps have no privilege or immunity as citizens of the United States that is infringed by the state law.

- The Equal Protection Clause of the Fourteenth Amendment was intended primarily to prevent state discrimination against blacks, although Congress may extend its scope to other areas. But Ps have not claimed a denial of equal justice in the state courts and therefore have no reason to have a remedy under the Equal Protection Clause.

- The restraint imposed by Louisiana upon the exercise of Ps' trade simply cannot be held, consistent with prior interpretations, to be a deprivation of property within the meaning of that provision.

Dissent (Field, J., Chase, C.J., Swayne, Bradley, JJ.). These amendments were intended to protect the citizens of the United States against the deprivation of their common rights by state legislation. The majority holding as to the Privileges and Immunities Clause would add no more protection than existed prior to adoption of the Amendment, making it meaningless. A distinguishing privilege of citizens of the United States is equality of right to the lawful pursuits of life throughout the whole country. To permit a state to interfere with such a basic privilege is to ignore the true purpose of the Fourteenth Amendment.

Dissent (Bradley, J.). Although the problems of blacks may have been the primary cause of the Fourteenth Amendment, its language extends protection to all citizens against violation of fundamental rights by the states. Prohibiting citizens from pursuing a lawful employment deprives them of both liberty and property, without due process of law. The fear that Congress will invade the internal affairs of the states through the Fourteenth Amendment is unjustified; very little legislation would be necessary to give effect to the Amendment.

Comment. The majority's view of "privileges and immunities" has prevailed to date, so that it protects a few rights of national citizenship but not state citizenship. These include the right to travel among the states, to vote for national officers, to petition Congress, and to enter public lands. The rights asserted by the dissenters in this case have come to be protected by the Due Process and Equal Protection Clauses.

---

3. **State Durational Residence Requirements and the Right to Travel.** A citizen has a constitutional right to travel freely from state to state. State durational residence requirements that would impair this right must be justified by a "compelling" state interest, at least where they affect the citizen's right to receive some vital government benefit or service. However, states may apply a requirement of residency at the time of (and during) receipt of governmental benefits, subject only to the "traditional" test. [*See, e.g.*, McCarthy v. Philadelphia Civil Service Commission, 424 U.S. 645 (1976)—requiring personal residence at place of governmental employment does not violate the right to travel]

---

a. **State welfare.**

1) **Limitation of benefits--**

Saenz v. Roe, 526 U.S. 489 (1999).

Facts. In response to high welfare benefit payments, California began limiting welfare benefits, for the first 12 months of a new citizen's residency in the state, to the level received by the individual in his previous state of residence. This change was apparently permitted by Congress in a statute titled Temporary Assistance to Needy Families ("TANF"). Roe and others (Ps) challenged the California statute. The lower courts held the California statute unconstitutional. The Supreme Court granted certiorari.

Issue. May a state limit the welfare benefits of a new citizen to the amount the new citizen would have received in his previous state of residency?

Held. No. Judgment affirmed.

- D claims that unlike the law in *Shapiro, infra,* the California statute here does not penalize the right of travel because new arrivals are not ineligible for benefits.

- The right to travel includes at least three components:

  (i) The right to enter and leave another state;

  (ii) The right to be treated as a welcome visitor; and

  (iii) The right to elect to become a permanent resident and to be treated like other citizens of the new state.

- The statute in this case does not directly impair the right to free interstate movement. As for visitor status, there are some situations in which a noncitizen may be treated differently from a citizen, such as in tuition fees for a state university. But this case involves the third aspect of the right to travel, since Ps became residents of the state.

- The Privileges and Immunities Clause of the Fourteenth Amendment protects the third element of the right to travel. Under that clause, a United States citizen can become a citizen of any state by a bona fide residence therein, with the same rights as other citizens of that state. The right to travel includes the citizen's right to be treated equally in the new state of residence, so the discriminatory classification is itself a penalty. The Citizenship Clause expressly equates citizenship with residence and does not allow for degrees of citizenship based on length of residence. California has created a hierarchy of subclasses based on the original state from which the immigrants came. Yet neither the duration of Ps' California residence, nor the identity of their prior states of residence, has any relevance to their need for benefits.

- D claims that the statute will save the state approximately $11 million per year, but the state's legitimate interest in saving money does not justify discrimination among equally eligible citizens.

Dissent (Rehnquist, C.J., Thomas, J.). The right to travel is distinct from the right to become a citizen. In fact, Ps had to stop traveling to become citizens of California. The Court has confused the right to travel with the right to enjoy the privileges of citizenship. The Court has ignored the state's need to assure that only persons who establish a bona fide residence receive the benefits provided to current residents of the state. States cannot determine an individual's subjective intent, so the Court has allowed states to impose durational residence requirements to test intention. States can impose a residence requirement prior to granting the right to educational benefits, the right to terminate a marriage, or the right to vote in primary elections, and they should be able to do the same for welfare benefits.

Dissent (Thomas, J., Rehnquist, C.J.). The Court's reliance on the Privileges and Immunities Clause is surprising because that clause had been drained of meaning by *The*

Slaughter-House Cases. The Court should consider how the Clause relates to equal protection and substantive due process.

Comment. The Court noted that Congress approved durational residence requirements, but held that Congress cannot authorize the states to violate the Fourteenth Amendment. The Citizenship Clause is a limitation on the powers of the federal government as well as the state governments.

---

2) **Denial of benefits.** In *Shapiro v. Thompson,* 394 U.S. 618 (1969), a case decided 30 years before *Saenz,* the Court struck down a Connecticut law similar to that in *Saenz*, except that the Connecticut law completely denied state welfare benefits to new Connecticut residents during their first year of residence. The Court stated that the purpose of inhibiting immigration by needy persons is constitutionally impermissible. The Court held that any classification that serves to penalize the exercise of a constitutional right, unless it is shown to be necessary to promote a compelling governmental interest, is unconstitutional.

b. **State medical care.** Relying on *Shapiro*, the Court in *Memorial Hospital v. Maricopa County*, 415 U.S. 250 (1974), struck down a state statute requiring a year's residency for receipt of nonemergency medical care. While some residency requirements are permissible (*e.g.*, certain waiting periods), strict scrutiny is triggered by restrictions that are, in essence, a penalty on a constitutional right. The existence of a penalty is generally determined by whether it affects a necessity of life.

c. **Domestic relations.** In *Sosna v. Iowa*, 419 U.S. 393 (1975), a one-year durational requirement for commencing a divorce action against a nonresident was sustained. Noting that domestic relations have long been considered a virtually exclusive province of the states, the Court found that the requirement may reasonably be justified on grounds other than budgetary or administrative factors such as those relied upon in *Shapiro* and *Maricopa County*. Furthermore, a plaintiff's access to the courts is merely delayed, not irretrievably foreclosed.

C. THE "INCORPORATION" OF THE BILL OF RIGHTS THROUGH THE DUE PROCESS CLAUSE

1. **Effect of Civil War Amendments.** The Civil War amendments changed the relationship between the federal and state governments. Application of these amendments was based largely on due process principles. Prior to the adoption of the Fourteenth Amendment, in *Murray v. Hoboken Land & Improvement Co.,* 59 U.S. (18 How.) 272 (1856), the Court noted that the Due

Process Clause of the Fifth Amendment was not further explained in the Constitution itself. Instead, the framers intended that the courts look to the settled usages and procedures existing in the common and statute law of England.

2. **Some Personal Rights Safeguarded Against State Action.** In *Twining v. New Jersey*, 211 U.S. 78 (1908), the Court held that the privilege against self-incrimination was not a necessary part of due process. However, the Court recognized that some of the personal rights safeguarded in the Bill of Rights were also safeguarded against state action because a denial of these rights would be a denial of due process itself.

3. **Due Process Under the Fourteenth Amendment.** The Fourteenth Amendment contains a clause that prevents any state from depriving any person of life, liberty, or property without due process of law. Although this clause appears to give Congress and the courts a means of protecting individual rights against improper state action, the scope of the clause was unclear for many years.

4. **The "Incorporation Doctrine" and "Fundamental Principles of Liberty."** Whether or not the Fourteenth Amendment Due Process Clause incorporated the rights guaranteed at the federal level by the Bill of Rights and made them applicable to the states was an important question. Some commentators and judges argued for total incorporation; *i.e.*, the Bill of Rights should apply fully to state action. Others argued that "due process" included only fundamental principles of liberty.

5. **Selective Incorporation.** *Palko v. Connecticut,* 302 U.S. 319 (1937), concerned a Connecticut statute permitting appeals by the prosecution. A jury in a state court had found Palko guilty of second degree murder. The state appealed, and Palko was tried again and was convicted of first degree murder. The Supreme Court held that the Fourteenth Amendment does not prevent a state from enacting a statute permitting the state to appeal in criminal cases. The Court noted that, while it is true that the Fifth Amendment prohibits retrial against the will of a defendant once convicted, no such protection extends to prosecution by a state. There is no general rule applying all of the protections of the original Bill of Rights to state action. The Court further explained that some immunities, such as those found in the First Amendment, have been extended to state action, but solely because of their indispensability to the concept of ordered liberty. Absorption of any of the Bill of Rights by the Fourteenth Amendment Due Process Clause is due solely to the belief that neither liberty nor justice would exist without them; the double jeopardy provision is not such an essential privilege. However, in *Benton v. Maryland*, 395 U.S. 784 (1969), the Court held that the guarantee against double jeopardy is fundamental to the American scheme of justice and overruled *Palko*.

6. **Argument for Total Incorporation.** In *Adamson v. California*, 332 U.S. 46 (1947), the Court decided that due process did not require reversal of a state criminal conviction where the prosecution had commented on the defendant's refusal to testify, although such a comment would be reversible error at the federal level because of the Fifth Amendment. Justices Black and Douglas dissented, arguing that the original purpose of the Fourteenth Amendment was to incorporate fully all of the Bill of Rights guarantees. They argued that failure to incorporate those specific guarantees would leave citizens without assured rights and would at the same time grant the Court an unauthorized broad power to expand or contract the scope of due process virtually at will. They also indicated a preference for selective incorporation over no incorporation at all.

7. **The Current Approach to Due Process and the Bill of Rights.**

    a. **Selective incorporation or total incorporation?** As indicated above, the Supreme Court has taken the position that the provisions of the Bill of Rights, through the Fourteenth Amendment, restrict the states only on a selective basis. Under this selective incorporation basis, the Court has held that most of the provisions of the Bill of Rights (although not all) apply to the states just as they do to the federal government. For example, the Fifth Amendment provisions concerning the privilege against self-incrimination and double jeopardy and the Eighth Amendment provision against cruel and unusual punishment have been held to apply to the states. But with the Court increasingly looking to the Bill of Rights and incorporating its provisions through the Fourteenth Amendment in application to the states, it may be that "selective incorporation may have proceeded to the point where it is essentially total incorporation."

    b. **Trial by jury--**

Duncan v. Louisiana, 391 U.S. 145 (1968).

Facts. Duncan (D) was convicted of simple battery, a misdemeanor in Louisiana punishable by up to two years' imprisonment and a $300 fine. D was fined $150 and sentenced to serve 60 days. D was refused a trial by jury under a Louisiana law, which he then challenged, but the state supreme court refused to review. D appeals.

Issue. May a state that provides trial by jury for all "felonies" try charges of simple battery to the court alone?

Held. No. Judgment reversed and case remanded.

♦ The right of trial by jury in serious criminal cases is fundamental to the American scheme of justice and qualifies for protection under the Due Process Clause against violation by the states. The authorized penalty is of major relevance in determining whether a particular crime is serious; the possibility of two years' imprisonment clearly indicates a serious offense, so it is within due process protection.

- ♦ The Sixth Amendment guarantee of a right to jury trial is hereby applicable through the Fourteenth Amendment to state criminal cases, which if tried in a federal court would be covered.

Concurrence (Black, Douglas, JJ.). The Court ought to make an absolute incorporation into the Fourteenth Amendment of all the Bill of Rights, but since the selective process adopted by the majority will eventually reach the same result, I concur. The Court ought to avoid the due process approach of Justices Fortas and Harlan, which would give due process an impermanent meaning subject to varying judges' predilections and understandings of what is best for the country.

Dissent (Harlan, Stewart, JJ.). The first section of the Fourteenth Amendment was meant neither to incorporate, nor to be limited to, the specific guarantees of the first eight amendments. The true intention was to assure due process, based on a gradual process of judicial inclusion and exclusion. The Court errs in focusing on the simple incorporation question. Examination of the true merits reveals that D has not been denied any element of fundamental procedural fairness. States should be free to experiment with alternatives (fair procedures that may prove more effective).

---

c. **Modifications to the jury trial guarantee.**

1) In *Williams v. Florida*, 399 U.S. 78 (1970), the Court upheld a Florida state law that permitted a six-member jury in noncapital cases, against the challenge that *Duncan* had made the Sixth Amendment jury trial guarantee applicable to the common law jury (including its 12-member panel).

2) In *Apodaca v. Oregon*, 406 U.S. 404 (1972), a sharply divided Court sustained the constitutionality of a state nonunanimous jury verdict (despite *Duncan*, which said that each element of the Sixth Amendment jury trial guarantee is fully applicable to the states by the Fourteenth Amendment, and a belief by five justices that the Sixth Amendment required unanimous jury verdicts in federal cases).

VIII. DUE PROCESS

A. SUBSTANTIVE DUE PROCESS AND ECONOMIC LIBERTIES

1. **Introduction.** As the *Palko* and *Adamson* cases illustrate, the Court can use the Due Process Clause as a basis for articulating fundamental rights. Those cases involved procedural fundamentals in an attempt to ensure a fair trial. However, the Court has also used the Due Process Clause to protect substantive rights. Beginning with *Lochner v. New York* (below), the Court invoked due process to protect economic and property rights. In more recent times, substantive due process has not been used to protect economic rights but instead has been invoked as a basis for protecting privacy and personal autonomy. The basic issue underlying the substantive due process cases is whether the Court may properly protect rights not specifically mentioned by the Constitution simply by declaring them "fundamental rights." If so, what guidelines exist to protect against purely subjective judicial lawmaking, and what accounts for changes in the types of liberties deemed "fundamental"?

2. **Economic Regulation.**

   a. **Background.** Although the Court did not expressly recognize substantive due process as protecting fundamental economic rights until *Allgeyer v. Louisiana*, 165 U.S. 578 (1897), arguments about the validity of governmental interference with personal liberty and property had long existed. In *Calder v. Bull*, 3 U.S. (3 Dall.) 386 (1798), Justice Chase argued that government existed to protect personal liberty and private property; an act by the legislature removing that protection would necessarily exceed the legislative authority. In the same case, Justice Iredell argued that constitutions were intended to limit the legislative power; a court may believe a statute violated natural law, but could not declare it void unless it was prohibited by the Constitution. In *Munn v. Illinois*, 94 U.S. 113 (1877), the Court deferred to legislative judgment in rejecting an attack on a state law regulating grain elevators, while suggesting the potential limits on legislative power. In that case, the Court refused to scrutinize the reasonableness of the rates levied against business owners with a near monopoly on grain storage because, under the police power, the state could regulate industrial use of property for the public good. Yet the Court noted that the reasonableness of merely private contracts must be ascertained judicially. Later, in *Mugler v. Kansas*, 123 U.S. 623 (1887), although the Court sustained a law prohibiting intoxicating beverages, it announced that it would examine the substantive reasonableness of state legislation. In *Allgeyer*, a state law had prohibited the insuring of Louisiana property by any company not licensed to do business in Louisiana. Allgeyer had insured his property with a New York insurer and was convicted of the offense. The Court held that the statute deprived Allgeyer of his liberty to contract without due process of law.

b. ***Lochner*** **and judicial intervention in economic regulation.**

1) **Leading case--**

Lochner v. New York, 198 U.S. 45 (1905).

Facts. Lochner (D) was convicted of permitting a bakery employee to work for him more than the statutory maximum of 60 hours per week. D challenges the law as a violation of the liberty to contract protected by the Fourteenth Amendment.

Issue. May a state generally prohibit private agreements to work more than a specified number of hours?

Held. No. Judgment reversed.

- The general right to contract in business is clearly part of the individual liberty protected by the Fourteenth Amendment. However, the right to hold both property and liberty is subject to such reasonable conditions as may be imposed by a government pursuant to its police powers.
- An earlier law restricting the work hours in certain dangerous occupations was upheld. The law here challenged, however, has no reference whatever to the health, safety, morals, nor welfare of the public. The state claims an interest in the individual worker's health, but this goes too far; the individual's liberty must impose some restraint on the police power.
- This is not a substitution of the Court's judgment for the legislature's, but merely a determination of whether the attempted regulation is within the state's police power.

Dissent (Harlan, White, Day, JJ.). Liberty of contract is subject to reasonable police regulations. The Court ought to take judicial notice of the injurious working conditions in bakeries; these conditions provided a reasonable justification for the state legislation.

Dissent (Holmes, J.). Many comparably restrictive uses of the police power have been upheld by the Court. The Constitution was not intended to embody a particular economic view, but was framed to permit expression of dominant opinions; *i.e.*, that the laws freely reflect the people's choices. The law is not clearly unrelated to public health and ought to be upheld.

2) **Substantive due process.** The Supreme Court said that substantive due process consisted of the following:

a) **Ends or purposes.** You must examine the purposes of the legislation. That is, is the object legitimate, appropriate, or necessary? Does the law promote in some way the health, safety, welfare, or morals of the people? This is answered from the language of the statute, the legislative record, and the history behind the passage of the statute, and is a question of law for the court.

b) **Means.** Are the means used to accomplish the legislation's purpose reasonable and appropriate? That is, is there a real and substantial relationship between the means used and the legitimate end?

c) **Effect.** What is the effect of the law on the liberty of the parties involved, on their property, and on their lives? If the effect is too drastic, the law might violate due process.

3) **Applications.**

a) **Maximum hours.** The Court upheld a law fixing maximum work hours for women, distinguishing *Lochner* by the special state interest in healthy women. [*See* Muller v. Oregon, 208 U.S. 412 (1908)] The Court later effectively overruled *Lochner* by upholding a general maximum work hour law in *Bunting v. Oregon*, 243 U.S. 426 (1917). However, the Court did not refer to *Lochner*, and substantive due process survived.

b) **"Yellow dog" contracts.** The Court invalidated a state law that prohibited employers from requiring employees to agree not to join a labor union ("yellow dog" contracts). [*See* Coppage v. Kansas, 236 U.S. 1 (1915)] The law violated due process because it interfered with the right to make contracts. *Adair v. United States*, 208 U.S. 161 (1908), invalidated a similar federal law.

c) **Minimum wages.** The Court invalidated a federal minimum wage law applicable only to the District of Columbia in *Adkins v. Children's Hospital*, 261 U.S. 525 (1923), again finding that interference with freedom to contract violated due process.

d) **Business entry and economic regulations.** In a series of decisions that have been undermined by developments since the 1930s, the Court invalidated restraints on competition that curtailed entry into a particular type of business. [*See* New York State Ice Co. v. Liebman, 285 U.S. 262 (1932)—manufacture of ice requiring a certificate of convenience and necessity; Adams v. Tanner, 244 U.S. 590 (1917)—employment agency fees collected from workers]

e) **Means scrutiny.** In *Weaver v. Palmer Brothers Co.*, 270 U.S. 402 (1926), although the Court recognized the validity of the state interest in curtailing business practices that might defraud or endanger consumers, the Court invalidated an absolute ban on the use of shoddy (cut up or torn) fabrics for bedding. The Court held that the ban was purely arbitrary since other secondhand materials could be used if sterilized and labeled.

c. **The modern era: decline of judicial intervention in economic regulation.**

1) **Due process.** Some time after *Lochner*, the Court changed its earlier view and began to apply less strict scrutiny to economic regulation. Instead it granted deference to legislative determinations of need and reasonableness.

2) **No area outside power of state to regulate--**

Nebbia v. New York, 291 U.S. 502 (1934).

Facts. New York (P) passed a law establishing minimum and maximum retail prices for milk. The purpose was to aid the dairy industry, which was in a desperate situation because the prices received by farmers for milk were below the cost of production. Nebbia (D), a retail grocer, sold milk below the minimum price and was convicted of violating the statute. D challenges the statute as a violation of due process.

Issue. May a state strictly control retail prices, even if such control inhibits the use of private property and the making of contracts?

Held. Yes. Judgment affirmed.

- As long as the Court finds the law to have a reasonable relationship to a proper legislative purpose, to be not arbitrary or discriminatory, and to have means chosen that are reasonably related to the ends sought, due process is not offended.

- No area is outside the province of state regulation for police power purposes, including the direct regulation of prices.

Dissent (McReynolds, Van Devanter, Sutherland, Butler, JJ.). This statute is not regulation but management. D is deprived of the fundamental right to conduct his business honestly and along customary lines, and consumers are deprived of their liberty to buy a necessity of life in an open market.

---

3) **Reasonable relationship to state's interests.** The Court overruled *Adkins* in *West Coast Hotel Co. v. Parrish*, 300 U.S. 379 (1937), by upholding a state minimum wage law for women. The Court found that the only issue for consideration was whether the legislative act was arbitrary or capricious and concluded that the legislature had the right to consider minimum wage requirements as an important means of implementing its policy of protecting abused workers.

    a) **Comment.** These cases were a sharp change from the *Lochner* approach of judicial intervention.

4) **Further retreat from *Lochner*.** In rejecting a due process challenge to a federal ban on interstate shipments of adulterated (filled) milk, the Court in *United States v. Carolene Products Co.*, 304 U.S. 144 (1938), noted that challenges to a rational basis underlying economic legislation would be difficult. The *Carolene* Court found that the statute was clearly within the commerce power and was reasonable and not reviewable.

    a) **Other cases.** Legislatures are given almost unlimited latitude in enacting economic legislation for such purposes and ends as they see fit. [*See* Olsen v. Nebraska, 313 U.S. 236 (1941)—upholding fixed maximum employment agency fees; Ferguson v. Skrupa, 372 U.S. 726 (1963)—permitting restrictive regulation of the business of debt adjusting, and Lincoln Federal Labor Union v. Northwestern Iron & Metal Co., 335 U.S. 525 (1949)—upholding state right to work laws because due process permits legislative protection of nonunion workers as well as union workers]

    b) **Footnote 4.** In a famous footnote in *Carolene*, Justice Stone pointed out that higher scrutiny would still be applied to legislation that implicates the Bill of Rights.

5) **Limits of nonintervention--**

Williamson v. Lee Optical Co., 348 U.S. 483 (1955).

Facts. Lee Optical Co. (P) challenged a state law that, among other things, (i) forbids an optician from fitting or duplicating lenses, even replacements, without a prescription from an ophthalmologist or optometrist; (ii) prohibits advertising of eyeglass frames; and (iii) prohibits optometrists from working in a general retail establishment. The district court held these three parts of the Act invalid under the Due Process Clause of the Fourteenth Amendment. Williamson (D), a state official, appeals.

Issue. Does the Fourteenth Amendment prohibit all state business regulation that is not essential and directly related to the harm it intends to cure?

Held. No. Judgment reversed.

- Although the law may exact a needless, wasteful requirement in many cases, the legislature, not the courts, must balance the advantages and disadvantages of a new requirement. There is ample reason for the legislative means adopted to correct an actual evil. The law need not be logically consistent with its aims in every respect to be constitutional.

- The Court will not strike down state laws regulatory of business and industrial conditions merely because they may be unwise, improvident, or out of harmony with a particular school of thought. The people as voters, not the courts, are the protection against legislative abuse.

Comment. The Court has not invalidated any economic regulation on substantive due process grounds since 1937. Compare this to the Court's expansive approach to substantive due process in the area of fundamental personal liberties.

B. TEXTUAL GUARANTEES OF ECONOMIC LIBERTIES: THE TAKINGS CLAUSE

1. The Takings Clause

a. **Constitutional provision.** There is no specific power of eminent domain in the federal government. Rather, it is an implied power. Also, the power of eminent domain may be exercised pursuant to the Necessary and Proper Clause whenever Congress is acting in accordance with one of its other specific powers.

1) **Constitutional limitation.** There is an express constitutional limitation on the exercise by Congress of this power. The Fifth Amendment states: ". . . nor shall private property be taken for public use, without just compensation." The requirement that just compensation be paid is likewise a constitutional limitation incorporated into the Fourteenth Amendment and applied to the states.

2) **Contrast: substantial diminution in value.** Despite this limitation, under the police power and other regulatory powers, government may impose restrictions on property that produce substantial diminution in value without having to compensate for losses incidental to these valid regulations. The question is—what is "taking" and what is merely "regulation"?

b. **Requirements for the exercise of eminent domain.**

1) **Public use.** The use for which the land is taken must be a "public" one. This notion is a broad one since the courts are willing to allow government to do pretty much what it wants to if it will pay for it. If the exercise of the power results in a public benefit, the government can delegate the power of eminent domain to private companies, educational institutions, government agencies, etc.

a) **Scope of "public use."** The Court's deferential stance toward a government's determination of what is a public use is analogous to the "ends" inquiries in economic due process cases. In one case, the Supreme Court upheld the use of eminent domain by Congress to redevelop a slum area in the District of Columbia. [Berman v. Parker, 348 U.S. 26 (1954)] State legislatures have used the eminent domain power to assist in commercial and industrial development as well, finding public use in the need to provide employment and tax bases for the localities involved. In *Hawaii Housing Authority v. Midkiff*, 467 U.S. 229 (1984), the Court upheld Hawaii's statute authorizing it to take title (with compensation) to large estates of land, of which ownership was concentrated in a few owners. The state then transferred title to the tenants living on smaller individual lots on the estates. A rational relationship to a conceivable public purpose is all the state need show. Federal courts may not second-guess legislative determinations in this area as long as the power is not used for a purely private purpose. In *Midkiff*, the state was attempting to reduce social and economic evils of a land oligopoly that interfered with the normal functioning of its residential land market.

2) **The necessity requirement.**

a) **Federal government.** The necessity question is not reviewable in federal condemnation cases. That is, the question of whether it was necessary or desirable to take the plaintiff's land will not be reviewed.

b) **State condemnation.** Many jurisdictions will not review the question of necessity. Other jurisdictions hold that the question is justiciable in some instances and not in others. In those states that permit a limited review, such review is normally limited to the question of whether there has been an excessive taking (*e.g.*, more land taken than needed).

3) **Just compensation.** Just compensation has usually been held to mean "fair market value" at the time and place of the taking. This price must be paid in cash. The test is the loss to the owner, not the gain to the taker.

c. **The "public use" requirement--**

Kelo v. New London, 545 U.S. 469 (2005).

Facts. State and local officials designated a portion of New London (D) for economic revitalization. Kelo (P) and other property owners in the area refused to sell their property to D. D initiated condemnation proceedings, using its power of eminent domain. Ps' properties were not in poor condition, but D sought to condemn them because they were in the redevelopment area. Ps sued, claiming the condemnation violated the Takings Clause. The Connecticut Supreme Court upheld the condemnation. The Supreme Court granted certiorari.

Issue. As part of a regional economic rejuvenation program, may a city take private property from one private party and give it to another private party?

Held. Yes. Judgment affirmed.

- ♦ The government cannot take the property of a private party for the sole purpose of transferring it to another private party, even with the payment of just compensation. However, the government may transfer property from one private party to another if future use by the public is the reason for the taking (*e.g.*, land for a railroad with common-carrier duties).

- ♦ Here, although D's taking is not to benefit specific individuals, D does not intend to open all of the condemned land to use by the general public. However, to satisfy the "public use" requirement, condemned property need not be put to use for the general public, but it must serve a public purpose. Thus, the disposition of this case rests on a determination of whether D's plan serves a public purpose.

- ♦ D determined that the area was sufficiently distressed to justify an economic rejuvenation plan. The plan clearly serves a public purpose. Therefore, the condemnation does not violate the Takings Clause.

- ♦ Ps ask us to adopt a rule that economic development does not qualify as a public use. This position is not supported by precedent or logic. Promoting economic development is a long-accepted governmental function.

♦ Nothing in our decision prevents the states from restricting the use of eminent domain powers.

Concurrence (Kennedy, J.). A taking that is intended to favor a particular private party, with only incidental and pretextual public benefit, would not be a valid taking. Although courts apply a rational basis review to this type of case, with a presumption that the government's actions are reasonable and intended to serve a public purpose, courts must treat plausible accusations of favoritism seriously.

Dissent (O'Connor, J., Rehnquist, C.J., Scalia, Thomas, JJ.). The majority concludes that incidental public benefit resulting from the subsequent ordinary use of private property renders economic development takings "for public use." But almost any lawful use of real private property can be said to generate some incidental benefit to the public. If this is enough to render transfer from one private party to another constitutional, the words "for public use" do not really exclude any takings and thus do not exert any constraint on the eminent domain power. To let the government itself define what is public and what is private use eliminates the protection provided by the Fifth Amendment. Economic development takings should not be constitutional.

Dissent (Thomas, J.). The Court is replacing the Public Use Clause with a "Public Purpose" clause. It is significant that the term "public use" contrasts with the very different phrase "general welfare" used elsewhere in the Constitution. This Court does not defer to legislative findings regarding what is a reasonable search, and it should not diminish the protection provided by the taking clause by deferring to a legislative finding about public purpose either. The government can only take property if it actually uses the property or gives the public a legal right to use the property.

---

d. **Regulatory takings--**

Pennsylvania Coal Co. v. Mahon, 260 U.S. 393 (1922).

Facts. Mahon (P) received title to the surface rights of a parcel of land from Pennsylvania Coal Co. (D), which reserved the rights to remove the coal under the surface. P also waived all claims for damages resulting from removal of the coal. D gave notice of intent to mine. P, knowing that D's activity would cause a subsidence of the surface and of P's house, sought an injunction based on a state statute that forbids coal mining in such a way as to cause subsidence of any human habitation. The lower court denied an injunction; the state supreme court held the statute a valid exercise of police power and granted an injunction. D appeals.

Issue. May a state exercise its police power to destroy previously existing property and contract rights without compensation?

Held. No. Judgment reversed.

- ♦ The general rule is that, while property may be regulated to a certain extent, if regulation goes too far it will be recognized as a "taking." One factor is the extent of the diminution in value of the property. Here, the statute would totally divest D of its properly reserved right to mine coal. Another factor is the extent of the public interest. Here, a single private house is involved, with no threat to personal safety since adequate notice was given.

- ♦ While there may be no doubt as to the need for the statute, the question is—who should pay for the changes initiated by the law? D's loss should not go uncompensated. The state may achieve its objectives properly only through eminent domain procedures. When private persons or communities take the risk of acquiring only surface rights they ought not be given greater rights than they bought merely because their risk has become an actuality.

Dissent (Brandeis, J.). Every restriction abridges property rights. Here, D is merely prohibited from a noxious use. Future events may render the use harmless; it is merely a temporary restriction, and need not be paid for.

---

e. **Destruction of public nuisance.** In *Miller v. Schoene*, 276 U.S. 272 (1928), the Court upheld a Virginia law that provided for the destruction of ornamental trees affected by a disease that could also damage apple orchards. Owners were compensated only for the cost of removing their trees. The state had to choose between preserving the trees or the orchards, and could properly determine that the public interest required preservation of the orchards.

f. **Extensive limitation on mining rights.** In *Keystone Bituminous Coal Association v. DeBendictis*, 480 U.S. 470 (1987), the Court cast serious doubt on the continuing validity of *Pennsylvania Coal* when it considered a state law that prohibited coal mining that caused subsidence damages to public buildings, dwellings, and cemeteries. The law required that 50% of the coal below these structures must remain for surface support. In finding that no taking had occurred, a closely divided Court noted that the *Pennsylvania Coal* ruling was an "uncharacteristic" advisory opinion based on the specific facts of that case, and that the *Keystone* case involved the protection of the public interest in health, the environment, and the fiscal integrity of the area. The prohibited actions were similar to a public nuisance. Moreover, the statute did not totally deprive the plaintiffs of their mining rights since all but 2% of the coal could be mined; such a minor limitation did not sustain treating the property as a separate segment for taking purposes.

g. **Interference with the use of land.** The government, by substantial interference with the use of land, may be held to have "taken" the land although it does not take actual possession. For example, in *United States v. Causby*, 328 U.S. 256 (1946), the federal government was held to have taken an easement over the plaintiff's land when it conducted continual low flights of army planes over the land in such a way as to destroy the plaintiff's poultry business. The distinction between a "taking" and merely an "injury" to the plaintiff's land may be very difficult to draw.

h. **Zoning and environmental regulation.** In *Goldblatt v. Town of Hempstead*, 369 U.S. 590 (1962), the Supreme Court upheld a city ordinance regulating mining in pits within the city limits. The regulation was aimed at one operation that was close to residences and schools. The mining operation was being conducted below the watermark; 25 feet of water had filled the pit, creating a lake of 20 acres. The ordinance completely prohibited the beneficial use of the land for mining. In denying the need to pay compensation, the Supreme Court cited the presumption in favor of constitutionality and the fact that the prohibition did not destroy all beneficial uses of the land.

1) **Comment.** A 1987 ruling in *Nollan v. California Coastal Commission* (discussed *infra*), suggested that the *Goldblatt* holding may no longer be effective since the decision was based on an incorrect assumption that due process, equal protection, and the Takings Clause restrictions were the same with regard to scrutiny of property rights.

i. **Historic landmark protection distinguished from taking regulation.** Because the Grand Central Terminal in New York City had been designated a landmark, its owner, Penn Central, was denied permission to construct an office building atop it on aesthetic principles. In addressing the assertion that an unconstitutional taking had occurred, the Court in *Penn Central Transportation Co. v. New York City*, 438 U.S. 104 (1978), concluded that a comprehensive historic landmarks preservation program can restrict further development of such structures without effecting a taking. Landmarks regulations are similar to zoning laws, which are ordinarily permissible restrictions on property interests for reasons of health, safety, morals, or general welfare.

j. **Per se rule.** The Court has indicated in subsequent cases that it is once again regarding the Takings Clause quite seriously. In *Loretto v. Teleprompter Manhattan CATV Corp.*, 458 U.S. 419 (1982), the Court rejected the balancing test used in earlier cases by articulating a per se rule of compensation when the government authorizes a permanent physical presence on private property.

k. **Complete destruction of property value.** In *Lucas v. South Carolina Coastal Council*, 505 U.S. 1003 (1992), Lucas had purchased two lots for nearly $1 million, intending to build single-family homes. South Carolina enacted the Beachfront Management Act, an anti-erosion law that effectively barred Lucas from building homes on the land. Lucas sued and the trial court found that he was entitled to compensation because his property was now valueless. The South Carolina Supreme Court reversed. On review, the Supreme Court explained that the functional basis for allowing the government, without making compensation, to affect property values through regulation is the recognition that the government could not operate if it had to pay for every change in the law that affected property values but that this basis does not apply where the government deprives a landowner of all economically beneficial uses. Such a regulation carries a risk that private property is being pressed into a form of public service under the guise of mitigating serious public harm. The state could avoid paying compensation only if the nature of the landowner's estate shows that the proscribed use interests were not part of his title to begin with. The Court held that confiscatory regulations cannot be newly legislated without compensation; they must inhere in the title itself, in the restrictions that background principles of the state's law of property and nuisance already place on land ownership. On remand, the South Carolina Supreme Curt ruled that Lucas was entitled to compensation.

l. **Remedies for de facto regulatory taking (inverse condemnation).** The Court, in *First English Evangelical Lutheran Church v. Los Angeles County*, 482 U.S. 304 (1987), determined when a land use regulation is so burdensome as to constitute a taking. Mere invalidation of the regulation is an insufficient remedy. A state must also pay damages for the temporary taking in effect before invalidation of the regulation.

m. **Challenge against regulation in place when property was purchased.** The Supreme Court has held that a property owner can challenge a regulatory taking even when the restriction was in place when he purchased the property. *Palazzolo v. Rhode Island*, 533 U.S. 606 (2001).

n. **Temporary restriction.** *Tahoe-Sierra Preservation Council, Inc. v. Tahoe Regional Planning Agency*, 535 U.S. 302 (2002), involved a temporary moratorium on development. The Supreme Court held that the question whether a temporary moratorium was a taking depended on the particular circumstances of the case. In some circumstances, it might be a per se taking under *Lucas*; in others, it would require case-by-case evaluation under *Penn Central*. The duration of the restriction is one of several factors for the courts to consider. The dissent noted that the moratoria in the case had lasted six years, a duration long enough to constitute a per se taking under *Lucas*.

o. **Conditions on building permits.**

1) **Beach access.** The trend to more frequently find compensable taking was apparent in *Nollan v. California Coastal Commission,* 483 U.S. 825 (1987), wherein the state had conditioned issuance of a building permit on agreement by the owners of beachfront property to allow public access to their beach. The Court concluded that the permit condition was, in essence, an easement that would have been a taking. In finding that there was no legitimate state interest to support the restriction, the Court stated that scrutiny in takings cases is more rigorous than the minimum rationality standard used in due process and equal protection analyses.

2) **Flood control and traffic improvement.** In *Dolan v. City of Tigard,* 512 U.S. 374 (1994), Dolan owned a plumbing and electric supply store that was on a 1.67-acre lot that bordered the Fanno Creek and was therefore in the floodplain. When Dolan applied for a permit to double the size of her store, the city's planning commission granted her application, subject to the dedication of part of her property for flood control and part for a pedestrian/bicycle pathway to improve traffic. Dolan challenged the dedication requirements, but the state courts upheld them. The Supreme Court reversed, explaining that under the doctrine of "unconstitutional conditions," the government may not require a person to give up a constitutional right (*e.g.*, the right to just compensation when property is taken for a public use) in exchange for a discretionary benefit conferred by the government if the property sought has little or no relationship to the benefit. The two-part test for takings cases requires: (i) a determination as to whether the "essential nexus" exists between the legitimate state interest and the permit requirement; and (ii) a sufficient degree of connection between the limitation and the projected impact of the proposed development. The Court found that the city's interests in preventing flooding and reducing traffic congestion are legitimate public purposes. As to the second part of the test, the Court noted that a variety of approaches were adopted to find the required degree of connection between the regulation and the proposed development. The Court decided that best approach is an intermediate one that requires the city to show a "reasonable relationship" between the required dedication and the impact of the proposed development. However, because of its concern that the term "reasonable relationship" is confusingly similar to "rational basis," the Court decided that the term "rough proportionality" should be applied. This requires the city to make some sort of individualized determination that the required dedication is related both in nature and extent to the impact of the proposed development. The Court found that the city never explained why a public greenway, as opposed to a private one, was required in the interest of flood control and

that the city failed to quantify its findings that purportedly supported the dedication for the pedestrian/bicycle pathway.

3) **Variances between courts.** Local governments have traditionally required developers to dedicate streets and utility easements within subdivisions, and frequently also require certain improvements that benefit the subdivision exclusively, such as paved streets or on-site utility facilities. However, some governments have required dedication of land for parks and schools, or a payment of money to develop parks and schools. Some courts disallow such requirements as not sufficiently attributable to the developer's activity to remove public responsibility for such improvements.

2. The Contract Clause.

a. **Constitutional provision.** Article I, Section 10 provides that "no ***state*** shall pass any law impairing the obligation of contracts." (Emphasis added.) Note that the Contract Clause is made applicable only to the states. There is no mention in the Constitution of a similar prohibition against the federal government. Despite this absence, the Due Process Clause of the Fifth Amendment has been held to be broad enough to extend the same prohibition to the federal government. [Lynch v. United States, 292 U.S. 571 (1934)]

b. **The Contract Clause in the nineteenth century.** The Contract Clause, for its first 100 years, was the major restraint on state economic action.

1) Its major purpose was to restrain state laws affecting private contracts, but it was extended in *Dartmouth College v. Woodward*, 17 U.S. (4 Wheat.) 518 (1819), to apply to public contracts as well. In that case, the college had, by its royal charter, given control of its board of trustees to the board itself. The state passed legislation attempting to pack the board; the Supreme Court held the state law unconstitutional.

2) Although early Contracts Clause cases were restrictive, their impact on economic and legal developments has probably been exaggerated. They did not compel legislative paralysis, were not the keystone of corporate development, nor did they effect an inflexible safeguard for all vested rights. The lack of statutory restrictions on corporations more likely resulted from legislators' unwillingness to enact them. However, some legislative action was taken.

3) For example, *Dartmouth College* recognized the legislature's power to reserve power to amend corporate charters; another case held that insolvency laws could be validly applied to contracts made after passage of the law. A further distinction established that the

clause did not prohibit changes by the legislature in "remedies," the scope of such changes depending on their "reasonableness," provided that no substantial right was impaired. Also, in publicly granted privileges, strict interpretations were the rule, not allowing anything not explicitly stated; there were no implied privileges. By later in the 19th century, the rule had developed that certain powers of the government could not be given away, nor be prevented by the Contracts Clause from operating, particularly the police power. All contract rights were subject to its fair exercise.

c. **Deference to state power--**

Home Building & Loan Association v. Blaisdell, 290 U.S. 398 (1934).

Facts. Minnesota passed a law that permitted extensions of the period of redemption from a foreclosure and sale of mortgaged real property. The Blaisdells (Ds) obtained such an extension. Home Building & Loan Association (P) sought to have the law invalidated as an improper state interference in private contracts. The state defended the law as a needed emergency measure to deal with the Depression. The state courts upheld the law; P appeals.

Issue. May a state alter existing contractual obligations in order to respond to emergency conditions?

Held. Yes. Judgment affirmed.

- ♦ An emergency does not create power, but it may justify the exercise of existing power. Maintenance of government is a necessary prerequisite to having enforceable contracts. Therefore, circumstances may arise when exercise of the police power to alter contracts is justified in order to maintain effective government. Here, the vital interests of the state were involved, and the police power is properly exercised.

- ♦ The policy behind the Contract Clause requires that any legislation affecting private contracts must be addressed to a legitimate end, as it was here. Additionally, the relief afforded must be appropriate to the emergency, and the means employed must be reasonable. The state's law satisfies these requirements.

- ♦ Finally, the legislation is temporary in operation, so that it deals specifically with the emergency and does not destroy the contractual obligations involved.

Dissent (Sutherland, J.). The history of the Contract Clause is clear; no state may act to impair the obligation of contracts, even if such action is to give relief to debtors during a time of emergency.

---

d. **Public interest justification.** In *El Paso v. Simmons*, 379 U.S. 497 (1965), the Supreme Court said that laws that restrict a party to those gains reasonably to be made from a contract are not subject to attack under the clause. The state had passed a law requiring that the privilege to reinstate land rights by paying overdue interest, granted under an early law making public land available for sale under contract, had to be exercised within five years. Confusion in land titles had caused the state legislature to pass the law.

e. **State obligations.** In *United States Trust Co. v. New Jersey*, 431 U.S. 1 (1977), the Court held that a state may not impair the obligation of its own contract based on its own determination of reasonableness and necessity. New York and New Jersey had formed the Port Authority of New York and New Jersey by interstate compact. In 1962, both states passed statutes prohibiting financing of railroad deficits with revenues pledged to pay the Authority's bonds, with minor exceptions. In 1974, the states retroactively repealed the 1962 covenant in order to permit greater subsidizing of mass transit. The Court held that the Contract Clause prohibited the retroactive repeal of the 1962 covenant. The Court explained that allowing a state to reduce its financial obligations whenever it wanted to spend the money for what it regarded as an important public purpose would negate all Contract Clause protection. For this reason, the Court found complete deference to legislative assessments of reasonableness and necessity to be inappropriate.

f. **Private obligations.** *Allied Structural Steel v. Spannaus*, 438 U.S. 234 (1978), involved a Minnesota law that subjected employers to a "pension funding charge" upon the termination of a pension plan or the closing of a Minnesota office. When Allied Structural Steel Company closed its Minnesota office, the law had the effect of making several of the company's otherwise unqualified employees pension obligees, resulting in a charge to the company of $185,000. The Court held that the Contract Clause precludes state legislation that significantly expands duties created by private contract. The Court explained that the law nullified express terms of the company's contractual obligations and imposed a completely unexpected liability in potentially disabling amounts. Furthermore, this severe change impacted not every Minnesota employer, but only those who had voluntarily agreed to establish pension plans for their employees.

C. SUBSTANTIVE DUE PROCESS AND PRIVACY

1. **Introduction.** Although substantive due process no longer imposes any serious restraints on economic regulations, the Court has revived the notion as a means of protecting certain fundamental ***personal rights*** not specifically enumerated in the Constitution, including the right of privacy. Early cases

began to recognize privileges recognized at common law but not specifically mentioned in the Constitution.

a. In *Meyer v. Nebraska*, 262 U.S. 390 (1923), the Court recognized the rights to marry, raise children, and acquire useful knowledge as essential to the liberty protected by due process.

b. In *Pierce v. Society of Sisters*, 268 U.S. 510 (1925), the Court invalidated a state law requiring attendance at public school as violative of parents' liberty to direct the education of their children.

c. In *Skinner v. Oklahoma*, 316 U.S. 535 (1942), the Court held that mandatory sterilization of certain felonious habitual criminals violated due process because it included relatively minor offenders and excluded major offenders, and because it involved a basic familial right.

d. The rulings in *Meyer* and *Pierce* may be explained as having been based on an implicit reliance on freedoms of association and religion. However, the *Skinner* decision was more likely a forerunner of the special protection of some fundamental interests under the new equal protection (discussed *infra*), although the actual opinion was based on something akin to substantive due process.

2. **General Familial Rights.** The right of personal choice in matters of marriage and the bearing and raising of children is protected from undue governmental intrusion in a variety of contexts and is so fundamental to society that it is afforded protection under the Due Process Clause. Hence, any regulation of familial rights must be justified by a compelling state interest and must be narrowly drawn so as to protect only the legitimate state interest at stake.

a. **Use of contraceptives--**

Griswold v. Connecticut, 381 U.S. 479 (1965).

Facts. Griswold and an associate (Ds) supplied information and medical advice to married persons on the use of contraceptives. They were convicted as accessories to the crime of using contraceptives in violation of a Connecticut statute prohibiting all such use. The conviction was upheld in all the state courts. Ds appeal.

Issue. Does a constitutional right of privacy exist that prohibits states from making use of contraceptives by a married couple a crime?

Held. Yes. Convictions reversed.

♦ The specific guarantees in the Bill of Rights have penumbras, or peripheral rights, which make the specific rights more secure. A right of privacy has been noted in earlier cases, and ought to especially protect the marriage relationship. The statute is overbroad and thus void.

Concurrence (Goldberg, J., Warren, C.J., Brennan, J.). The Ninth Amendment expressly recognizes fundamental personal rights not specifically mentioned in the Constitution. Privacy in the marital relation is clearly one of these basic personal rights "retained by the people."

Concurrence (Harlan, J.—relying on his dissent in *Poe v. Ullman*, 367 U.S. 497 (1961)). The Due Process Clause independently requires rejection of the Connecticut statute without reference to the Bill of Rights.

Concurrence (White, J.). Application of the law to married couples deprives them of "liberty" without due process of law.

Dissent (Black, Stewart, JJ.). While the law is offensive, it is not prohibited by any specific constitutional provision and therefore must be upheld. Constitutional amendments, not judge-made alterations, are the correct means of modernizing the Constitution.

Dissent (Stewart, Black, JJ.). The law is silly since it is obviously unenforceable, but there is no general right of privacy found in the Constitution, so we cannot hold that it violates the Constitution.

Comment. Later, in *Eisenstadt v. Baird*, 405 U.S. 438 (1972), the Court held that the decision whether to use contraceptives was one of individual privacy, and hence that the right belonged to single as well as married persons. In *Carey v. Population Services International*, 431 U.S. 678 (1977), the Court held that a state could not prohibit distribution of nonmedical contraceptives to adults except through licensed pharmacists, nor prohibit sales of such contraceptives to persons under 16 who did not have approval of a licensed physician.

---

b. **Distribution of contraceptives.** In *Carey v. Population Services International*, 431 U.S. 678 (1977), the Court invalidated a New York law that prohibited advertising or display of contraceptives, distribution of contraceptives by other than licensed pharmacists, and distribution of contraceptives to persons under age 16. Applying strict scrutiny, the Court found that the statute violated the First Amendment and intruded on the right to decide whether to bear children, and the ban on distribution was not clearly relevant to the state's interest in discouraging premarital sexual activity among minors.

3. **Abortion.**

a. **Blanket prohibitions--**

Roe v. Wade, 410 U.S. 113 (1973).

Facts. Roe (P), unmarried and pregnant, sought declaratory and injunctive relief against Wade (D), a county district attorney, to prevent enforcement of Texas criminal abortion statutes. The district court invalidated the statute, and the Supreme Court granted review.

Issue. May a state constitutionally make it a crime to procure an abortion except to save the mother's life?

Held. No. Judgment affirmed.

- P claims a constitutional right to terminate her pregnancy, based on the Fourteenth Amendment concept of personal "liberty," the Bill of Rights penumbras, and the Ninth Amendment. D claims a state interest in regulating medical procedures to ensure patient safety and in protecting prenatal life.

- The right of privacy generally relates to marriage, procreation, and contraception, and includes the abortion decision, but is not without restraint based on the state's compelling interests. The state's interest in prenatal life cannot be based on the fetus's right to life, for a fetus cannot be considered a "person" in the constitutional sense. Unborn children have never been recognized in any area of the law as persons in the whole sense. However, the pregnant woman cannot be isolated in her privacy. The state may decide that at some point in time another interest, that of health of the mother or that of ***potential*** human life, becomes significantly involved. The woman's right of privacy must be measured accordingly.

- The state's interest in the health of the mother becomes "compelling" at approximately the end of the first trimester, prior to which mortality in abortion is less than mortality in normal childbirth. Only from this point forward may the state regulate the abortion procedure as needed to preserve and protect maternal health.

- The state's interest in potential life becomes "compelling" at viability. A state interested in protecting fetal life after viability may proscribe abortion except when necessary to preserve the life or health of the mother.

- The Texas statute challenged here is overbroad and cannot be upheld.

Concurrence (Stewart, J.). The Court has generally recognized freedom of personal choice in matters of marriage and family life as a liberty protected by the Fourteenth Amendment. The Texas statute directly infringes on that right and is correctly invalidated.

Concurrence (Douglas, J.). The right of privacy is broad and needs to be protected.

Dissent (White, Rehnquist, JJ.). There is nothing in the language or history of the Constitution to support the Court's judgment. The decision is an improvident and extravagant exercise of the Court's power of judicial review. The Court ought not impose its order or priorities upon the people and legislatures of the states. The issue ought to be left with the people and their political processes.

Dissent (Rehnquist, J.). An abortion is not "private" in the ordinary use of the word. The Court seems to define "privacy" as a claim of liberty from unwanted state regulation of consensual transactions, protected by the Fourteenth Amendment. But that liberty is not guaranteed absolutely against deprivation, only against deprivation without due process of law. The traditional test is whether the law has a rational relation to a valid state objective, but this test could not justify the Court's outcome. Instead, the Court adopts the "compelling state interest test," which is more appropriate to a legislative judgment than to a judicial one. The Court's conclusions are more like judicial legislation than determination of the intent of the drafters of the Fourteenth Amendment. Further, the fact that most states have had restrictions on abortion for over a century indicates that the asserted right to an abortion is not so universally accepted as P claims.

Comment. In the companion case to *Roe*, *Doe v. Bolton*, 410 U.S. 179 (1973), Doe and other interested parties challenged the Georgia abortion statutes, which made abortion a criminal offense except when pregnancy would endanger the mother's life or health or resulted from rape, or when the fetus would very likely have severe defects at birth. Even in these circumstances, several conditions had to be met to legalize the abortion. The Court struck down three procedural requirements. First, the law required that all legal abortions be performed in accredited hospitals. However, the state made no showing that alternative facilities were incapable, and had no such requirement for nonabortion surgery. The Court held that the requirement did not reasonably relate to valid state objectives. Second, all legal abortions were to be certified by a hospital abortion committee, but the Court found this to be unnecessary. Finally, separate confirmation by two doctors was required, but the Court found that the judgment of a licensed attending physician should be adequate. The condition unduly infringed upon the physician's right to practice, without being rationally connected to the patient's need.

---

b. **Implications of *Roe* and *Griswold*.** Based on these opinions, claims that an individual has a fundamental right to personal autonomy in other areas have been advanced. The Court has recently recognized such a right in consensual sexual relations. [*See* Lawrence v. Texas, *infra, overruling* Bowers v. Hardwick, *infra*]

c. **O'Connor's dissent in *Akron*.** The Court has reviewed several cases involving restrictions on access to abortions. *Akron v. Akron Center for Reproductive Health*, 462 U.S. 416 (1983), basically reaffirmed *Roe v. Wade*. The majority relied in large part on stare decisis; the dissenters argued for a new approach to abortion cases. Justice O'Connor's dissent criticized *Roe's* trimester approach. She argued that constitutional interpretation could not depend on the trimester approach when the standards of review for each stage changed with medical technology; because technology will make viability possible earlier in pregnancy, the *Roe* framework is "on a collision course with itself." O'Connor's recommended approach would require that state interference heavily burden the right to an abortion before heightened scrutiny would be applied. She would have held that *Akron's* requirement that a second trimester abortion be performed in a hospital did not constitute a significant obstacle to obtaining an abortion and was rationally related to a valid state objective.

d. **Other attempts to discourage abortion through regulation.** In addition to *Akron*, a narrowly divided Court in *Thornburgh v. American College of Obstetricians and Gynecologists*, 476 U.S. 747 (1986), affirmed a lower court's rejection of restrictions on doctor-patient relations (*e.g.*, informed consent; reporting of patient and doctor identities) that were intended to discourage performance of abortions. Although constitutional rights may not have easily ascertainable boundaries, the Court is bound to uphold a law even when it is subject to bitter dispute. A woman's right to end her pregnancy is fundamental. [*See also* Webster v. Reproductive Health Services (discussed *infra*)]

4. **Problems with Abortion and Contraceptives Since *Roe v. Wade*.**

a. **Consent requirements.** In *Planned Parenthood v. Danforth*, 428 U.S. 52 (1976), the Court held that a woman's decision whether to terminate her pregnancy is within her constitutionally protected right of privacy, and cannot be made subject to parental or spousal consent. However, it did uphold a requirement that the woman give written, informed consent to the abortion and that she be of certain age or maturity in order to consent. Also, in *Bellotti v. Baird*, 443 U.S. 622 (1979), the Court invalidated a provision that required parental consent, but held that parental involvement was permissible if the state provided an alternative procedure for approval of the abortion (usually a judicial determination). In *H.L. v. Matheson*, 450 U.S. 398 (1981), the Court upheld a parental notice requirement to protect family integrity and the unemancipated minors it was directed toward.

b. **Regulation of medical practices.** The Court has strictly scrutinized state attempts to regulate various aspects of medical care relating to abortions. In *Colautti v. Franklin*, 439 U.S. 379 (1979), the Court struck down a state law that prescribed a certain standard of care when the fetus was determined to be viable, on grounds that it was unconstitutionally vague. In *Akron v. Akron Center for Reproductive Health*, 462 U.S. 416 (1983), the Court, in addition to reaffirming *Roe* (discussed *supra*), held unconstitutional a number of restrictions on the abortion process, including a requirement that abortions performed after the first trimester must be performed in a hospital, detailed guidelines as to information physicians must give a woman before the procedure, and a 24-hour waiting period. [*See also* Thornburgh v. American College of Obstetricians and Gynecologists, *supra*]

c. **Government funding.**

1) **Generally.** Despite its strict scrutiny of regulation of abortion, the Court has held that the government may choose not to fund abortions.

2) **1977 cases.** *Maher v. Roe*, 432 U.S. 464 (1977), was the first major case in this area. The state had excluded nontherapeutic abortions from its Medicaid-funded program, although it did cover childbirth. The Court applied a rationality standard of review instead of strict scrutiny. The Court held that *Roe v. Wade* did not preclude the states from favoring childbirth over abortion, as long as they did not unduly interfere with the woman's freedom to choose an abortion. The dissent argued that the exclusion effectively forced indigent women to bear children instead of procuring a desired abortion. *Beal v. Doe*, 432 U.S. 438 (1977), and *Poelker v. Doe*, 432 U.S. 519 (1977), applied the same rationale to other programs.

3) **Public funding of medically necessary abortions.** *Harris v. McRae*, 448 U.S. 297 (1980), involved the Hyde Amendment, which denied public funding for most medically necessary abortions. The Court held that Congress may, consistent with the Due Process Clause, deny public funding for certain medically necessary abortions while funding substantially all other medical costs. The Court explained that the government may not place obstacles in the path of a woman's exercise of her freedom of choice to terminate her pregnancy, but it need not remove those not of its own creation, such as indigency. The Court stated that a woman's freedom of choice does not confer an entitlement to such funds as may be necessary to realize all the advantages of that freedom.

4) **Policy-based funding.** In *Rust v. Sullivan*, 500 U.S. 173 (1991), a federal statute provided that federal funds could not be used for family service programs in which abortion was a method of family planning. The Court held that the federal government may condition the acceptance of federal funds by a particular project on the

project's agreement to refrain from promoting or even discussing abortion. The Court reasoned that Congress's refusal to fund abortion counseling and advocacy leaves a pregnant woman with the same choices as if Congress had chosen not to fund family-planning services at all.

5) **Use of public facilities and state employees.** In *Webster v. Reproductive Health Services*, 492 U.S. 490 (1989), the Court held that a state's prohibitions on the use of public facilities and employees are constitutional, since the Due Process Clause generally confers no affirmative right to government aid. The Court reasoned that under this provision, an indigent woman seeking an abortion has at least the same range of choices she would have if the state had chosen not to operate public hospitals at all.

d. **Permissible state regulation of abortion--**

Planned Parenthood of Southeastern Pennsylvania v. Casey, 505 U.S. 833 (1992).

Facts. The Pennsylvania Abortion Control Act required that a woman seeking an abortion be given certain information at least 24 hours before the abortion; that the woman give informed consent prior to the abortion; that, if a minor, the woman obtain the informed consent of her parents unless a judicial bypass option is followed; that, if married, the woman certify she informed her husband; and that facilities providing abortion services must make certain reports about each abortion, including the woman's age, gestational age, type of abortion procedure, medical conditions and results, and the weight of the aborted fetus. Compliance with the requirements is not required in certain medical emergencies. Planned Parenthood of Southeastern Pennsylvania (P) challenged the Act on its face by suing Casey (D), the Governor. The district court held all the provisions unconstitutional, but the court of appeals upheld everything except the husband notification requirement. The Supreme Court granted certiorari.

Issue. May a state impose notification and consent requirements as prerequisites for obtaining an abortion?

Held. Yes. Judgment reversed in part.

♦ The three parts of the essential *Roe* holding are reaffirmed. These are: (i) the woman's right to have an abortion before viability without undue state interference; (ii) the state's power to restrict abortions after fetal viability, so long as there are exceptions to protect a woman's life or health; and (iii) the state's legitimate interests from the outset of the pregnancy in protecting the health of the woman and the life of the fetus that may become a child.

♦ Substantive due process claims require courts to exercise reasoned judgment, and the Court must define the liberty of all, not mandate a moral code. The

Constitution has been interpreted to protect personal decisions regarding marriage, procreation, and contraception. Defining one's own concept of existence, meaning, and the mystery of human life is at the heart of liberty. At the same time, abortion has consequences for persons other than the woman who is pregnant.

- *Roe* should be upheld under the principle of stare decisis because it has not proven unworkable, because people have relied on the availability of abortion, because under *Roe* women have been better able to participate equally in the economic and social life of the country, because no evolution of legal principle has left *Roe's* doctrinal footings weaker than they were in 1973 when the decision was announced, and because there have been no changed circumstances or new factual understandings. Even if *Roe* is wrong, the error involves only the strength of the state interest in fetal protection, not the liberty of women. Overruling *Roe* simply because of a change in philosophical disposition would undermine the Court's legitimacy.

- Although *Roe* has been criticized for drawing lines, the Court must draw specific rules from the general standards in the Constitution. The trimester approach was not part of the essential holding in *Roe* and it both misconceived the nature of the pregnant woman's interest and undervalued the state's interest in potential life. It is therefore overruled and replaced with a line drawn only at viability. Under this approach, a law that serves a valid purpose not designed to strike at the right of abortion itself may be sustained even if it makes it more difficult or more expensive to obtain an abortion, unless the law imposes an undue burden on a woman's ability to make an abortion decision. Thus, the state may further its interest in potential life but cannot place a substantial obstacle in the path of a woman's choice.

- The state may adopt health regulations to promote the health or safety of a woman seeking an abortion. It may not prohibit any woman from making the ultimate decision to terminate her pregnancy before viability. After viability, the state may promote its interest in the potentiality of human life by regulating and even proscribing abortion except where it is necessary to preserve the life or health of the mother.

- With regard to the specific provisions of D's Act, the definition of medical emergency does not impose an undue burden on a woman's abortion right. The informed consent requirement is also permissible because it furthers the legitimate purpose of reducing the risk that a woman may elect an abortion, only to discover later, with devastating psychological consequences, that her decision was not fully informed. The 24-hour waiting period does not impose substantial obstacles, and it is not unreasonable to conclude that important decisions will be more informed and deliberate if they follow some period of reflection. The exception for cases in which a physician reasonably believes that furnishing the information would have a severely adverse effect on the woman's physical or mental health accommodates the interest in allowing physicians to exercise their medical judgment.

- ♦ The spousal notification requirement does impose an undue burden on a woman's choice to undergo an abortion and cannot be sustained. In well-functioning marriages, the spouses discuss important intimate decisions such as whether to bear a child, and the notification requirement adds nothing in such situations. However, millions of women are the victims of physical and psychological abuse from their husbands, and requiring spousal notification in these situations can be tantamount to preventing the woman from getting an abortion. The husband's interest in the life of the child his wife is carrying does not permit the state to empower him with a veto over the abortion decision. Men do not have the kind of dominion over their wives that parents have over their children.

- ♦ The parental consent provision has been sustained before, and provided there is an adequate judicial bypass procedure, its constitutionality is reaffirmed. The recordkeeping and reporting requirements are also permissible, with the exception of whether the spouse was notified of the abortion.

Concurrence and dissent (Stevens, J.). The Court properly follows the principle that a developing organism that is not yet a "person" does not have a "right to life." The state's interest in protecting potential life is not grounded in the Constitution, but reflects humanitarian and pragmatic concerns, including the offense taken by a large segment of the population at the number of abortions performed in this country and third-trimester abortions specifically. But the woman's interest in liberty is constitutional; the Constitution would be violated as much by a requirement that all women undergo abortion as by an absolute ban on abortions. The 24-hour delay requirement should not be upheld because it presumes that the abortion decision is wrong and must be reconsidered. The state may properly require physicians to inform women of the nature and risks of the abortion procedure and the medical risks of carrying to term, but it should not be allowed to require that the woman be provided with materials designed to persuade her to choose not to undergo the abortion.

Concurrence and dissent (Blackmun, J.). The Court's decision preserves the liberty of women that is one vote away from being extinguished. The Court also leaves open the possibility that the regulations it now approves may in the future be shown to impose an unconstitutional burden.

Concurrence and dissent (Rehnquist, C.J., White, Scalia, Thomas, JJ.). *Roe* was wrongly decided, and it can and should be overruled consistently with the traditional approach to stare decisis in constitutional cases. Stare decisis is not a reason to retain *Roe*; the Court's legitimacy is enhanced by faithful interpretation of the Constitution. The Court's revised "undue burden" standard is an unjustified constitutional compromise that allows the Court to closely scrutinize all types of abortion regulations despite the lack of any constitutional authority to do so. The new "undue burden" approach is still an imposition on the states by the Court of a complex abortion code. Abortion involves the purposeful termination of potential life and is thus different in kind from the other areas of privacy recognized by the Court, including marriage, procreation, and contraception. Prohibitions on abortion have been part of the law of many of the states since before the Fourteenth Amendment was adopted; there is no deeply rooted tradition of unrestricted abortion in our history that justifies characterizing the right as "fundamental." A woman's interest in having an abortion is a form of liberty protected by the Due Process Clause, but states may regulate abortion procedures in ways rationally related to a legitimate state interest. D's Act should be upheld in its entirety.

Concurrence and dissent (Scalia, J., Rehnquist, C.J., White, Thomas, JJ.). The states may permit abortion on demand, but the Constitution does not require them to do so. It is a legislative decision. The issue is not whether the right to an abortion is an absolute liberty, or whether it is an important liberty to many women, but whether it is a liberty protected by the Constitution. It is not, because the Constitution says nothing about it and because long-standing traditions of American society have permitted it to be prohibited. Under the rational basis test, D's statute should be upheld. Instead, the Court perpetuates the premise of *Roe*, which is a value judgment, not a legal matter. The "undue burden" standard lacks meaningful content, and may be summed up by concluding that a state may regulate abortion only in such a way as to not reduce significantly its incidence. *Roe* nourished the deeply divisive issue of abortion by elevating it to the national level where it is much more difficult to resolve than it was at the state level. Political compromise is now impossible, and *Roe* has been a major factor in selecting Justices to the Court. The Court should not be concerned with predicting public perceptions but should do what is legally right by asking whether *Roe* was correctly decided and whether it has succeeded in producing a settled body of law. The answer to both questions is no, and *Roe* should therefore be overruled. The Court's reliance on value judgments instead of interpreting text has created political pressure directed to the Court, whereby various groups of people demonstrate to protest that the Court has not implemented the respective group's values.

---

e. **Post-*Casey* anti-abortion measures.**

1) **Ban on partial birth abortion struck down.** In *Stenberg v. Carhart*, 530 U.S. 914 (2000), the Court struck down a Nebraska statute that prohibited "dilation and extraction" ("D&X") partial birth abortions and that lacked an exception for the preservation of the health of the woman. The Court found that D&X significantly prevents health risks in certain circumstances and that a statute forbidding D&X could endanger women's health. Also, the statute did not distinguish between D&X and D&E, the most commonly used method for performing previability second trimester abortions. The Court reasoned that the statute imposed an undue burden on a woman's right to make an abortion decision,

because those who perform abortion procedures using the D&E method would fear prosecution, conviction, and imprisonment.

2) **Ban on partial birth abortion upheld--**

Gonzales v. Carhart, 127 S. Ct. 1610 (2007).

Facts. Most of the 1.3 million abortions performed annually in the United States occur during the first trimester. Of the remaining 10% to 15%, most occur in the second trimester, usually by a procedure called "dilation and evacuation" or D&E. The doctor grabs the fetus in the womb and tears it apart, removing it piece by piece. A variation of D&E called "partial birth abortion" extracts the fetus's entire body. In response to *Stenberg*, Congress enacted the Partial-Birth Abortion Ban Act. The Act prohibits anyone from knowingly performing this type of abortion, which is specifically defined in the statute in terms of how much of the fetus's body can be removed before the procedure constitutes a partial birth abortion. Carhart and other abortion doctors (Ps) challenged the constitutionality of the Act on its face. The lower courts held the Act unconstitutional. The Supreme Court granted certiorari.

Issue. May Congress prohibit a specific form of abortion as long as it does not impose a substantial obstacle to late-term, but previability, abortions?

Held. Yes. Judgment reversed.

- The Act is materially different from the statute in *Stenberg*. The Act adopts the phrase "delivers a living fetus," instead of "delivering ... a living unborn child, or a substantial portion thereof"; its language expresses the usual meaning of "deliver" when used in connection with "fetus," which is the extraction of an entire fetus, rather than removal of fetal pieces; it identifies specific anatomical landmarks to which the fetus must be partially delivered; and the interpretation of the Act so that it does not prohibit standard D&E is the most reasonable reading and understanding of its terms.

- The state has a regulatory interest in protecting the life of a fetus that may become a child. *Casey*'s requirement of a health exception should not be interpreted as allowing a doctor to choose whatever abortion method he prefers. Where the state has a rational basis to act, and it does not impose an undue burden, it may bar certain procedures in furtherance of its legitimate interests in regulating the medical profession.

- The Act's ban on abortions that involve partial delivery of a living fetus furthers the government's objectives. The Act expresses respect for the dignity of human life. Congress determined that partial birth abortion has a disturbing similarity to the killing of a newborn infant. The Act draws a bright line between abortion and infanticide.

- ♦ A woman's decision to have an abortion is fraught with emotional consequences, and some doctors may prefer not to disclose details of the means that will be used. However, this lack of information concerning the way in which the fetus will be killed is of legitimate concern to the state, which has an interest in ensuring that such a serious decision is well informed.

- ♦ It is argued that the congressional purpose of the Act was to place a substantial obstacle in the path of a woman seeking an abortion and that the standard D&E is as brutal, if not more, than the intact D&E. However, partial birth abortion occurs when the fetus is partially outside the mother, and thus differs from a standard D&E. It was reasonable for Congress to think that partial birth abortion, more than the standard D&E, undermines the public's perception of the appropriate role of a physician during the delivery process.

- ♦ There is medical uncertainty as to whether the Act creates significant health risks for women. The evidence presented demonstrates that both sides have medical support for their position. The Court has traditionally given state and federal legislatures wide discretion to pass legislation in areas where there is medical and scientific uncertainty. This Act is not invalid on its face because of uncertainty over whether the barred procedure is ever necessary to preserve a woman's health, since there are other abortion procedures that are considered to be safe alternatives.

- ♦ The Act does not on its face impose a substantial obstacle to late-term, previability abortions. It may, however, be challenged on an as-applied basis.

Concurrence (Thomas, Scalia, JJ.). The Court's abortion jurisprudence has no basis in the Constitution.

Dissent (Ginsburg, Stevens, Souter, Breyer, JJ.). The majority opinion does not take *Casey* and *Stenberg* seriously. Instead, it encourages federal intervention to ban a procedure that medical experts find necessary and proper in certain cases. It blurs the line between previability and postviability abortions, and does not include an exception for a woman's health. Instead, it bans intact D&E, which provides safety benefits over D&E by dismemberment. The Act does not save a single fetus from destruction; it merely requires doctors to use a brutal and more risky method. The Court is simply chipping away at the right to abortion.

---

5. Marriage and Family Relations.

a. **Right to marry.** In *Zablocki v. Redhail*, 434 U.S. 374 (1978), the Court invalidated a Wisconsin law that required that an applicant with a support obligation for a child not in his custody prove that the child was not a public charge and that he had complied with the support obligation. The Court stated that the right to marry is part of the fundamental right of privacy implicit in the Due Process Clause. A law that interferes directly and substantially with the right to marry cannot be upheld unless it is closely tailored to effectuate sufficiently important state interests. The Court concluded that, assuming the state's interests in protecting out-of-custody children and motivating applicants to fulfill prior support obligations are valid, the state has numerous other effective means for exacting compliance with support obligations that do not restrict the right to marry.

b. **Extended family relationships.**

1) **Housing.** In *Moore v. City of East Cleveland,* 431 U.S. 494 (1977), the Court struck down a local zoning ordinance that restricted occupation of dwelling units to certain categories of related individuals, excluding other categories of related individuals. The Court explained that the extended family has a strong tradition in our history, and the United States Constitution prohibits the government from forcing its people to live in certain narrowly defined family patterns. The Court distinguished *Belle Terre v. Boraas*, 416 U.S. 1 (1974), on the grounds that *Belle Terre* involved restrictions on unrelated individuals.

2) **Visitation.** *Troxel v. Granville*, 530 U.S. 57 (2000), involved a mother's challenge to a Washington statute that allowed anyone to petition for visitation rights at any time and authorized state superior courts to grant visitation when it would serve the best interest of the child. The Troxels had petitioned for the right to visit the two daughters of their deceased son. The girls' mother was not against all visitation, but she objected to the amount sought by the grandparents. After the superior court ordered more visitation than the mother thought was appropriate, the Washington Supreme Court struck down the statute, the court of appeals reversed, and the United States Supreme Court granted certiorari. The Court found that the Washington statute, as applied in this case, violated the mother's due process rights. The Court held that a judge may not override a fit parent's decision regarding third-party visitation merely because he feels that a "better" decision could be made or that visitation would be in the best interest of the child.

c. **The role of tradition.** *Michael H. v. Gerald D.*, 491 U.S. 110 (1989), involved a challenge to a California presumption that a child born to a married woman is a child of the marriage. The Court upheld the California law based on an assessment of substantive due process that required the fundamental interest to be protected to also be an interest traditionally protected by American society. Historically, the family relationship was protected against the type of claims asserted in this case; therefore, the claimant did not have an interest protected by due process.

6. **Sexuality.**

a. **Adultery.** In *Hollenbaugh v. Carnegie Free Library*, 439 U.S. 1052 (1978), the Court refused to grant certiorari in a case sustaining the discharge of public employees who were living together in open adultery. Justice Marshall's dissent stated that the right to pursue an open rather than a clandestine personal relationship and to rear a child in that environment is a right of personal privacy requiring constitutional protection.

b. **Restrictions on homosexual conduct upheld.** In *Bowers v. Hardwick*, 478 U.S. 186 (1986), the Court upheld a Georgia law forbidding sodomy by any person. The Court defined the issue narrowly, as applying only to homosexuals. The Court noted that prior cases had recognized a right of privacy in matters of child rearing, family relationships, procreation, contraception, and abortion. But the Court stated that none of those rights bore any resemblance to the right to engage in homosexual sodomy. Also, the Court pointed out that sodomy was a common law offense that was still forbidden by 24 states.

c. ***Bowers* overruled--**

Lawrence v. Texas, 539 U.S. 558 (2003).

Facts. Police officers responding to a reported weapons disturbance entered an apartment where Lawrence resided. The officers found Lawrence and another man (Ds) engaging in a sexual act. Ds were arrested and convicted of deviate sexual intercourse with a member of the same sex. Ds claimed that the applicable statute was unconstitutional under the Due Process Clause of the Fourteenth Amendment. The Texas state courts upheld the statute. The Supreme Court granted certiorari.

Issue. May a state criminalize private and consensual sexual activity between two persons of the same sex?

Held. No. Judgment reversed.

♦ In *Bowers, supra*, the Supreme Court held that there was no fundamental right for homosexuals to engage in sodomy, so the Constitution did not prevent the states from making such activity illegal. This framing of the issue, however, limited the claim to the right to engage in certain sexual conduct. In reality, criminal statutes prohibiting certain sexual activity have more far-reaching consequences because they control a personal relationship that is within the liberty of persons to choose without being punished as criminals.

- The *Bowers* Court based its decision in part on proscriptions against homosexual conduct that have ancient roots. The historical premises relied on by the Court, however, have been reevaluated by scholars. Legal prohibitions against homosexual conduct did not actually emerge until the late 19th century. Prior to that, sodomy laws were designed to prohibit non-procreative sexual activity, regardless of gender. Laws against same-sex couples were not enacted until the last third of the 20th century.

- The *Bowers* Court did note that societies have condemned homosexual conduct as immoral for many centuries. While many people may consider this a moral issue, the legal issue is whether the majority may use the power of the state to enforce these views on the whole society through the operation of the criminal law.

- In recent years, society has recognized that liberty gives substantial protection to adults in deciding how to conduct their private sex lives. The European Convention on Human Rights has been interpreted to preclude laws against consensual homosexual conduct in Europe, for example. Since the *Bowers* decision, 12 states have abandoned their laws against sodomy, and the remaining 13 states have a pattern of non-enforcement against consenting adults acting in private.

- *Romer v. Evans*, *infra*, recognized that class-based legislation directed at homosexuals violates the Equal Protection Clause. This undermines the central holding of *Bowers* because the continued validity of *Bowers* demeans the lives of homosexual persons.

- The erosion of *Bowers* under *Romer*, the invalidity of many of the premises upon which *Bowers* was based, and the substantial criticism of *Bowers* by the states and the European Court of Human Rights suggest that *Bowers* should be overruled. Despite the importance of stare decisis, it is time to recognize that *Bowers* was incorrectly decided, and it is hereby overruled.

Concurrence (O'Connor, J.). I do not join the Court in overruling *Bowers*, but I agree the Texas statute here is unconstitutional under the Equal Protection Clause instead of the Due Process Clause. The Texas statute prohibits sodomy between homosexual partners, but not between opposite-sex partners. This makes homosexuals unequal in the eyes of the law. The Court need not decide whether a sodomy law violates the substantive component of the Due Process Clause. So long as the Equal Protection Clause requires a sodomy law to apply equally to the private consensual conduct of homosexuals and heterosexuals alike, the democratic process would soon dispense with such a law.

Dissent (Scalia, J., Rehnquist, C.J., Thomas, J.). The Court has strongly rejected overruling *Roe v. Wade* out of stare decisis concerns, but the very conditions the Court finds applicable to *Bowers* also apply to *Roe*. The Court now allows us to overrule precedent if (i) its foundations have been "eroded" by subsequent decisions; (ii) it has been subject to substantial and continuing criticism; and (iii) it has not induced individual or societal reliance that counsels against overturning. The Court's reasoning in this case calls into question laws against bigamy, prostitution, adultery, and related conduct. Until today, only fundamental rights qualify for heightened scrutiny protection, and all others may be abridged if the law is rationally related to a legitimate state interest. Homosexual sodomy is not such a fundamental right. The Court today effectively decrees the end of all morals legislation by holding that majoritarian sexual morality is not even a legitimate state interest.

Dissent (Thomas, J.). The Texas law is uncommonly silly and a waste of law enforcement resources, but there is no constitutional right of privacy that invalidates such laws.

Comment. The *Lawrence* opinion is the first Supreme Court majority opinion to cite an authority from European law as a factor in the decision. The Court took judicial notice of the laws in Europe, apparently concluding that it was useful to determine the extent of the governmental interest in proscribing such conduct.

---

7. **Other Privacy and Autonomy Concerns.**

   a. **Personal appearance.** Applying rationality review, the Court rejected a challenge based on privacy and autonomy grounds to a hair grooming regulation applied to police officers. The Court held that all the state needed to show was a rational connection between the regulation and the promotion of safety of person and property. [Kelley v. Johnson, 425 U.S. 238 (1976)]

   b. **Mentally retarded persons.** The Court has recognized that mentally retarded persons have a right to safe conditions of confinement, freedom from bodily restraints, and training, although these interests are subject to relevant state interests. [Youngberg v. Romeo, 457 U.S. 307 (1982)] The courts must defer to the judgments of professionals in this area, however.

   c. **Computerized data banks.** In *Whalen v. Roe*, 429 U.S. 589 (1977), the Court discussed the privacy impact of computerized data banks. The state of New York passed a statute requiring that centralized records be kept of the names and addresses of all persons who obtain certain drugs pursuant to a doctor's prescription. The drugs have both a lawful and unlawful market. The Court reversed the district court's injunction against enforcement of the law. As stated by the Court: "Constitutional 'privacy' involves two kinds of interests: avoiding disclosure of personal matters ***and*** retaining independence in making certain kinds of important decisions. [The plaintiff] claims both interests are at stake here. However, the only possibilities of public disclosure created by the statute arise from improper administration of its security provisions and inadequacy of judicial supervision of the evidentiary use of the information in judicial proceedings. Neither possibility is substantial enough to invalidate the entire program."

d. **Intimate association.** In *Roberts v. United States Jaycees*, 468 U.S. 609 (1984), *infra*, the Court hinted at a fundamental freedom of intimate association, separate from the First Amendment freedom of association.

8. **Rights over Death.** In most states, patients may refuse even lifesaving medical treatment, or accept pain medication that can hasten death, but it is a crime to aid another to commit or attempt suicide. Many physicians assert that the assisted suicide ban prevents them from providing lethal medication for mentally competent, terminally ill patients who are suffering great pain and desire a doctor's help in taking their own lives, although it would be consistent with the standards of their medical practices to provide this type of service.

a. **The right to die.** In *Cruzan v. Director, Missouri Department of Health*, 497 U.S. 261 (1990), the Court held that a state may require proof by clear and convincing evidence of an incompetent patient's wishes as to the withdrawal of life-sustaining medical treatment. Nancy Cruzan was injured in an automobile accident and entered a persistent vegetative state, her body kept functioning by artificial nutrition and hydration procedures. Her parents asked that the medical procedures be terminated, which would cause Nancy's death. Based on evidence suggesting that Nancy would not want to continue to live in a vegetative state, the trial court ordered that her parents' request be carried out. The Missouri Supreme Court reversed on the ground that the evidence was insufficient to constitute clear and convincing proof of Nancy's desire to have hydration and nutrition withdrawn. The Supreme Court affirmed that ruling, finding that a competent person has a constitutionally protected right to refuse lifesaving hydration and nutrition, but an imcompetent person cannot exercise that right; it must be exercised on her behalf by someone else. The Court explained that the choice between life and death is a deeply personal decision, and the state, having an important interest in the protection and preservation of human life, may safeguard the personal element by requiring a high standard of proof. The Court found that the state did not violate the Constitution by placing the increased risk of an erroneous decision on those seeking to terminate the incompetent patient's life. The dissent asserted that the liberty interest in being free of unwanted medical treatment is fundamental, and no state interest can outweigh the rights of a person in Nancy's position.

b. Due process analysis--

Washington v. Glucksberg, 521 U.S. 702 (1997).

Facts. Washington (D) enacted a statute that prohibited assisting suicide. Glucksberg and other physicians (Ps) occasionally treated terminally ill, suffering patients and would assist these patients in ending their lives if not for D's ban on assisted suicide. Ps brought suit seeking a declaration that the statute violates the Fourteenth Amendment, because Ps' patients have a liberty interest in a personal choice to commit physician-assisted suicide. The district court held the statute unconstitutional. The court of appeals initially reversed, but after an en banc hearing, affirmed the district court. The Supreme Court granted certiorari.

Issue. Is there a constitutional right to assistance in committing suicide?

Held. No. Judgment reversed.

- ♦ It is a crime to assist a suicide in almost every state and almost every western democracy. This reflects the states' commitment to protect and preserve all human life. For over 700 years, the Anglo-American common law tradition has punished both suicide and assisting suicide.

- ♦ In modern times, the states' bans on assisted suicide have been reexamined and mostly reaffirmed. There have been modifications to reflect current medical technology, which can prolong life. For example, states permit "living wills," surrogate health care decisionmaking, and withdrawal or refusal of life-sustaining medical treatment. However, the states continue to prohibit assisted suicide. D's voters rejected a ballot initiative that would have permitted a form of physician-assisted suicide.

- ♦ The Court has previously applied the Due Process Clause so as to protect the right to marry, have children, educate one's children, enjoy marital privacy, use contraception, and have abortions. Under *Cruzan*, the Clause protects the traditional right to refuse unwanted lifesaving medical treatment. However, the extension of constitutional protection to an asserted right or liberty interest is only appropriate for those areas that are rooted in the nation's history and tradition, and even then only where there is a careful description of the asserted fundamental liberty interest.

- ♦ To recognize the right asserted by Ps, the Court would have to reverse centuries of legal doctrine and practice, including the policy choices of almost every state. In contrast, the right to refuse medication recognized in *Cruzan* reflected a long legal tradition. Forced medication was a battery at common law.

- ♦ Given that the right to assisted suicide is not a fundamental liberty interest, the Constitution still requires that D's ban be rationally related to legitimate government interests. That is satisfied here, where D has an interest in the preservation of human life, an interest in protecting the integrity and ethics of the medical profession, an interest in protecting vulnerable groups, and an interest in not opening the door to euthanasia, both voluntary and involuntary.

Concurrence (O'Connor, J.). There is no generalized right to "commit suicide." A terminal patient who suffers great pain may obtain medication to alleviate that suffering, even to the point of hastening death. Therefore, the state's interest in protecting those who are not truly competent or facing imminent death is sufficiently weighty to justify a prohibition against physician-assisted suicide. The democratic process will strike the proper balance in this area.

Concurrence (Stevens, J.). The value to others of a person's life is far too precious to allow the individual to claim a constitutional entitlement to complete autonomy in making a decision to end that life. But there may be situations where the individual's interest in choosing how to die might be paramount.

Concurrence (Souter, J.). The appropriate test would be to determine whether D's statute sets up an arbitrary imposition or a purposeless restraint contrary to the Due Process Clause. Substantive due process analysis requires a court to assess the relative weights of the contending interests. Statutes must give way when the legislation's justifying principle is so far from being commensurate with the individual interest as to be arbitrary or pointless. This case involves the right of a narrow class to help others in a narrow class under a set of limited circumstances. Ps note that D has largely repudiated the common law of suicide by decriminalizing suicide. A right to physician assistance in committing suicide is analogous to the right to physician assistance in abortion. D already allows doctors to administer pain relief medication that may hasten death. D could address its legitimate interests through a regulatory system.

Concurrence (Breyer, J.). Justice O'Connor's approach is persuasive. There may be a right to die with dignity, or a right to personal control over the manner of death, professional medical assistance, and the avoidance of unnecessary and severe physical suffering. Changes in medical technology may affect these types of cases in the future.

Comment. The Court noted that at one time, Oregon voters enacted a ballot initiative that legalized physician-assisted suicide. This prompted proposals in many other states. The Court specifically noted that its decision would allow the debate about physician-assisted suicide to continue.

---

c. **Equal protection analysis.** In *Vacco v. Quill*, 521 U.S. 793 (1997), decided at the same time as *Glucksberg*, the Court held that a ban on physician-assisted suicide does not violate the Equal Protection Clause. New York made it a crime to assist suicide, but it was legal for a patient to refuse lifesaving medical care. The Court discussed the distinction, widely recognized in the medical and legal traditions, between assisting suicide and withdrawing life-sustaining treatment. A patient who refuses life-sustaining medical treatment dies from the underlying disease or pathology, but a patient who ingests lethal medication dies from that medication. In the latter case, the doctor's intent is to end the patient's life, while in the former, it is merely to respect the patient's wishes. The Court pointed out that the law has long used a person's intent to distinguish between two acts that have the same result. The Court noted that the distinction between letting a patient die and making that patient die was reflected in *Cruzan*, which recognized, not that patients have the right to hasten death, but instead that patients have a right to bodily integrity and unwanted touching. The Court stated that the distinction between the two types of care is not arbitrary or irrational and that New York had the same reasons to recognize and act on this distinction as did the state of Washington in *Glucksberg*. The Court found that these important public interests satisfy the constitutional requirement that the classification bear a rational relation to a legitimate end.

D. PROCEDURAL DUE PROCESS AND THE RIGHT TO A HEARING

1. Defining "Property" and "Liberty."

a. **Property.** As used in the Due Process Clause of the Fourteenth Amendment, the term "property" denotes more than just actual ownership of realty, chattels, or money—it includes "interests already acquired in specific benefits." However, there must be more than a mere abstract need or desire for (or unilateral expectation of) the benefit: There must be a legitimate claim to the benefit under state (or federal) law. [Board of Regents of State Colleges v. Roth, 408 U.S. 564 (1972)—termination of nontenured public employee does not affect a property right.]

1) **Welfare benefits.** In *Goldberg v. Kelly*, 397 U.S. 254 (1970), the Court held that welfare benefits are an entitlement. By definition, a person entitled to receive welfare needs the assistance for essentials such as food, clothing, housing, and medical care. Termination of benefits despite a controversy over eligibility may deprive an eligible recipient of the necessities of life. Thus, welfare benefits may not be terminated without an evidentiary hearing.

2) **Public employment.** Whether there is a "property" interest in continued public employment is determined by state (or federal) law. There must be a legitimate claim to the benefit. [Board of Regents of State Colleges v. Roth, *supra*] In *Perry v. Sindermann*, 408 U.S. 593 (1972), a companion case to *Roth*, the Court held that if the state has a program of de facto tenure, *i.e.*, teachers are assured that they have the equivalent of tenure, even a non-tenured teacher

is entitled to a hearing. A statute (or ordinance), the employment contract, or some clear practice or understanding must provide that the employee can be terminated only "for cause." [Arnett v. Kennedy, 416 U.S. 134 (1974)—federal law mandated removal only "for cause," but did not provide for an adversary hearing] There is no "property interest" if the position is held "at the will of" the public employer. [Bishop v. Wood, 426 U.S. 341 (1976)—police officer dismissed without a pretermination hearing] In *Cleveland Board of Education v. Loudermill*, 470 U.S. 532 (1985), the Court rejected the notion that due process rights, which arise under the Constitution, could be limited by the state statute creating the property interest.

3) **No property interest in enforcement of restraining order.** In *Town of Castle Rock v. Gonzales*, 545 U.S. 748 (2005), a mother brought a section 1983 action against Castle Rock and the police officers who failed to enforce a domestic abuse restraining order against her estranged husband, who then killed their three children. The Supreme Court held that there was no liability under section 1983 because the officers had discretionary power as to when to enforce an order. The Court further held that the enforcement of the order was not something that the mother was entitled to, nor did she have a property interest in its enforcement. The dissent argued that the mother had a "legitimate claim of entitlement" to the enforcement of the restraining order because Colorado law had eliminated the police's discretion to deny enforcement.

b. **Liberty.** In *Paul v. Davis*, 424 U.S. 693 (1976), the Court held that the plaintiff suffered no deprivation of liberty as a result of his identification as an active shoplifter in a flyer produced by the local police and distributed to local merchants. Defamation resulting only in damage to one's reputation was held not to be a denial of protected "liberty." As a result, the definition of liberty was assumed to depend on state determinations.

2. **Procedural Due Process Requirements.** Whether a prior hearing is required and the extent of procedural requirements are determined by weighing (i) the importance of the individual interest involved, (ii) the value of specific procedural safeguards to that interest, and (iii) the governmental interest in fiscal and administrative efficiency. [*See* Mathews v. Eldridge, 424 U.S. 319 (1976)—evidentiary hearing not required before termination of disability benefits]

IX. EQUAL PROTECTION

A. INTRODUCTION

The Fourteenth Amendment provides that no state shall "deny to any person within its jurisdiction the equal protection of the laws." However, most laws necessarily classify groups and individuals as a means of burdening or benefiting appropriate objects of the law. The courts have long wrestled with the proper meaning of the Equal Protection Clause. Certainly it prohibits classifications on racial grounds. It also requires some standard of rationality in legislative action. But over the years the interpretation of the clause has changed significantly.

1. **Early View.** Historically, courts used equal protection only to insure that the legislative means were reasonably related to the legislative purpose. This approach supported only minimal judicial intervention. Judicial intervention instead was grounded in due process.

2. **The Warren Court's "New" Equal Protection.** The Warren Court utilized the traditional equal protection analysis in most areas of economic and social regulation. However, it also articulated a new, higher level of scrutiny applicable when legislation affected one of two areas: a "suspect" classification or a "fundamental" right or interest.

   a. **Old standard.** In the absence of a suspect classification or fundamental right, equal protection requires that the legislative means must be "reasonably" related to "legitimate" state ends. This is also called the "rational basis" standard.

   b. **New standard.** When a suspect classification (*e.g.*, race) or a fundamental interest (*e.g.*, voting or criminal appeals) is involved, the legislative means must be "necessary" to achieve "compelling" state interests. This standard of review—also called "strict scrutiny"—has resulted in significant judicial intervention.

3. **The Burger and Rehnquist Courts.** The Burger and Rehnquist Courts generally accepted the old and new standards of equal protection, although they have given greater effect to the old standard. But the Court has also added a third tier of scrutiny for certain classifications that fall between the two Warren Court extremes, including classifications based on sex, alienage, and illegitimacy. This intermediate standard requires that the legislative means be "substantially related" to "important" governmental objectives. In actuality, the whole equal protection jurisprudence is confusing and at times inconsistent. The Court has never expressly adopted Justice Marshall's "sliding scale" approach to the problem, but clearly there are no rigid guidelines with which to decide every equal protection case.

B. RACE DISCRIMINATION

1. **Background.** Soon after the *Slaughter-House Cases* (*supra*), the Court decided *Strauder v. West Virginia*, 100 U.S. 303 (1880), in which a state statute indicating that only white persons could serve on juries was held to violate equal protection.

2. **The Unconstitutionality of Racial Segregation.**

   a. **Separate but equal doctrine.** In *Plessy v. Ferguson*, 163 U.S. 537 (1896), the Court upheld a Louisiana law that required separate railway carriages for the white and black passengers. Plessy, who was seven-eighths white and one-eighth black, refused to comply with a demand that he sit in the black railway carriage rather than the one for whites. He was convicted of violating the state statute. The Court stated that although the Fourteenth Amendment provides for equality under the law, it was not intended to abolish distinctions based on color or to enforce social equality or a commingling of the two races. The Court said that laws requiring separation do not imply the inferiority of either race to the other and that such laws were recognized as properly within the exercise of states' police power. The Court noted that the establishment of separate schools for white and black children was held to be a valid exercise of the legislative power. Every exercise of the police power must be reasonable and extend only to those laws enacted for the public good, with the intention of preserving the public peace and good order. The Court maintained that legislation could not overcome social prejudices and that the attempt to do so could only result in accentuating difficulties. According to the Court, the Constitution could act to equate civil and political rights of the races but could not affect social standing. In his dissent, Justice Harlan argued that no legislature or court could properly regard the race of citizens where personal freedom and civil rights are involved. He asserted that every citizen, regardless of color, has a right to occupy the public transportation of his choice and that governmental infringement of that right is unconstitutional. Justice Harlan pointed out that the Constitution is color-blind, and neither knows nor tolerates classes among citizens. And he cautioned that the thin disguise of "equal" accommodations would not mislead anyone.

   b. **Repudiation of the separate but equal doctrine--**

Brown v. Board of Education (Brown I), 347 U.S. 483 (1954).

Facts. Brown (P) and other black schoolchildren (the opinion consolidates appeals from four states) were denied admission to schools attended by white children under laws requiring or permitting segregation based on race. P challenged the law but was denied relief under the "separate but equal" doctrine. (In the Delaware case, P was admitted solely because the white school was superior; *i.e.*, separate was not equal.) P appeals.

Issue. May children be segregated in essentially "equal" public schools solely on the basis of race?

Held. No. Judgments vacated and reargument ordered on the issue of appropriate relief.

- The circumstances surrounding adoption of the Fourteenth Amendment are not conclusive to its interpretation, especially here where public education, which barely existed then, is at issue. The effect of segregation on public education in its current setting is therefore determinative.

- Granted that black and white schools are substantially "equal" in tangible factors, there yet exists an invidious effect when black and white children are segregated. Namely, segregation creates a feeling of inferiority, which may significantly affect a child's motivation to learn; separate educational facilities are therefore inherently unequal, and their maintenance by government authority denies equal protection of the law.

Comment. This holding applied to the states through the Fourteenth Amendment. The federal government is similarly restrained via the Due Process Clause of the Fifth Amendment. [*See* Bolling v. Sharpe, 347 U.S. 497 (1954)—holding that due process precludes segregation of public schools in the District of Columbia]

---

c. **Implementation of desegregation.**

1) **Public facilities.** While most public facilities were ordered integrated at once [*see* Johnson v. Virginia, 373 U.S. 61 (1963)], the Court initially permitted gradual desegregation of public schools in recognition of the difficulties inherent in school desegregation [*see* Brown v. Board of Education (Brown II), 349 U.S. 294 (1955)]. The *Brown II* opinion addressed solely the manner in which the relief granted in *Brown I* was to be accorded. In *Brown II*, the Court stated that the full implementation of the constitutional principles required solution of various local school problems to be solved by school authorities and reviewed by courts to assure good faith compliance. The cases were remanded to the lower courts, who were to be guided by equitable principles in fashioning decrees. The competing interests involved plaintiffs' rights to ad-

mission at the earliest date and the need for systematic, effective, and orderly removal of obstacles to full integration.

2) **Acceleration of desegregation.** In *Green v. New Kent County School Board*, 391 U.S. 430 (1968), the Court held that the school board had an affirmative duty to take immediate steps to desegregate schools.

3) **Federal court intervention.** At least where there is a finding that the segregation is deliberate (so-called "de jure segregation"), the Court has held that federal district courts are empowered to fashion whatever remedies are necessary to desegregate local schools. [*See* Swann v. Charlotte-Mecklenburg Board of Education, 402 U.S. 1 (1971)]

d. **Desegregation outside the South.** Most school systems in the South were characterized by de jure segregation. In the northern states, however, claims of segregation normally were based on the de facto approach. The ground rules for such cases were set forth in *Keyes v. School District*, 413 U.S. 189 (1973). A finding that school authorities intentionally segregated any significant portion of the school district creates a presumption that the entire school district is being operated on a segregation basis.

e. **Limits on remedies.** A federal court may not order busing of students between school districts to remedy de jure segregation in only one of the districts unless discriminatory acts of one school district have been a substantial cause of interdistrict segregation; *e.g.*, the district boundaries were drawn so as to foster such segregation, or one district had engaged in racial discrimination that caused the segregation to exist in the other district. [Milliken v. Bradley, 418 U.S. 717 (1974)]

1) The impact is that the federal courts cannot achieve desegregation of urban schools by ordering the children bused to suburban school districts (and vice versa), as long as the suburban school districts had nothing to do with causing the segregation that exists in the city school district.

2) In *Missouri v. Jenkins*, 495 U.S. 33 (1990), a school desegregation case, the Supreme Court held that the $450 million necessary to implement the lower court's plan could not be raised by the court directly imposing a property tax increase, but the lower court could direct the school district to levy the necessary taxes itself and could enjoin state laws that would otherwise prevent this. The majority opinion found that the difference was more than a matter of form.

3) In *Board of Education of Oklahoma City v. Dowell*, 498 U.S. 237 (1991), the Court considered continuing judicial involvement with long-standing desegregation decrees. Federal supervision was intended to be a temporary measure that was no longer necessary after local authorities had complied with the decree and vestiges of past discrimination had been eliminated. [*See also* Freeman v. Pitts, 503 U.S. 467 (1992)—applying *Dowell*]

3. Eliminating Other Vestiges of Segregation.

a. Interracial marriage--

Loving v. Virginia, 388 U.S. 1 (1967).

Facts. Loving (D), a white man, married a black woman in Washington, D.C., and returned to Virginia. D was convicted of violating a Virginia antimiscegenation statute. The state courts upheld the conviction. D appeals, claiming that the statute violates the Equal Protection and Due Process Clauses of the Fourteenth Amendment.

Issue. May a state prevent marriages between persons solely because they are of different races?

Held. No. Judgment reversed.

- ♦ The state claims that equal protection is afforded when any penalties due to interracial elements of an offense are applied equally to members of both races. However, equal protection means more than mere "equal application."
- ♦ The Court must consider whether statutory classifications constitute arbitrary and invidious discrimination. Racial classifications, especially in criminal statutes, are subject to the most rigid scrutiny and must be essential to the accomplishment of some permissible state objective to be constitutional.
- ♦ The state has failed to show any legitimate overriding purpose for the distinction between one-race and interracial marriages other than invidious discrimination. The statute cannot be upheld.

Concurrence (Stewart, J.). It is impossible for a state law that makes the criminality of an act dependent on the race of the actor to be constitutional.

---

b. Interracial remarriage and child custody. In *Palmore v. Sidoti*, 466 U.S. 429 (1984), the Court held that a mother cannot be divested of the custody of her child merely because of her remarriage to a person of a different race. Upon her divorce from Sidote, Palmore was awarded custody of their three-year-old daughter. However, when Palmore subsequently married an African-American, the state court awarded custody to the father, applying the "best interests of the child" standard. Reversing the ruling, the Supreme Court explained that even if the child may suffer from social stigmatization because of the racially mixed household, such private biases are not permissible considerations under the Constitution. Private biases may be beyond the reach of the law, but the law cannot give them effect.

4. **Facial Discrimination Against Racial Minorities.** Racial classifications were not articulated as being suspect, and hence subject to the most rigid scrutiny, until *Korematsu v. United States*, 323 U.S. 214 (1944). Congress had provided for the creation of military areas where all persons of Japanese ancestry were forbidden. Although the law would have been clearly invalid under normal circumstances, the Court upheld it because of the exigencies of war and the need for quick action. The classification was reasonable in light of the circumstances. Justice Jackson's dissent argued that the order violated the Equal Protection Clause because the class was not general enough. American citizens of German or Italian origin were not regulated. Justice Murphy dissented on the ground that there were no reasonable grounds for an order regulating all citizens of Japanese origin.

5. **Racially Discriminatory Purpose and Effect.**

   a. **Racially discriminatory application of facially neutral laws.** In *Yick Wo v. Hopkins*, 118 U.S. 351 (1886), the Supreme Court held that discriminatory application of a statute that is fair and impartial on its face constitutes denial of equal protection under the Fourteenth Amendment. San Francisco had passed an ordinance requiring that all laundries housed in wooden buildings be licensed before operating. Yick Wo, a Chinese citizen, was convicted and imprisoned for violation of the ordinance. He petitioned for a writ of habeas corpus, proving that his equipment was not a fire hazard and that, while he and 200 other Chinese laundrymen had been denied permits, virtually all non-Chinese who made application received permits. The Court found that although the statute appeared fair and impartial on its face, its administration made illegal and unjust discriminations of a material character among people in similar circumstances. Discriminatory application such as this denies equal protection of the law and cannot be sanctioned.

   b. **Racially discriminatory motivation.** In *Palmer v. Thompson*, 403 U.S. 217 (1971), the city of Jackson, Mississippi, closed its public swimming pools after a court order to desegregate. The purpose for the closure was "to preserve peace and order and because the pools could not be operated economically on an integrated basis." The Court found no equal protection violation, reasoning that it could not declare a law invalid "because of the motivations of its sponsors" and that there was no showing of "state action affecting blacks differently from whites."

c. **Proving purposeful discrimination.**

1) **Introduction.** Although it is necessary to show purposeful discrimination to prove a violation of the Constitution, the Court has been unable to state exactly what must be proven. The following cases illustrate the problem and articulate what guidance there is.

2) **Racial impact of qualification tests, by itself, is not enough--**

Washington v. Davis, 426 U.S. 229 (1976).

Facts. Davis (P), a black police officer (and other interested black officers) challenged the promotion policies and recruiting practices of the District of Columbia Police Department. P filed for partial summary judgment on the recruiting question, specifically challenging a qualification test that allegedly discriminated against blacks in violation of the Fifth Amendment Due Process Clause. The district court denied P's motions; the court of appeals reversed. The Supreme Court granted certiorari.

Issue. Does a qualification test that has not been established as a reliable measure of job performance and that fails a higher percentage of blacks than whites violate Fifth Amendment due process?

Held. No. Judgment reversed.

- A disproportionate impact on different races resulting from a general qualification test does not, by itself and independent of any discriminatory purpose, establish a constitutional violation. Government action is not unconstitutional solely because it has a racially disproportionate impact; there must be a racially discriminatory purpose to justify invalidation. The purpose need not be express, but it must exist, whether on the face of the statute or in its application.

- When a disproportionate racial impact is proved, the government must show that the law is neutral on its face and serves proper governmental ends, but the burden is not high. The test involved here has a reasonable relation to the need for competent police officers. Additionally, D has made affirmative efforts to recruit black officers, indicating a lack of intent to discriminate.

- Even though the test was not shown to relate directly to eventual job performance, it is closely related to the requirements of the training program for new recruits.

Concurrence (Stevens, J.). The link between discriminatory purpose and impact is not bright, and not determinative since dramatic discriminatory impact is unacceptable.

---

3) **Denial of an application for zoning variance.** In *Village of Arlington Heights v. Metropolitan Housing Development Corp.,* 429 U.S. 252 (1977), the Supreme Court held that without proof of improper intent, a mere showing of disproportionate impact on a racial minority is inadequate to the constitutional question. In that case, the plaintiff applied for rezoning in order to build units for low-income tenants, many of whom would be racial minorities. When the city denied the application pursuant to standard procedures, the plaintiff sued, claiming the denial was racially discriminatory. The Supreme Court found for the city and reaffirmed the *Davis* requirement that governmental action having a racially disproportionate impact must also have a discriminatory purpose to justify judicial invalidation. The challenged action need not rest solely on such a racially discriminatory purpose; it is enough to show that such a purpose was a motivating factor in the decision.

4) **Circumstantial and historical evidence.**

   a) **Voting dilution of at-large elections.** Black citizens of Burke County, Georgia, brought suit challenging the county's system of at-large elections. Over 53% of the county population was black, but only about 38% of the registered voters were black. The Burke County Board of Commissioners governed the county and consisted of five members elected at large. No black person had ever been elected to the commission. The trial court found that the election system was racially neutral when adopted, but was being maintained for invidious purposes, and ordered that the county be divided into five districts for purposes of electing commissioners. In *Rogers v. Lodge,* 458 U.S. 613 (1982), the Supreme Court found that evidence of bloc voting along racial lines, and the fact that no black person had ever been elected to the commission, was insufficient by itself to prove purposeful discrimination. However, the trial court also considered the impact of past discrimination, which resulted in low black voter registration and the absence of blacks in various governmental positions; the voting scheme has served to maintain the status quo.The Court held that there was no reason to overturn the district court's order to utilize single-member districts.

b) **Disenfranchisement for crimes involving moral turpitude.** In *Hunter v. Underwood*, 471 U.S. 222 (1985), the Court held that the disenfranchisement of persons convicted of any crime "involving moral turpitude" was unconstitutional because it had produced disproportionate effects along racial lines. The evidence clearly showed that the motivation for the provision in the Alabama Constitution was to discriminate against blacks.

6. Affirmative Action and Race Preferences--

Regents of the University of California v. Bakke, 438 U.S. 265 (1978).

Facts. Bakke (P) was denied admission to the Medical School of the University of California at Davis in two consecutive years. Regents (D) maintained both a regular admissions system and a special admissions program intended to assist disadvantaged minorities in getting admitted. P claimed that because he was white, he was denied consideration for the places reserved for minorities in the special program, denying him equal protection and violating Title VI of the 1964 Civil Rights Act. The California Supreme Court altered lower court decisions and found that D's admissions program was illegal, that P must be admitted to the Medical School, and that D may not accord any consideration to race in its admissions process. D appeals.

Issue. May a state school use race as a factor in its admissions process?

Held. Yes. Judgment affirmed in part and reversed in part.

- Title VI of the Civil Rights Act of 1964 must be held to proscribe only those racial classifications that would violate the Equal Protection Clause of the Fifth Amendment.

- D claims that since its procedure does not disadvantage minorities, it should not be subject to strict judicial review. However, D does disadvantage a specific race—whites; equal protection requires that racial and ethnic distinctions of any sort be examined by the most exacting judicial scrutiny. It is incorrect to assert that the Fourteenth Amendment justifies "benign" preference for one race over another due to past discriminations, since its language is inconsistent with such an interpretation and the kind of variable sociological and political analysis necessary to produce and enforce such rankings is beyond judicial competence. Such an interpretation would be manifestly unjust. The Court has approved preferential classifications in some instances (school desegregation, employment discrimination) but only after proof of constitutional or statutory violations, absent here, and only when the remedy was closely related to the violation.

♦ The use of a suspect classification may be justified if the state can show that its purpose or interest is both constitutionally permissible and substantial, and that its use of the classification is necessary to the accomplishment of its purpose or the safeguarding of its interest. D's reasons for using its special admissions process are inadequate under this standard. Although D does have a valid interest in seeking diversity among its student body, its program, focusing as it does solely on ***ethnic*** diversity, hinders rather than promotes genuine diversity. An admissions process seeking diversity may properly consider race as one of many characteristics of an applicant that are compared with all other applicants to decide who is to be admitted, such as the procedure used at Harvard. But reservation of a fixed number of seats to a minority group unnecessarily denies other persons an equal chance to be considered, and is therefore unconstitutional.

♦ The California court's judgment that D's special admissions program is unlawful and that P must be admitted is affirmed. Its judgment that D be enjoined from any consideration of race in its admissions process is reversed.

Concurrence and dissent (Brennan, White, Marshall, Blackmun, JJ.).

♦ The central meaning of the decision is that government may take race into account when it acts not to demean or insult any racial group but to remedy disadvantages caused by past discrimination, when supported by appropriate findings.

♦ D's affirmative action program is constitutional. Congress has enacted legislation under Title VI incorporating racial quotas. Prior decisions of this Court suggest that remedial use of race is permissible. D's goal of admitting minority students disadvantaged by the effects of past discrimination is sufficiently important to justify use of race-conscious admissions criteria. D ought not be forced to abandon its reasonable and effective procedure.

Concurrence and dissent (Marshall, J.). For several hundred years, blacks have suffered discrimination, yet the Court is unwilling to hold that a class-based remedy for that discrimination is permissible. It is difficult for me to accept that blacks cannot now be afforded greater protection to remedy the effects of past discrimination.

Concurrence and dissent (Blackmun, J.). It is ironic that we are so disturbed over using race as an element when schools have conceded preferences for athletes, children of alumni, the affluent, etc.

Concurrence and dissent (Stevens, J., Burger, C.J., Stewart, Rehnquist, JJ.). The California court judgment should be affirmed in its entirety based on the plain language of Title VI of the Civil Rights Act, which specifies that "No person . . . on the ground of race, color, or national origin, be excluded from participation in . . . any program . . . receiving federal assistance." There is no need to reach the constitutional issues.

Comment. The holding and effect of *Bakke* can be illustrated by the following table:

	Specific System Was Unconstitutional	States Can Consider Race as a Factor
J. Brennan and three others	No	Yes
J. Powell	Yes	Yes
J. Stevens and three others	Yes	No

In summary, the less formal and specific the admissions system, the more likely it will be constitutional.

---

7. **Race Preferences in Employment and Contracting.**

   a. **Teacher layoffs.** In *Wygant v. Jackson Board of Education*, 476 U.S. 267 (1986), the Court considered a collective bargaining agreement that limited the percentage of minority personnel laid off to the percentage of minorities employed at the time of the layoff. The effect was to protect recently hired minority teachers at the expense of more senior white teachers. The Court held that the provision was unconstitutional because it was not related to specific prior discrimination by the government unit involved and did not necessarily bear a relationship to the harm caused by prior discriminatory hiring practices.

   b. **Public contracts.** In *Fullilove v. Klutznick*, 448 U.S. 448 (1980), the Court held that Congress may affirmatively require a minimum minority participation as a condition of the expenditure of federal funds. Congress had enacted a statute that required that federal grants to local governments for local public work projects be awarded only to applicants who assured that at least 10% of the grant would be spent for minority business enterprises. The Court held that the objective of the legislation—to prohibit traditional procurement practices that perpetuate the effects of prior discrimination—was within the constitutional scope of congressional power.

   c. **State and local set-aside programs.** In *City of Richmond v. J.A. Croson Co.*, 488 U.S. 469 (1989), the city of Richmond, citing the authority of *Fullilove, supra,* required prime contractors on city projects to set aside at least 30% of their subcontracts to minority business enterprises, using the *Fullilove* definition of minority group members. The program was adopted based on evidence that minority businesses had received a significantly lower percentage of contracts (.67%) than the percentage of minorities living in the city (50%). However, there was no evidence of racial discrimination on the city's part or on the part of any of its prime contractors. The Court pointed out that unlike the states and their subdivisions, Congress has a specific constitutional mandate to enforce the Fourteenth Amendment. Furthermore, the Richmond plan denied certain citizens the opportunity to compete for a fixed percentage of public contracts based solely on their race, and thereby implicated the personal rights of the excluded persons. The Court also explained that the overinclusiveness of the Richmond plan, which covered Spanish-speaking, Oriental, Indian, Eskimo, and Aleut persons, suggested that Richmond's purpose was not to remedy past discrimination. The Court found that the plan was not narrowly tailored—there had been no consideration of the use of race-neutral means to increase minority business participation in city contracting. Justice Stevens, concurring in part and in the judgment, contended that the plan did not address the specific characteristics of the racial groups involved; it relied merely on a stereotypical analysis that could not be condoned under the Equal Protection Clause. Justice Kennedy, also concurring in part and in the judgment, stated that any racial preferences must face the most rigorous scrutiny by the courts. Concurring only in the judgment, Justice Scalia asserted that there is only one circumstance in which the states may act by race to undo the effects of past discrimination—to eliminate their own maintenance of a system of unlawful racial classification (*e.g.*, school desegregation). Justice Marshall, joined by Justices Brennan and Blackmun, argued that Richmond, the former capital of the Confederacy, had an interest in remedying past discrimination and an interest in preventing its own spending decision from furthering racial discrimination. According to Justice Marshall, Richmond's plan was patterned after the *Fullilove* plan and was substantially related to these interests.

d. Strict scrutiny of affirmative action--

Adarand Constructors, Inc. v. Pena, 515 U.S. 200 (1995).

Facts. Adarand Constructors, Inc. (P) submitted the low bid for a guardrail subcontract on a federal road project. The prime contract's terms provided for additional compensation if subcontractors were hired who were certified as small businesses controlled by "socially and economically disadvantaged individuals." P's competitor, Gonzales Construction Company, certified as such a business and received the subcontract, although its bid was higher than P's. Under federal law, general contractors must presume that socially and economically disadvantaged individuals include specified racial minorities. P sued Pena (D), Secretary of Transportation, claiming he was deprived of property without due process of law under the Fifth Amendment. The court of appeals upheld the law. P appeals.

Issue. Is the federal government's use of race-based classifications subject to strict scrutiny even for affirmative action?

Held. Yes. Judgment reversed and remanded.

- The Fifth Amendment protects against arbitrary treatment by the federal government, but it does not guarantee equal treatment.

- In *Croson*, the Court held that the Fourteenth Amendment requires strict scrutiny of all race-based action by state and local governments. Thus, any person, of whatever race, has the right to demand that the government justify any racial classification subjecting that person to unequal treatment under the strictest judicial scrutiny.

- In *Metro Broadcasting*, the Court held that "benign" racial classifications made by Congress required only intermediate scrutiny. This holding undermined the basic principle that the Fifth and Fourteenth Amendments protect persons, not groups. Group classifications must be subject to detailed inquiry to assure that the personal right to equal protection has not been infringed. Therefore, it is inconsistent to treat "benign" racial classifications differently from other types of racial classifications, and all racial classifications shall now be subject to strict scrutiny. *Metro Broadcasting* is thus overruled to the extent that it is inconsistent with this rule.

- This holding does not preclude the government from acting in response to the lingering effects of racial discrimination. When race-based action is necessary to further a compelling interest, it is permitted so long as it satisfies the "narrow tailoring" test of strict scrutiny.

Concurrence (Scalia, J.). There can never be a compelling interest in discriminating on the basis of race to compensate for past racial discrimination in the opposite direction. Under the Constitution, there can be neither a creditor nor a debtor race.

Concurrence (Thomas, J.). The government may not make distinctions on the basis of race, whether the objectives are to oppress a race or to help a race. Affirmative action programs undermine the moral basis of the equal protection principle and arouse resentment by those not benefited. The targeted minorities are stamped with a badge of inferiority and are prompted to develop dependencies or an attitude that they are "entitled" to preferences.

Dissent (Stevens, Ginsburg, JJ.). There is a clear distinction between policies designed to oppress minorities and policies designed to eradicate racial subordination.

Dissent (Ginsburg, Breyer, JJ.). The judiciary should defer to Congress, as the political branches are better suited to respond to changing conditions.

---

8. **Affirmative Action After *Croson* and *Adarand*.**

a. **Race as a factor for law school admission--**

Grutter v. Bollinger, 539 U.S. 306 (2003).

Facts. Grutter (P), who was white, applied for admission to the University of Michigan Law School. P had a 3.8 grade point average and an LSAT score of 161. P was denied admission. P sued Bollinger (D), the President of the University, and other officials, claiming their admissions policy discriminated against her on the basis of race. D's admissions policy sought to achieve diversity in the student body and therefore enrolled a "critical mass" of minority students, including African-Americans, Hispanics and Native Americans. The district court found that D's use of race as a factor in admissions decisions was unlawful, but the court of appeals reversed. The Supreme Court granted certiorari.

Issue. Does a state university have a compelling state interest in obtaining the educational benefits that flow from a diverse student body, sufficient to justify the use of race as a factor in admissions criteria?

Held. Yes. Judgment affirmed.

- Under the Equal Protection Clause, a racial classification must survive strict scrutiny review. Justice Powell's decision in *Bakke* recognized that student body diversity is a compelling state interest that can justify the use of race in university admissions.

- The Court has never held that only remedial objectives can provide a basis for consideration of race. D in this case was not seeking to remedy past discrimination, but was seeking diversity in its student body which D considers essential to its educational mission.

- Given the important purpose of public education and the expansive freedoms of speech and thought associated with the university environment, universities have a special niche under the Constitution. D's consideration of race is not simply to assure racial balancing, which is patently unconstitutional, but instead focuses on the educational benefits that diversity produces. In addition, law schools are the training ground for a large number of civil leaders. To cultivate a set of leaders that the citizens deem legitimate, the path to leadership must be open to talented and qualified individuals of every race and ethnicity.

- D's admissions policy is narrowly tailored to further the compelling state interest. There is no quota. Admissions decisions are based on individual considerations. Race is considered as a "plus" factor during consideration of each individual candidate. Race is not the defining feature of an application. There are many other diversity considerations, including living or traveling abroad, speaking other languages, etc. At the same time, D's program does not unduly burden individuals who are not members of the favored racial and ethnic groups.

♦ D's race-conscious admissions program must be limited in time, however. In 25 years, racial preferences will likely be unnecessary to further the diversity interest.

Concurrence (Ginsburg, Breyer, JJ.). Minority students still encounter inadequate and unequal educational opportunities, which hopefully will be remedied within the next generation.

Concurrence and dissent (Scalia, Thomas, JJ.). The Court invites further litigation about the scope of a "good faith effort" and the extent of the permissible "critical mass." The government should simply not discriminate on the basis of race.

Concurrence and dissent (Thomas, Scalia, JJ.). Minorities can achieve in every avenue of American life without the meddling of university administrators. The Court has deferred to D in an unprecedented way that is inconsistent with the concept of "strict scrutiny." The Court is correct in holding that racial discrimination that does not help a university to enroll a "critical mass" of underrepresented minority students is unconstitutional. However, the Court should not uphold discrimination even to achieve the critical mass.

Dissent (Renhquist, C.J., Scalia, Kennedy, Thomas, JJ.). D's admissions program is not narrowly tailored to the interest D asserts. Over five years, D has admitted 91 to 108 African-Americans to achieve "critical mass," so that members of that race would not feel isolated or like spokespersons for their race. During the same time, D admitted 13 to 19 Native Americans and between 47 and 56 Hispanics. D offers no explanation why fewer Hispanics and Native Americans are needed to achieve "critical mass." It turns out that the percentage of students admitted in each of these groups corresponds very closely to the percentage of applicants who were in the same groups. This is the type of racial balancing that is not permissible.

b. Race as a preferential factor for undergraduate admission--

Gratz v. Bollinger, 539 U.S. 244 (2003).

Facts. Gratz and other Caucasian students (Ps) were denied admission to the University of Michigan as undergraduates. They sued Bollinger (D), the university president, claiming that D's policy of including race as a factor in making admissions decisions was unconstitutional. Under D's policy, an applicant needed 100 points to guarantee admission. Applicants who were African-American, Hispanic, or Native American automatically received 20 points. The district court certified Ps as a class and granted Ps summary judgment on the basis that D's policy was the equivalent of a quota. While the case was under appeal, the Sixth Circuit decided *Grutter*, *supra*. The Supreme Court granted certiorari in both cases even though the Sixth Circuit had not rendered a judgment in *Gratz*.

Issue. May an undergraduate university automatically confer 20 points, out of the 100 needed to guarantee admission, to every applicant who is a member of a specified race?

Held. No. Judgment affirmed.

- D's policy grants preferences to every minority applicant, solely on the basis of race. This policy is not narrowly tailored to achieve the interest in educational diversity that D claims as justification.

- Under Justice Powell's *Bakke* opinion, each applicant should be assessed as an individual. No single characteristic automatically ensures a specific and identifiable contribution to a university's diversity. D's policy does not include such individualized consideration.

- Although D's policy may be easier to administer than an individualized consideration process, administrative challenges cannot make constitutional an otherwise problematic system.

Concurrence (O'Connor, J.). D's policy also awarded points for other diversity contributions, including high school leadership, but these awards were capped at 5 points. D's policy is in sharp contrast to the law school admissions program in *Grutter*, which did allow admissions officers to make individualized judgments.

Concurrence (Thomas, J.). Any use of racial discrimination in higher education admissions is unconstitutional.

Dissent (Souter, J.). D's policy is closer to *Grutter* than to what *Bakke* prohibits. There is no quota, and the 20 points does not convert race into a decisive factor comparable to reserving minority places as prohibited by *Bakke*.

Dissent (Ginsburg, Souter, JJ.). D's policy was designed to help achieve equality in light of the history of discrimination against these minorities. D has not limited or decreased enrollment by any particular racial or ethnic group, and it has not reserved places on the basis of race.

---

9. Racial Diversity in K-12 Public Education--

Parents Involved in Community Schools v. Seattle School District, 127 S. Ct. 2738 (2007).

Facts. The Seattle school district and the Jefferson County school district in Louisville, Kentucky (Ds) voluntarily adopted student assignment plans that used race to determine which public school certain children could attend. The Seattle school district classified children as "white" or "nonwhite," and used its plan to allocate slots in oversubscribed high schools. The Jefferson County school district classified children as "black" or "other," and used its plan to make certain elementary school assignments and to rule on transfer requests. Both school districts sought to maintain a racial balance within a predetermined range based on the racial composition of the school district as a whole. Seattle used a series of tiebreakers when its schools were oversubscribed by students. The first tiebreaker was whether the student had a sibling at the school. The second tiebreaker was based on race. If an oversubscribed school was not within 10 percentage points of the district's overall white/nonwhite racial balance, it selected students who would bring the school into balance. Seattle had never operated segregated schools. The Jefferson County district, after achieving unitary status, adopted a voluntary assignment plan that required nonmagnet schools to maintain black enrollment between 15% and 50%. Parents whose children were denied assignments to desired schools solely because of race (Ps), sued. The appellate courts upheld the plans. The Supreme Court granted certiorari.

Issues.

(i) May a public school that has not operated legally segregated schools choose to classify students by race and rely upon that classification in making school assignments?

(ii) May a public school that has been found to have achieved unitary status choose to classify students by race and rely upon that classification in making school assignments?

Held. (i) No. (ii) No. Judgment reversed.

- Government action that distributes benefits or burdens on the basis of individual racial classification is subject to strict scrutiny. Thus, Ds' use of racial classifications in this case must be narrowly tailored to achieve a compelling government interest.

- In the school context, one compelling interest is remedying the effects of past intentional discrimination, but that interest does not apply to either D in this case. The other compelling interest is diversity in higher education, as upheld in *Grutter*. But *Grutter* approved the use of racial classifications as part of a broader assessment of diversity, not merely as an effort to achieve racial balance. And since *Grutter* applied to higher education, it does not govern cases involving Ds.

- ♦ In this case, Ds' plans are directed only to racial balance and are not narrowly tailored to achieve educational and social benefits that allegedly flow from racial diversity. The plans are tied solely to racial demographics. Racial balancing is unconstitutional and may not be sought for its own sake. If racial balancing was a compelling state interest, it could be imposed throughout American society.

- ♦ Ds claim that they have to use these classifications to achieve their stated ends, but in fact they have used the racial classifications to shift only a small number of students. This suggests that the racial classifications are not really necessary. They failed to show that they considered methods other than explicit racial classifications.

- ♦ Both parties debated the *Brown* case, but the plaintiffs in *Brown* asserted that "[t]he Fourteenth Amendment prevents states from according differential treatment to American children on the basis of their color or race." The way to achieve a system of determining admission to public schools on a nonracial basis is to stop assigning students on the basis of race.

Concurrence (Thomas, J.). Neither of these districts is threatened with resegregation. Racial imbalance is not segregation. It has not been shown that coerced racial mixing has any educational benefits or that black achievement depends on integration. Furthermore, our Constitution is color-blind.

Concurrence in part (Kennedy, J.). The government has a legitimate interest in ensuring that all people have equal opportunity regardless of race. School districts cannot ignore the problem of de facto resegregation. However, the small number of students affected by Ds' plans suggests that they could have achieved their stated ends through different means, without treating students differently based solely on race. There are dangers presented by individual classifications based on racial typologies; this can cause new divisiveness.

Dissent (Stevens, J.). *Brown* applied to situations in which only black children were told where to go; white children were not striving to get into black schools.

Dissent (Breyer, Stevens, Souter, Ginsburg, JJ.). We have approved of narrowly tailored plans that are no less race-conscious than these plans. And the Constitution permits local communities to adopt desegregation plans even where it does not require them to. Local government efforts to prevent growing de facto resegregation will be impeded. No prior case has held that the test of strict scrutiny means that all racial classifications must be treated as the same; the strict scrutiny test forbids racial classifications that harmfully exclude, not those that include. Furthermore, there are three essential elements to the interest at stake: (i) an interest in setting right the consequences of prior conditions of segregation; (ii) an interest in overcoming the adverse educational effects of highly segregated schools; and (iii) an interest in producing an educational environment that reflects the pluralistic society in which our children will live. These interests are of a compelling nature, and Ds' plans satisfy strict scrutiny.

---

10. Race Preferences in Electoral Districting.

a. State redistricting plan designed only to separate voters on the basis of race--

---

Shaw v. Reno, 509 U.S. 630 (1993).

Facts. After the 1990 census, North Carolina became entitled to a twelfth congressional seat. Forty of the state's 100 counties were covered by the Voting Rights Act, which required approval from a federal court or from Reno (D), the United States Attorney General, for any changes to voting districts. Blacks made up 20% of the state's population and were the majority in five of the counties. The state legislature submitted a redistricting plan that included one majority-black congressional district. After D objected to the plan, the legislature enacted a revised plan that had two majority-black districts. To include sufficient black citizens to fill the district, the second district was 160 miles long and, for much of its length, was only as wide as the freeway corridor it followed from black neighborhood to black neighborhood. Shaw (P) challenged the redistricting, claiming that the deliberate segregation of voters into separate districts on the basis of race violated the right to vote in an electoral process not tainted by racial discrimination. The district court held that P did not state a claim under the Equal Protection Clause. P appeals.

Issue. May a state legislature create a voting district that is so irrational on its face that it can be understood only as an effort to segregate voters into separate voting districts because of their race alone?

Held. No. Judgment reversed.

- ♦ Redistricting legislation that is so bizarre on its face that it is unexplainable on grounds other than race requires close scrutiny. A reapportionment plan that includes groups who have little or nothing in common other than their race has the appearance of political apartheid. It reinforces the stereotype that all members of a particular racial group think alike and vote alike.

- ♦ When a district is created solely to create a majority of one racial group, the representative from that district may believe that the primary objective is to represent only the members of that group instead of their entire constituency.

Accordingly, the courts should recognize an equal protection claim such as P's challenging the intentional creation of a majority-minority district that has no nonracial justifications.

- D claims that a jurisdiction covered by the Voting Rights Act may have a compelling interest in creating majority-minority districts. These states may have a strong interest in creating these districts, but they are still subject to constitutional challenges such as P's. Racial classifications of any type pose the risk of long-term harm to society by reinforcing the belief that citizens should be judged by the color of their skin.

Dissent (White, Blackmun, Stevens, JJ.). P has no cognizable claim, and the case should be dismissed. There are only two types of state voting practices that can give rise to a constitutional claim. The first is a direct deprivation of the right to vote and the second affects the political strength of various groups, such as where legislation unduly diminishes the group's influence on the political process. The second type, which is usually a gerrymandering case, is involved here. But the Court has previously required that an identifiable group show more than a mere lack of success at the polls to have a justiciable claim. In this case, P relies only on the irregular shape of the district, but this is not a sufficient ground for a claim.

Dissent (Blackmun, J.). It is ironic that the case in which the majority chooses to abandon settled law is a challenge by white voters to a plan under which North Carolina has sent black representatives to Congress for the first time since Reconstruction.

Dissent (Stevens, J.). There is no constitutional requirement of compactness or contiguity in a voting district. Equal protection is violated when a state creates an uncouth district for the sole purpose of making it more difficult for minorities to win an election, but it is not violated when the majority acts to facilitate the election of a member of a group that lacks power because it remains underrepresented in the state legislature. If it is permissible to draw districts to provide adequate representation for rural voters, union members, Hasidic Jews, Polish Americans, or Republicans, it is permissible to do the same thing for the very minority group whose history gave birth to equal protection.

Dissent (Souter, J.). There is no justification to depart from our prior decisions; we can have one equal protection analysis for electoral districting and another for most other types of state governmental decisions. Electoral districting in a mixed race area necessarily calls for decisions that require some consideration of race. Also, the mere placement of an individual in one district instead of another does not deny another individual of a right or benefit. Only if a cognizable harm such as vote dilution or the abridgement of the right to participate in the electoral process is shown is there a violation of equal protection.

Comment. After remand, the Court again reviewed the North Carolina plan and determined that neither the race-based redistricting nor the actual shape of the district were required by the Voting Rights Act, so the redistricting did not serve a compelling interest through narrowly tailored means. [Shaw v. Hunt (Shaw II), 517 U.S. 899 (1996); *see also* Bush v. Vera, 517 U.S. 952 (1996)—strict scrutiny is applicable upon proof that other legitimate districting principles were subordinated to race]

b. **Race as predominant factor.** *Miller v. Johnson*, 515 U.S. 900 (1995), also involved redistricting legislation. The 1990 Census gave Georgia an Eleventh Congressional District. After two redistricting plans were rejected by the Department of Justice under the Voting Rights Act, the state legislature adopted one that included three majority-black districts. This redistricting plan was cleared by the Department of Justice, but white voters challenged the reapportionment, claiming racial gerrymandering. The Supreme Court held that the redistricting plan was unconstitutional. The Court stated that the claim in *Shaw* was an equal protection claim, based on the state's use of race as a basis for separating voters into districts. A state may not separate its citizens into different voting districts on the basis of race any more than it may separate them on the basis of race in its parks, buses, golf courses, beaches, and schools. The Court noted that *Shaw* does not require that the challenged district be bizarre on its face but that shape may be circumstantial evidence of intent to use race for its own sake. The Court explained that a plaintiff has the burden to show that race was the predominant factor motivating the legislature's decision to place a significant number of voters within or outside a particular district. This means showing that the traditional race-neutral districting principles, such as compactness, contiguity, respect for political subdivisions or communities defined by actual shared interests, were subordinated to racial considerations. The Court found that Georgia's legislature was motivated by a predominant desire to assign black populations to the Eleventh District, permitting the creation of a third majority-black district. Thus, the standard of strict scrutiny applied. The Court held that the redistricting plan did not satisfy that standard and, thus, was unconstitutional.

C. OTHER ARGUABLY "SUSPECT" CLASSIFCATIONS

All classifications based on suspect criteria are subject to the strict equal protection standard of review. The traditional indicators of a suspect class are that the class is determined by characteristics that are solely an accident of birth, or the class has been subjected to such a history of purposefully unequal treatment, or relegated to a position of such political powerlessness, as to command extraordinary protection from the majority.

1. **Sex Discrimination.** Although early decisions dealt with sex classifications under the traditional equal protection tests [*see, e.g.*, Goesaert v. Cleary, 335

U.S. 464 (1948)], more recent cases have judged these classifications under a higher standard, but not so high a test as would apply to the inherently suspect classes.

a. **Heightened scrutiny under the traditional approach.** In *Reed v. Reed*, 404 U.S. 71 (1971), the Court declined to make sex a suspect classification. However, it did hold that a state could not prefer men over women in appointing estate administrators simply to reduce the workload of probate courts. This was considered an arbitrary choice forbidden by the Equal Protection Clause.

b. **Heightened scrutiny of military benefits plan.** *Frontiero v. Richardson*, 411 U.S. 677 (1973), concerned a federal law under which male members of the armed forces could claim wives as dependents without any showing, but women in the service had to show that their spouses were actually dependent on them for over one-half of their support. The government claimed that the differential treatment of men and women served the purpose of administrative convenience. Writing for four justices, Justice Brennan argued that classifications based on gender are suspect and, therefore, are subject to close scrutiny. Justice Powell, joined by two other justices, concurred, but asserted that since the statute was unconstitutional under *Reed*, *supra*, there was no need to go further and characterize sex as a suspect classification. He contended that to do so would unnecessarily preempt the prescribed constitutional processes of amending the Constitution, which he said were being utilized on that very issue in the guise of the Equal Rights Amendment.

c. **Liquor regulation--**

Craig v. Boren, 429 U.S. 190 (1976).

Facts. Craig (P), a male, challenged an Oklahoma statute that denied beer sales to males under 21 and females under 18. The three-judge district court dismissed P's action; P appeals.

Issue. May a state properly impose gender-based differentials in regulating sales of alcoholic drinks?

Held. No. Judgment reversed.

♦ Classifications by gender must serve important governmental objectives and must be substantially related to the achievement of those objectives to withstand constitutional challenge. The state objective—the enhancement of traffic safety—is clearly important. However, the relation between this objective and the challenged statute is based on statistical evidence fraught with shortcomings and is inadequate to show that sex represents a legitimate, accurate proxy for the regulation of drinking and driving.

- Failure to show a substantial relation between the gender-based classification and achievement of the state's objectives requires that the statute be invalidated as unconstitutional. The operation of the Twenty-First Amendment, limited as it is when applied outside Commerce Clause issues, does not alter application of the equal protection standards that govern here.

Concurrence (Powell, J.). The Court has added confusion to the appropriate standard for equal protection analysis. The statistics do tend to support the state's view, but are inadequate to support the classification.

Concurrence (Stevens, J.). I believe that the two-tiered standard is really a method the Court has used to explain decisions that actually apply a single standard. The classification here is not totally irrational, but it punishes all males for the abuses of only 2% of their class.

Dissent (Rehnquist, J.).

- Men challenging a gender-based statute unfavorable to themselves should not be able to invoke a more stringent standard of review than normally pertains to most other types of classifications, since men, as a group, have not suffered the type of prior discrimination that has always supported a standard of special scrutiny. Nor is the interest involved—beer purchasing—"fundamental" in the constitutional sense of invoking strict scrutiny.

- The Court has added a new standard to the norm of "rational basis" and the "compelling state interest" required when a "suspect classification" is involved—that of the "important governmental objectives" and "substantial relation to achievement of those objectives." This new standard is unneeded and invites judicial confusion and interference into the proper roles of the legislature.

- The correct standard here is the rational basis test, under which a classification is invalid only if it rests on grounds wholly irrelevant to the achievement of the state's objective. The state has shown sufficient evidence to show a rational basis, and the statute should be upheld.

---

d. **Women's college.** In *Mississippi University for Women v. Hogan*, 458 U.S. 718 (1982), the Court invalidated a state statute that prevented males from enrolling in the Mississippi University for Women ("MUW"), a state-supported nursing school. Hogan, a male registered nurse, applied for admission to MUW to obtain a degree. He was denied admission but was allowed to audit classes. The Court stated that the state had to show that the classification served important governmental objectives and that the discriminatory means employed were substantially related to the achievement of those objectives. The state claimed that its policy compensated for discrimination against women and was educational affirmative action. However, the Court pointed out that while a compensatory purpose might justify an otherwise discriminatory classification in some situations, this argument was unpersuasive with respect to the nursing school. Women had earned the large majority of nursing degrees in the state and in the nation as a whole. The actual effect of the policy was to perpetuate the stereotyped view of nursing as a woman's job. The state also failed to show that the classification was substantially and directly related to its compensatory objective. Men were allowed to audit classes. This undermined the state's claim that women were adversely affected by the presence of men.

e. **Jury selection.** In *J.E.B. v. Alabama*, 511 U.S. 127 (1994), the Court held that gender-based peremptory challenges to jurors are unconstitutional. In that case, a paternity suit, the state had used its challenges to exclude male jurors, leading to an all-female jury. The Court held that equal protection prohibits discrimination in jury selection on the basis of gender, because this would reinforce prejudicial views of the relative abilities or inclinations of men and women.

f. **Single-sex public school prohibited--**

United States v. Virginia, 518 U.S. 515 (1996).

Facts. The Virginia Military Institute ("VMI") was founded in 1839 and at the time of the litigation was the only single-sex school among Virginia's (D's) public schools of higher learning. VMI's mission was to produce "citizen-soldiers" who are prepared for leadership in civilian and military life. The school's training used an "adversative method" designed to instill physical and mental discipline in its cadets. This involves complete lack of privacy, wearing uniforms, and eating and living together, all in a high-pressure environment comparable to Marine Corps boot camp. VMI excluded women from its program, although neither the school's goals nor teaching methodologies were inherently unsuitable to women. When one woman complained about being denied admission, the United States (P) sued, alleging that D's single-sex policy violated equal protection. In response to an earlier remand from the federal court of appeals, D proposed a separate but parallel program for women, called Virginia Women's Institute for Leadership ("VWIL"), which would have a goal of producing "citizen-soldiers" but still differed significantly from VMI's program. The court of appeals approved this approach, and the Supreme Court granted both parties' petitions for certiorari.

Issue. May a state sponsor a single-sex school of higher learning?

Held. No. Judgment reversed.

- Under *J.E.B.* and *Hogan*, those who seek to defend gender-based government action must demonstrate an "exceedingly persuasive justification" for that action. Gender classifications have not been equated with racial or national origin classifications for all purposes, but official action that denies opportunities to an individual because of gender must be carefully inspected by the courts. Gender is not a proscribed classification; physical differences between men and women are enduring. These differences may not be used to denigrate the members of either sex or to artificially constrain their opportunities.

- To prevail against a challenge, the government must show that the classification serves "important governmental objectives" and that the discriminatory means used are "substantially related" to the achievement of those objectives. In this case, D has shown no "exceedingly persuasive justification" for its exclusion of all women from VMI. D claims the single-sex education contributes to diversity in education. While that may be true, diversity was not the reason VMI excluded women. D's plan to provide a unique educational benefit only to males is not equal protection when there is no corresponding plan for females.

- D also claims that VMI's adversative method of training provides educational benefits that cannot be made available to women without modification. To accommodate women, VMI claims it would have to "destroy" its program. In fact, the VMI methodology could be used for some women, and the only accommodation necessary would be in housing assignments and physical training programs for female cadets. But while most women may not choose VMI's adversative method, many men would also not choose it. D simply cannot constitutionally deny entrance to women who have the will and capacity to attend VMI.

- D presented its remedial plan to establish VWIL, but this plan still does not address the categorical exclusion of women from the extraordinary educational opportunity afforded to men by VMI. The VWIL program was premised on the same generalizations about women that the exclusion policy was, which is that the VMI methodology is inherently unsuitable to women.

Concurrence (Rehnquist, C.J.). The Court should continue to follow the *Craig* approach, and not introduce new terminology such as "exceedingly persuasive justification." D's justifications may have been after the fact, but D should have been entitled to reconsider its policy after *Hogan*. The true constitutional violation was not the exclusion of women, but the maintenance of an all-men school without providing a comparable institution for women. D might have cured the violation if VWIL was truly comparable to VMI.

Dissent (Scalia, J.). The Court has rejected the fact findings of two courts below, has drastically revised the established standards for reviewing sex-based classifications, and has disregarded the long tradition of men's military colleges. The Court should be preserving our society's values, not revising them. A change that forbids men's military colleges should be implemented by the voters not the Courts. As a result of the Court's opinion, single-sex public education is functionally dead.

---

2. **Sex Equality and Sex Differences.**

   a. **Pregnancy classifications.** A state law that excluded from state disability insurance benefits "disabilities arising from normal pregnancy and childbirth" has been upheld. This provision did not violate equal protection because it furthered the state policy of making the disability insurance program self-supporting by excluding certain physical conditions from coverage thereunder. The fact that this particular condition (pregnancy) happens to apply to only one sex does not render the exclusion invalid. [Geduldig v. Aiello, 417 U.S. 484 (1974)]

   b. **Statutory rape laws.** In *Michael M. v. Sonoma County Superior Court*, 450 U.S. 464 (1981), the Court upheld California's statutory rape law, which made the man alone criminally liable for the act of sexual intercourse where the female was not his wife and was under 18 years of age. The Court noted that a legislature may not make overbroad generalizations based on sex that are entirely unrelated to any differences between men and women or that demean the ability or social status of the affected class; however, legislation may realistically reflect the fact that the sexes are not similarly situated in certain circumstances. The asserted purpose of the statute is to prevent illegitimate pregnancy and its attendant social harms, a valid state purpose. The Court rejected the claim that the statute was underinclusive because a gender-neutral statute would serve the state's goal equally well. The Court explained that it did not redraw constitutionally permissible lines and that even if it were so inclined, it could not say that a gender-neutral statute, attended by increased enforcement difficulties, would be equally effective.

   c. **Exclusion of women from the military draft.** In *Rostker v. Goldberg*, 453 U.S. 57 (1981), the Court upheld the Military Selective Service Act, which required only men to register for the draft. The Court pointed out that Congress has authority over national defense and military affairs and is accorded broad deference in this area. Congress determined that the purpose of registration was to prepare for a draft of combat troops. Because women were not eligible for combat, the Court found that the exemption of women from registration was not only sufficiently but closely related to Congress's purpose in authorizing registration.

   d. **Discrimination against fathers of nonmarital children.** Discrimination against the fathers of nonmarital children has been scrutinized under the intermediate standard of review. [Caban v. Mohammed, 441 U.S. 380 (1979)] In the *Caban* ruling, the Court invalidated a state provision granting the mother but not the father of a nonmarital child the right to block the child's adoption by withholding consent. The Court determined that the law was an overbroad generalization and that there was no showing that the differentiation bears a substantial relation to the state's interest in encouraging adoption. In contrast, in *Nguyen v. I.N.S.*, 533 U.S. 53 (2001), the Court upheld a law providing that if an unmarried American woman gives birth abroad, her child is automatically granted United States citizenship. But when the child of an unmarried American man is born abroad, the man must take specific steps to establish his paternity in order to make his child a United States citizen. This discrimination based on the gender of the parent was held permissible because it promotes the important governmental interest of avoiding proof of parentage problems, which is more difficult to resolve for fathers than mothers.

3. **Gender-Based Purpose and Effect.** In *Personnel Administrator of Massachusetts v. Feeney*, 442 U.S. 256 (1979), the Court upheld a veterans preference law, although 98% of the veterans were male. The Massachusetts statute gave veterans an "absolute lifetime preference" for consideration for state civil service positions. Veterans with passing scores were automatically ranked above all other candidates. The Court rejected a challenge from Helen Feeney, a nonveteran, who claimed that the law discriminated against women and denied them equal protection. The Court explained that although a neutral law may have a disparate impact upon a group, the Fourteenth Amendment guarantees equal laws, not equal results. The Court articulated a two-step analysis of facially neutral statutes alleged to have a discriminatory impact. First, is the classification really neutral, *i.e.*, not gender based? If so, does the adverse effect on the group reflect invidious discrimination? If so, the law is invalid, because purposeful discrimination is the condition that offends the Constitution. Finding the statute to be neutral, the Court pointed out that many men are nonveterans and are thus also excluded from preference, and some women are veterans. Thus, the distinction is between veterans and nonveterans, not between men and women. The Court also explained that although the legislature was certainly aware that most veterans are male, "discriminatory purpose" implies more than intent as awareness of consequences. It implies action taken "because of," not merely "in spite of," its effect. The Court found that nothing indicated that the legislature acted in order to prevent women from getting the civil service jobs and that the record showed a valid interest in assisting veterans. Justice Stevens, joined by Justice White, concurred, adding that the number of males disadvantaged was sufficiently large to refute Feeney's claim. Justice Marshall, joined by justice Brennan, dissented, contending that because of the disproportionate impact, the state should have had the burden to affirmatively prove that sex-based considerations played no part in the adoption of the scheme.

4. **Sex Preferences.**

a. **Property tax exemptions.** In *Kahn v. Shevin,* 416 U.S. 351 (1974), the Court upheld a property tax exemption for widows that did not apply to widowers. The Court found that the law was reasonably designed to assist the sex for whom the loss of a spouse is a disproportionately heavy burden. The classification was not a mere administrative convenience as in *Frontiero.*

b. **Alimony after divorce.** The Court invalidated a state law authorizing the state court to impose alimony obligations on husbands but not on wives. [*See* Orr v. Orr, 440 U.S. 268 (1979)]

c. **Social Security benefits.**

1) **Survivors' benefits.** The Court has struck down a provision in the Social Security Act that granted "survivors' benefits" to widows, but not widowers, while they care for minor children of the deceased wage earner. The disqualification of widowers was held "irrational," since the purpose of the benefits was to enable the surviving parent to stay at home and care for the children. The classification thus discriminated against the ***children*** based on the gender of the surviving parent. [Weinberger v. Wiesenfeld, 420 U.S. 636 (1975)]

2) **Proof of dependency requirement.** In *Califano v. Goldfarb*, 430 U.S. 199 (1977), the plurality held that *Wiesenfeld* applied to a requirement that a widower, but not a widow, must prove dependency on the deceased spouse in order to collect benefits. The dissent distinguished *Wiesenfeld* on the grounds that the statute did not totally foreclose widowers and that favoring aged widows was not invidious discrimination.

3) **Old age benefits.** The Court has upheld a Social Security Act formula entitling women wage earners to greater benefits than males. The Court recognized reduction of the disparity in economic condition between men and women, caused by the long history of discrimination against women, as an important governmental objective. [Califano v. Webster, 430 U.S. 313 (1977)]

4) **Workers' compensation.** In *Wengler v. Druggists Mutual Insurance Co.*, 446 U.S. 142 (1980), the Court invalidated a state workers' compensation provision that automatically provided death benefits to widows but required widowers to show dependence on their wives' earnings in order to collect benefits. Finding that the provision discriminated against ***both*** men and women, the Court rejected a claim of benign discrimination because the discrimina-

tory means was not substantially related to an important legislative purpose, *i.e.*, providing for needy spouses.

d. **Military promotions.** The Court has upheld the Navy's mandatory discharge procedure, which accords different treatment for male and female line officers (*i.e.*, male officers are automatically discharged if twice denied promotion, whereas women officers are not). This was upheld because the different promotional opportunities offered by the Navy to male and female officers made the procedure consistent with the Navy's overall goal of treatment of both sexes. [Schlesinger v. Ballard, 419 U.S. 498 (1975)]

5. **Other Classifications Arguably Warranting Heightened Scrutiny.**

a. **Alienage.** Although Congress has plenary power over admission or exclusion of aliens, state laws discriminating against aliens once admitted are inherently suspect. The courts have recognized an exception for governmental functions, however.

1) **Heightened scrutiny.** Strict scrutiny for alienage classifications emerged in *Graham v. Richardson*, 403 U.S. 365 (1971), in which the Court held that states could not deny welfare benefits to aliens because such classifications are inherently suspect and thus subject to strict scrutiny. The state statutes also interfere with federal power. Since Congress has placed no restrictions on aliens who become indigent after entry to the United States, state welfare restrictions based merely on alienage conflict with an overrriding federal policy. States likewise cannot exclude aliens from all civil service jobs [Sugarman v. Dougall, 413 U.S. 634 (1973)]; nor may they prescribe citizenship as a requirement for the practice of law [*In re* Griffiths, 413 U.S. 717 (1973)]. The *Dougall* opinion noted that Court scrutiny of citizenship requirements would be less strict regarding governmental positions that fall within a state's constitutional prerogatives.

2) **Deferential review under governmental function exception.** In the late 1970s, a number of cases relied on the *Dougall* exception, interpreting it broadly. In the first case, *Foley v. Connelie*, 435 U.S. 291 (1981), it was held that aliens could be denied employment as state troopers if a state could show a rational relationship between citizenship and the special demands of the job. Police officers exercise broad discretion in enforcing laws. Similarly, a state may require citizenship of elementary and secondary public school teachers if they are eligible for citizenship, because public education is one of the most important governmental functions. [Ambach v. Norwick, 441 U.S. 68 (1979)] However, the func-

tions of a notary public are mainly clerical and ministerial and thus do not fall within the governmental function exception. [Bernal v. Fainter, 467 U.S. 26 (1984)]

3) **Federal preemption grounds.** In *Toll v. Moreno*, 458 U.S. 1 (1982), the Court struck down a policy of granting preferential tuition treatment to in-state residents attending the state university, but excluding in-state resident aliens. Since Congress clearly had not barred aliens from acquiring domicile, the university's policy violated the Supremacy Clause.

4) **Federal restrictions on aliens.** The Court invalidated a regulation by the Civil Service Commission that barred resident aliens from the federal competitive civil service. In *Hampton v. Mow Sun Wong*, 426 U.S. 88 (1976), the Court held that although the federal government has power over immigration and naturalization, it cannot exercise that power arbitrarily once aliens are admitted. The Commission had failed to specify what federal interest justified the regulation. In *Mathews v. Diaz*, 426 U.S. 67 (1976), by contrast, the Court upheld the limitation of federal Medicare benefits to aliens who had been admitted for permanent residence and who had lived in the United States continuously for five years. The Court deferred to congressional judgment that the distinctions drawn within the class of aliens were appropriate.

b. **Disability, age, poverty.**

1) **Discrimination against the mentally retarded--**

Cleburne v. Cleburne Living Center, Inc., 473 U.S. 432 (1985).

Facts. Under a city zoning ordinance, group homes for the mentally retarded could operate only with a special permit that required the signatures of property owners within 200 feet of the property to be used. The applicants were unable to obtain the required signatures in a residential neighborhood. The lower courts held the ordinance unconstitutional. The Supreme Court granted certiorari.

Issue. Is mental retardation a suspect class for equal protection analysis?

Held. No. Judgment affirmed on other grounds.

♦ Generally, under the Equal Protection Clause, legislation is presumed valid and will be upheld if the classification drawn by the statute is rationally related to a legitimate state interest. Certain types of classifications are subject to strict scrutiny, others to heightened scrutiny.

- The court of appeals held that mental retardation is a quasi-suspect classification. However, the legislature has a legitimate interest in providing for the various problems of the mentally retarded, and courts are ill-equipped to make substantive judgments about legislative decisions in this area. Legislatures have addressed the problems of the mentally retarded and need the flexibility of the rational basis test to be effective.

- Under the rational basis test, however, the ordinance is defective. It does not apply to nursing homes for the aged or convalescents, apartment houses, sanitariums, or boarding houses. Nothing in the record explains how the permit requirement for only facilities for the mentally retarded is rationally related to any governmental purpose.

Concurrence (Stevens, J., Burger, C.J.). The mentally retarded have historically been subject to unfair mistreatment. This ordinance reflects the irrational fears of neighboring property owners, not a concern for the welfare of the mentally retarded.

Concurrence and dissent (Marshall, Brennan, Blackmun, JJ.). The Court has created a "second order" rational basis review. Normally under the rational basis test, the legislature does not have to address all ills at once. Thus, zoning plans based on fears of proximity to a high school, location in a flood plain, and crowded living conditions or increased congestion are perfectly valid, even if applied one step at a time. However, the class of mentally retarded persons deserves heightened scrutiny, and the Court reaches the correct result.

Comment. In *Schweiker v. Wilson*, 450 U.S. 221 (1981), the Court did not reach the issue of whether the mentally ill were a discrete group entitled to a heightened standard of review because the statute, which excluded institutionalized patients from welfare comfort payments, did not classify directly on the basis of mental illness.

---

2) **Age classifications.** Rationality standards were applied in *Massachusetts Board of Retirement v. Murgia*, 427 U.S. 307 (1976), wherein the Court rejected a police officer's challenge to mandatory retirement at age 50. The Court explained that strict scrutiny is required only when a classification impermissibly interferes with the exercise of fundamental rights or operates to disadvantage a suspect class. Age is not a suspect class nor is a right to continued public employment a fundamental right. A state does not violate equal protection merely because its classifications are imperfect.

3) **Poverty and wealth classifications.** The Court has clearly ruled that poverty, standing alone, is not a suspect classification [*See, e.g.*, James v. Valtierra, 402 U.S. 137 (1971)—upholding require-

ment for local referendum approved prior to state development of low-rent housing], but some dicta have suggested that such classifications will invite scrutiny.

c. **Sexual orientation--**

Romer v. Evans, 517 U.S. 622 (1996).

Facts. Colorado voters adopted an amendment to the Colorado Constitution that prohibited all legislative, executive, or judicial action at any level of state or local government designed to confer a protected status upon, or to allow claims of discrimination by, any person based on homosexual, lesbian, or bisexual orientation. Evans (P) initiated litigation to have the amendment declared unconstitutional. The Colorado Supreme Court held that the amendment was subject to strict scrutiny because it infringed the fundamental right of homosexuals to participate in the political process, and, after remand to the trial court, held the amendment unconstitutional. The Supreme Court granted certiorari.

Issue. May a state prohibit governmental action that confers a protected status upon, or allows claims of discrimination by, any person based on homosexual, lesbian, or bisexual orientation?

Held. No. Judgment affirmed.

♦ D claims that the amendment simply puts homosexuals in the same position as all other persons; *i.e.*, it does no more than deny homosexuals special rights. However, the actual effect of the amendment is to put homosexuals in a solitary class with respect to transactions and relations in both the private and governmental spheres. It imposes a special disability upon these persons by forbidding them to seek or enjoy the safeguards against discrimination that other groups can enjoy.

♦ To reconcile the Equal Protection Clause with the reality that most legislation creates classes, the Court has held that legislation that neither burdens a fundamental right nor targets a suspect class will be upheld so long as the classification bears a rational relation to some legitimate end. The amendment in this case has the peculiar property of imposing a broad and undifferentiated disability on a single named group, and its breadth is so discontinuous with the purported reasons for it that it cannot be explained by anything but animus toward homosexuals. As such, it lacks a rational relationship to legitimate state interests.

♦ Animus toward a politically unpopular group cannot constitute a legitimate state interest. The interest asserted by D is respect for other citizens' freedom of association, such as the liberties of employers or landlords who oppose homosexuality. But the breadth of the amendment is so far removed from these justifications that they cannot reasonably be deemed the true legitimate purpose of the amendment.

Dissent (Scalia, J., Rehnquist, C.J., Thomas, J.). This amendment is a modest attempt to preserve traditional sexual mores against the efforts of a politically powerful minority to revise those mores through the use of the laws. The majority has made the Court accept the proposition that opposition to homosexuality is as reprehensible as racial or religious bias. But the Constitution says nothing about the subject, and the resolution of such public values should be left to the democratic processes, not the courts. The only denial of equal treatment articulated by the Court is that homosexuals may not obtain preferential treatment without modifying the state constitution. Furthermore, there was a legitimate rational basis for the amendment. In *Bowers v. Hardwick*, 478 U.S. 186 (1986), the Court held that the Constitution does not prohibit making homosexual conduct a crime. If a state may make homosexual conduct criminal, it should be allowed to enact laws disfavoring homosexual conduct; and if so, it should certainly be allowed to adopt a provision that does not even disfavor homosexual conduct but merely prohibits special protections for homosexuals. The animus toward homosexuals—moral disapproval of homosexual conduct—is the same "animus" that for centuries led to criminalization of homosexual conduct. Congress itself required the states of Arizona, New Mexico, Oklahoma, and Utah to adopt, as a condition of statehood, a ban against polygamy. The Court has approved this criminalization of polygamy; thus the Court has today concluded that the perceived social harm of polygamy is a legitimate concern of government, and the perceived social harm of homosexuality is not. The amendment is simply designed to prevent piecemeal deterioration of the sexual morality favored by a majority of Coloradans, and should be upheld.

D. MINIMUM RATIONALITY REVIEW OF ECONOMIC REGULATION

1. **Introduction.** Racial and other suspect classifications merit a stringent standard of review, while other classifications are upheld as long as they pass a rational basis review. A statute's legislative purpose usually may be defined so that the statutory classification is rationally related to it. The classification will necessarily be rationally related to such a purpose because the reach of the purpose is derived from the classification itself. The courts may still find that the purpose was illegitimate, or that while the purpose was legitimate, the classification did not rationally further the specified purpose.

2. **Judicial Deference to Economic Regulation.**

   a. **Deference to ends--**

Railway Express Agency v. New York, 336 U.S. 106 (1949).

Facts. The city of New York (P) passed a traffic regulation that prohibited advertising on vehicles except for "business notices upon business delivery vehicles" engaged in the usual business of the vehicle's owner. Railway Express Agency (D), a nationwide express business, sold the space on its trucks for advertising by other businesses, and was convicted for violation of P's regulation. The trial court found a reasonable basis for the regulation and upheld the conviction. D appeals.

Issue. May a local business regulation make distinctions based on practical considerations but which are theoretically discriminatory?

Held. Yes. Judgment affirmed.

- D's equal protection argument is based on the allegedly irrational distinction between allowing owner-advertising but banning advertising-for-hire. However, P may have concluded that the former type of advertising is less distracting and possibly necessary for business. Equal protection questions are answered by such practical considerations based on experience rather than by purely theoretical inconsistencies.

Concurrence (Jackson, J.). The Equal Protection Clause is properly invoked as the best measure to assure just laws.

Comment. The ends—safety—were arguably served by the means—prohibition on advertising. Still, this opinion reflects extreme deference to the legislature's judgment.

---

b. **Deference to means-ends relationships.**

1) **One step at a time.** In *Williamson v. Lee Optical Co.*, 348 U.S. 483 (1955), the Court held that the legislature could take one step at a time in solving problems, as long as it made no invidious discrimination. Thus, the state could regulate opticians while exempting sellers of ready-to-wear glasses.

2) **Preservation of appearance and custom.** In determining that state economic regulations are not subject to strict judicial scrutiny, the Burger Court in *New Orleans v. Dukes*, 427 U.S. 297 (1976), overruled the only decision since the late 1930s that had struck down an economic regulation on equal protection grounds. [*See* Morey v. Doud, 354 U.S. 457 (1957)] The Court in *Dukes* upheld an exception to a general prohibition against pushcart foodstuff vendors in the French Quarter of New Orleans. The exception, a "grandfather provision," permitted vendors who had been in business for at least eight years to continue selling.

c. **Exception for classifications based on "animus."**

1) **Exclusion of households with unrelated persons.** *United States Department of Agriculture v. Moreno*, 413 U.S. 528 (1973), concerned a provision in the food stamp program that excluded any household containing an individual who was unrelated to any other members of the household. In finding the provision unconstitutional, the Court stated that a legislative classification must be sustained if it is rationally related to a legitimate government interest. However, the purposes of the Food Stamp Act were to "raise levels of nutrition among low-income households," and to increase utilization of food to "strengthen [the] agricultural economy." The Court found that the classification excluding households with nonrelatives was clearly irrelevant to the statute's purposes. The Court further observed that there were no other legitimate governmental interests that the classification rationally furthered. The legislative history indicated that the rule was intended to prevent "hippies" and "hippie communes" from receiving food stamps. Intent to harm a politically unpopular group cannot constitute a legitimate governmental interest.

2) **Exclusion of methadone users.** In *New York City Transit Authority v. Beazer*, 440 U.S. 568 (1979), the Court upheld the city's exclusion of all methadone users from any employment by the Transit Authority. Even though this could exclude methadone users who were actually qualified to work, the Court found that the classification served the general objectives of safety and efficiency and did not define a class based on an unpopular trait or affiliation.

d. **Property taxes.**

1) **Property tax scheme struck down.** In *Allegheny Pittsburgh Coal v. Webster County*, 488 U.S. 336 (1989), the Court held that it was unconstitutional, in light of West Virginia's requirement that property be taxed in proportion to its value, to assess one owner's property on the basis of a recent purchase price without also updating the assessments on neighboring property. The disparity caused the plaintiff to bear an unreasonably unequal tax burden.

2) **Property tax preferences upheld.** In *Nordlinger v. Hahn*, 505 U.S. 1 (1992), the Court upheld California's Proposition 13, which capped real property taxes at 1% of a property's "full cash value," defined as the assessed valuation as of the 1975-1976 tax year, or thereafter, the appraised value of the property when purchased or newly constructed. In 1988, Nordlinger purchased a house in California for $170,000. She then found out her property taxes were five times what her neighbors paid who owned their homes since 1975, and in fact were about the same as those paid by the owners

of a $2.1 million Malibu beachfront home. The Supreme Court applied the rational basis standard and found that there was a legitimate state interest in local neighborhood preservation, continuity, and stability, and that the tax system accomplished this by discouraging rapid turnover in ownership of homes and businesses. A second legitimate interest was protecting the reliance interest and expectations of existing owners who have vested expectations in their property. The Court distinguished *Allegheny Pittsburgh Coal Co. v. Webster County, supra*, where the Court invalidated a property tax scheme whereby the assessor modified only the assessments of recently purchased property, increasing the values up to 35 times those properties that had not been sold. According to the Court the difference between *Allegheny Pittsburgh* and Proposition 13 is that in *Allegheny Pittsburgh*, the inconsistent treatment was not rationally related to a legitimate purpose, and the West Virginia Constitution required that all property be taxed at a uniform rate according to its estimated market value. Here there was no suggestion that the unequal assessment practice was intended to achieve the benefits of an acquisition-value tax scheme. Justice Thomas thought that *Allegheny Pittsburgh* should be overruled. Justice Stevens dissented. He felt that Proposition 13 creates severe inequalities that are arbitrary and unreasonable and do not rationally further a legitimate state interest.

e. **Extent of deference accorded--**

United States Railroad Retirement Board v. Fritz, 449 U.S. 166 (1980).

Facts. In 1974, Congress fundamentally altered the railroad retirement system that had been in effect since 1937. Essentially, Congress acted to place the system on a sound financial basis by eliminating future accruals of "windfall" benefits, resulting from concurrent qualification for railroad retirement and social security. The new system established several classes of employees whose benefits would be computed differently. Fritz (P) represented a class of employees who had between 10 and 25 years of railroad employment but who would be denied "windfall" benefits because they had no "current connection" with the railroad industry in 1974 or as of the date of retirement. P claimed the new system violated the equal protection component of the Fifth Amendment. The district court agreed, and the United States Railroad Retirement Board (D) appeals.

Issue. May the Court uphold legislation by inquiring whether, based on the plain language of the statute, there is a plausible reason for the classification made without inquiring into the actual reason the statute was enacted?

Held. Yes. Judgment reversed.

- The district court held that a differentiation based on whether an employee was "active" in the railroad business in 1974 was not "rationally related" to the congressional purposes of ensuring the solvency of the railroad retirement system and protecting vested benefits. However, in recent years we have refused to invalidate economic legislation on equal protection grounds just because it was unwise or inartfully drawn.

- Congress could have eliminated "windfall" benefits entirely, so it is not improper to draw lines in order to phase out such benefits.

- D has advanced plausible reasons for Congress's action. Thus, this Court's inquiry is at its end. It is constitutionally irrelevant whether this reasoning in fact underlays the legislative decision. We cannot say that Congress was unaware of what it accomplished or that it was misled by the groups that appeared before it.

Concurrence (Stevens, J.).

- The dissent correctly points out that a test using any "conceivable basis" reduces judicial review to a meaningless exercise. P represents a small class of persons deprived of vested rights while others in a substantially similar position have those rights enhanced. The proper inquiry should be whether there is a correlation between the classification and either the actual purpose or a purpose we may legitimately presume to have motivated an impartial legislature.

- The determinative questions are whether Congress may deprive some persons of benefits while enhancing other persons' benefits, and whether it can classify persons based on how recent their employment was. Both questions must be answered affirmatively.

Dissent (Brennan, Marshall, JJ.).

- The Court's approach here virtually immunizes social and economic legislative classifications from judicial review. The rational basis standard is not "toothless." The test requires examination of both the purposes of the statute and the relationship of the classification to that purpose. The classification here is not only rationally unrelated to the congressional purpose; it is inimical to it.

- The Court avoids serious analysis by, first, assuming purpose from result (Congress intended to do what it did do); second, by disregarding Congress's actual stated purpose for an unsupported justification that conflicts with the stated purpose; and third, by failing to ascertain whether the classification is rationally related to the identified purpose.

- Equitable considerations of need, reasonable expectation and reliance, and contribution to the system show that P has as great a claim to earned dual benefits as those permitted to retain such benefits. The fortuity of one day of employment in a particular year is an irrational basis for classification.

♦ Application of the Court's new analysis will mean that in future cases, we will defer not to the considered judgment of Congress, but to the arguments of skilled government litigators.

E. THE "FUNDAMENTAL INTERESTS" BRANCH OF EQUAL PROTECTION

1. **Introduction.** In addition to the suspect classifications that merit strict scrutiny, the Court has also applied heightened review when a classification impinges on a "fundamental" interest. Such fundamental interests include voting and access to the courts.

2. **Fundamental Interest in Voting.**

   a. **Constitutional provisions.**

      1) **Fourteenth Amendment.**

      "Section 1. . . . No State shall . . . deny to any person within its jurisdiction the equal protection of the laws."

      "Section 5. The Congress shall have power to enforce, by appropriate legislation, the provisions of this article."

      2) **Fifteenth Amendment.**

      "Section 1. The right of the citizens of the United States to vote shall not be denied or abridged by the United States or by any State on account of race, color, or previous condition of servitude."

      "Section 2. The Congress shall have power to enforce this article by appropriate legislation."

      3) **Nineteenth Amendment.** "The right of citizens of the United States to vote shall not be denied or abridged by the United States or by any State on account of sex."

      4) **Twenty-Fourth Amendment.** "The right of citizens of the United States to vote in any primary or other election for President or Vice President, for electors for President or Vice President, or for Senator or Representative in Congress, shall not be denied or abridged by the United States or any State by reason of failure to pay any poll tax or other tax."

5) **Twenty-Sixth Amendment.** "The right of citizens of the United States, who are eighteen years of age or older, to vote shall not be denied or abridged by the United States or any State on account of age."

b. **Denial of right to vote.**

1) **Voter qualifications—general elections--**

Harper v. Virginia State Board of Elections, 383 U.S. 663 (1966).

Facts. Harper (P) and other Virginia residents brought suit to have Virginia's poll tax declared unconstitutional. The district court, under *Breedlove v. Suttles*, 302 U.S. 277 (1937), dismissed P's complaint; P appeals.

Issue. May a state exact a poll tax as a condition for exercise of the right to vote?

Held. No. Judgment reversed.

♦ Once the franchise is granted to the electorate, lines may not be drawn that are inconsistent with the Equal Protection Clause of the Fourteenth Amendment. Lines drawn by the affluence of the voter or by the payment of any fee violate equal protection, which requires equal participation by all voters. Undoubtedly states may impose reasonable voter qualifications, but these must pass careful scrutiny since the franchise is a fundamental political right. Wealth or payment of a fee is an irrelevant factor in measuring a voter's qualifications. Notions of what constitutes equal treatment for purposes of the Equal Protection Clause change, and *Breedlove* is overruled.

Dissent (Black, J.). The Court has ignored the original meaning of the Constitution and has instead given the Equal Protection Clause a new meaning according to the Court's idea of a better governmental policy. Such changes are unjustifiable; they should be made only through the proper amendment procedure.

Dissent (Harlan, Stewart, JJ.). The decision to abolish state poll taxes for state elections ought to be made by the states, not the United States Supreme Court.

2) **Voter qualification—limited purpose elections--**

Kramer v. Union Free School District No. 15, 395 U.S. 621 (1969).

Facts. Kramer (P) challenged a state law that restricted eligibility to vote in certain school district elections to those who either own or lease taxable real property within the district, or who are parents (or have custody of) children enrolled in the local public schools. The lower courts upheld the law; P appeals.

Issue. May a state restrict the franchise for limited purpose elections merely on a showing of a rational basis for the restrictions?

Held. No. Judgment reversed.

- Statutes denying some residents the right to vote impinge on one of the most fundamental rights of a democratic society. Accordingly, such exclusions must be necessary to promote a compelling state interest.

- Even if the state interests here are substantial enough to justify limiting the exercise of the franchise to those "primarily interested" or "primarily affected" (which is not decided), this statute is not narrowly drawn to effectuate that purpose. It is both underinclusive and overinclusive. Therefore, it cannot stand.

Dissent (Stewart, Black, Harlan, JJ.). If a state may impose valid restrictions based on residence, literacy, and age, it ought to be able to impose these requirements, which are rational. The Court should apply only the traditional equal protection standard.

---

3. Strict Scrutiny of Vote Denials.

a. **Special purpose elections.** In *Cipriano v. City of Houma*, 395 U.S. 701 (1969), a state law granted only property taxpayers the right to vote in elections to approve municipal utility bonds. The Court held the restriction invalid since all citizens have an interest in the quality of utility services and rates. In *Phoenix v. Kolodziejski*, 399 U.S. 204 (1970), the Court held that a statute limiting the vote for the issuance of general obligation bonds to real property owners was unconstitutional even though only property taxes would pay for the improvements, since all residents were said to have a substantial interest in the municipal improvements to be made. But in *Salyer Land Co. v. Tulare Lake Basin Water Storage District*, 410 U.S. 719 (1973), the Court upheld an election scheme in which only landowners could vote for the members of the district board, because costs were assessed against land benefited. The board had a special limited purpose, and its activities disproportionately affected landowners as a group.

b. **Disenfranchisement of felons.** In *Richardson v. Ramirez*, 418 U.S. 24 (1974), the Court held that the states may disenfranchise convicted felons because section 2 of the Fourteenth Amendment specifically permits such a limitation on the right to vote.

4. Vote "Dilution": Reapportionment and Gerrymandering.

a. **Reapportionment.**

1) **Pre-1962—nonjusticiable.** The decision in *Colegrove v. Green*, 328 U.S. 549 (1946), reflected the Court's early attitude regarding state districting disputes. It refused to consider the merits of an equal protection challenge to a state's congressional districting plan on the grounds that the issue was nonjusticiable.

2) **Equal participation by voters--**

Reynolds v. Sims, 377 U.S. 533 (1964).

Facts. Sims (P) and others challenged the apportionment of the Alabama Legislature, which was based on the 1900 federal census and thus seriously discriminated against voters who lived in the area whose population had grown disproportionately in the intervening years. The district court ordered temporary reapportionment; Reynolds (D) and other state officials appeal.

Issue. Must a state apportion its legislative districts on the basis of population?

Held. Yes. Judgment affirmed.

- ♦ The right to vote is essential to a democratic society, and is denied by abasement or dilution of a citizen's vote just as effectively as by wholly prohibiting the free exercise of the franchise. The fundamental principle of representative government is one of equal representation for equal numbers of people, regardless of race, sex, economic status, or place of residence within a state.

- ♦ The Equal Protection Clause guarantees the opportunity for equal participation by all voters in the election of state legislators. Therefore, votes cannot be weighed differently on the basis of where the voters happen to reside. This applies whether the state legislature is unicameral or bicameral.

- ♦ Congress cannot be taken as a guide for state legislative district apportionment because it arose from unique historical circumstances, and represents a union of sovereigns. Political subdivisions of states never have been sovereign entities in that sense.

- ♦ Each state district must contain as nearly an equal population as possible, although precision, being impossible, is not required. Substantial equality of population must be the overriding objective. States need not perpetually update their apportionment plans, but there must be a reasonable plan for periodic readjustment.

Dissent (Harlan, J.). The history of the adoption of the Fourteenth Amendment shows that the Equal Protection Clause was not meant to limit the power of the states to apportion their legislatures as they saw fit.

Dissent (Stewart, Clark, JJ.). A state's plan for legislative apportionment must be rational and not permit the systematic frustration of the will of a majority of the electorate. So long as a plan achieves effective and balanced representation of the variety of social and economic interests of the state, it cannot be considered irrational.

Comment. In one of the five companion cases to *Reynolds* involving the Colorado apportionment scheme, *Lucas v. Forty-Fourth General Assembly*, 377 U.S. 713 (1964), the Court held that the fact that a scheme had been approved by the state's voters is without constitutional significance.

---

b. **Political gerrymandering.**

1) **Political factors permissible.** In *Gaffney v. Cummings*, 412 U.S. 735 (1973), the Court held that a state may consider political factors as well as census data in creating its legislative districts. The Court pointed out that the very essence of districting is to produce a more "politically fair" result than elections at large, in which the winning party would take all legislative seats; political considerations are inseparable from districting and apportionment. The Court explained that the danger arises from manipulation intended to minimize or eliminate the political strength of any group or party.

2) **Political gerrymandering justiciable--**

Davis v. Bandemer, 478 U.S. 109 (1986).

Facts. Indiana's 1981 state apportionment was enacted by the Republican-controlled state legislature and signed by the Republican governor. Democrats claimed that the apportionment was a gerrymander intended to disadvantage Democrats on a statewide basis. The lower courts agreed. The Supreme Court granted certiorari.

Issue. Is a threshold showing of discriminatory vote dilution required for a prima facie case of an equal protection violation?

Held. Yes. Judgment reversed.

- ♦ Ps have the burden to prove both intentional discrimination against an identifiable political group and an actual discriminatory effect on that group. The intention requirement was satisfied by the district court's findings, and at any rate, is virtually inherent in the legislative process of redistricting.

- ♦ However, the district court's findings that the plan had such an adverse effect on Ps as to constitute a violation of the Equal Protection Clause is not sustainable. The Constitution does not require proportional representation, nor does it require a plan that draws lines as near as possible to allocating seats to the contending parties in proportion to what their anticipated statewide vote will be.

- Winner-take-all district-based elections inherently present the potential for disproportionate party representation as compared with the popular vote. Challenges to multi-member districts require a showing much greater than mere lack of proportional representation. One consideration is the responsiveness of elected officials to the concerns of the groups involved, because even defeated parties have influence on the winning candidate. The test is whether the electoral system is arranged so as to consistently degrade a voter's or a group's influence on the political process as a whole.

- The district court relied primarily on the results of the 1982 election. One election is not enough to prove unconstitutional discrimination. There was no finding that the plan would render the Democrats a minority party throughout the 1980s.

Concurrence (O'Connor, J., Burger, C.J., Rehnquist, J.). Political gerrymandering is a political question and the Court should avoid these cases lest it mandate a system of proportional representation for political parties.

Dissent (Powell, Stevens, JJ.). A partisan political gerrymander violates equal protection only when it is intentionally and actually discriminatory against an identifiable political group. While it may be difficult for courts to protect against this form of discrimination, appropriate judicial standards can and should be developed to prevent creation of voting districts that are distorted deliberately and arbitrarily to achieve illegitimate ends.

Comments.

- The Court was initially reluctant to consider purely political gerrymandering as a possible equal protection violation in *Gaffney v. Cummings*, *supra*, because political fairness is the essence of districting.

- In *Vieth v. Jubelirer*, 541 U.S. 267 (2004), in an opinion by Justice Scalia, a plurality would have held that political gerrymandering claims are nonjusticiable because there are no judicially discernible and manageable standards for adjudicating such claims. Justice Kennedy, concurring in the judgment, agreed that there were no existing manageable standards for adjudicating political gerrymandering claims. But he concluded that the courts should continue to adjudicate such claims because such a standard might one day be discovered.

---

5. Fundamental Right to Access to Courts.

a. **Source of interest.** The Court has shown sensitivity to burdens placed on the access of litigants, especially criminal defendants, to the courts. Both procedural due process and equal protection have been invoked for analysis.

b. **Right to a record on appeal.** The "access to courts" principle evolved in *Griffin v. Illinois*, 351 U.S. 12 (1956), wherein the Supreme Court relied on equal protection to hold that in a state prosecution where no appeal was possible without a transcript from the trial court, the state must provide indigent defendants a free transcript in all felony criminal cases. The rationale is that in criminal prosecutions (where the defendant is involuntarily involved), matters of "justice" are charged with too much social interest to be decided on the basis of some defendants being poor and others being rich. The dissent argued that due process did not require this result, since there is no constitutional right to an appeal, and equal protection was not applicable because the state was treating everyone the same.

c. **Right to counsel on appeal.** The Court in *Douglas v. California*, 372 U.S. 353 (1963), extended the *Griffin* holding to include an indigent's right to appointed counsel in a first appeal when the right to a first appeal has been granted by the state. In *Ross v. Moffit*, 417 U.S. 600 (1974), the Court refused to extend the *Douglas* approach to discretionary appeals.

d. **Economic barriers and civil litigation.** In many of these cases, there is some disagreement as to the appropriate theory on which to proceed (equal protection or due process).

1) For example, in the civil area in *Boddie v. Connecticut*, 401 U.S. 371 (1971), the Court used the Due Process Clause to hold that states may not require the payment of court fees, as a condition for judicial dissolution of marriage, from indigents who in good faith seek a divorce. The Court limited the scope of the decision by noting (i) the basic position of the "marriage relationship" in society, and (ii) the "state monopolization of the means for legally dissolving this relationship." It reasoned that due process requires that "absent a countervailing state interest of overriding significance, persons forced to settle their claims . . . through the judicial process must be given a meaningful opportunity to be heard."

2) When the issue of the applicability of *Boddie* in other civil contexts reached the Court, the Court read *Boddie* narrowly. In *United States v. Kras*, 409 U.S. 434 (1973), the Court held that the Bankruptcy Act filing fee requirement as a condition for discharge is

"rational" and does not violate equal protection as applied to indigent persons who seek voluntary bankruptcy. The right to bankruptcy is not a "fundamental" interest but is in the "area of economics and social welfare."

3) The same rationale was used for *Ortwein v. Schwab*, 410 U.S. 656 (1973) (filing fee for judicial review of administrative ruling on welfare decision).

4) In *Little v. Streater*, 452 U.S. 1 (1981), the Court applied *Boddie* to hold that an indigent defendant in a paternity action is entitled to state-subsidized blood grouping tests. Such tests can be exculpatory, and the proceedings have quasi-criminal aspects.

e. **Termination of parental rights--**

M.L.B. v. S.L.J., 519 U.S. 102 (1996).

Facts. M.L.B. (D) had her parental rights to her two young children terminated by a Mississippi court. D tried to appeal, but the state required payment of record preparation fees of over $2,300 in advance. D could not afford this fee, and her appeal was dismissed. D appeals, claiming the fee requirement deprived her of due process and equal protection.

Issue. May a state require payment of fees for a party to appeal the termination by the state of her parental rights?

Held. No. Judgment reversed and remanded.

- Under *Griffin, supra*, a state may not make access to appellate processes dependent on the convicted defendant's ability to pay. *Griffin* applies to criminal cases, but in some civil cases, the state must also provide access to its judicial processes regardless of the party's ability to pay fees, such as in divorce cases. In civil cases, this is the exception, not the rule.

- Parental status termination decrees are unlike other civil actions, even those involving divorce, paternity, and child custody. Termination decrees work a unique kind of deprivation because through them, the state permanently destroys all legal recognition of the parental relationship. For that reason, Mississippi may not withhold from D "a record of sufficient completeness" to permit proper appellate consideration of D's claims.

Concurrence (Kennedy, J.). This case can be decided exclusively on due process.

Dissent (Thomas, J., Rehnquist, C.J., Scalia, J.). Under *Washington v. Davis, supra*, the Equal Protection Clause protects only against purposeful discrimination, not disparate impact. The Clause seeks to guarantee equal laws, not equal results. The state had no requirement to give D an opportunity to appeal, so it should not have to also pay for that appeal. The requirement of prepaid transcripts in civil appeals is facially neutral and does not create a classification.

---

6. No Fundamental Interest in Food, Shelter, Education.

a. **Welfare benefits.** There is no constitutional right to receive public welfare. Welfare classifications are subject only to the traditional equal protection test; *e.g.*, in *Dandridge v. Williams*, 397 U.S. 471 (1970), the Court upheld a state regulation that placed an absolute limit on the ***amount*** of welfare assistance, regardless of need.

b. **Housing.** The right to housing is not guaranteed in the Constitution. State classifications in housing laws are subject only to the traditional test of reasonableness; *e.g.*, a state may permit landlords to bring summary actions to evict tenants from rented premises but cannot require posting of a bond for twice the amount of rent in order to appeal. [Lindsey v. Normet, 405 U.S. 56 (1972)]

c. **Education.**

1) **School financing--**

San Antonio Independent School District v. Rodriguez, 411 U.S. 1 (1973).

Facts. Rodriguez (P), a Mexican-American, challenged the Texas system of financing public education. The system involved a combination of state, local, and federal funding, and was operated such that state and local expenditures per pupil varied according to the market value of taxable property per pupil within the various districts. P claims the system denies equal protection by invidiously discriminating against the poor. The district court found the system unconstitutional. The San Antonio School District (D) appeals.

Issue. Must a state system of financing public education, which closely correlates spending per pupil and the value of local taxable property, pass strict judicial scrutiny to be valid?

Held. No. Judgment reversed.

- D's system might be regarded as discriminating against functionally indigent persons, against persons relatively poorer than others, or against all who, regardless of their personal incomes, happen to reside in relatively poorer school districts. However, there is no evidence to support a finding that any persons in the first two groups are discriminated against, and the third group clearly cannot fit the traditional definition of a suspect class.

- ♦ Although the system does not operate to the peculiar disadvantage of any suspect class, strict review is still required where the state's action impermissibly interferes with the exercise of a "fundamental" right, which P claims includes education. Although education is an important state service, that importance is not determinative of equal protection examination. Only those rights explicitly or implicitly guaranteed by the Constitution are "fundamental" for purposes of equal protection. Education is neither explicitly nor implicitly guaranteed. Additionally, D's system was implemented to extend public education, not to interfere with any rights. Finally, courts ought not interfere with state fiscal policies if not necessary. Therefore, D's system is not subject to strict judicial scrutiny.

- ♦ D concedes that its system is not perfect, yet claims that it bears the necessary rational relationship to a legitimate state purpose. It is based on the state's experience and extensive consideration. Because the statute rationally furthers a legitimate state purpose, it is justifiable under the Equal Protection Clause.

Concurrence (Stewart, J.). The Equal Protection Clause confers no substantive rights but merely measures the validity of classifications created by state laws.

Dissent (White, Douglas, Brennan, JJ.). The Court merely requires D to establish that unequal treatment is in furtherance of a permissible goal, but it should also require D to show that the means chosen to effectuate that goal are rationally related to its achievement.

Dissent (Marshall, Douglas, JJ.). The Court appears to find only two standards of equal protection review—strict scrutiny or mere rationality. In reality, there is a wide spectrum of review depending on the constitutional and societal importance of the interest adversely affected and the recognized invidiousness of the classification. The amount of review accorded to unconstitutional rights or interests varies according to the nexus between those rights and specific constitutional guarantees. Discrimination on the basis of group wealth in this case calls for careful judicial scrutiny.

---

2) **Education of children of illegal aliens.** In *Plyer v. Doe*, 457 U.S. 202 (1982), the Court held that a state may not deny to undocumented school-age children the free public education it provides to citizens and legally admitted aliens. Texas had enacted a statute that withheld state funds for the education of illegal alien children and that allowed local school districts to deny enrollment to such children. The Court noted that an equal protection analysis does

not require that illegal aliens be treated as a suspect class because, unlike most suspect classifications, entry into this class is the product of voluntary action. However, this case presented another consideration; the Texas law was directed against the minor children of such illegal entrants, and it imposed its discriminatory burden on the basis of a legal characteristic that the children did not control. The Court explained that although public education is not a fundamental right, it is more than a mere government benefit. Moreover, denying these children a basic education would impose a lifetime hardship and the stigma of illiteracy on a discrete class of innocent children. The Court applied heightened scrutiny and found that the discrimination contained in the Texas statute could not be considered rational unless it furthered a substantial goal. Justice Blackmun, concurring, added that because of the political disadvantage incurred by uneducated persons, denial of an education is the analogue of denial of the right to vote. Justice Powell also concurred, saying that the legislative classification threatened the creation of an underclass of future residents.

X. THE RECONSTRUCTION AMENDMENTS: STATE ACTION AND CONGRESSIONAL POWER TO ENFORCE CIVIL RIGHTS

A. CIVIL RIGHTS LEGISLATION

1. Introduction.

a. **The post-Civil War amendments.** As previously discussed, each of the post-Civil War amendments gives Congress power to enforce its provisions by appropriate legislation. The Fourteenth and Fifteenth Amendments are directed at governmental behavior; the Thirteenth Amendment is not so limited. When Congress acts under the Fourteenth or Fifteenth Amendment, therefore, the question of what constitutes "state action" becomes important. The other main issue in this area is the actual scope of the power conferred on Congress.

b. **Legislative framework.** Congress has acted under the post-Civil War amendments in two phases—just after the Civil War, and again starting in the 1950s.

1) **Reconstruction statutes.** To counteract the state "black codes" impairing the legal rights of blacks, Congress passed the 1866 Civil Rights Act, which spelled out certain rights held by all persons born in the United States. [*See* 42 U.S.C. §§1981, 1982] Depriving another person of these rights was a criminal offense. [18 U.S.C. §242] The 1870 Act enforced voting rights, but also outlawed private conspiracies to violate federal rights. [*See* 18 U.S.C. §241] The Civil Rights Act of 1871 provided a civil cause of action for the deprivation, under color of state law, of a person's federal rights. [*See* 42 U.S.C. §1983]

2) **Modern statutes.** The 1964 Civil Rights Act covered voting rights, school desegregation, and desegregation of public accommodations. The 1965 Voting Rights Act further ensured equal access to the franchise.

B. THE REQUIREMENT OF STATE ACTION

1. State Action in the Nineteenth Century.

a. **In general.** Both the Fourteenth and Fifteenth Amendments indicate that only "state action" (as opposed to private, nongovernmental action) that violates the amendments is prohibited. The early cases held that these amendments therefore did not apply to private acts of discrimination; *i.e.*, that individuals were free to discriminate if they chose to do so.

b. **The Civil Rights Act of 1875--**

The Civil Rights Cases, 109 U.S. 3 (1883).

Facts. The Civil Rights Act of 1875 made it unlawful for anyone to deny a person the enjoyment of accommodations at inns, on public transportation, etc., on the basis of race. These cases arose when certain black persons (Ps) were excluded from hotels, theatres, and railroad cars. The cases were consolidated before the Supreme Court.

Issue. May Congress prohibit private discriminatory actions?

Held. No.

- The Fourteenth Amendment prohibits only state action, and the Thirteenth Amendment term "slavery" does not include the kind of discrimination involved here.

- Congress had no power to pass the Civil Rights Act of 1875, and Ps must seek their remedy in state law for any cause of action against private individuals or corporations who are discriminating.

Dissent (Harlan, J.). The Court has ignored the substance and spirit of these amendments. Freedom includes immunity from and protection against racial discrimination, particularly in the use of public, albeit privately owned, accommodations and facilities licensed by the state.

Comment. The common law of all states at the time of the Civil Rights Act of 1875 held that it was unlawful to deny the facilities of inns and carriers to any person. Therefore, Ps did have a remedy in state law. The major premise of the *Civil Rights Cases*—that the Fourteenth Amendment prohibits state, not private, action—is still good law. The definition of state action has undergone change, however.

---

c. **Private conduct.** In *United States v. Cruikshank*, 92 U.S. 542 (1875), the Court stated that the Fourteenth Amendment does not add anything to the rights of one citizen against another; *i.e.*, it does not reach private action. However, private conduct that affected constitutional rights not subject to the state action limitation could still be regulated by Congress.

2. State Action in the Twentieth Century.

a. The "public function" analysis.

1) **The private company town.** In *Marsh v. Alabama*, 326 U.S. 501 (1946), a private corporation owned a town and posted signs prohibiting peddlers. Marsh (a Jehovah's Witness) distributed religious literature on the streets of the company town and was convicted of violating a state trespass law that made it a crime "to enter or remain on the premises of another" after being warned not to do so. The conviction was reversed because the town's streets, although privately owned, were in effect a public place. The Court held that neither the state nor any private owner can totally ban freedom of expression in public places; nor can state trespass laws be applied to enforce such a ban. "Ownership does not always mean absolute dominion. The more an owner opens up his property for use by the public in general, the more do his rights become circumscribed by the statutory and constitutional rights of those who use it." In other words, this case shows that state action includes not only any action taken directly by the state executive, legislative, or judicial branches, but also any such action taken indirectly by delegating public functions to private organizations or by controlling, affirming, or to some extent becoming involved in that private action.

2) **Shopping centers.** The Court has since held that the "company town" rationale does not extend to the passageways in a privately owned shopping center. [Hudgens v. NLRB, 424 U.S. 507 (1976), *overruling* Amalgamated Food Employees Union v. Logan Valley Plaza, 391 U.S. 308 (1968)]

3) **Parks.** In *Evans v. Newton*, 382 U.S. 296 (1966), the Court held that a park, which had been created pursuant to a trust, could not be operated on a racially restrictive basis as required by one of the trust provisions, even if the city, the original trustee, no longer operated it. In so ruling, the Court stated that although there was a private trustee, the operation of the park on a racially restrictive basis violated the Fourteenth Amendment because the city still provided maintenance and the service rendered by the park is municipal in nature. Later, in *Evans v. Abney*, 396 U.S. 435 (1970), the Court upheld the state court's termination of the trust creating the park because the decedent's intention that the park be operated for whites only was impossible to fulfill. The Court held that the reverter to the heirs violated no federal rights since the state court

decision to eliminate the park impacted equally on both black and white citizens. Compare this with *Shelley v. Kraemer, infra.*

b. **Conduct of elections—The White Primary Cases.** Since the conduct of elections is an exclusively public function, the Court has consistently invalidated state attempts to vest in private boards or political parties any effective control over the selection of candidates or the exercise of voting rights, as by:

1) Giving authority to a political party to determine who can vote in primary elections from which the party nominee for the general election is chosen [*see* Smith v. Allwright, 321 U.S. 649 (1944)]; or

2) Structuring the state's electoral apparatus to vest in a political party the power to hold a primary from which blacks are excluded, or to determine who shall run in the party primary in which blacks are permitted to participate [*see* Terry v. Adams, 345 U.S. 461 (1953)].

c. **The "nexus" analysis.**

1) **Enforcement of private contracts--**

Shelley v. Kraemer, 334 U.S. 1 (1948).

Facts. Shelley (D), a black person, purchased residential property that, unknown to D, was encumbered by a restrictive agreement that prevented ownership or occupancy of the property by non-Caucasians. Kraemer (P), a neighbor and owner of other property subject to the restriction, brought suit to restrain D from possessing the property and to divest title out of D. The trial court denied relief, but the Missouri Supreme Court reversed. D appeals.

Issue. Does the Fourteenth Amendment Equal Protection Clause prohibit judicial enforcement by state courts of restrictive covenants based on race or color?

Held. Yes. Judgment reversed.

♦ Property rights clearly are among those civil rights protected from discriminatory state action by the Fourteenth Amendment. Early decisions invalidated any government restrictions on residency based on race. Here the restrictions are purely private and, standing alone, are not precluded by the Fourteenth Amendment.

♦ Actions of state courts are state actions within the meaning of the Fourteenth Amendment. Judicial enforcement of these private racial restrictions constitutes state discrimination contrary to the Fourteenth Amendment, and denies D equal protection.

Comment. *Shelley* and other cases indicate that what is essentially a private act of discrimination may become illegal state action if somehow the state or its officers are in any way involved in carrying out the private action. Possibly any private action that gets into court may then amount to state action.

---

2) **Additional cases.** In *Barrows v. Jackson*, 346 U.S. 249 (1953), a case involving a damages action against a co-covenantor, the Court applied the *Shelley* reasoning to block enforcement of the restrictive covenant. The Court stated that it would not require a state to coerce a covenantor to respond in damages for failure to observe a covenant that the state would have no right to enforce. In *Pennsylvania v. Board of Trusts*, 353 U.S. 230 (1957), the Supreme Court held that a will that had discriminatory provisions might be infused with state action when enforced by a state court. There a private citizen willed his property to be used for a school for poor white orphan children, with the city council to serve as the board of trustees. Later, in a 3 to 3 decision rendered in a case involving a restaurant sit-in, the Court reversed trespass convictions on the basis of *Shelley*. The Court stated that the discrimination was done for business reasons and the property was associated with serving the public. The dissent, construing section 1 of the Fourteenth Amendment more narrowly, argued that without cooperative state action, no property owner was forbidden from banning people from his premises, even if the owner was acting with racial prejudice. [Bell v. Maryland, 378 U.S. 226 (1964)]

3) **Leasing of public property.** In *Burton v. Wilmington Parking Authority*, 365 U.S. 715 (1961), the Court held that a private lessee of state property is required to comply with the Fourteenth Amendment if the lease furthers state interests and forms an integral part of a state operation. In that case, Burton, a black person, was denied service at a private restaurant, the Eagle, located within a building owned and operated by the Wilmington Parking Authority, a state agency.

4) **Public use by private groups.** Following the particularized approach set forth in *Burton*, the Court remanded *Gilmore v. Montgomery*, 417 U.S. 556 (1974), an action involving a federal injunction barring a city from permitting private segregated school groups and racially discriminatory non-school groups from using the city's recreational facilities. The Court held that although exclusive temporary use interfered with a school desegregation order, the lower court's ruling against nonexclusive use by the groups,

especially the private non-school groups, was invalid without a proper finding of state action.

d. **State involvement through licensing.** In *Moose Lodge No. 107 v. Irvis*, 407 U.S. 163 (1972), the Court held that state alcoholic licensing of a private club does not constitute sufficient state action to require that the club observe Fourteenth Amendment prohibitions against discrimination. Irvis, a black person, had been refused service by Moose Lodge. Irvis claimed that the Lodge's refusal was state action because the Lodge was licensed by the state liquor board to sell alcoholic beverages. The Court reasoned that a private entity is not covered by the Fourteenth Amendment when it merely receives any sort of benefit or service at all from the state, or is subject to any state regulation. Otherwise, the distinction between private and public would be meaningless. If the impetus for the discrimination is private, state involvement must be significant to implicate constitutional standards. The Court found that, in this case, the state's liquor regulation in no way fostered or encouraged racial discrimination.

e. **Broadcast licenses.** In *CBS, Inc. v. Democratic National Committee*, 412 U.S. 94 (1973), a case sustaining the FCC's refusal to compel broadcasters to accept editorial advertisement, three of the Justices also concluded that the action of the licensee was not governmental action for purposes of the First Amendment, since the FCC had not fostered the policy and thus was not a partner to the action and did not profit from it.

f. **Facilitation or encouragement.** After California had enacted fair housing laws barring discrimination, voters passed an initiative (Proposition 14) amending the state constitution so as to prohibit the state from denying any person the right to sell, lease, or rent to whomever he chose. In *Reitman v. Mulkey*, 387 U.S. 369 (1967), a 5 to 4 Court affirmed the state supreme court's invalidation of Proposition 14. The Court stated that, while mere repeal of an antidiscrimination law is not per se unconstitutional state action, here the state was encouraging and significantly involved with private discrimination. The dissent opined that the provision merely assured state neutrality and no more violated the Fourteenth Amendment than would have failure to pass antidiscrimination laws in the first place.

1) **Comment.** "State action" exists whenever a state has affirmatively facilitated, encouraged, or authorized acts of discrimination by its citizens. States are not required to outlaw discrimination, but they cannot do anything to encourage it. [*See also* Jackson v. Metropolitan Edison Co., *infra*, and Flagg Brothers, Inc. v. Brooks, *infra*] Those cases rejected both the "public function" argument and the assertion that the state's authorization of the activity made the activity attributable to the state.

g. **Limitation of public function approach.**

1) **Utilities--**

Jackson v. Metropolitan Edison Co., 419 U.S. 345 (1974).

Facts. Metropolitan Edison (D), a private utility regulated by the state, terminated Jackson's (P's) electric service for nonpayment before affording P notice, hearing, and an opportunity to pay. P sued, contending D's action constituted state action depriving her of property without due process of law. The lower courts dismissed P's complaint; P appeals.

Issue. Does termination of service by a heavily regulated private utility, using procedures permitted by state law, constitute state action?

Held. No. Judgment affirmed.

- State regulation of a private business, even if extensive and detailed, does not by itself convert private action to state action for Fourteenth Amendment purposes. There must be a close nexus between the state and the actual activity of the regulated entity. D's monopoly status, by itself, fails to show such a nexus. Nor is D's service a public function, since the state has no obligation to furnish such service. The limited notion that businesses "affected with a public interest" are state actors cannot be expanded to include private utilities.

- The state concededly approved D's termination procedures, but not upon specific consideration. The state's approval amounts merely to a finding that the procedures are permissible under state law. For these reasons, D's actions cannot be considered to be state action.

Dissent (Marshall, J.). The essential nature of D's service requires that D be subject to the same standards as other governmental entities. The interests of diversity and flexibility that favor protection of private entities from constitutional standards are irrelevant in monopoly situations like D's. Finally, the majority's opinion would appear to apply to a broad range of claimed constitutional violations by the company, including racial discrimination.

2) **The insufficiency of state acquiescence.** In *Flagg Brothers, Inc. v. Brooks*, 436 U.S. 149 (1978), the Court held that a warehouseman's sale of goods entrusted to him for storage does not constitute state action merely because it is permitted by state law. When Brooks had failed to pay storage charges, Flagg Brothers, Inc. threatened to sell her possessions, pursuant to procedures established by

the New York Uniform Commercial Code ("U.C.C."). Brooks claimed that Flagg Brothers's action was state action because the state had authorized and encouraged it by enacting the U.C.C. The Court held that, while private action compelled by a state is properly attributable to the state, mere acquiescence by the state is insufficient.

h. **Further developments.** *Blum v. Yaretsky*, 457 U.S. 991 (1982), involved the transfer of nursing home patients from privately owned—but publicly subsidized—nursing homes to lower-cost facilities. As a result, the patients' Medicaid benefits were reduced. The Court held that, because the decisions were made by private physicians, no state action was involved and no violation of procedural due process had occurred. In *Rendell-Baker v. Kohn*, 457 U.S. 830 (1982), the Court held that a decision to fire a teacher, made by a small private school that was publicly subsidized and regulated, was not state action. However, in *Lugar v. Edmondson Oil Co.*, 457 U.S. 922 (1982), the Court upheld damages under section 1983 for conduct done "under color of state law" when the creditor had attached the debtor's property in an ex parte proceeding. The Court held that this was state action because the writ was issued and executed by state officials.

i. **Promulgation of rules adopted by state university.** In *NCAA v. Tarkanian*, 488 U.S. 179 (1988), the Court held that a public university's disciplinary action against its employee, taken in response to encouragement by the NCAA, a private organization, would not render the NCAA's action "state action." The Court noted that the NCAA and the university were adversaries, not partners, and that the university's adoption of NCAA standards did not mean the NCAA acted under color of state law in establishing those standards. [*See also* San Francisco Arts and Athletics v. United States Olympic Committee, 483 U.S. 522 (1987)—United States Olympic Committee not a governmental actor by exercise of right, granted by Congress, to prohibit certain commercial uses of word "Olympic"]

j. **Peremptory juror challenges.** Contrary to most of the recent state action decisions, the Court in *Edmonson v. Leesville Concrete Co.*, 500 U.S. 614 (1991), found state action in a nongovernmental decision where a private civil litigant used peremptory challenges to exclude jurors on the basis of race. The state was overtly participating in a significant manner because peremptory challenges were creatures of statutory authorization and have no significance outside a court of law.

k. **Failure to act.** A state agency's failure to intervene and take custody of a minor after receiving reports of child abuse did not constitute actionable state action because the Due Process Clause does not require the government to protect the life, liberty, and property of its citizens against invasion by private actors. [DeShaney v. Winnebago County Social Services Department, 489 U.S. 189 (1989)]

C. CONGRESSIONAL POWER TO REACH PRIVATE INTERFERENCE WITH CONSTITUTIONAL RIGHTS

1. **Introduction.** As discussed *supra*, Congress has enacted civil and criminal statutes aimed at preventing private interference with constitutional rights. 18 U.S.C. section 241 makes private conspiracies illegal, for example. Three basic issues arise when these laws are applied. First, what is the constitutional source of the power exercised by Congress? Second, is the statute sufficiently specific to be enforceable? Third, should the statute be enforced by its terms or is the state action limitation implicit? The basic statutes may be kept straight by referring to the following table:

	Criminal	Civil
Color of law	18 U.S.C. 242	42 U.S.C. 1983
Conspiracy	18 U.S.C. 241	42 U.S.C. 1985(3)

2. **Criminal Sanctions.**

   a. **Private action without state action--**

United States v. Guest, 383 U.S. 745 (1966).

Facts. Guest (D) and others were indicted for criminal conspiracy to deprive black citizens of the right to equal utilization of public facilities and of the right to travel. The district court dismissed the indictment for failure to charge an offense under the laws of the United States. The government appeals.

Issue. May Congress include Fourteenth Amendment rights within the scope of a criminal statute prohibiting private action?

Held. Yes. Judgment reversed.

- ♦ The statute is not unconstitutionally vague. The rights under the Equal Protection Clause, endangered by D's conspiracy, are firmly and precisely established by prior decisions.

- ♦ No determination of the threshold level of state action necessary to create equal protection rights is required here, because the indictment alleges that D sought, among other things, to have blacks falsely arrested; such activity sufficiently implicates the state.

- Interference with the right to travel (and to use highway facilities) also implicates a basic constitutional right, long recognized, which Congress has authority to protect.

Concurrence (Clark, Black, Fortas, JJ.). Congress has authority to punish all conspiracies, with or without state action, that interfere with Fourteenth Amendment rights.

Concurrence and dissent (Harlan, J.). The Constitution creates no rights of private individuals as against other private individuals. Because there was no state action involved with D's attempt to interfere with the right to travel, the Court is wrong on this point.

Concurrence and dissent (Brennan, Warren, Douglas, JJ.). Congress may reach purely private activity under the Enabling Clause of the Fourteenth Amendment, even though only governmental activity is restricted by the Constitution itself. This also applies to the right to travel, which Congress, not the Constitution, protects as against purely private infringement.

---

b. **State-involved private interference.**

1) When private individuals willfully engage in a "joint activity" with state officials to infringe the civil rights of others, the private individuals as well as the state officers are subject to sanctions under federal law passed pursuant to the enabling provisions of the Fourteenth Amendment. [*See* United States v. Price, 383 U.S. 787 (1966)]

2) In *Williams v. United States*, 341 U.S. 97 (1951), the Supreme Court affirmed the conviction of the defendant (under 18 U.S.C. section 242) where he, as a private detective who had been issued a special police officer's badge, was employed by a lumber company to investigate thefts of its property, and along with a regular police officer took four suspects to a shack and beat them until they confessed.

3) In *Screws v. United States*, 325 U.S. 91 (1945), the Supreme Court held that Congress can enforce the limitations of the Fourteenth Amendment by enacting legislation (here 18 U.S.C. section 242—persons, under color of law, that subject inhabitants of a state to deprivation of constitutional rights on the basis of race or color, other than those prescribed by law, can be fined or imprisoned) authorizing civil or criminal convictions of state authorities acting on behalf of or clothed with government authority who misuse their authority, even though such misuse also violates state law.

The case upheld a federal statute as applied to a state officer who arrested a black man on false pretext and then beat him to death without provocation.

3. **Civil Sanctions for Private Conspiracies.** In *Griffin v. Breckenridge*, 413 U.S. 88 (1971), a unanimous Court discarded its prior narrow interpretation of 42 U.S.C. section 1985(3) (formerly 1985(c)) that denial of "the equal protection of the laws, or of equal privileges and immunities under the laws" was applicable only to conspiracies under color of state law. *Griffin* concluded that Congress has the power under the Enabling Clause of the Thirteenth Amendment to reach private conduct, thus interpreting section 1985(3) as being applicable to private conspiracies where an invidiously discriminatory motivation is shown.

   a. **Labor dispute.** In *United Brotherhood of Carpenters v. Scott*, 463 U.S. 825 (1983), the Court declined to apply section 1985(3) to an alleged conspiracy to interfere with an employee's First Amendment right not to associate with a union. Outside of the racial area, some proof of state involvement is necessary to state a cause of action under 1985(3). Infringement of First Amendment rights does not violate section 1985(3) unless the state is involved or the conspiracy's aim is to influence the state.

   b. **Blockades of abortion clinics.** In *Bray v. Alexandria Women's Health Clinic*, 506 U.S. 265 (1993), the Court reversed a lower federal court's issuance of an injunction preventing obstruction of access to abortion clinics by various groups. Animus toward abortion did not constitute a class-based animus toward women that could support a section 1985(3) claim. The lower court's interpretation of the statute would convert it into a general federal tort law, which it was the very purpose of the animus requirement to avoid.

      1) **Civil damages.** A year later, a unanimous Court upheld civil damages against those who would unlawfully obstruct access to abortion clinics under RICO. [National Organization for Women, Inc. v. Scheidler, 510 U.S. 249 (1994)]

      2) **42 U.S.C. section 1983.** Section 1983 provides civil remedies for actions arising under color of state law. In *Monroe v. Pape*, 365 U.S. 167 (1961), damages were permitted against police officers for violation of a plaintiff's Fourth Amendment rights; the specific intent needed in criminal cases was not required. Under *Monroe*, local governments were immune from section 1983 actions. That immunity has been substantially diminished after *Monroe*. [*See, e.g.*, Monell v. Department of Social Services, 436 U.S. 658 (1978); Owen v. Independence, 445 U.S. 622 (1980)]

4. Private Conduct Under the Thirteenth Amendment.

a. Private sales--

Jones v. Alfred H. Mayer Co., 392 U.S. 409 (1968).

Facts. Alfred H. Mayer Co. (D) refused to sell a home to Jones (P), solely because P was black. P sued for injunctive and other relief under 42 U.S.C. section 1982. The lower courts dismissed P's complaint, concluding that section 1982 applies only to state action and does not reach private refusals to sell. P appeals.

Issue. Does the authority of Congress to enforce the Thirteenth Amendment "by appropriate legislation" include the power to eliminate all racial barriers, including private actions, to the acquisition of real and personal property?

Held. Yes. Judgment reversed.

- The plain language of section 1982 appears to prohibit ***all*** discrimination, private and public, against blacks in the sale or rental of property.
- The Thirteenth Amendment authorizes Congress to enact appropriate legislation to abolish all badges and incidents of slavery, and such laws may operate upon the unofficial acts of private individuals. Congress has determined that free exercise of property rights is essential to abolition of all badges and incidents of slavery; therefore, section 1982 may properly act upon actions of private individuals such as D.
- Were Congress denied the power to enforce the Thirteenth Amendment to this extent, that amendment would constitute a promise that the nation could not keep.

Dissent (Harlan, White, JJ.). This case is unimportant in light of the recently passed Fair Housing Act, and the Court should have dismissed P's writ as improvidently granted.

b. **Interference with right to lease.** In *Sullivan v. Little Hunting Park, Inc.*, 396 U.S. 229 (1969), the Court found that a black tenant and a member of a corporation that operated a community park and playground facilities could sue for damages and injunctive relief under section 1982 to challenge the corporation's refusal to approve assignment of the shares to the tenant. The Court held that the corporation's action interfered with the member's right to lease. The dissent argued that the Court's ruling had ignored the existence of the Fair Housing Act and the complexities of the Civil Rights Act of 1866.

c. **Admission to private school.** In *Runyon v. McCrary*, 427 U.S. 160 (1976), the Court held that 42 U.S.C. section 1981 prohibits private, commercially operated, nonsectarian schools from denying admission to prospective students solely because of race. The First Amendment right of freedom of association allows parents to send their children to schools that promote racial segregation, but it does not protect the actual practice of excluding certain races from such schools.

D. CONGRESSIONAL POWER TO ENFORCE CIVIL RIGHTS UNDER SECTION 5 OF THE FOURTEENTH AMENDMENT

1. **Basic Question.** Is Congress limited to remedying what the Court finds unconstitutional, or may it remedy what it itself deems unconstitutional? In other words, does section 5 of the Fourteenth Amendment confer remedial or substantive powers?

2. **Congressional Protection of Voting Rights.** The right to vote for federal, state, and local officials is protected from both state and federal government infringement by the provisions of the Fifteenth and Nineteenth Amendments, as well as from state infringement of this right by the Due Process, Equal Protection, and Privilege and Immunities Clauses of the Fourteenth Amendment. Also note that the Twenty-Fourth Amendment protects the right to vote, but only in federal elections, and only from intrusions on this right imposed by poll or other taxes imposed by either state or federal governments.

   a. **Literacy tests—early interpretation.** In *Lassiter v. Northampton County Board of Elections,* 360 U.S. 45 (1959), the Supreme Court upheld a North Carolina law that required a nondiscriminatorily applied literacy test (ability to read and write any section of the state constitution) in order to register to vote.

   b. **The Voting Rights Act of 1965.** Congress has the power by the Enabling Clauses of the Fourteenth and Fifteenth Amendments to pass legislation to enforce the provisions of these amendments. In 1965, Congress passed the Voting Rights Act, which essentially created a rebuttable presumption that literacy tests in certain states were used to perpetrate racial discrimination.

      1) In *South Carolina v. Katzenbach*, 383 U.S. 301 (1966), the Supreme Court sustained the constitutionality of the Act, which had been enacted by Congress pursuant to its power to enforce the Fifteenth Amendment (racial discrimination in voting).

      2) For certain states (determined by a formula of voter registration), where past discrimination against blacks in voting had been found

to be most flagrant, the Act suspended all literacy and other tests or devices for screening eligible voters, provided for the appointment of federal voting registrars, and made new state voting regulations subject to review by federal authorities.

3) The Court held that Congress could use any rational means of effectuating or ensuring the constitutional prohibition of racial discrimination in voting; that Congress was not limited to forbidding violations of the Fifteenth Amendment in general terms (but could fashion specific remedies); that the remedies provided by Congress were "necessary and proper" to Congress's powers under the Fifteenth Amendment; and that any inconsistent standard set up by the state must fall under the Supremacy Clause regardless of whether those state standards were in fact aimed at or resulted in racial discrimination in voting.

c. **The Voting Rights Act Amendments of 1970.** These amendments, inter alia, extended the 1965 Act for five years and also suspended use of literacy tests nationwide. The suspension of literacy tests was upheld by the Court in *Oregon v. Mitchell, infra.*

d. **English literacy requirement prohibited--**

Katzenbach v. Morgan, 384 U.S. 641 (1966).

Facts. Morgan (P), a registered voter in the city of New York, challenged section 4(e) of the Voting Rights Act of 1965, which provides that any person who has successfully completed sixth grade in an accredited school in Puerto Rico cannot be denied the right to vote because of lack of English proficiency. P claims that the law pro tanto prohibits enforcement of New York election laws based on English proficiency. A three-judge district court granted P relief; Katzenbach (D), the United States Attorney General, appeals.

Issue. May Congress prohibit enforcement of a state English literacy voting requirement by legislating under section 5 of the Fourteenth Amendment, regardless of whether the judiciary would find such a requirement unconstitutional?

Held. Yes. Judgment reversed.

- Congress need not wait for a judicial determination of unconstitutionality before prohibiting the enforcement of a state law. Congress may enact any legislation that is appropriate.

- The test for appropriateness is whether (i) the end is legitimate, and (ii) the means are not prohibited by and are consistent with the letter and spirit of the Constitution.

- Section 4(e) is plainly adapted to the legitimate end of assuring equal protection to all, including non-English-speaking citizens. D claims section 4(e) works an invidious discrimination violation of the Fifth Amendment by failing to include persons attending schools not covered by the law. But section 4(e) extends the franchise and does not restrict or deny P. The fact that Congress went no further than it did does not imply a constitutional violation.

Concurrence (Douglas, J.). The question of whether section 4(e) encompasses means not prohibited by but consistent with the Constitution should not be addressed until presented by a member of the class against which that particular discrimination is directed.

Dissent (Harlan, Stewart, JJ.). The Court has confused the issue of the extent of the section 5 (of the Fourteenth Amendment) enforcement power with the distinct issue of what questions are better resolved by the judiciary than by the legislature. Congress should not be permitted to enact remedial legislation where there is no constitutional infringement to be remedied, and the judiciary alone ultimately determines whether a practice or statute is unconstitutional. This Court has previously held that a state English literacy test is permissible; here, the Court grants Congress authority to override that judicial determination and define the substantive scope of the Fourteenth Amendment.

Comment. The *Morgan* decision is a far-reaching decision that may exempt the Fourteenth Amendment from the principle of Court-Congress relationships enunciated in *Marbury v. Madison* (that the judiciary is the final arbiter of the Constitution), thus allowing Congress to act independently. Another view is that Congress was merely acting to strengthen the judicially declared right of equal access to government services.

---

e. **Challenge to the 1970 amendments.** In *Oregon v. Mitchell*, 400 U.S. 112 (1970), the Court held that Congress could constitutionally abolish literacy tests as a requirement to vote. The Court also held that Congress could enfranchise 18-year-olds in federal elections, but struck down a section of the federal act that required states to grant the franchise to 18-year-olds in state and local elections. The following year, the Twenty-Sixth Amendment was ratified, which guarantees citizens age 18 or older the right to vote in federal, state, and local elections.

f. **Prohibiting voting plans that have no discriminatory purpose.** *Rome v. United States*, 446 U.S. 156 (1980), involved section 5 of the Voting Rights Act of 1965. Georgia and its municipalities were covered jurisdictions under the 1965 Act; thus, the city of Rome, Georgia, had to comply with the preclearance provisions of section 5. When Rome sought to alter its electoral scheme, the Attorney General denied preclearance, finding no discriminatory purpose behind the alteration but finding discriminatory effect. The Supreme Court held section 5 constitutional as applied to changes in the electoral scheme of Rome. The Court explained that the Act permits preclearance only when the new voting plan has neither the purpose nor the effect of discriminating. The city of Rome claimed that this exceeds congressional authority under section 1 of the Fifteenth Amendment, which expressly prohibits only purposeful discrimination. However, the Court pointed out that earlier cases had interpreted section 2 as authorizing Congress to do what is necessary, if not expressly prohibited by the Constitution, to prohibit state action that perpetuates the effects of past discrimination.

3. Limits on Congressional Enforcement of Reconstruction Amendments--

City of Boerne v. Flores, 521 U.S. 507 (1997).

Facts. In *Employment Division, Department of Human Resources of Oregon v. Smith*, 494 U.S. 872 (1990), the Court held that, except in special circumstances, the Free Exercise Clause was not violated by a facially neutral and secular law, drafted without legislative animus, that had the effect of interfering with a given religious practice. In that case, Smith had been denied unemployment benefits because he had used peyote in a sacramental ceremony. The Court rejected application of the *Sherbert v. Verner* (*infra*) balancing test. In response, Congress passed the Religious Freedom Restoration Act of 1993 ("RFRA") that required courts to apply the balancing test. Under RFRA, courts would have to determine whether a statute substantially burdened a religious practice, and if it did, whether the burden was justified by a compelling government interest. The city of Boerne (D) denied a building permit to enlarge a church, based on an ordinance governing historic preservation in the area. Flores (P), the Archbishop of San Antonio, challenged the denial under RFRA. The district court held that in enacting RFRA, Congress exceeded the scope of its section 5 enforcement power under the Fourteenth Amendment. The Fifth Circuit reversed. The Supreme Court granted certiorari.

Issue. May Congress impose a rule of constitutional interpretation on the Supreme Court through its enforcement of the Fourteenth Amendment?

Held. No. Judgment reversed.

- ♦ Congress relied on the Fourteenth Amendment to impose the RFRA requirements on the states. The Fourteenth Amendment gives Congress power to enforce the constitutional guarantee that no state shall deprive any person of "life, liberty, or property, without due process of law; nor deny any person . . . equal protection of the laws." In enacting RFRA, Congress sought to protect the free exercise of religion.

- While congressional authority under the Fourteenth Amendment is broad, it is not unlimited. Congress does have power to enforce the constitutional right to the free exercise of religion, since the First Amendment liberties are included within the Due Process Clause of the Fourteenth Amendment. This power extends only to enforcement, however. It does not extend to changing or defining what the right of free exercise is. There is a distinction between enforcement and changing governing law.

- The power to interpret the Constitution in a case or controversy is in the judiciary, not in Congress. Congress does not have a substantive, nonremedial power under the Fourteenth Amendment. If Congress could define its own powers by altering the meaning of the Fourteenth Amendment, the Constitution would no longer be a superior paramount law that cannot be changed by ordinary means.

- Preventive rules may sometimes be appropriate remedial measures, but the means must be appropriate to the ends to be achieved. In this case, there was no record of generally applicable laws that were passed because of religious bigotry. The provisions of RFRA are so out of proportion to a supposed remedial objective that it cannot be treated as responsive to unconstitutional behavior. RFRA is applicable to all state and federal law, whenever enacted. The substantial costs RFRA imposes on government far exceed any pattern or practice of unconstitutional conduct under the Free Exercise Clause as interpreted by *Smith.*

- Each branch of the government must respect both the Constitution and the proper determination of the other branches. RFRA was designed to control cases and controversies, but it is the interpretation of the Constitution that must govern cases and controversies, not RFRA.

Comment. It could be argued that since Congress is specifically mentioned in the Fourteenth Amendment, it does have special authority to determine what rights to enforce. It has such authority under the Thirteenth Amendment.

---

4. **Civil Remedy Not Part of Congress's Remedial Power.** In *United States v. Morrison, supra*, the Court held that the Commerce Clause did not give Congress authority to enact the federal civil remedy for the victims of gender-motivated violence under the Violence Against Women Act of 1994. The Court also held that the civil remedy could not be upheld as an exercise of Congress's remedial power under section 5 of the Fourteenth Amendment. The civil remedy in this case was not aimed at proscribing discrimination by state officials, but at individuals.

XI. FREEDOM OF SPEECH—WHY GOVERNMENT RESTRICTS SPEECH—UNPROTECTED AND LESS PROTECTED EXPRESSION

A. INTRODUCTION

1. **The Constitutional Provision—the First Amendment.** "Congress shall make no law . . . abridging the freedom of speech, or of the press; of the right of the people peaceably to assemble, and to petition the Government for a redress of grievances."

2. **Balancing Interests.** The right to freedom of expression is not an absolute right to say or do anything that one desires; rather, the interests of the government in regulating such expression must be balanced against the very strong interests on which this right is based.

    a. **Rationale.** The rationale behind freedom of speech is that (i) such freedom will lead to the discovery of truth and better ideas through the competition of differing viewpoints, and (ii) such speech and action is a necessity for a free society that is to be governed by democratic principles (*i.e.*, change can be brought about by the will of the people, expressed in nonviolent ways).

    b. **Presumption of validity.** Legislation, even legislation that imposes limitations on freedom of expression, is presumed valid until the person attacking such legislation can show otherwise (*i.e.*, that the interests of the government are outweighed by those interests restricted by the regulation).

    c. **Invalid on its face.** Note that sometimes the Supreme Court will hold that a statute is invalid on its face (*i.e.*, that the statute in all of its possible applications is unconstitutional); in other cases, and far more frequently, the Supreme Court will hold that the statute is unconstitutional only as applied to a particular fact situation (the one before the Court at that time).

    d. **Special scrutiny.** There has been considerable debate over the years about whether First Amendment rights have a "preferred position" or whether restraints on freedom of expression are reviewed with special care (*i.e.*, whether the Court gives more careful scrutiny to alleged infringements of personal, noneconomic liberties than to restrictions on property use and economic interests). Most Justices agree that the First Amendment rights are special. The issue concerns how or in what way this "specialness" is implemented. To say that restrictions on First Amendment rights receive special scrutiny may be saying that they are presumptively unconstitutional or that Justices in this area have wider latitude for enforcing their own prejudices—and certainly this should not be true.

B. REGULATION OF POLITICAL SPEECH

1. The World War I Cases.

a. The clear and present danger test--

Schenck v. United States, 249 U.S. 47 (1919).

Facts. The Espionage Act of 1917 made it a crime to cause or attempt to cause insubordination in the military forces or to obstruct recruitment. Schenck (D) was charged with such an attempt as a result of publishing a pamphlet that attacked the Conscription Act and encouraged disobedience to it. D appeals the conviction under the Act.

Issue. May Congress outlaw speech that presents a clear and present danger to an important government interest?

Held. Yes. Judgment affirmed.

- ♦ The right of free expression is not absolute but varies with the circumstances; *i.e.*, one is not free to falsely yell "fire" in a crowded theater.

- ♦ The first question is whether Congress is pursuing a proper end or purpose in the legislation. Here it is—Congress has the right to prohibit the evils at which this statute is aimed, especially in time of war.

- ♦ The next question is to what extent Congress can go in seeking to effectuate its purpose; that is, how far can it go before it is prohibited by the First Amendment? Congress cannot make speech a crime (because the effect on free speech is too great) unless there is a "clear and present danger" of action resulting from the defendant's words that would lead to the legitimately proscribed evil.

Comment. Shortly after *Schenck* was decided, the Court held that newspaper articles may create a clear and present danger [Frohwerk v. United States, 249 U.S. 204 (1919)] and that political speeches denouncing public policy and advocating an alternative may constitute illegal activity [Debs v. United States, 249 U.S. 211 (1919)].

---

b. Intent--

Abrams v. United States, 250 U.S. 616 (1919).

Facts. After the Russian revolutionary government signed a peace treaty with Germany, the United States sent military forces to northern cities of the Soviet Union. A group of Russian immigrants (Ds), who were avowed revolutionists and anarchists, believing the military action was an attempt to crush the revolution, wrote and distributed leaflets advocating a general strike and urging workers in munitions factories to stop production. Ds were convicted under amendments to the Espionage Act that prohibited encouragement of any curtailment of necessary war material with intent to do so.

Issue. Is the Act's requisite intent present where Ds' goal was to aid the Russian Revolution?

Held. Yes. Judgment affirmed.

- Even if Ds' primary intent was to aid the revolutionary cause in Russia, they must have intended and must be held accountable for the effects that their acts were likely to produce; here, Ds' plan, if effective, would defeat the war program of the United States.

Dissent (Holmes, Brandeis, JJ.). It is only the present danger of immediate evil or an intent to bring it about that supports congressional interference with expressions of opinion. Neither was present in this case. The free trade of ideas is necessary to the attainment of truth. Contrary to the government's argument, the First Amendment did not leave the common law as to seditious libel in force.

Comment. Subsequent to *Abrams*, Justice Holmes continued to dissent from affirmances of convictions under the Act. [*See* Pierce v. United States, 252 U.S. 239 (1920); Schaefer v. United States, 251 U.S. 466 (1920)]

c. Incitement--

Masses Publishing Co. v. Patten, 244 F. 535 (S.D.N.Y. 1917).

Facts. Patten (D), the New York postmaster, refused to accept for mailing a magazine published by Masses Publishing (P). D claimed that the publication violated the Espionage Act. P seeks an injunction.

Issue. May the government refuse to permit use of the mails by private magazines that criticize public policy?

Held. No. Injunction granted.

- The Act prohibits false statements that interfere with the military or aid its enemies. P has not made such false rumors, but has published political arguments.

- The Act forbids anyone from willfully causing disloyalty among the military. Although anyone who adopts P's views would be more prone to insubordination than one having faith in the existing policies, such an interpretation of causation would prohibit any expression of views counter to those currently prevailing, an impermissible restriction in a democratic society. Of course, one may not counsel or advise violation of the law as it now stands, but everyone is free to advocate changing the law.

- The Act also forbids willful obstruction of the enlistment service. But here only direct advocacy of resistance, or actual incitement, is prohibited. P has not done such an incitement.

Comment. The decision by Judge Learned Hand was reversed on appeal. The circuit court did not agree with the incitement test, and deferred to the Postmaster General's discretion. [*See* Masses Publishing Co. v. Patten, 246 F. 24 (2d Cir. 1917)]

---

2. **Post-World War I Legislation—"Red Scare" Cases (1920s and 1930s).**

   a. **Legislative facts--**

Gitlow v. New York, 268 U.S. 652 (1925).

Facts. Gitlow (D) was convicted and imprisoned for violating a New York law that prohibited language advocating, advising, or teaching the overthrow of organized government by unlawful means. D appeals. There was no evidence of any effect resulting from D's actions.

Issue. May states prohibit advocacy of criminal anarchy when there is no concrete result, or likelihood of such a result, flowing from such advocacy?

Held. Yes. Judgment affirmed.

- The state has penalized not doctrinal exposition or academic discussion but language urging criminal action to overthrow the government. D's expressions clearly fit the statutory prohibition; his words were the language of direct incitement. The state has determined that such activity is so inimical to the general welfare that it may be penalized in the exercise of its police power. The state has sought to suppress the threatened danger in its incipiency. Because the statute is not arbitrary or unreasonable, it must be upheld.

♦ If the statute itself is constitutional and the use of language falls within its reach, absence of actual results is irrelevant. The state has determined that these utterances involve sufficient likelihood of causing harm that they must be discouraged, and that determination cannot be shown to be clearly erroneous.

Dissent (Holmes, J.). D's words did not constitute a present danger of an actual attempt to overthrow the government; they were too indefinite and ineffective. To say D's words were an incitement proves nothing, for every idea is an incitement and may move the recipient to action depending on outside circumstances.

---

b. The rationale for free speech--

Whitney v. California, 274 U.S. 357 (1927).

Facts. Whitney (D) helped organize and became a member of the Communist Labor Party of California, an organization that advocated, taught, and aided criminal syndicalism as defined by the Criminal Syndicalism Act of California. She was convicted, and appeals, claiming that although she remained a member, she did not intend that the party be an instrument of terrorism or violence.

Issue. May the state outlaw mere membership in a criminal organization even if the individual member intends no criminal acts?

Held. Yes. Judgment affirmed.

♦ The Act is not void for vagueness, and its purpose is clearly proper. The state may exercise its police power to outlaw organizations menacing the peace and welfare of the state.

♦ A person who abuses the right of association by joining such an organization is not protected by the Due Process Clause from punishment.

Concurrence (Brandeis, Holmes, JJ.). Freedom of expression is an end in itself. It is a safety valve for frustration and it is a means for finding the truth through the competition of ideas. Suppression of free speech can be justified only if there exist reasonable grounds to fear that a serious evil would otherwise result, and reasonable grounds exist for believing that there is imminent danger that the serious evil will occur.

c. **The Smith Act.**

1) **Introduction.** The Smith Act [18 U.S.C. §2385] makes it unlawful for any person (i) to knowingly or willfully advocate, abet, advise, or teach the duty, necessity, desirability, or propriety of overthrowing any government in the United States by force or violence; or (ii) to attempt to commit, or to conspire to commit any of such acts; or (iii) to become a member of any organization advocating such acts, knowing its purposes.

2) **Validity upheld--**

Dennis v. United States, 341 U.S. 494 (1951).

Facts. Dennis and others (Ds) were convicted of participating in a conspiracy to organize the Communist Party in the United States. The party participated in activity prohibited by the Smith Act. Ds appeal.

Issue. May Congress pass a law forbidding association with organizations advocating overthrow of the government?

Held. Yes. Judgment affirmed.

- Congress clearly has the power to protect the government from violent overthrow, and in exercising this power could properly limit any expression or utterance aimed at inciting such a result.

- The gravity of the evil (the possible overthrow of the government) is to be discounted by the improbability of its occurrence in order to determine whether a clear and present danger exists.

- In the trial court the jury is to decide whether the defendant in fact violated the Act, and the judge is to decide the question of application of the Act to the defendant's conduct in the light of the clear and present danger test.

Concurrence (Frankfurter, J.). The First Amendment does not provide absolute immunity for all expression; some balancing of the competing interests is necessary. Congress has prime responsibility to adjust these interests; the Court merely decides whether the Constitution permits Congress to enact the Smith Act.

Concurrence (Jackson, J.). The "clear and present danger" test was designed as a rule of reason for isolated incidents. It is not a limitation on the power of Congress to deal with the threat of a conspiracy dedicated to overthrowing the government.

Dissent (Black, J.). "Reasonableness" is an inadequate standard for reviewing restrictions on First Amendment rights.

Dissent (Douglas, J.). Mere advocacy of Communism should not be a crime. Free speech should not be eliminated unless there is a showing that the evils advocated are imminent. The clear and present danger test should apply.

Comment. After *Dennis* held the Smith Act constitutional, the government brought many actions against alleged Communists. In *Dennis*, Ds had been holding classes, giving speeches, and writing articles that advocated overthrow of the government. This was the illegal advocacy involved. Although in *Dennis* Ds were ringleaders, it was thereafter thought that all that need be shown for a conviction of any person was that he was linked with the organization (which advocated overthrow as fast as possible). In all cases, of course, there had to be shown some connection between the advocacy and the proscribed evil (this was the clear and present danger aspect of the case). This connection could be supplied by judicial notice, however.

---

d. **Opposition to Vietnam policy and the draft.** Most political activities by government employees may be reasonably curtailed; however, this is not true with respect to freedom of political expression. So, for example, the Supreme Court unanimously held in *Bond v. Floyd*, 385 U.S. 116 (1966), that a state legislature could not refuse to seat a duly elected representative on the basis of his speeches critical of Vietnam War policy and the selective service system. [*See also* Watts v. United States, 394 U.S. 705 (1969)—"If they ever make me carry a rifle, the first man I want to get in my sights is L.B.J." interpreted as political hyperbole]

e. **The modern incitement test: Advocacy vs. incitement--**

Brandenburg v. Ohio, 395 U.S. 444 (1969).

Facts. Brandenburg (D), a Ku Klux Klan leader, invited a television crew to cover a private rally. He was convicted under an Ohio statute for advocating criminal terrorism and criminal syndicalism. The state courts upheld the conviction. D appeals.

Issue. May a state law prohibit advocacy of civil disruption without distinguishing between mere advocacy and incitement to imminent lawless action?

Held. No. Conviction reversed.

- The constitutional guarantees of free speech and free press do not permit a state to forbid or proscribe advocacy of the use of force or of law violation except where such advocacy is directed to inciting or producing imminent lawless action and is likely to incite or produce such action. Ohio's law fails to make the required distinction, and cannot be upheld.

Concurrence (Black, J.). The Court cites the *Dennis* case but properly does not agree with the *Dennis* "clear and present danger" doctrine.

Concurrence (Douglas, J.). The line between permissible and impermissible acts is the line between ideas and overt acts. The "clear and present danger" test has no place in the Constitution.

Comment. Applying the *Brandenburg* incitement standard, the court reversed a disorderly conduct conviction in *Hess v. Indiana*, 414 U.S. 105 (1973), a case involving a campus antiwar demonstration. The Court held that since the appellant's statement could be interpreted in various ways, there was no rational inference from the language that the words were intended to produce imminent disorder. The Court stated that words that only had a ***tendency*** to lead to violence could not be punished by the state. The Court also applied *Brandenburg* in setting aside a large damage award against participants in an economic boycott by black citizens in *NAACP v. Claiborne Hardware Co.*, 458 U.S. 886 (1982). The Court concluded that a public speech by Charles Evers (one of the defendants) did not incite subsequent lawless action. Mere advocacy of the use of force or violence does not abrogate First Amendment protection. The subsequent violence was not immediate, but rather occurred weeks or months after the speech.

C. FIGHTING WORDS AND HOSTILE AUDIENCES

1. Fighting Words.

a. **General attacks.** The Court invalidated a conviction for inciting breach of the peace in *Cantwell v. Connecticut*, 310 U.S. 296 (1940). Cantwell, while on public streets, played a record that embodied a general attack on all organized religious systems except his religion. The Court concluded that Cantwell had no intent to assault or offend listeners in a manner that would incite violence since, upon their objections, he left the area. Cantwell expressed no epithets or personal abuse so as to create a clear and present menace to public peace and order.

b. **Categorization approach.** In contrast, the Court in *Chaplinsky v. New Hampshire*, 315 U.S. 568 (1942), held that a state may forbid the use of words in a public place that would be likely to cause an addressee to fight—so-called fighting words. Chaplinsky had called the city marshal a "damned Fascist" and a "God-damned racketeer." The Court held that fighting words are one of the "well-defined and narrowly limited classes of speech" not protected by the Constitution. Other classes include bribery, perjury, and criminal solicitation.

c. **Balancing approach.** Because categorization presents such a high risk of being overinclusive, the Court has adopted a balancing approach to most content-based restrictions on speech. Balancing presents the danger of being susceptible to manipulation by those who apply the law.

d. **Current status of fighting words analysis.** The *Chaplinsky* approach appears to retain validity so long as the statute involved is narrowly construed. However, the Court has not upheld a conviction on the basis of the fighting words doctrine since *Chaplinsky*. In *Gooding v. Wilson*, 405 U.S. 518 (1972), the Court reversed a conviction for using provocative words because the statute was overbroad. The Court apparently would uphold a statute applicable only to words that "have a direct tendency to cause acts of violence by the person to whom, individually, the remark is addressed."

e. **Offensive words.** In vacating and remanding three convictions for the use of offensive language in *Rosenfeld v. New Jersey, Lewis v. New Orleans*, and *Brown v. Oklahoma*, 408 U.S. 901, 913, 914 (1972), the Court articulated a narrow view of the governmental power to restrain offensive words. Several dissents were written in the actions; Chief Justice Burger argued that the law should protect against fighting words and profane and abusive language such as the utterances in these cases.

f. **Offensive conduct.** *Chaplinsky* defined fighting words as ***either*** those that inflict injury merely by utterance or those that tend to incite an immediate breach of peace. Later cases have focused only on the latter definition. For example, in *Texas v. Johnson*, 491 U.S. 397 (1989), a political protester's conviction for burning a United States flag was reversed. The Court found that it would be unreasonable to interpret the conduct expressing dissatisfaction with government policies as a direct personal insult inviting violence.

g. **Offensive sign--**

Cohen v. California, 403 U.S. 15 (1971).

Facts. Cohen (D) wore a jacket in a Los Angeles courthouse corridor bearing the words "Fuck the Draft." He was convicted of violating a state statute that prohibited disturbing the peace by offensive conduct. He appeals after the state courts upheld his conviction.

Issue. May a state excise as "offensive conduct" public use of an offensive word?

Held. No. Judgment reversed.

- Government has special power to regulate speech that is obscene, that constitutes "fighting words," or that intrudes on substantial privacy interests in an essentially intolerable manner. D's expression falls within none of these categories. D's jacket could not be considered erotic. Nor would D's jacket violently provoke the common citizen in the manner of fighting words. Finally, persons present in the courthouse were not unwilling captives of the offensive expression; they could simply avert their eyes.

- ♦ The state's regulatory attempt must fail because it would permit the state to outlaw whatever words officials might deem improper, thus running a substantial risk of suppressing ideas. Such power would permit official censorship as a means of banning the expression of unpopular views.

Dissent (Blackmun, J., Burger, C.J., Black, J.). D's antic was mainly conduct and involved little speech. As such, it could be regulated.

Comment. The test for fighting words requires that the speech have a direct tendency to cause immediate acts of violence by the person or group to whom addressed. Thus, a statute prohibiting "abusive language . . . tending to cause a breach of the peace" is overbroad. [*See* Gooding v. Wilson, 405 U.S. 518 (1972)]

---

2. **Hostile Audiences.** Free speech does not include the right to disrupt the community. The question is whether hostile audience reactions justify curtailment of otherwise protected speech. For example, speech or writing that by its very utterance tends to incite an immediate breach of the peace is not constitutionally protected, and may be prevented or punished by the state. *See Chaplinsky v. New Hampshire,* 315 U.S. 568 (1942), where the conviction of a Jehovah's Witness, whose personal attack on the city marshal with fighting words resulted in a physical fight, was upheld. On the other hand, reiterating the clear and present danger standard, the Court in *Terminiello v. Chicago*, 337 U.S. 1 (1949), held that a breach of the peace statute that included a restriction on speech that stirs the public to anger, invites dispute, or causes unrest was unconstitutional because one of the functions of free speech, which is often provocative and challenging, is the invitation to dispute.

    a. **Protective suppression--**

Feiner v. New York, 340 U.S. 315 (1951).

Facts. Feiner (D) was addressing a street meeting and attracted a crowd, but there was no disorder. One man told the police officers that if they did not stop D, he would. The police asked D to stop speaking, and arrested him when he refused to obey. He was convicted of disorderly conduct and appeals.

Issue. May police act to suppress speech that in their judgment is causing a breach of the peace?

Held. Yes. Judgment affirmed.

- ♦ D was accorded a full, fair trial, the result of which was a determination that D was arrested and convicted not for his speech but for the reaction it caused. The police were justified in acting to preserve peace and order.

Dissent (Black, J.). The police had a duty to protect D's right to talk, even to the extent of arresting the man who threatened to interfere.

Comment. The problems of freedom of expression in public places really have two aspects—one is the idea of the content of the speech. For example, political dialogue or comment is clearly going to receive greater protection than is business advertising (*i.e.*, the Court might allow distribution of handbills concerning American involvement in the Middle East in circumstances in which it would not permit the distribution of advertising matter). The second element is clearly that of the conduct involved (this is the *Feiner* case); *i.e.*, when there is a clear and present danger that the conduct involved will lead to harmful results (riot, etc.).

---

b. **Actual threat required.** In *Edwards v. South Carolina*, 372 U.S. 229 (1963), Edwards and others peaceably assembled at the state capitol to protect against racial discrimination. Although ordered to disperse, they failed to do so. Instead, they listened to speakers, sang songs, etc. There was no violence or threat thereof by the demonstrators or the crowd watching them, and there was adequate police protection. The Court reversed convictions for "breach of the peace," since there was no actual interference or threat to public order or safety. [*See also* Cox v. Louisiana, 379 U.S. 536 (1965)—breach of peace conviction for an appeal to stage sit-ins at segregated lunch counters did not threaten or result in violence]

c. **Street demonstrations and hostile audiences.** In *Gregory v. Chicago*, 394 U.S. 111 (1969), the Court reversed a disorderly conduct conviction of peaceful demonstrators who had refused to disperse upon police demand following hostile reactions in the crowd. Chief Justice Warren stated that peaceful conduct was protected by the First Amendment and that, in such situations, the conviction is not only based upon the refusal to move but also the demonstration itself. The concurring opinions noted that while the Court had always warned that dragnet statutes like the disorderly conduct provision were too vague and overbroad, the Constitution did not bar a narrowly drawn law that specifically barred forbidden conduct.

d. **Permit requirement.** In *Kunz v. New York*, 340 U.S. 290 (1951), the Supreme Court struck down a New York City ordinance that made it unlawful to hold public worship meetings on city streets without first obtaining a permit to do so from the city police commissioner. Since the ordinance vested absolute discretion in the commissioner without adequate standards to guide his decisions, the Court held that this was a prior restraint on the exercise of First Amendment rights. [*See also* Forsyth County, Georgia v. Nationalist Movement, 505 U.S. 123 (1992)—ordinance assessing varying fees on demonstrators to cover increased public costs held facially invalid]

D. INJURY TO REPUTATION AND SENSIBILITY

1. **Introduction.** Libelous speech is in somewhat the same category as obscenity—it receives little constitutional protection. However, the same difficult questions exist here also; that is (i) what is libelous, and (ii) what tests are to be used to distinguish protected from unprotected speech?

2. **Group Libel.** Speech or writing that is defamatory is not constitutionally protected and may be punished through criminal libel laws or civil laws awarding damages based on such publications. [*See* Beauharnais v. Illinois, 343 U.S. 250 (1952)—convictions for circulating anti-black literature were upheld under a state "group criminal libel" statute; publications aimed at a group of individuals]

3. **Libel.**

   a. **Public officials--**

New York Times Co. v. Sullivan, 376 U.S. 254 (1964).

Facts. Sullivan (P) was a commissioner of the city of Montgomery, Alabama, and supervised the police department. The New York Times Co. (D) carried a full-page advertisement that included several false charges of repressive police conduct in Montgomery. P sued for damages on grounds that D libeled him; although P's name was not mentioned, the accusations of the ad could be read as referring to him. The trial court awarded damages of $500,000, which were upheld in the state courts. The controlling state rule of law dealt with libel per se, established here by merely showing that D's statements reflected upon the agency P supervised. Once libel per se is demonstrated, the only defense is truth. D appeals.

Issue. Do the First and Fourteenth Amendments prohibit state rules that would allow a public official to recover damages for a defamatory falsehood relating to his official conduct without proof of actual malice?

Held. Yes. Judgment reversed.

- ♦ The Constitution expresses a profound commitment to uninhibited debate on public issues. This protection does not turn on the truth of the ideas or beliefs expressed, nor does concern for official reputation remove defamatory statements from the constitutional shield.

- ♦ The deterrent effect of damage awards—without the need for any proof of actual pecuniary loss—is so great as to severely chill public criticism, which should be openly permitted under the First Amendment.

- ♦ Despite First Amendment considerations, a public official may recover damages for a defamatory falsehood relating to his official conduct if he proves the statement was made with actual malice (knowledge of falsity or reckless disregard of truth). P's proof falls short.

Concurrence (Black, Douglas, JJ.). D had an absolute, unconditional privilege to criticize official conduct despite the harm that might flow from excesses and abuses.

---

b. **Public figures.** The Supreme Court has stated that the same privilege to make statements about "public officials" exists for statements made about "public figures." In *Curtis Publishing Co. v. Butts*, 388 U.S. 130 (1967), Wally Butts, the former director of athletics at the University of Georgia, had sued after he was reported to have thrown a football game while at the University. In *Associated Press v. Walker* (decided with *Butts*), the Court held that General Walker, a retired army general, was a public figure. However, a person is ***not*** a public figure simply because she is extremely wealthy and engaged in divorce proceedings of interest to the reading public. The fact that she files for divorce (and even holds a press conference during the proceedings) does not mean that she voluntarily chooses to publicize her married life—since going to court is the only way she can legally dissolve her marriage. [*See* Time, Inc. v. Firestone, 424 U.S. 448 (1976)]

c. **Private individuals.**

1) **General rule.** If the defamed person is neither a public figure nor a public official (or candidate for public office), "free speech" considerations are not as strong. Private individuals are more susceptible to injury because they usually do not have media access to counteract false statements published about them. Consequently, the states may impose whatever standard of defamation liability they choose, except that, for matters of public concern:

a) The factual misstatement must be such as would warn a reasonably prudent editor or broadcaster of its defamatory potential;

b) There must be a finding (by the trier of fact or the appellate court) that the publisher or broadcaster was at least negligent in publishing the misstatement (*i.e.*, liability without fault cannot be imposed); and

c) Damages must be limited to "actual injury" (which includes any out-of-pocket loss plus impairment of reputation, personal humiliation, and mental anguish). An award of "presumed" or punitive damages is permissible only if the publication was made with knowledge of its falsity or in reckless disregard for the truth (*i.e.*, actual malice).

2) **Persons involved in public issues.** In *Gertz v. Robert Welch, Inc.*, 418 U.S. 323 (1974), the Court considered the standard of liability for defamation of a private person involved in a public issue. Gertz, an attorney, represented the family of a victim murdered by a police officer, in the family's civil suit against the officer. After Robert Welch, publisher of *American Opinion*, printed a concededly untrue article discrediting Gertz's reputation and motives, Gertz sued for libel. The Court pointed out that the need to avoid self-censorship by the news media must be balanced against the legitimate interest in permitting compensation for harm resulting from defamatory falsehoods. However, the Court recognized that defamation plaintiffs are not all in the same class—public officials and public figures have more access to the media to counteract falsehoods than do private individuals. Also, private individuals are more deserving of recovery because their public exposure is not voluntary. Therefore, the Court found that the rationale behind the *New York Times* rule does not extend to private individuals. States may define their own standards of liability for defamation by a publisher or broadcaster, but may not impose liability without fault. And states may allow compensation for actual injury, but may not permit recovery of presumed or punitive damages in the absence of proof of "actual malice" (knowledge of falsity or reckless disregard for the truth).

d. **Speech on matters of private concern.** In *Dun & Bradstreet, Inc. v. Greenmoss Builders, Inc.*, 472 U.S. 749 (1985), the Court held that a defamed person may recover presumed and punitive damages, even without proving actual malice, if the defamation is not speech on a public matter. The Court stated that when defamatory statements involve no issue of public concern, the Court must balance the state's interest in compensating injured parties against the First Amendment interest in protecting the expression. Speech on private matters does not merit the highest First Amendment protection; thus there are fewer constitutional limits on state libel law in this area. In this case, the credit report was intended only for the benefit of Greenmoss and its business audience of five subscribers; it did not constitute speech on a public issue.

4. **Non-Defamation Torts.**

a. **Intentional infliction of emotional distress.** In *Hustler Magazine v. Falwell*, 485 U.S. 46 (1988), Hustler magazine published an advertisement parody featuring an alleged interview with Falwell, a nationally known minister. The ad contained a disclaimer. An award of damages for intentional infliction of emotional distress was reversed by the Court, which concluded that, although the speech was offensive to Falwell and probably to many others, and was intended to inflict emotional injury, this was of no constitutional relevance. Even if motivated by ill-will, the First Amendment requires a showing of falsity made with actual malice, the standard used when public figures are involved.

b. **Invasions of privacy.** The Supreme Court has held that "matters of public interest" may be commented on, safe from an action for invasion of privacy, unless the plaintiff can show that the person making the publication was motivated by actual malice.

1) **Public matter.** In *Time, Inc. v. Hill*, 385 U.S. 374 (1967), the Supreme Court reversed a lower court judgment for damages for invasion of privacy ("false light") that had been based on a magazine article about a Broadway play. The article alleged that the plot of the play was based on the actual experiences that the plaintiff and his family suffered at the hands of some escaped convicts.

2) **Disclosure of victims' names.** In *Cox Broadcasting Corp. v. Cohn*, 420 U.S. 469 (1975), the Court held that because of public interest in a vigorous press, a broadcaster could not be liable for accurately publishing information regarding a rape victim, which information was already contained in a public record. [*See also* Florida Star v. B.J.F., 491 U.S. 524 (1989)—state may not prohibit publication of victim's name obtained from police report made available in police press room; dissent distinguished *Cox* as involving judicial records]

3) **Privacy and electronic eavesdropping.** During contentious union negotiations between a teachers' union and the school board, the union's chief negotiator used a cell phone to talk with the union's president. An unknown person intercepted and recorded their conversation. Vopper, a radio commentator, played a tape of the intercepted conversation on his radio show. In *Bartnicki v. Vopper*, 532 U.S. 514 (2001), the Court held that Vopper could not be held liable for damages under antiwiretap laws for broadcasting the phone call. The Court acknowledged that Vopper knew or should have known that the recording was illegal. However, the Court

explained that although the government has a legitimate interest in protecting privacy, it cannot suppress speech by a law-abiding possessor of information in order to deter the conduct of a non-law-abiding third party. Furthermore, the tape involved a matter of public concern, and the Court decided that, in balancing the competing interests, privacy concerns must yield to the interest in publishing matters of public importance.

4) **Appropriation torts.** The plaintiff in *Zacchini v. Scripps-Howard Broadcasting Co.*, 433 U.S. 562 (1977), claimed a right of publicity in his act as a human cannonball. The Court agreed, explaining that this tort protects a proprietary interest of the individual and is analogous to patent and copyright law. Dissemination of information to the public is not limited; the only issue is who gets to do the publishing.

5. Hate Speech.

a. **Nazi demonstrations.** Emphasizing the need for strict procedural safeguards in First Amendment areas, the Court in *National Socialist Party v. Skokie*, 432 U.S. 43 (1977), held unconstitutional an order of the state supreme court denying the petition of Nazi Party demonstrators for a direct expedited appeal following the refusal of the appellate court to stay an injunction pending appeal. The Court held that if the state imposes a restraint in this action barring a march in a city with a large Jewish population, it must provide such procedural safeguards as immediate appellate review. And in *Smith v. Collin*, 439 U.S. 916 (1978), the Court denied certiorari to review the Seventh Circuit decision invalidating later-enacted ordinances that (i) established a permit system for demonstrations like those proposed by the Nazis, (ii) prohibited the dissemination within the city of materials inciting racial hatred, and (iii) barred the wearing of military-style uniforms by political groups in demonstrations. In dissent, two Justices urged that the Court grant certiorari so that the Court could consider possible limits on the exercise of free speech in a context such as the Skokie-Nazi situation, which might be in the same category as the *Schenck* cry of "fire" in a theatre.

b. **Racist speech on campus.** Several universities have sought to regulate speech that victimizes on the basis of race, sex, religion, etc. These attempts have caused considerable controversy as the parties balance First Amendment considerations with the desire to prevent or minimize harm.

c. **Content of "fighting speech"--**

R.A.V. v. City of St. Paul, Minnesota, 505 U.S. 377 (1992).

Facts. R.A.V. (D) and several other teenagers assembled a cross from broken chair legs and burned it inside the fenced yard of a black family that lived across the street from D's house. The city of St. Paul, Minnesota (P) charged D with disorderly conduct pursuant to an ordinance that provided: "Whoever places on public or private property a symbol, object, appellation, characterization or graffiti, including, but not limited to, a burning cross or Nazi swastika, which one knows or has reasonable grounds to know arouses anger, alarm or resentment in others on the basis of race, color, creed, religion or gender commits disorderly conduct and shall be guilty of a misdemeanor." D moved to dismiss the charge on the ground that it was invalid under the First Amendment because it was overbroad and impermissibly content-based. The trial court granted D's motion, but the Minnesota Supreme Court reversed, construing the ordinance to apply only to conduct that amounts to "fighting words," *i.e.*, "conduct that itself inflicts injury or tends to incite immediate violence." The Supreme Court granted certiorari.

Issue. May the government regulate "fighting words" based on the subjects the speech addresses?

Held. No. Judgment reversed.

- Content-based speech regulations are presumptively invalid, but, as the Court held in *Chaplinsky* (*supra*), there are exceptions in a few limited areas that are "of such slight social value as a step to truth that any benefit that may be derived from them is clearly outweighed by the social interest in order and morality."

- Certain categories of expression are not within the area of constitutionally protected speech (obscenity, defamation, etc.), which means that they may be regulated because of their constitutionally proscribable content. This does not mean they may be used to discriminate on the basis of content unrelated to their distinctively proscribable content; *i.e.*, the government may proscribe libel, but it cannot proscribe only libel critical of the government.

- The exclusion of "fighting words" from the scope of the First Amendment means that the unprotected features of the words are essentially a "nonspeech" element of communication. But there is a "content discrimination" limitation on the government's prohibition of proscribable speech; the government may not regulate use based on hostility or favoritism towards the underlying message expressed.

- When the basis for the content discrimination consists entirely of the very reason the entire class of speech at issue is proscribable, no significant danger of idea or viewpoint discrimination exists. The government may prohibit only the most patently offensive obscenity, but it cannot prohibit only obscenity that includes offensive political messages. Or, the government may regulate price advertising on one industry and not in others, because the risk of fraud is greater there, but it cannot prohibit only that commercial advertising that depicts men in a demeaning fashion.

- The government could properly give differential treatment to even a content-defined subclass of proscribable speech if the subclass happens to be associated with particular "secondary effects" of the speech; *e.g.*, prohibiting only those obscene live performances that involve minors. And laws against conduct instead of speech may reach speech based on content, such as sexually derogatory "fighting words" that violate Title VII's prohibition against sexual discrimination. The key element is that the government does not target conduct on the basis of its expressive content.

- In this case, P's ordinance is facially unconstitutional because it applies only to "fighting words" that insult, or provoke violence, "on the basis of race, color, creed, religion or gender." It does not apply to abusive invective on other topics, but singles out those speakers who express views on disfavored subjects. Instead of singling out an especially offensive mode of expression, P has proscribed fighting words of whatever manner that communicate messages of racial, gender, or religious intolerance. This creates the possibility that P is seeking to handicap the expression of particular ideas.

- P's content discrimination is not reasonably necessary to achieve P's compelling interests; an ordinance not limited to the favored topics would have precisely the same beneficial interest.

Concurrence (White, Blackmun, O'Connor, Stevens, JJ.).

- P's ordinance is overbroad because it criminalizes expression protected by the First Amendment as well as unprotected expression. The majority's rationale is a new doctrine that was not even briefed by the parties and is a departure from prior cases. The Court has long applied a categorical approach that identifies certain classifications of speech as unprotected by the First Amendment because the evil to be restricted so overwhelmingly outweighs the expressive interests, if any, at stake. The Court now holds that the First Amendment protects these categories to the extent that the government may not regulate some fighting words more strictly than others because of their content. Now, if the government decides to criminalize certain fighting words, it must criminalize all fighting words.

- The Court also refuses to sustain P's ordinance even though it would survive under the strict scrutiny applicable to other protected expression. In *Burson v. Freeman*, 504 U.S. 191 (1992), the Court applied the strict scrutiny standard and upheld a statute that prohibited vote solicitation and display or distribution of campaign materials within 100 feet of the entrance to a polling place, even though it could have been drafted in broader, content-neutral terms. Under the Court's decision today, the *Burson* law would have been found unconstitutional.

- Although the Court's analysis is flawed, the conclusion is correct because P's ordinance is overbroad. Even as construed by the Minnesota Supreme Court, the ordinance criminalizes a substantial amount of expression that is protected by the First Amendment. That court held that P may constitutionally prohibit expression that "by its very utterance" causes "danger, alarm or resentment," but such generalized reactions are not sufficient to strip expression of its constitutional protection.

Concurrence (Blackmun, J.). The ordinance is overbroad.

Concurrence (Stevens, White, Blackmun, JJ.). P's ordinance regulates conduct that has some communicative content, and it raises two questions: Is it "overbroad" because it prohibits too much speech, and if not, is it "underbroad" because it does not prohibit enough speech? The majority and concurring opinions deal with the basic principles that (i) certain categories of expression are not protected, and (ii) content-based regulations of expression are presumptively invalid. But both principles have exceptions. The majority applies the prohibition on content-based regulation to "fighting words"—speech that previously had been considered wholly "unprotected." Now, fighting words have greater protection than commercial speech, which is often regulated based on content. Assuming arguendo that the ordinance regulates only fighting words and is not overbroad, it regulates speech not on the basis of its subject matter or the viewpoint expressed, but rather on the basis of the harm the speech causes—injuries based on "race, color, creed, religion or gender." It only bans a subcategory of the already narrow category of fighting words. It is not an unconstitutional content-based regulation of speech, and should be upheld, except that it is overbroad.

---

6. **Hate Crimes Distinguished.** In *Wisconsin v. Mitchell*, 508 U.S. 476 (1993), the Supreme Court limited the *R.A.V.* holding to viewpoint-selective laws specifically aimed at unprotected words or symbols by upholding a penalty enhancement statute for hate crimes convictions, *i.e.*, crimes committed because of a victim's race, religion, etc. The Court explained that the *R.A.V.* ordinance was directed to expression, while this law is aimed at conduct unprotected by the First Amendment.

7. **Statutory Inference of Intent from Conduct Not Allowed--**

Virginia v. Black, 538 U.S. 343 (2003).

Facts. The state of Virginia prohibited the burning of a cross with "an intent to intimidate a person or group of persons." Black and others (Ds) were tried for violating the statute. At the trial, the jury was instructed that Ds' burning of the cross, by itself, was sufficient evidence from which the jury could infer the required intent to intimidate. Ds were convicted, and the court of appeals affirmed. The Virginia Supreme Court held that the cross-burning statute was facially unconstitutional under the First Amendment. The Supreme Court granted certiorari.

Issue. May a criminal statute provide that the burning of a cross is prima facie evidence of an intent to intimidate when such an intention is one of the elements of the crime?

Held. No. Judgment affirmed in part, vacated in part, and remanded.

- Cross burning was originally used by Scottish tribes to signal one another in the 14th century. In the United States, however, cross burning has been closely tied to the Ku Klux Klan, which uses cross burnings to communicate threats of violence and intimidation. The Klan also uses cross burnings as symbols of shared group identity and ideology. Thus, although the cross burning does not inevitably convey a message of intimidation, when it is used to intimidate, it is a powerful message.

- The government may regulate categories of expression including fighting words and incitement, as well as true threats. Intimidation is a type of true threat, where the speaker directs a threat to a person with the intent of making the victim fear bodily harm or death. Some cross burnings fit within this definition of intimidating speech.

- The Supreme Court of Virginia held that the statute was unconstitutional because it discriminates on the basis of content and viewpoint under *R.A.V. v. City of St. Paul (supra). R.A.V.* does not hold that all forms of content-based discrimination within a proscribable area of speech are unconstitutional. The Virginia statute here, unlike the statute in *R.A.V.*, does not single out only that speech directed at one of the specified disfavored topics. The Virginia statute is aimed at burning a cross with intent to intimidate regardless of the victim's race, gender, religion, or other characteristics.

- Virginia may properly outlaw cross burnings done with the intent to intimidate because such activity is a particularly virulent form of intimidation, given its history as a signal of impending violence.

- However, the statute is unconstitutional because the prima facie evidence provision allows a conviction without proof of the very element that makes it constitutional for Virginia to ban cross burning—the intent to intimidate. Virginia could not ban cross burning alone, without the intimidation intent as an element of the offense, so it cannot simply provide that cross burning constitutes prima facie evidence of the required intent. The statute does not distinguish between cross burning with intent to intimidate and cross burning as a political statement not intended to intimidate.

Concurrence (Stevens, J.). Cross burning with an intent to intimidate is the kind of threat that is not protected by the First Amendment.

Concurrence and dissent (Scalia, Thomas, JJ.). The prima facie evidence part of the statute is not unconstitutional, at least on a facial challenge. Only a limited class of persons, those who abstain from presenting a defense to rebut the prima facie evidence, could be wrongly convicted under that statute; so the statute is not overbroad.

Concurrence (Souter, Kennedy, Ginsburg, JJ.). The statute makes a content-based distinction within the category of punishable intimidating expression, which is unconstitutional. This content-based proscription of cross burning could be an effort to ban not only intimidation, but also the messages communicated by non-threatening cross burning. No content-based statute should survive under *R.A.V.* without a high probability that no official suppression of ideas is afoot. The statute here is not narrowly tailored, since a content-neutral statute banning intimidation would accomplish the same objective without singling out particular content.

Dissent (Thomas, J.). The statute addressed conduct only, not speech, and should not fall within the First Amendment protections.

E. SEXUALLY EXPLICIT EXPRESSION

1. Introduction--Unprotected Speech.

a. Obscene publications are not protected by the constitutional guarantee of freedom of speech and press. Both federal and state governments may halt such expression. The difficulty, of course, is in defining obscenity.

b. The problem is in finding and defining the social interest that is to be weighed against the limitation on free speech. Supposedly when speech reaches the obscenity stage, there is no interest in protecting it. The implication is that freedom of expression is not an end in itself; that is, the kind of speech involved must have some content that has value to society in order to be given the freedom to express it, and "obscene" speech supposedly has no such value.

2. Obscenity.

a. Defining obscenity--

Roth v. United States; Alberts v. California, 354 U.S. 476 (1957).

Facts. Roth (D) was convicted of mailing obscene materials in violation of a federal obscenity statute. Alberts (D) was convicted of a similar state offense. Ds appeal their convictions.

Issue. Is obscenity, judged by the proper standard, outside the protection of the First Amendment?

Held. Yes. Convictions affirmed.

- ♦ The unconditional phrasing of the First Amendment was not intended to protect every utterance; *e.g.*, libel is unprotected. Obscenity is utterly without redeeming social importance; therefore it cannot claim constitutional protection.

- ♦ Ds claim that their material does not create a clear and present danger to society, but merely incites impure sexual thoughts. It is true that mere portrayal of sex does not deny the material constitutional protection. But obscenity is not synonymous with sex. Obscenity deals with sex in a manner appealing to prurient interest. As such, it is unprotected.

- ♦ The test for obscenity then is: whether to the average person, applying contemporary community standards, the dominant theme of the material taken as a whole appeals to the prurient interest.

Concurrence (Warren, C.J.). Ds' conduct is properly subject to government punishment.

Concurrence and dissent (Harlan, J.). We deal with different statutes. The states may properly regulate in this area, but federal regulation must be more narrow, since Congress has no substantive power over sexual morality. Also, each challenged item must be examined individually to determine whether it is suppressible.

Dissent (Douglas, Black, JJ.). The First Amendment protects all speech and precludes the courts from weighing the values of speech against silence.

---

b. **Post-*Roth* decisions.** In *Kingsley International Pictures Corp. v. Regents*, 360 U.S. 684 (1959), the Court invalidated a New York motion picture licensing law that banned films portraying acts of sexual immorality or presenting such acts as proper behavioral patterns. The Court held that the concept of sexual immorality differed from the concepts of obscenity or pornography and that the state law prevented the advocacy of an idea protected by the basic guarantee of the First Amendment. The Court also reversed a conviction for knowingly possessing obscene materials found in the appellant's home in *Stanley v. Georgia*, 394 U.S. 557 (1969). In so ruling, the Court held that the First Amendment grants the right to receive information and ideas and that there is a fundamental right to be free from unwanted governmental intrusion in one's home. However, in *United States v. Reidel*, 402 U.S. 351 (1971), the Court reversed the lower court's dismissal of an indictment under the federal law prohibiting the mailing of obscene materials. The Court rejected the lower court's contention, based upon the ruling in *Stanley*, that if a person has a right to possess obscene material, then a person also has a right to deliver it. The Court held that the indictment was not an infringement of the right to freedom of mind and thought or of the right to privacy in one's home; commerce implicates no privacy interests.

c. **The modern standard for defining obscene materials--**

Miller v. California, 413 U.S. 15 (1973).

Facts. Miller (D) was convicted under a California statute of knowingly distributing obscene matter to unwilling recipients. The statute incorporated the *Memoirs v. Massachusetts* test of obscenity, namely, that to be unprotected by the First Amendment, the material must meet three criteria: (i) the dominant theme of the material taken as a whole appeals to a prurient interest in sex; (ii) the material is patently offensive because it affronts contemporary community standards relating to the description or representation of sexual matters; and (iii) the material is utterly without redeeming social value. [Memoirs v. Massachusetts, 383 U.S. 413 (1966)] D appeals the conviction.

Issue. Is the *Memoirs* test the appropriate measure of obscene expressions?

Held. No. Judgment vacated and remanded.

- Obscenity is not within the area of constitutionally protected speech or press. *Roth v. United States* (*supra*), presumed obscenity to be "utterly without redeeming social value," but the *Memoirs* case transformed that presumption into a necessary element of proof. *Memoirs* thus requires the prosecution to prove a negative, and that test cannot be upheld.

- Regulation of obscene material is restricted to works that depict or describe sexual conduct, and must specifically define that conduct. The basic guidelines for the trier of fact must be: (i) whether the average person, applying contemporary community standards, would find that the work, taken as a whole, appeals to the prurient interest; (ii) whether the work depicts or describes, in a patently offensive way, sexual conduct specifically defined by the applicable state law; and (iii) whether the work, taken as a whole, lacks serious literary, artistic, political, or scientific value. Thus, material can be regulated without a showing that it is "utterly without redeeming social value."

Dissent (Douglas, J.). The people through constitutional amendment, and not the courts, should decide what is and is not obscene.

Dissent (Brennan, Stewart, Marshall, JJ.). The challenged statute is unconstitutionally overbroad, hence invalid on its face.

d. **Permissible extent of state regulation--**

Paris Adult Theatre I v. Slaton, 413 U.S. 49 (1973).

Facts. Slaton (P), a state district attorney, filed civil complaints against Paris Adult Theatre I (D), seeking to enjoin exhibition of films claimed to be obscene. The films were available only to "consenting adults." The trial judge dismissed the complaint but the Georgia Supreme Court reversed, holding that the films were without First Amendment protection. D appeals.

Issue. May a state prohibit commercial exhibition of "obscene" films to consenting adults?

Held. Yes. Judgment vacated and remanded.

- ♦ The state afforded D the best possible notice, as no restraint on exhibition was imposed until after a full judicial proceeding determined that the films were obscene and therefore subject to regulation.
- ♦ Obscene, pornographic films do not acquire constitutional immunity from state regulation merely because they are shown to consenting adults only. The states have power to make a morally neutral judgment that public exhibition of obscene material, or commerce in such material, has a tendency to injure the community as a whole, even if actual exposure is limited to a few consenting adults.
- ♦ While the right of privacy may preclude regulation of use of obscene materials within the home, commercial ventures such as D's are not "private" for the purpose of civil rights litigation. Commerce in obscene material is unprotected by any constitutional doctrine of privacy.
- ♦ Incidental effects on human "utterances" or "thoughts" do not prevent state action to protect legitimate state interests where the communication is not protected by the First Amendment and where the right of privacy is not infringed. Such state action is permitted as long as it conforms to the standards of *Miller*.

Dissent (Brennan, Stewart, Marshall, JJ.). The Court's attempts to define obscenity have clearly failed. Government cannot constitutionally bar the distribution even of unprotected material to consenting adults.

---

e. **Review of jury determinations of obscenity.** Finding that nudity alone is not enough to meet the *Miller* standard for legal obscenity, the Court held, in *Jenkins v. Georgia,* 418 U.S. 153 (1974), that the film *Carnal*

Knowledge was not obscene. In rejecting the state court's belief that a jury verdict precluded further review of the elements of obscenity, the Court noted that a jury does not have unbridled discretion in determining what is patently offensive, because the *Miller* illustrations, although not exhaustive, did establish constitutional limitations for the type of material that could be found obscene.

1) In a separate dissenting opinion in *Smith v. United States*, 431 U.S. 291 (1977), Justice Stevens delineated his objection to criminal prosecution for obscenity, although advocating civil sanctions for obscene, offensive, and indecent displays. Justice Stevens argued that, although the variable, inconsistent nature of a standard dependent on a jury's subjective determination of community attitudes is defective if used to identify criminal conduct, civil rules that protect an individual's right to select a desirable environment should be so flexible.

f. **Community standards.** In *Miller*, the Court recognized that the degree of tolerance towards sexually explicit materials would differ, depending on the locales. Although *Miller* used a statewide standard, the Court in *Hamling v. United States*, 418 U.S. 87 (1974), employed a local rather than statewide or national standard in federal obscenity prosecutions. However, *Smith* made clear that the literary, artistic, political, or scientific value factor was ***not*** to be measured by local community standards. [*See also* Pope v. Illinois, 481 U.S. 497 (1987)—a work's value does not vary from community to community depending on the degree of local acceptance]

3. Child Pornography.

a. **Distribution of child pornography.** In *New York v. Ferber*, 458 U.S. 747 (1982), the Court upheld a New York statute that outlawed production and promotion (including distribution) of child pornography, regardless of whether the material was legally obscene. The Court explained that states have great leeway in dealing with child pornography because of the compelling state interest in safeguarding their children's physical and psychological well-being. Distribution of child pornography is intrinsically related to sexual abuse of children because the distribution aggravates the harm to the child and because, without a market, the pornography would not be produced. Prohibiting distribution of obscene materials would not adequately promote the state's interest because the harm of abuse is unrelated to any possible literary, artistic, political, or social value of the material. Production of child pornography, of which distribution is an integral part, is illegal; the First Amendment does not protect against commission of a crime. There is no cognizable value in permitting production of child pornography.

b. **Possession of child pornography.** In *Osborne v. Ohio*, 495 U.S. 103 (1990), the Court distinguished *Stanley v. Georgia, supra,* from a state statute that prohibited the possession of material showing a minor in a state of nudity on the ground that the interests underlying prohibitions on child pornography were much greater than the interests involved in *Stanley*.

c. **Virtual child pornography.** *Ashcroft v. Free Speech Coalition*, 535 U.S. 234 (2002), involved the Child Pornography Prevention Act of 1996 ("CPPA"). The CPPA expanded the federal prohibition of child pornography to include "virtual child pornography," which is sexually explicit images that appear to depict minors but are produced without using any real children. The CPPA did not require such pornography to be obscene under *Miller v. California*, *supra*, but prohibited all child pornography, real or virtual. The government argued that pedophiles might use the materials to encourage children to participate in sexual activity and that virtual child pornography might whet the sexual appetites of pedophiles. The government also claimed that the CPPA was needed because modern imaging technology makes it harder to prosecute pornographers who use real minors. However, the CPPA prohibited the depiction of sexually explicit activity, even if in a psychology manual or in a movie about the horrors of sexual abuse, and it applied to depictions of persons under 18 years of age. The Court noted that teenage sexual activity has been the topic of countless literary works, from Shakespeare to acclaimed modern movies. The Court held that Congress cannot prohibit speech that adults have a right to hear in an attempt to shield children from that speech. It also cannot prohibit otherwise protected speech because pedophiles might use it for illegal purposes. The Court stated that the mere tendency of speech to encourage unlawful acts is not a sufficient reason for banning it. The Court described the argument that virtual pornography makes it difficult to prosecute actual child pornography as an argument that protected speech may be banned as a means to ban unprotected speech. The Court ruled that the government may not suppress lawful speech as the means to suppress unlawful speech.

4. **Pornography as Subordination of Women--**

American Booksellers Association, Inc. v. Hudnut, 771 F.2d 323 (7th Cir. 1985), *aff'd mem.*, 475 U.S. 1001 (1986).

Facts. American Booksellers Association, Inc. (P) sued Hudnut (D), the mayor of Indianapolis, to prevent enforcement of an ordinance that defined "pornography" as a practice that discriminates against women, subjecting it to regulation and remedies used for other forms of discrimination. Rather than applying the "obscene" definition of *Miller*, the ordinance defined pornography as "the graphic sexually explicit subordination of women, whether in pictures or words, that also includes one or more of the following: (i) women are presented as sexual objects who enjoy pain or humiliation; (ii) women are presented as sexual objects who experience sexual pleasure in being raped; (iii) women are presented as sexual objects tied up or cut up or mutilated or bruised or physically hurt, or as dismembered or truncated or fragmented or severed into body parts; (iv) women are presented as being penetrated by objects or animals; (v) women are presented in scenarios of degradation, injury, abasement, torture, shown as filthy or inferior, bleeding, bruised, or hurt in a context that makes these conditions sexual; or (vi) women are presented as sexual objects for domination, conquest, violation, exploitation, possession, or use, or through postures or positions of servility or submission or display." The ordinance precludes trafficking in pornography, coercing others into performing in pornographic works, forcing pornography on a person, or assaulting anyone in a way that is directly caused by specific pornography, for which a right of action arises under the statute against pornography makers or sellers. The district court held that the ordinance was unconstitutional and prevented its enforcement. D appeals.

Issue. May the government restrict pornographic speech that conveys a message of discrimination against women?

Held. No. Judgment affirmed.

- D's ordinance does not judge the work as a whole, but focuses on particular depictions, so that it is irrelevant whether the work has literary, artistic, political, or scientific value. D notes that the ordinance is not intended to vindicate community standards of offensiveness, but to alter the socialization of men and women.

- There are many arguments for and against the ordinance, but basically the ordinance discriminates against expression on the ground of the content of the speech. Speech treating women in the approved way, with sexual encounters premised on equality, is lawful regardless of how sexually explicit, while speech treating women in an unapproved way is unlawful, regardless of the literary, artistic, or political qualities of the work taken as a whole.

- The First Amendment prevents the government from evaluating ideas and regulating based on content. Yet this statute expressly regulates speech based on its viewpoint. D claims that the regulation is justified because the prohibited form of pornography is not an idea but an injury because it does not persuade people but it changes them and socializes them by establishing what conduct is permissible.

- D's position demonstrates the power of pornography as speech. Its adverse effects depend on mental intermediation. This is also true of speech advocating racial bigotry, anti-semitism, violence, and other undesirable social activity. Many types of speech have the effect of social conditioning, including religious ceremonies and school curriculum. If the government could regulate speech based on its effect on people, there would be no free speech.

- ♦ D also claims that women are harmed while making pornographic films and pictures. To the extent that there is actual harm to the actors, these harms may be unlawful. But the image of pain is not necessarily pain. It is common in films to show violent or painful images, but the actors are not actually harmed.

- ♦ D's argument is that pornography is low value speech, similar to obscenity. But the Supreme Court's definition of obscenity is not based on the point of view of the particular work. D's approach focuses on the message of the speech, and is therefore unconstitutional. Any rationale to support D's ordinance could not be limited to sex discrimination. There is no way to construe D's ordinance that would make it constitutional.

---

5. **Nonobscene, Sexually Explicit Expression.**

   a. **Nudity bans.** In *Erznoznik v. City of Jacksonville*, 422 U.S. 205 (1975), the Court found facially invalid an ordinance prohibiting the showing of films containing nudity by drive-in movie theaters with screens visible from public streets. The ban was too broad since it banned all nudity, no matter how educational or innocent. Similarly, the Court reversed a prosecution for live nude dancing in an area zoned to exclude all live entertainment. The ordinance lacked justification for its broad ban of protected expression. [Schad v. Borough of Mount Ephraim, 452 U.S. 61 (1981)]

   b. **"Erogenous zoning."**

      1) **Introduction.** The Court has used an approach to offensive displays and speech which applies a less stringent standard of review than is normally applicable to speech. This approach does not go as far as the categorization approach used for "fighting words," however.

      2) **Low value speech.** In *Young v. American Mini Theatres, Inc.*, 427 U.S. 50 (1976), the Court held that a city may use exhibition of sexually explicit "adult" movies as a basis for statutory classification of theaters. The city of Detroit had adopted amendments to an Anti-Skid Row Ordinance that regulated the locations of theaters showing sexually explicit "adult" movies. The operators of two adult movie theaters challenged the ordinance. The Court rejected the challenge, finding that the location regulations were clearly within the city's police power and did not, by themselves,

violate the First Amendment. The Court explained that the question of whether speech is, or is not, protected by the First Amendment often depends on the content of the speech. Society's interest in protecting expression of erotic material is wholly different, and lesser, than its interest in protecting political or philosophical discussion. Although the First Amendment does not permit total suppression of erotic material, it does permit the states to use content as a basis for classification.

3) **Secondary effects.** The Court upheld a zoning ordinance that regulated adult theaters by concentrating them in certain areas in *Renton v. Playtime Theatres, Inc.*, 475 U.S. 41 (1986). The ordinance was a time, place, and manner regulation and was content neutral since it was not directed at the film contents, but rather at the secondary effects of such theaters on the surrounding community.

c. **Indecency bans in the communications media.**

1) **Control of airwaves--**

FCC v. Pacifica Foundation, 438 U.S. 726 (1978).

Facts. A New York radio station owned by Pacifica Foundation (D) broadcast a monologue by George Carlin that contained several indecent words. A listener complained to the FCC (P), which issued a declaratory order finding the monologue indecent as broadcast and therefore subject to regulation. The district court reversed P's determination. P appeals.

Issue. Does the federal government have power to regulate a radio broadcast that is indecent but not obscene?

Held. Yes. Judgment reversed.

- The statute upon which P based its power to regulate D's broadcast [18 U.S.C. §1464] forbids the use of any "obscene, indecent, or profane" language; since the disjunctive is used, each word has a separate meaning, and language need not be obscene to be indecent. D's words were admittedly not obscene, but P could still properly find them indecent.
- Broadcasting, of all forms of communication, has the most limited First Amendment protection because of its unique ability to penetrate privacy and its accessibility to children.
- The First Amendment does not prohibit all governmental regulation that depends on the content of speech. Nor is P's action invalidated by its possible deterrent effect on similar broadcasts.

Concurrence (Powell, Blackmun, JJ.). While P's holding does not violate the First Amendment, the Court should not decide on the basis of content which speech is less "valuable" and hence less deserving of protection.

Dissent (Brennan, Marshall, JJ.). The word "indecent" must be construed to prohibit only obscene speech. Since the broadcast was concededly not obscene, and since it does not fit within the other categories of speech that are totally without First Amendment protection, it should not be subject to government control. The government does not have a duty to protect its citizens from certain broadcasts merely because some citizens, even if a majority, object to the broadcast.

Dissent (Stewart, Brennan, White, Marshall, JJ.). Since "indecent" properly means no more than "obscene," P had no authority to ban D's broadcast.

---

2) **The limits of *Pacifica*.**

a) **Captive audiences.** The *Pacifica* decision relied on *Rowan v. United States Post Office Department*, 397 U.S. 728 (1970), which upheld a federal law permitting recipients of pandering advertisements to request a postal order requiring removal of names from the mailing list and to stop all future mailings. No one has the right to press even "good" ideas on an unwilling recipient. Subsequently, *Rowan's* captive audience rationale was limited in *Consolidated Edison v. Public Service Commission*, 447 U.S. 530 (1980), which struck down a utility regulation prohibiting the inclusion in monthly bills of inserts discussing controversial issues, *e.g.*, nuclear power, as a content regulation. However, the utility was allowed to send its views on noncontroversial issues. The Court noted that customers could escape exposure to mailed materials by transferring the insert from the bill envelope to a wastebasket.

(1) **Contraceptive products.** The *Consolidated Edison* principle was extended to unsolicited ads for contraceptive products in *Bolger v. Youngs Drug Products Corp.*, 463 U.S. 60 (1983), in which a proscribing federal law was invalidated. The First Amendment does not allow the government to prohibit speech as intrusive unless objectionable speech cannot be avoided. Once again, it is a short journey from mailbox to trash can.

b) **Total indecency bans.** In *Sable Communications, Inc. v. FCC*, 492 U.S. 115 (1989), the Court refused to uphold a ban on indecent recorded telephone messages, distinguishing *Paci-*

fica on the ground that there are alternative, less burdensome means of controlling access to phone messages.

c) **Segregation of sexual materials on cable television.** *Denver Area Educational Telecommunications Consortium, Inc. v. FCC*, 581 U.S. 727 (1966), concerned the Cable Television Consumer Protection and Competition Act of 1992 ("Cable Act"). The Court upheld a provision of the Cable Act that authorized cable operators to prohibit "indecent" programming on leased access channels, although cable operators could not exercise any other editorial control over the content of programs. The Court invalidated a different provision that required cable operators carrying "indecent" programming to segregate such programming on a single channel, to block that channel from viewer access, and to unblock it only on a subscriber's written request. The Court reasoned that, although the protection of children is a compelling interest, the latter provision significantly differed from the former because it did not merely permit, but rather required cable operators to restrict speech.

d) **Regulation of time for cable programming.** Section 505 of the Telecommunications Act of 1996 required cable operators who provided sexually-oriented programming to either fully scramble sexually-oriented channels or to limit their transmission to between 10 p.m. and 6 a.m. The technology to fully scramble signals was so expensive that most cable operators chose the limited transmission option. When the regulation was challenged in *United States v. Playboy Entertainment Group, Inc.*, 529 U.S. 803 (2000), the Court invalidated section 505. The Court reasoned that cable television systems can block unwanted channels on a household-by-household basis, which is less restrictive than banning. The Court held that the government cannot ban speech if targeted blocking is a feasible and effective means of furthering its compelling interests.

e) **The Internet--**

Reno v. American Civil Liberties Union, 521 U.S. 844 (1997).

Facts. Certain provisions of the Communications Decency Act of 1996 ("CDA") prohibited the knowing transmission of obscene or indecent messages to any recipient under 18 years of age and the knowing sending or displaying of patently offensive messages in a manner that is available to a person under 18 years of age. These provisions were designed to prevent Internet obscenity. An affirmative defense was available for those who take good faith, reasonable, effective, and appropriate actions to restrict minor access to such material, or who require certain designated forms of age proof, such as a verified credit card or an adult identification number. The American Civil Liberties Union (P) challenged the Act. A three-judge district court enjoined enforcement of the Act, except with respect to obscenity and child pornography, on the ground that it violated freedom of speech. Reno (D), the United States Attorney General, appeals.

Issue. May Congress suppress certain types of web pages to deny minors access to potentially harmful speech?

Held. No. Judgment affirmed.

- Previous cases do not support D's position. *Ginsberg v. New York*, 390 U.S. 629 (1968) upheld a New York prohibition on selling obscene material to minors, but this did not prohibit their parents from buying the material for their children, as does the CDA. The New York statute was also better defined and applied to persons under the age of 17. *Pacifica, supra*, applied to the timing of a radio broadcast and did not involve a criminal prosecution. *Renton, supra*, applied to a zoning ordinance that was aimed at "secondary effects," unlike the CDA, which is a content-based blanket speech restriction, not a time, place, and manner regulation.

- Previous cases have recognized special justifications for regulation of broadcast media that do not apply to other speakers. Broadcast media have a history of extensive government regulation, they have scarce available frequencies, and they are invasive in nature. The Internet, which does not have a history of government regulation, allows anyone to "publish" information, which is then accessible to anyone who accesses the Internet unless the publisher imposes restrictions; *i.e.*, there is no scarcity of broadcast spectrums. Unlike radio or television communications that can be received passively, Internet communications require deliberate effort on the part of the recipient. There are methods to allow parents to block access to undesired web sites.

- The CDA contains undefined terms and different phrases for different sections, raising uncertainty about how the two standards relate to each other. The vagueness of the CDA is of special concern because as a content-based regulation, it has a chilling effect on free speech. It is also a criminal statute. The CDA attempts to use just one of the three *Miller* prongs, but all three are necessary.

- The CDA also lacks the necessary precision required by a content regulation. To deny minors access to potentially harmful speech, the CDA suppresses a large amount of speech that adults have a constitutional right to receive. Such a broad content-based restriction on adult speech is unacceptable if less restrictive alternatives would be equally effective. Currently available user-based software is a reasonably effective method that parents can use to prevent their children from accessing inappropriate material.

- ♦ The CDA's severability clause allows deletion of the term "or indecent" such that knowing transmission of "obscene" messages to any recipient under 18 years of age may continue to be punishable.

Concurrence and dissent (O'Connor, J., Rehnquist, C.J.). The CDA is an attempt to create "adult zones" on the Internet. A zoning law is valid if (i) it does not unduly restrict adult access, and (ii) minors have no right to read or view the banned material. As technology exists today (1997), the CDA fails the first part of this test. Currently the only way for a speaker on the Internet to prevent a child from being exposed to indecent material is to refrain completely from using indecent speech.

F. COMMERCIAL SPEECH

1. **Introduction.** Before 1976, the Court assumed that most commercial speech was not protected. [Valentine v. Chrestensen, 316 U.S. 52 (1942); Pittsburgh Press Co. v. Pittsburgh Human Relations Commission, 413 U.S. 376 (1973)] However, the Court changed direction in *Bigelow v. Virginia*, 421 U.S. 809 (1975), which held that commercial speech merits some First Amendment protection. Commercial speech is now entitled to some degree of protection under the First Amendment, although subject to more stringent regulation than would be permissible with respect to noncommercial speech. In determining the degree of protection, the free speech interest in the contents of the speech must be weighed against the public interest served by the governmental regulation.

2. **Scope of Protection--**

Virginia Pharmacy Board v. Virginia Citizens Consumer Council, Inc., 425 U.S. 748 (1976).

Facts. The Virginia Pharmacy Board (D) prohibited advertisement of the retail prices of prescription drugs by pharmacists. The Virginia Citizens Consumer Council (P), for itself and on behalf of users of prescription drugs, sought an injunction against the enforcement of D's rule. The three-judge district court granted the injunction; D appeals.

Issue. Is purely commercial speech wholly outside First Amendment protection?

Held. No. Judgment affirmed.

- First Amendment protection extends to the communication, to its source, and to its recipients. P, as a potential recipient, has standing to bring this action.

- The speech in question—commercial advertising—is not disqualified from protection merely because the speaker's interest is purely economic. The particular consumer has a vital interest in the free flow of commercial information, possibly a greater interest than in current political debates, which are clearly protected. Society in general also has a strong interest in the free flow of commercial information. Actually, such a free flow is essential to the proper functioning of our economic system; it is likely that no line can properly be drawn between "important," and hence protected, advertising and the opposite kind.

- D claims an interest in protecting the public from unscrupulous pharmacists who would use advertising to their own advantage and the public's detriment. But the choice between the dangers of suppressing information, and the dangers of its misuse if it is freely available, has been made by the First Amendment. Therefore, D cannot prohibit commercial advertising of the type involved here.

- Although commercial speech is protected, it remains subject to proper restrictions, *e.g.*, time, place, and manner restrictions, false and misleading advertising prohibitions, and prohibitions against advertising illegal transactions.

Dissent (Rehnquist, J.). The Court expands the standing requirements and extends First Amendment protection beyond what is necessary. This ruling prevents the states from protecting the public against dangers resulting from excessive promotion of drugs that should be used only with professional guidance.

Comment. The Court emphasized the importance of a free flow of information by invalidating an ordinance that prohibited the posting of "for sale" signs on real estate. The township had justified the ordinance as a means of preventing "white flight" from racially integrated neighborhoods, but this justification was inadequate. [*See* Linmark Associates, Inc. v. Township of Willingboro, 431 U.S. 85 (1977)]

---

3. **Defining Commercial Speech.** *Virginia Pharmacy Board* defined commercial speech as that which does no more than propose a commercial transaction, making clear that it did not include all speech produced for profit. [*See, e.g.*, First National Bank of Boston v. Bellotti, *infra*—business interests included with political views] However, the definition was subsequently narrowed. For example, in *Bolger v. Youngs Drug Products Corp.*, *supra*, it was held that mailings of advertising flyers accompanied by informational pamphlets was commercial speech. [*See also* Board of Trustees v. Fox, 492

U.S. 469 (1989)—promotional speech combined with home economics information constitutes commercial speech]

4. **Regulating the Legal Profession.** In ruling that a state could not prohibit a lawyer from advertising routine legal services in a truthful and nonmisleading manner, the Court rejected the state's contention that such advertisement, which did not concern the quality of service or personal solicitation, had an adverse effect on professionalism and was inherently misleading. [Bates v. State Bar of Arizona, 433 U.S. 350 (1977); *see also In re* R.M.J., 455 U.S. 191 (1982)]

   a. A state may discipline lawyers for in-person solicitation of clients for personal gain, at least under circumstances likely to present dangers of misrepresentation, overreaching, invasion of privacy, or stirring up litigation. Unlike advertising legal services, such solicitation may pressure clients without providing time for reflection. [*See* Ohralik v. Ohio State Bar Association, 436 U.S. 447 (1978)] However, in *In re Primus*, 436 U.S. 412 (1978), disciplinary action was dismissed against a lawyer who had solicited a client, not for pecuniary gain, but rather for political ideological reasons.

   b. In *Zauderer v. Office of Disciplinary Council*, 471 U.S. 626 (1985), the Court held that media solicitation by attorneys with respect to a specific legal problem is permissible, and rejected Ohio's attempt to apply the principles of *Ohralik* to large-scale advertising. The Court later struck down a ban on direct-mail solicitation of clients known to need a particular kind of legal service. [Shapero v. Kentucky Bar Association, 486 U.S. 466 (1988)]

   c. In *Peel v. Illinois Attorney Registration and Disciplinary Commission of Illinois*, 496 U.S. 91 (1990), it was held that a lawyer cannot be prohibited from stating that he has been certified as a specialist by a legitimate organization. However, the representation must be truthful and not misleading. A divided Court did uphold certain restrictions in *Florida Bar v. Went For It, Inc.* 515 U.S. 618 (1995), finding that a state may bar personal injury lawyers from soliciting victims for 30 days following an accident. Such advertising invades victims' privacy and casts disrepute on lawyers.

      1) In contrast, state regulations of uninvited solicitation and advertising by certified public accountants were struck down in *Edenfield v. Fane*, 507 U.S. 761 (1993). Accountants are not trained in the art of persuasion and, unlike attorneys' clients, clients of accountants are less susceptible to manipulation. Additionally, an attorney may advertise truthfully that she is also a certified public accountant. [Ibanez v. Florida Board of Accountancy, 512 U.S. 136 (1994)]

5. Four-Part Analysis of Commercial Speech--

Central Hudson Gas v. Public Service Commission, 447 U.S. 557 (1980).

Facts. The Public Service Commission (D), in response to an energy shortage, temporarily banned all advertising by electric utilities that "promotes the use of electricity." Over the objections of Central Hudson Gas (P), D extended the ban and distinguished between promotional advertising, which was totally prohibited, and institutional and informational advertising, which P permitted. The state courts upheld D's order; P appeals.

Issue. Does a public service commission's prohibition of promotional advertising by an electric utility violate the utility's First Amendment rights?

Held. Yes. Judgment reversed.

- Although D's regulation applies only to commercial speech, such speech is protected by the First Amendment because of its informational functions. Thus, a four-part analysis has developed regarding commercial speech.
- First, is the expression protected? If it concerns lawful activity and is not misleading, it generally is; P's speech is protected.
- Second, is the asserted governmental interest in regulation substantial? D based its regulation on the need for energy conservation, clearly a substantial interest.
- Third, does the regulation directly advance the governmental interest? If demand for electricity were unaffected by advertising, P would not have brought this suit. Therefore D's regulation does advance the governmental interest.
- Fourth, is the regulation more extensive than necessary? Here D's regulation fails, since it would prohibit information about electric devises or services that would not increase net energy use, although they might increase electric use, *e.g.*, use of electricity as a backup to solar heating. D's rule is overbroad, and in the absence of a showing that a more limited rule could not serve D's interests, it cannot be upheld.

Concurrence (Blackmun, Brennan, JJ.). The four-part test is inadequate in that it permits deprivation of information needed by the public to make a choice. D attempts to manipulate choices of private persons by withholding information rather than by persuasion or direct regulation. Such covert attempts are illegal regardless of their "necessity."

Concurrence (Stevens, Brennan, JJ.). The issue is whether D has banned nothing but commercial speech. D's ban covers more than purely commercial speech and is therefore invalid, regardless of the four-point analysis.

Dissent (Rehnquist, J.). D here is placing an essentially economic regulation on a heavily regulated state-created monopoly. Economic regulation traditionally merits virtually complete deference by the Court; D's regulation should also.

6. **Regulation After *Central Hudson*.** In *Board of Trustees v. Fox, supra*, the Court interpreted the "no more extensive than necessary" element of *Central Hudson* to mean that the least restrictive alternative was mandated. The majority of the Court would uphold a restriction on commercial billboards to further the aesthetic and traffic safety interests of a city. [Metromedia, Inc. v. San Diego, 453 U.S. 490 (1981)] However, commercial speech may not be treated differently than noncommercial speech for aesthetic or safety reasons, absent distinctively commercial harm. [City of Cincinnati v. Discovery Network, Inc., 507 U.S. 410 (1993)]

7. **Ban on Avertising of Specific Type of Legal Activity.**

   a. **Ban upheld.** In *Posadas de Puerto Rico Associates v. Tourism Co. of Puerto Rico*, 478 U.S. 328 (1986), the Court upheld a Puerto Rican statute that legalized casino gambling but prohibited advertising of casino gambling to the public. The Court held that the government had a substantial interest in preventing the seriously harmful effects of excessive casino gambling and declared that the law directly advanced that interest within the meaning of *Central Hudson, supra*. Since the government could have completely prohibited casino gambling, the Court reasoned that it could take the less intrusive step of prohibiting its advertising.

   b. **The rise and fall of the vice exception.** The Court's deferential approach to regulation of "harmful" activities, begun in *Posadas*, continued in *United States v. Edge Broadcasting Co.*, 509 U.S. 418 (1993), which upheld the prohibition by a nonlottery state of broadcasting of lottery advertisements. However, in *Rubin v. Coors Brewing Co.*, 514 U.S. 476 (1995), and *44 Liquormart, Inc. v. Rhode Island* (below), the Court clearly rejected the presumption that there existed a vice exception to protection of commercial speech.

   c. **Ban on truthful advertising of legal activity rejected--**

44 Liquormart, Inc. v. Rhode Island, 517 U.S. 484 (1996).

Facts. Rhode Island (D) prohibited advertising of the retail price of alcoholic beverages, except for price tags or displays within licensed premises and not visible from the street. In addition, news media within D could not broadcast any advertisements referring to the price of such beverages, even if they referred to sales in other states. 44 Liquormart, Inc. (P) operated a liquor store in D. Peoples Super Liquor Stores, Inc. ("Peoples") operated stores in Massachusetts that were patronized by D's residents. P placed an ad in a Rhode Island newspaper. D began enforcement proceedings and eventually fined P $400. P sought a declaratory judgment that the advertising ban was unconstitutional. The district court found for P, but the court of appeals reversed. The Supreme Court granted certiorari.

Issue. May a state prohibit advertising about retail prices for alcoholic beverages?

Held. No. Judgment reversed.

- In *Central Hudson (supra)*, the Court noted that special concerns arise from regulations that entirely suppress commercial speech in order to pursue a nonspeech-related policy.

- A state regulation of commercial speech that is intended to protect consumers from misleading or deceptive information is consistent with the reasons such speech is protected by the Constitution and thus receives less than strict review. But when a state prohibits the dissemination of truthful, nonmisleading commercial messages for other public policy reasons, there is less reason to depart from ordinarily rigorous First Amendment review.

- Complete bans serve to obscure an underlying governmental policy that could be implemented in other ways without regulating speech. As such, they typically are based on the assumption that the public will respond to the truth in a manner disfavored by the government. The First Amendment clearly disfavors regulations that seek to keep people in the dark for what the government perceives to be their own good.

- D's rationale for the ban is that it advances D's substantial interest in promoting temperance. Theoretically, a ban on price advertising mitigates competition, thus keeping prices higher and demand lower. But D has produced no evidence of any connection between the ban and a significant change in alcohol consumption. Besides, there are several actions D could take to accomplish its objective without restricting speech, such as increasing prices through higher taxation or educational campaigns.

- D argues that under *Posadas de Puerto Rico Associates v. Tourism Co. of Puerto Rico* (*supra*), the Court should give particular deference to D's choice because D could, if it chose, ban the sale of alcoholic beverages outright. While *Posadas* did hold that a state could reduce gambling by suppressing in-state casino advertising, that case erroneously performed the First Amendment analysis. The Court should not have held that the legislature could choose suppression over a less speech-restrictive policy. *Posadas* was also erroneous in applying a "greater-includes-the-lesser" approach that would allow a state that can ban activity outright to ban speech regarding the activity. The power to prohibit an activity is not necessarily greater than the power to suppress speech about it. Under the First Amendment, it should be more difficult for the government to suppress speech than to suppress conduct.

- *Posadas* also held that an advertising ban was permissible if it targets commercial speech that pertains to a "vice" activity. The scope of any "vice" exception to First Amendment protections would be impossible to define. Labeling activity a "vice" cannot permit greater speech restrictions, especially where there is no corresponding prohibition against the commercial behavior involved.

- The Twenty-First Amendment grants the states authority over commerce that might otherwise be reserved to the federal government, but it does not limit other constitutional provisions.

Concurrence (Scalia, J.). Both sides in this case accepted the *Central Hudson* approach, which should be reexamined in favor of a test based on state legislative practices prevalent at the time the First and Fourteenth Amendments were adopted.

Concurrence (Thomas, J.). When the government asserts an interest to keep legal users of a product or service ignorant in order to manipulate their choices in the marketplace, the interest should be deemed per se illegitimate without applying the *Central Hudson* test. The majority implies that if the ban had been more successful in decreasing alcohol consumption by keeping consumers ignorant, it might have been upheld under *Central Hudson*.

Concurrence (O'Connor, J., Rehnquist, C.J., Souter, Breyer, JJ.). The Court should apply *Central Hudson* to these facts. Even assuming the first three prongs are satisfied, D's ban does not meet the final prong because the ban is more extensive than necessary to serve the state's interest. There are several readily available alternatives that would not suppress speech. Since *Posadas*, the Court has required a closer look at this prong.

XII. FREEDOM OF SPEECH—HOW GOVERNMENT RESTRICTS SPEECH

A. DISTINCTION BETWEEN CONTENT-BASED AND CONTENT-NEUTRAL REGULATIONS

1. **Content-Based Restrictions.** If a restriction on speech relies on the content of the speech, the Court will scrutinize it much more carefully than if the restriction is content-neutral. This analysis underlies many of the Court's recent cases.

    a. **Ban on labor picketing.** In *Police Department v. Mosley*, 408 U.S. 92 (1972), the Court struck down a disorderly conduct ordinance prohibiting picketing at certain times near public schools, except for peaceful labor picketing. Picketing is protected by the First Amendment but may be subject to reasonable time, place, and manner regulations. However, regulations based on subject matter is tantamount to government censorship and violates both equal protection and the First Amendment.

        1) **Picketing against racial discrimination.** The Court relied on *Mosley* to invalidate another picketing restriction in *Carey v. Brown*, 447 U.S. 455 (1980), which involved a peaceful picket outside the mayor's home to protest racial discrimination in schools. At issue was a law banning picketing outside residences but exempting peaceful labor dispute picketing outside places of employment, even if residences. The Court ruled that the content-based restriction has no bearing on privacy, since it allows labor picketing, but bans all other types and thus, violates the First Amendment. The dissent argued that the law was not based on content but rather, the character of the picketed residence.

    b. **Crime victims and publishing profits.** The Court, in *Simon & Schuster, Inc. v. Members of New York State Crime Victims Board*, 502 U.S. 105 (1991), invalidated New York's "Son of Sam" law that required payment to a crime victim's board of any profits derived from books by criminals about their crimes. The law was unconstitutional because it imposed a burden on speech of only a particular content and was not narrowly tailored to the state's undisputed compelling interest. It was also overinclusive and would include such works as Malcolm X's autobiography and Thoreau's *Civil Disobedience*. A concurring opinion by Justice Kennedy found the law invalid per se.

c. **Polling place restrictions.** The Court considered a conflict between free speech rights and the fundamental right to vote in *Burson v. Freeman*, 504 U.S. 191 (1992). The Court concluded that this was that rare case under which a law limiting speech survives strict scrutiny. The challenged law imposed a ban on all electioneering activities within 100 feet of polling place entrances. It was held that, although the law was a facially content-based restriction on political speech in a public forum, it was valid because of a long history of election reform to combat fraud and intimidation, a substantial consensus, and common sense, which shows that the restricted area is necessary to protect the fundamental right and does not constitute an unconstitutional compromise.

d. **Impact on audience.** In *Boos v. Barry*, 485 U.S. 312 (1988), the Court invalidated a law banning displays critical of foreign governments within 500 feet of foreign embassies. Listeners' reactions to the content-based restriction is not the type of secondary effects considered in *Renton*, *supra*.

2. **Content-Neutral Laws and Symbolic Conduct.** The protection afforded unpopular words extends to symbolic conduct that can be considered expression—*i.e.*, conduct undertaken to communicate an idea.

a. **Draft card burning--**

United States v. O'Brien, 391 U.S. 367 (1968).

Facts. O'Brien and others (Ds) publicly burned their draft cards, in violation of federal law. Ds claim their action was intended to influence others to adopt their antiwar beliefs. Ds were convicted, but the court of appeals held that the statute was an unconstitutional abridgement of freedom of speech. The United States (P) appeals.

Issue. When conduct contains both "speech" and "nonspeech" elements, may an important governmental interest in regulating the nonspeech element justify incidental limitations on First Amendment freedoms?

Held. Yes. Judgment reversed.

- ♦ The statute does not abridge free speech on its face, but deals with conduct having no connection with speech, *i.e.*, destruction of draft cards.
- ♦ Although freedom of expression includes certain symbolic speech, it does not include any and all conduct intended to express an idea. Even conduct that contains a protected communicative element is not absolutely immune from government regulation. A sufficiently important governmental interest in regulating the nonspeech element of conduct can justify incidental limitations on the speech element.

♦ A government regulation is justified if: (i) it is within constitutional authority; (ii) it furthers an important governmental interest; (iii) the interest is unrelated to the suppression of free expression; and (iv) the incidental restriction on First Amendment freedoms is no greater than is essential to the furtherance of that interest. The draft card laws meet these tests; therefore, D may properly be prosecuted for his illegal activity.

---

b. **Incidental restrictions.** The *O'Brien* Court formulated a less-than-strict-scrutiny analysis for examining incidental limitations on protected speech. However, this heightened scrutiny is not required on all "incidental" restrictions. For example, in *Arcara v. Cloud Books, Inc.*, 478 U.S. 697 (1986), the Court found no First Amendment implications in the closure of an adult bookstore, where prostitution was occurring, as a nuisance under a law defining places of prostitution, assignation, and lewdness to be public health nuisances. Unlike the symbolic conduct in *O'Brien*, the sexual activity was not protected expression, nor were bookstores singled out. The burden, if any, on bookselling could be mitigated by selling books at another location. Civil and criminal sanctions are not traditionally subject to least restrictive means scrutiny simply because a remedy may have some effect on First Amendment activities. Rather, such scrutiny is applied only to conduct specifically directed at expression.

c. **Flag desecration.** The earlier flag cases did not reach the issue of whether flag desecration was protected speech. In a 5 to 4 decision in *Street v. New York*, 394 U.S. 576 (1969), the Court struck down a law making it a crime to publicly defile or cast contempt on an American flag. Not reaching the issue of the constitutionality of flag burning as political protest, the Court found that the law was unconstitutionally applied to the defendant as punishment for his speech, not for his conduct. In 1974, under a similar law, the Court reversed a conviction based on a flag sewn to the seat of trousers. The holding was based on a due process doctrine of vagueness. [Smith v. Goguen, 415 U.S. 566 (1974); *see also* Spence v. Washington, 418 U.S. 405 (1974)—law unconstitutional as applied to removable peace symbol attached to flag because it was a peaceful, nondestructive means of communication]

d. **Flag burning--**

Texas v. Johnson, 491 U.S. 397 (1989).

Facts. During the 1984 Republican National Convention, Johnson (D) doused an American flag with kerosene and set it on fire, to chants of "America, the red, white, and blue, we spit on you." Several witnesses were seriously offended, but no one was physically injured or threatened with injury. D was convicted of desecration of the flag and sentenced to a year in prison and a $2,000 fine. The Texas Court of Criminal Appeals reversed. Texas (P) appeals.

Issue. May a state make it a criminal offense to burn the American flag?

Held. No. Judgment affirmed.

- D's burning of the flag constitutes expressive, overtly political conduct, so he can invoke the First Amendment under *Spence*. The government has greater latitude to regulate expressive conduct than written or spoken words, but it may not prohibit conduct because of the conduct's expressive elements.

- The standard established in *O'Brien* applies when the government interest in regulating conduct is unrelated to the suppression of expression. P here claims an interest in preventing breaches of the peace and in preserving the flag as a symbol of nationhood and national unity. On these facts, the first interest is not implicated, and the second is related to the suppression of expression. Accordingly, the *O'Brien* test does not apply.

- P's interest in preserving the symbolism of the flag is aimed not at the flag's physical integrity (because burning is a permitted means of disposing of an old flag), but at the likely offense D's conduct would cause. Because P's restriction is content-based, it is subject to the most exacting scrutiny.

- The government clearly may not prohibit the expression of an idea simply because society finds the idea offensive. No exceptions to this principle have ever been permitted. The government is not empowered to ensure that a symbol be used to express only one view, nor does the Constitution recognize any special judicial category for the American flag. Therefore, the government may not criminally punish a person for burning the flag as a means of political protest.

Dissent (Rehnquist, C.J., White, O'Connor, JJ.). The American flag is not just another idea competing for recognition in the marketplace of ideas. The flag has a special status. D could have conveyed his message in any of a number of alternative ways. In fact, D's form of protest was relatively inarticulate, and he was punished not for the idea he sought to convey, but only for the use of this particular symbol.

Dissent (Stevens, J.). The flag symbolizes not just nationhood, but also freedom, equal opportunity, and other fundamental values. The government may protect the flag as much as it may protect the Washington Monument against even political graffiti. Sanctioning public desecration of the flag will tarnish its value. This case involves disagreeable conduct, not disagreeable ideas.

Comment. The same majority held unconstitutional a federal statute enacted by Congress in reaction to *Johnson* that was intended to prevent any mutilation, including burnings, of any flag of the United States, except during proper disposal. [United States v. Eichman, 496 U.S. 310 (1990)]

---

e. **Public indecency and the prohibition of nude dancing.** In *Barnes v. Glen Theatre, Inc.*, 501 U.S. 560 (1991), the Court upheld an Indiana public indecency statute that prohibited complete nudity in public places and required that dancers at adult entertainment establishments wear pasties and G-strings. The plurality stated that nude dancing is expressive conduct, even if it is only marginally protected by the First Amendment. But under the four-part *O'Brien* test, the plurality found that the statute was justified despite its incidental limitations on some expressive activity. They reasoned that the public indecency statute furthered substantial governmental interests in protecting societal order and morality and that it was within the traditional police power of a state. The plurality contended that the governmental interests were unrelated to the suppression of free expression and that the statute did not proscribe nudity because of the erotic message conveyed by the dancers; erotic performances could be performed, as long as the performers wore a scant amount of clothing. The plurality held that a state may properly prevent public nudity, even if it is combined with expressive activity, and that the statute was narrowly tailored because requiring the wearing of pasties and G-strings was the bare minimum necessary to achieve the state's purposes. Justice Scalia, concurring in the judgment only, asserted that the statute was not subject to First Amendment scrutiny at all because it was a general law that regulated conduct and was not specifically directed at expression. Justice Souter also concurred in the judgment only, finding that the *O'Brien* test properly applied in this case and that the state's interest in preventing "secondary effects" such as prostitution, sexual assault, and other criminal activity was sufficient to justify enforcement of the statute. Justice White, joined by Justices Marshall, Blackmun, and Stevens, argued that the purpose of a ban on public nudity, which is to protect others from offense, is inapplicable in establishments where people pay to see nude dancing. The dissent maintained that nudity is an expressive component of the dance, not incidental conduct, and that the statute was therefore related to expressive conduct.

f. **Prohibition of public nudity to avoid harmful secondary effects.** In *City of Erie v. Pap's A.M.*, 529 U.S. 277 (2000), the Court upheld a municipal ordinance similar to the statute in *Barnes, supra*. However, the plurality in this case found that the ordinance's purpose of combating the negative secondary effects, such as crime, caused by the presence of nude dancing establishments satisfied the *O'Brien* standard.

B. GOVERNMENT POWER TO LIMIT SPEECH IN PARTICULAR SETTINGS

1. Speech in Public Forums.

a. **Early cases.** Since the 1930s, the Court has imposed some limits on restrictions of speech in the public forum. [*See, e.g.*, Hague v. CIO, 307 U.S. 496 (1939)—privilege to use public places for communication of views concerning national issues has been part of the rights and liberties of citizens since ancient times] Several early cases invalidated standardless licensing regulations for granting public officials too much discretion [*see* Saia v. New York, 334 U.S. 558 (1948)], but permit requirements that contain objective standards have been upheld [*see* Cox v. New Hampshire, 312 U.S 569 (1941)]. Total bans on distribution were usually found to be an unconstitutional interference with free speech. [*See* Schneider v. State, 308 U.S. 147 (1939) and Martin v. Struthers, 319 U.S. 141 (1943)—flat ban on leaflets] However, in *Kovacs v. Cooper*, 336 U.S. 77 (1949), a ban on loud and raucous outside loudspeakers was upheld, but it was noted that prohibition of all loudspeakers would probably violate the First Amendment. The *Kovacs* dissent argued that the First Amendment protected all means of public communication from government censorship or prohibition. Thereafter, the Court seldom used the reasoning of *Schneider* and *Martin* or of the *Kovacs* dissent to invalidate content-neutral regulations, but extended the antidiscrimination rule of the standardless licensing decisions to invalidate nearly all content-based restrictions. In 1994, the Court resurrected the presumption against total medium bans in *City of Ladue v. Gilleo*, 512 U.S. 43 (1994), which held that a ban on the posting of most signs was unconstitutional because it banned too much speech.

b. **The "time, place, and manner" test.**

1) **Introduction.** While the government has the power to regulate the time, place, and manner of speech, the scope of this power depends in part on the governmental interest asserted.

2) **Public order and safety.** The government has a legitimate interest in maintaining public order and safety, but this interest may not be used to ban public expression entirely, or to regulate it in an arbitrary manner that may allow censorship.

a) **Need for guidelines.** In *Cox v. Louisiana, supra*, the Court reversed Cox's conviction under the law that prohibited the obstruction of any public sidewalk or street. While recognizing that the state had a duty to keep public passageways open, the Court noted that the law had been applied so as to allow parades and meetings on the street, upon prior approval. But there were no standards to guide local officials in issuing permits, which permitted the official to act as a censor.

b) **Restriction to specified space.** In *Heffron v. International Society for Krishna Consciousness, Inc.*, 452 U.S. 640 (1981), the Court held that a state fair may restrict distribution of literature and solicitation of funds to assigned booths. The Court noted that the First Amendment does not guarantee the right to communicate one's views at all times and places or in any manner that might be desired. The Court found that the restrictive rule was a proper time, place, and manner restriction because it was not based on content and served the significant governmental interest in protecting the "safety and convenience" of persons using a public forum. Also, the rule did not foreclose all means of expression, since the restriction did not apply outside the fair.

3) **Zoning for aesthetics.** Government aesthetic interests have been recognized as substantial or significant in many cases. For example, in *Metromedia, Inc. v. San Diego*, 453 U.S. 490 (1981), the Court upheld a ban on billboards, excepting signs on the advertiser's business site, but invalidated a ban on noncommercial billboards. The plurality were deferential to the city's determination that the ban on off-site signs was necessary to eliminate distracting hazards to motorists and pedestrians and to preserve and improve the city's appearance. However, the noncommercial regulation was struck down because it gave commercial speech more protection than noncommercial speech. Additionally, the exceptions to the noncommercial signs provision resulted in content-based regulation.

a) **Utility poles--**

Members of City Council v. Taxpayers for Vincent, 466 U.S. 789 (1984).

Facts. Taxpayers for Vincent (P) attached political signs to utility poles in the city of Los Angeles (D). D had an ordinance that prohibited the posting of signs on public property, and D's employees routinely removed all posters attached to utility poles, including P's posters. P brought suit in federal court for an injunction against enforcement of the ordinance. The trial court granted D's motion for summary judgment, holding that the ordinance was constitutional. The court of appeals held that D did not justify its total ban on posting signs. D appeals.

Issue. May a city prohibit the posting of all signs on public property?

Held. Yes. Judgment reversed and remanded.

- The First Amendment forbids governments from regulating speech so as to favor some viewpoints at the expense of others. D's rule here does not violate this principle; the text of the ordinance is silent as to any particular point of view and it has been applied equally to all violators. Such a viewpoint-neutral regulation is justified if:

  It is within the constitutional power of the government;

  It furthers an important or substantial governmental interest;

  The governmental interest is unrelated to the suppression of free expression; and

  The incidental restriction on alleged First Amendment freedoms is no greater than is essential to furtherance of that interest.

- P admits that D has the constitutional power to enhance its appearance, and that this interest is basically unrelated to the suppression of ideas. In *Metromedia, Inc. v. San Diego* (*supra*), the Court held that a city's interest in avoiding visual clutter is a substantial governmental interest. Likewise, D's ordinance here furthers a significant governmental interest.

- In another case, the Court had held that the city's interest in preventing general littering of the streets cannot support a prohibition against all distribution of leaflets on the public streets and sidewalks. Such an ordinance was too broad; the same objective could have been attained by penalizing those who litter. Here, however, D's ordinance does no more than eliminate the exact source of the evil; the signs themselves have the adverse impact on the appearance of the city. As D's ordinance responds precisely to D's problem, the incidental restriction on alleged First Amendment freedoms is no greater than is essential.

- D was not required to extend the ban to private property. Private owners' interest in controlling their own land justifies different treatment, and private owners will likely keep clutter on their property under control. P has alternative means available to communicate its message. Nor was D required by the Constitution to make exceptions that would allow P to post signs.

Dissent (Brennan, Marshall, Blackmun, JJ.). The Court's permissive approach toward restriction of speech for aesthetic purposes undermines the protections of the First Amendment. Aesthetics are too subjective to allow meaningful judicial review; the Court should scrutinize the validity of D's bare declaration of an aesthetic objective. D should be required to pursue its objective comprehensively if it is to impose a total ban on a particularly valuable method of communication.

b) Sleeping in public parks--

Clark v. Community for Creative Non-Violence, 468 U.S. 288 (1984).

Facts. The Community for Creative Non-Violence (P) obtained a permit from Clark (D), Secretary of the Interior, to conduct a wintertime demonstration in Lafayette Park and the Mall in Washington, D.C. The demonstration consisted of two symbolic tent cities, intended to show the plight of the homeless. However, D denied P's request that demonstrators be allowed to sleep in the tents. D's regulations prohibited camping in national parks except in designated campgrounds. P sued to prevent application of the regulations to its demonstration. The district court granted D summary judgment, but the court of appeals reversed. D appeals.

Issue. May the federal government prevent demonstrators from sleeping in national parks pursuant to general regulations when the sleeping is asserted to be expression?

Held. Yes. Judgment reversed.

- Assuming that overnight sleeping is expressive conduct, it is subject to reasonable time, place, and manner restrictions. In addition, symbolic expression may be regulated or forbidden if: (i) the regulation is narrowly drawn to further a substantial governmental interest; and (ii) the interest is unrelated to the suppression of free speech.

- D's regulations are defensible both as time, place, and manner restrictions on expressive conduct and as regulations of symbolic conduct. The regulation is clearly content neutral. It narrowly focuses on D's interest in maintaining the parks in a suitable condition.

- Although D could have issued more restrictive regulations, these regulations are valid and reasonable as long as the parks would be more exposed to harm without the sleeping prohibitions than with them. The court of appeals determined that other alternatives, less restrictive on speech, were available. This is a disagreement with D, but the judiciary does not manage the national parks.

Concurrence (Burger, C.J.). Sleeping is conduct, not speech entitled to First Amendment protection.

Dissent (Marshall, Brennan, JJ.). The symbolic speech involved here is subject to reasonable time, place, and manner restrictions. D's regulations do not advance substantial government interests in this case. The Court has adopted a two-tiered approach to First Amendment cases. Once the regulation has been shown to be content neutral, the Court applies a lower level of scrutiny, thus diminishing First Amendment protections.

4) **Tranquility, privacy, and repose.**

a) **Noise regulations.** New York City required use of city-provided sound systems and technicians for concerts in Central Park. The Court rejected a First Amendment challenge in *Ward v. Rock Against Racism*, 491 U.S. 781 (1989). In construing the least intrusive means requirement considered in *United States v. O'Brien*, *supra*, the *Ward* Court relied on the rephrasing enunciated in *Clark*, *supra*, that the means must be "narrowly drawn" to further a substantial governmental interest. The Court found that this standard was the same as the narrowly tailored requirement for time, place, and manner restrictions, which was met in this case. Such restrictions are not invalid just because there may be a less burdensome alternative. The dissent contended that a least-restrictive-alternative analysis was built into the narrowly tailored requirement.

b) **Targeted residential picketing.** In *Frisby v. Schultz*, 487 U.S. 474 (1988), the Court upheld a municipality's flat ban on "focused picketing" of an individual residence. The Court noted the content neutrality of the ordinance, the alternative channels of communication that remained available, and the governmental interest in the protection of residential privacy; and it distinguished the focused nature of the picketing here from the more generally directed communication involved in the leafleting and door-to-door solicitation cases. Two of the dissenters believed that a municipality could regulate such aspects of residential picketing as noise level, hours, etc., but could not prohibit it entirely.

c) **Abortion clinic protests.** *Madsen v. Women's Health Center, Inc.*, involved a challenge to a Florida state injunction that limited the picketing and demonstrating of antiabortion protestors on the public streets outside an abortion clinic. The Court in part upheld and in part struck down the injunction, ruling that when a court evaluates a content-neutral injunction, as opposed to a general statute, the court must apply a more stringent test than the standard time, place, and manner analysis. The Court explained that because an injunction carries greater risks of censorship and discriminatory application than does a general ordinance, the courts must inquire whether the challenged provisions of an injunction "burden no more speech than necessary to serve a significant government interest." The Court found several significant government interests protected by the injunction in this case, including protection of a woman's freedom to seek lawful medical or counseling services for her pregnancy, ensuring public safety and order, and protecting residential privacy.

5) **Invalidation of time, place, and manner regulation—Supreme Court grounds.** In *United States v. Grace*, 461 U.S. 171 (1983), the Court invalidated a portion of federal law that banned the display of certain types of devices and banners in the Supreme Court building or on its grounds, including public sidewalks or the perimeter of the property. The Court found the public sidewalk prohibition unconstitutional because the walks are a public forum historically open to expressive activities and there is no substantial governmental interest served by the ban.

6) **Speaker access to other public places.**

   a) **Libraries, jails, and schools.** In *Brown v. Louisiana*, 383 U.S. 131 (1966), a sharply divided Court reversed breach of the peace convictions arising from a peaceful sit-in in a segregated public library. The plurality opinion rested on due process grounds and the right of speech and assembly. However, the Court upheld convictions of students for trespassing on the premises of a county jail where they had gone to protest against the arrests of student civil rights demonstrators. [Adderley v. Florida, 385 U.S. 39 (1966)] The sheriff's objections rested on the students' presence on that part of the grounds used for jail purposes, not on the expressive content or motivation for their conduct. A state has the right to preserve property for the use for which it was intended. The dissent argued that a prison is an obvious place to petition for redress of grievances. Similarly, a prohibition on demonstrations near schools during school hours was upheld since the activity materially disrupted the classwork. [Grayned v. Rockford, 408 U.S. 104 (1972)]

   b) **Public transportation.** In *Lehman v. Shaker Heights*, 418 U.S. 298 (1974), the Court upheld a city rule against political advertising on city-owned buses; commercial ads were allowed. The court observed that a bus was not a park or public sidewalk. The nature of the forum was commercial—although city-owned, the city was engaging in commercial activity and could limit its advertising just as a newspaper, etc., can. Moreover, the distinction between commercial and political advertising advances the legislative objectives of minimizing chances for abuse, appearances of favoritism, and imposing on a captive audience.

c) **Municipal theaters.** First Amendment rights were violated when a municipal managing board refused permission to present the musical *Hair* on the ground of obscenity. The Court, in *Southeastern Promotions, Ltd. v. Conrad*, 420 U.S. 546 (1975), noted that municipal theaters are public forums designed for expressive activities. As such, unbridled discretion to determine obscenity is censorship, *i.e.*, prior restraint.

d) **Military bases.** Military bases may be closed to political speeches and distribution of leaflets, if done evenhandedly. This is true even if the public is generally permitted to visit the base, because of the strong government interest in keeping the military free of partisan political entanglements. [*See* Greer v. Spock, 424 U.S. 828 (1976)] The government may also bar persons with records of past disruptions from entering the base even during a public open house. [United States v. Albertini, 472 U.S. 675 (1985)]

7) **Traditional, designated, and nonpublic forums.**

a) **Mailboxes.** In *Postal Service v. Council of Greenburgh Civic Associations*, 453 U.S. 114 (1981), the Court held that the First Amendment does not guarantee a civic association the right to deposit literature, without payment of postage, in home mail boxes approved by the United States Postal Service. The Court explained that although a postal customer pays for the depository, he agrees to abide by the regulations of the Postal Service in exchange for the service's handling his mail. The Postal Services's authorization of such depositories does not make them a "public forum." Property owned or controlled by the government that is not a public forum may be subject to a prohibition of speech, picketing, etc., without violating the First Amendment.

b) **Teachers' mailboxes.** A school district may restrict access to its interschool mail system so that an exclusive labor bargaining representative may use the mail system and teachers' mailboxes, but a challenger may not. [Perry Education Association v. Perry Local Educators' Association, 460 U.S. 37 (1983)] The public school mail system fell within the category of public property that is not by tradition or designation a public forum. Access to such property may be limited as long as the restriction on speech is reasonable, and not an arbitrary suppression of ideas.

c) **Charitable campaigns in federal offices.** An executive order limited participation in the Combined Federal Campaign

("CFC"), an annual fundraising drive conducted during working hours in the federal workplace, to charitable organizations; political advocacy groups were excluded. In *Cornelius v. NAACP Legal Defense and Education Fund, Inc.*, 473 U.S. 788 (1985), the Court upheld the executive order, finding that participation in the "CFC" was a form of charitable solicitation of funds, which is protected speech, but that the CFC was a nonpublic forum.

d) **Post Office sidewalks.** In *United States v. Kokinda*, 497 U.S. 720 (1990), the Court upheld a Postal Service regulation that prohibited people from soliciting contributions on postal premises. Political volunteers had set up a table on a sidewalk next to a post office entrance to collect contributions. The sidewalk was adjacent to the post office building and connected it to the parking lot, but the sidewalk was not on the main street. The Court held that this sidewalk was not the kind of sidewalk that constituted a traditional public forum. This sidewalk was used only for entrance to the post office. The restriction was not based on content and was reasonable under the circumstances. Justice Kennedy considered the restriction to be an appropriate time, place, and manner regulation. Four justices dissented on the ground that a public sidewalk adjacent to a public building should be a public forum.

e) **Airport terminals.** Members of the International Society for Krishna Consciousness ("ISKCON") challenged a Port Authority regulation that prohibited the repetitive sale of merchandise, the solicitation of money, or the distribution of literature within the interior areas of buildings at the major airports in the New York City area. Such activities were permitted on the sidewalks outside the terminal buildings. In *International Society for Krishna Consciousness v. Lee*, 505 U.S. 672 (1992), the Court held that an airport terminal operated by a public authority may prohibit solicitation in the interior of its buildings. Writing for the Court, Chief Justice Rehnquist explained that airports do not meet the requirements of traditional public forums. They were not historically made available for speech activity, and their purpose is to facilitate travel and to make a regulated profit, not to promote expression. Because an airport is not a public forum, the Court ruled that regulations are permissible as long as they are reasonable. The Court found that face-to-face solicitation presents a risk of duress and fraud and that ISKCON's proposed solicitation had a disruptive effect on airport travelers who are typically in a hurry and for whom a delay can mean a lost flight and severe inconvenience. Therefore, the ban on solicitation was sustained. However, in the companion case of *Lee v. International Society for Krishna Consciousness, Inc.*, 505 U.S. 830 (1992), the Court held that the ban on the distribution of literature was invalid.

8) **Religious speech on public property.** The Establishment Clause has been interpreted to prohibit government from establishing religion both overtly and through symbolic endorsement or financial support. While the Establishment Clause does not require government to exclude religious speech from fora opened to expression, the First Amendment prohibits government from discriminating against religious expression.

   a) **School facilities as a public forum.** [*See also* Grayned v. Rockford, *supra*] In exercising the strict scrutiny usually applied to content-based exclusions from public places, the Court in *Widmar v. Vincent*, 454 U.S. 263 (1981), held that when state university facilities are generally available for use by registered student groups, the university becomes a public forum. Consequently, a group's use of the facilities for religious worship and discussion cannot be barred, even on the basis of promoting the separation of church and state. However, the Court did state that the university had a right to establish reasonable time, place, and manner restrictions. In his dissent, Justice White objected to the Court's view that religious worship is protected by the free speech provision because such worship uses speech. Justice White argued that the challenge to the ban must rest solely on a claim that the state's action impermissibly interferes with the free exercise of religious practices.

   b) **Religious use of school property permitted.** In *Lamb's Chapel v. Center Moriches Union Free School District*, 508 U.S. 384 (1993), the Court held that if a school permitted the use of school property for social, civic, and recreational meetings, it could not prohibit the use of school property by student bible clubs.

   c) **Religious speech in public forums.** In *Capitol Square Review and Advisory Board v. Pinette*, 115 U.S. 753 (1995), the Court allowed the Ku Klux Klan to erect a cross on a public square where other unattended displays had been permitted.

2. First Amendment Access Rights to Private Property.

a. In *Amalgamated Food Employees Union v. Logan Valley Plaza*, 391 U.S. 308 (1968), the Court held that a state trespass law could not be applied to enjoin union picketing of a supermarket in a private shopping center. The premises resembled those of the business area of a municipality—and "public places" are historically associated with the exercise of First Amendment rights. Such exercise cannot be constitutionally denied broadly and absolutely, which the state law did. Such rights, however, cannot unduly interfere with the normal use of the property.

b. In *Lloyd Corp. v. Tanner*, 407 U.S. 551 (1972), the Court distinguished *Logan Valley* and upheld a shopping center ban on antiwar handbill distribution. The Court reasoned that *Logan Valley* involved union picketing, which was related to the shopping center's activity, but that antiwar handbills were not so related and could therefore be prohibited. Four justices dissented, arguing that *Logan Valley* was controlling and that areas such as a community's business district should be open to public communication.

c. In *Hudgens v. NLRB*, 424 U.S. 507 (1976), the Court ruled that *Lloyd* had in effect overruled *Logan Valley*. *Hudgens* involved labor picketing of a store in a private shopping center by employees of a warehouse located outside the center but owned by the same store owner. The Court reasoned that if the *Lloyd* respondent had no First Amendment right to distribute "Vietnam" handbills, then respondents in this case had no right to advertise their strike on the premises.

3. Speech in Public Schools.

a. **Introduction.** Public schools by necessity control speech. Administrators and classroom teachers determine what subjects are to be studied and discussed. However, students also participate in noncurricular activities while at school. Generally, students are allowed to engage in expression that does not materially disrupt the educational purpose of the school.

b. **Black armbands as nondisruptive symbolic conduct.** In *Tinker v. Des Moines School District*, 393 U.S. 503 (1969), the Court held that a public school could not discipline students for wearing black armbands to school to protest the Vietnam War because such conduct is a symbolic act protected by the First Amendment. The students' expression was passive and did not interfere with the educational process. Prohibition of a particular expression of opinion is only justified by showing a material interference with the school's discipline. Avoidance of controversy attending unpopular opinion is an inadequate reason for a ban.

c. **Book removal from public school libraries.** Members of a school board obtained a list of "objectionable" books and removed eight out of nine of the books from the high school library. The board based its decision on claims that the books were anti-American and presented moral danger to the students. In *Board of Education v. Pico*, 457 U.S. 853 (1982), the Court held that the First Amendment imposes limitations on a local school board's discretionary removal of books from a high school library. The Court pointed out that local school boards' discretion in managing school affairs is subject to the First Amendment rights of the students. A board's discretion may not be exercised so as to deny students access to ideas with which the board members disagree, although they could remove books that were pervasively vulgar or educationally unsuitable. The evidence as to the board's motive in removing the books was unclear. Thus, the Court remanded the case for trial.

d. **Sexual innuendo at student assembly.** In *Bethel School District No. 403 v. Fraser*, 478 U.S. 675 (1986), the Court upheld the right of a school district to discipline a high school student who made a lewd speech at a school assembly. This speech was contrasted with the political message involved in *Tinker, supra.*

e. **Articles on pregnancy and divorce in school newspaper.** In *Hazelwood School District v. Kuhlmeier*, 484 U.S. 260 (1988), a high school principal had deleted two articles from the school newspaper, which was produced by the school journalism class and funded by the school. One article dealt with three students' experiences with pregnancy, and the other dealt with the impact of divorce on students. The Court held that a high school may exercise control over the content of a student-produced high school paper. The Court found that the newspaper was not a public forum; thus, school officials were entitled to regulate the contents of the paper in any reasonable manner. Also, this case involved the question of whether the First Amendment requires a school affirmatively to promote particular student speech, a different question from that involved in *Tinker* (*i.e.*, whether a school must tolerate particular student speech). Because the newspaper was school-sponsored, the public might have reasonably perceived it to bear the imprimatur of the school; educators may exercise greater control over this type of student expression to preserve its educational value as well as protect against attribution of the expression to the school. The Court ruled that the principal in this case acted reasonably in deleting the specific articles involved.

4. **Speech and Association by Public Employees and Contractors.**

a. **Introduction.** Political activity by government employees raises free speech and free association issues unlike those faced by employees in private industry. The public interest in freeing government from graft and political favoritism justifies reasonable restrictions on the political activities of government employees.

b. **Public employee speech.**

1) **Balancing approach.** The Court set forth a balancing approach in *Pickering v. Board of Education*, 391 U.S. 563 (1968). This approach recognizes that the governmental interest in regulating government employees differs from its interest in regulating citizenry in general. The interest in promoting the efficiency of government must be balanced against the employee's rights, as a citizen, to comment on matters of public interest. The Court held that a teacher could not be fired for writing a letter to a newspaper criticizing the school board.

2) **Internal office affairs--**

Connick v. Myers, 461 U.S. 138 (1983).

Facts. Myers (P) worked as assistant district attorney under Connick (D), the local district attorney. Despite her objections, P was to be transferred to another section. She prepared a questionnaire intended to solicit her fellow employees' opinions about transfer policy, office morale, the level of confidence in named supervisors, and pressure to work in political campaigns. D fired P for insubordination. P sued, claiming wrongful termination based on her exercise of free speech. The lower courts upheld P's claim. The Supreme Court granted certiorari.

Issue. Do the First and Fourteenth Amendments prohibit the discharge of a state employee for circulating a questionnaire concerning internal office affairs?

Held. No. Judgment reversed.

- ♦ Questions of a public employee's right to free speech involve a balance between the employee's interests as a citizen in commenting on matters of public concern, and the state's interest as an employer in promoting the efficiency of the public services it provides through its employees.
- ♦ The focus of P's questionnaire is to gather ammunition for her controversy with D. Such speech dealing with matters of personal interest is normally not the type that federal courts should pass on as to whether the termination was unconstitutional. The matter of pressure to work on political campaigns does touch a public concern, though.
- ♦ The state's burden to justify a termination depends on the nature of the employee's speech. Here, P's limited First Amendment interest did not require

D to tolerate disruptive activity. The evidence indicates that P's actions carried the potential to undermine office relations. Therefore, P's dismissal was not unconstitutional.

Dissent (Brennan, Marshall, Blackmun, Stevens, JJ.). P's questionnaire dealt with the manner in which the government is, or should be, operated. Such communication is essential for self-governance, which is a major basis for the First Amendment. The public interest of a statement does not depend on where it is said or why. The district court found that the questionnaire was not disruptive. The deference given by the majority to D's judgment is unjustified. The effect of the decision will be to deter public employees from speaking out.

Comment. In *Rankin v. McPherson*, 483 U.S. 378 (1987), a 5 to 4 decision found that a clerical employee in a city constable's office could not be discharged for remarking, in a private conversation, that "[i]f they go for him again, I hope they get him," after the attempted assassination of President Reagan. The state's interest in content-related sanctions was minimal where the employee is not in a confidential, policymaking, or public contact role. The speech did not interfere with the functioning of the office nor was it made in a manner that would discredit the office.

---

3) **Public or private concern.** The Court held in *Waters v. Churchill*, 511 U.S. 661 (1994), that the discharge of a public employee for what the employer reasonably believed was speech on a matter of private concern, even if erroneous, does not violate the First Amendment. The scope of what is public speech of matters on public concern was considered in *United States v. National Treasury Employees Union*, 513 U.S. 454 (1995), which involved a federal ethics act barring a wide range of federal employees from receiving compensation for speeches, appearances, or articles. *Pickering* rather than *Conrad* governed the ruling that the ban imposed a significant burden on expressive activity and was facially invalid since it applied to lower echelon employees whose actions had no nexus to their employment and since it referred only to speech, while expressive conduct was not sanctioned.

c. **Public employee political party affiliation.**

1) **The Hatch Act.** The Hatch Act of 1940 [5 U.S.C. §7324(a)(2)] prohibits federal employees from taking "an active part in political management or in political campaigns." The Act was upheld in *United Public Workers v. Mitchell*, 330 U.S. 75 (1947). [*See also* United States Civil Service Commission v. National Association of Letter Carriers, 413 U.S. 548 (1973)—prohibition of

government employees from political management and campaigning upheld where only marginal applications would violate the First Amendment]

2) **Political patronage.** In *Elrod v. Burns*, 427 U.S. 347 (1976), the Court prohibited dismissals from public employment based solely on political beliefs and associations as violating those rights. The Court rejected the government interests asserted in defense of patronage practices. For example, the Court found that there were other means available for dealing with poor job performance that were not based on patronage (*e.g.*, a politically-motivated, insubordinate employee could be dismissed for cause). In *Branti v. Finkel*, 445 U.S. 507 (1980), the Court held that the question of whether a public employee could be dismissed solely on partisan political grounds depended on whether party affiliation was an appropriate requirement for the effective performance of the public office involved. *Elrod* and *Branti* have been extended to decisions regarding hiring, promotion, transfers, and recalls after layoffs. [*See* Rutan v. Republican Party of Illinois, 497 U.S. 62 (1990)]

3) **Independent contractor speech and party affiliation.** While independent contractors may be less dependent on the government than government employees, the Court held that the *Pickering* and *Elrod* rules should apply to independent contractors as well as to government employees. Job labels are not determinative. Otherwise, the government could avoid constitutional liability simply by attaching different labels to particular jobs. [Board of Commissioners, Wabaunsee County v. Umbehr, 518 U.S. 668 (1996) and O'Hare Truck Service, Inc. v. City of Northlake, 518 U.S. 712 (1996)]

5. **Public Subsidies of Speech.**

a. **Government cannot condition benefits on speech content.** The Court has held that the government cannot penalize an individual for the content of his speech by withholding benefits for certain speech. In *Speiser v. Randall*, 357 U.S. 513 (1958), the Court disapproved a state law limiting property tax exemptions for veterans to those who would declare that they did not advocate the forcible overthrow of the government. Denying the exemption was equivalent to punishment for the content of speech.

b. **Restraint in exercising rights.** In some circumstances, the government may condition benefits on a person's or group's restraint in exercising First Amendment rights. Thus, the IRS may withdraw the tax-exempt status of an organization that engages directly in lobbying. [Regan v. Taxation with Representation of Washington, 461 U.S. 540 (1983)]

c. **Editorials on public broadcasting.** Congress created the Corporation for Public Broadcasting ("CPC") to disburse federal funds to noncommercial, educational television and radio stations. Those receiving funds were prohibited from editorializing. In *FCC v. League of Women Voters*, 468 U.S. 364 (1984), that provision was invalidated because it resulted in a content-based penalty on broadcasters' protected speech, not a mere nonsubsidy of speech as in *Regan*. The broadcasting of editorial opinion lies at the core of the First Amendment. The public interest in receiving a reasonable and fair presentation of controversial issues may be insured by the fairness doctrine.

d. **Conditioning federal funds on refraining from speaking.** In *Rust v. Sullivan*, 500 U.S. 173 (1991), the Court upheld Title X of the Public Health Service Act, which provided federal funding for family-planning services, provided that none of the funds could be used in programs where abortion was a method of family planning. Challengers to the regulations claimed that the regulations discriminated based on viewpoint because they promoted childbirth over abortion. But the Court explained that the government had merely chosen to fund one activity to the exclusion of the other. The government has no obligation to subsidize counterpart rights once it decides to subsidize one protected right. The Court found that the regulations did not deny anyone a benefit, but merely required that public funds be spent for the purposes for which they were authorized. The Court also found that the regulations applied to the project, not to the grantee, who could perform abortions and advocate for abortion in other contexts.

e. **Reimbursement of student newspaper with religious expression.** In *Rosenberger v. Rector & Visitors of the University of Virginia*, 515 U.S. 819 (1995), the Court held that a public university could not deny reimbursement to a student newspaper solely on the ground that the newspaper expresses a religious viewpoint. *See* further discussion, *infra*.

C. IMPERMISSIBLE METHODS OF RESTRICTING SPEECH: OVERBREADTH, VAGUENESS, AND PRIOR RESTRAINT

1. Overbreadth.

a. **Introduction.** Even where the government is authorized to restrict constitutional activity, the regulation may not be unnecessarily broad so as to invade areas of protected freedoms. For example, in *Gooding v. Wilson*, *supra*, the Court held that a statute prohibiting the use of "opprobrious words or abusive language, tending to cause a breach of the peace," was too broad because it was not limited to reach fighting words.

b. **Requirement of "substantial" overbreadth.** In *Broadrick v. Oklahoma,* 413 U.S. 601 (1973), the Court changed course and sustained state law restrictions on partisan political activity by public employees against challenges of overbreadth and vagueness. The Court refused to consider the possible effect of the restriction on parties not before the Court. As to those before the Court, the restriction was constitutionally valid. "Although such laws, if too broadly worded, may deter protected speech to some unknown extent, there comes a point where that effect—at best a prediction—cannot, with confidence, justify invalidating a statute on its face and so prohibiting a state from enforcing the statute against conduct that is admittedly within its power to proscribe. To put the matter another way, particularly where conduct and not merely speech is involved, we believe that the overbreadth of a statute must not only be real, but substantial as well, judged in relation to the statute's plainly legitimate sweep." A challenge based on overbreadth may still succeed. [*See* Village of Schaumburg, *infra*, and Schad, *supra*]

c. **No substantial overbreadth in child pornography law.** The Court applied *Broadrick* to find no substantial overbreadth in a child pornography law in *New York v. Ferber*, *supra*, even though it applied not only to hard core pornography, but also to nonpornographic materials (*e.g.*, medical textbooks), which could arguably constitute only a fraction of all materials covered. Case-by-case analysis could cure such over-breadth.

d. **Limits on overbreadth analysis.** In *Brockett v. Spokane Arcades, Inc.*, 472 U.S. 491 (1985), the Court found unconstitutional a law defining obscenity to include nonobscene materials. However, despite an apparent overbreadth finding, the Court refused to invalidate it on its face, limiting the challenger, whose rights were violated under the law, to an invalid-as-applied remedy. In effect, the Court left it to the state to appropriately rewrite the unconstitutional portions.

e. **Invalidation of laws involving charitable solicitation.** The Court facially invalidated a law barring the prohibition of solicitation of charitable contributions by organizations that failed to prove that at least 75% of the receipts were used for charitable purposes. [Village of Schaumburg v. Citizens For a Better Environment, 444 U.S. 620 (1980)] The *Schaumburg* restriction was a direct and substantial limitation of protected activity, which was not sufficiently related to the government's interests of protecting the public from fraud, crime, and annoyance. Alternative means, such as disclosure of use of the funds, were available. Similarly, although the regulation in *Secretary of State v. J.H. Munson Co.*, 468 U.S. 947 (1984), had criminal penalties instead of permit requirements and the 25% limitation on noncharitable use of proceeds was subject to waiver, the Court followed *Schaumburg* in invalidating the restriction on charitable solicitation. The Court held that the activity itself was protected by the First Amendment and that the statute was overbroad and operated on the invalid premise that high solicitation costs accurately measured fraud.

f. **Overbreadth and due process.** In *Massachusetts v. Oakes,* 491 U.S. 576 (1989), a substantially overbroad law was amended by the state legislature to cure the overbreadth subsequent to the defendant's conviction. The Court upheld the defendant's challenge because to hold otherwise would result in significantly reduced incentives for legislators to pay heed to constitutional restraints while legislating. However, in *Osborne v. Ohio*, *supra*, it was held that a ***judicial*** narrowing of an overbroad law ended the problem and permitted application of the statute as construed to prior unprotected conduct as long as the person had fair warning the conduct was covered.

g. **Continued use.** The Court continues to use overbreadth invalidation, which has become a useful technique for reaching an agreement among justices who would otherwise disagree about whether particular conduct is within First Amendment protection. [*See e.g.*, Houston v. Hill, 482 U.S. 451 (1987); Board of Airport Commissioners v. Jews for Jesus, 482 U.S. 569 (1987)]

2. **Vagueness.** A statute that provides inadequate notice of its meaning is considered vague and unenforceable. In *Coates v. Cincinnati*, 402 U.S. 611 (1971), the Court invalidated a ban on sidewalk gatherings that were "annoying" to passersby. This standard was so vague that it actually specified no standard of conduct at all.

3. **Prior Restraint.**

a. **Introduction.** Prior restraint on expression has a heavy presumption against its constitutional validity. Prior restraint can be held unconstitutional even if the speech involved could be constitutionally restricted through subsequent civil liability or criminal punishment. The deterrent effect of such punishment is considered sufficient to protect individual and public rights that might be affected by the speech involved.

b. **Licensing.**

1) **Introduction.** While the government may apply appropriate time, place, and manner restrictions, it may not condition the right of a person to express his views publicly on first obtaining a permit to do so from local authorities where such permits are given on a purely discretionary basis. There must be some reasonable stan-

dard established on which to decide who gets a permit, when, and why.

2) **Unlimited discretion.** In *Lovell v. Griffin*, 303 U.S. 444 (1938), the Court invalidated as a prior restraint an ordinance requiring all distributors of literature to obtain a permit from the city manager. Freedom of the press includes a right to publish without a license. A statute that gives licensing officials undue discretion is void on its face. [*See also* Lakewood v. Plain Dealer Publishing Co., 486 U.S. 750 (1988)—mayor had complete discretion to grant annual permits for placement of newsracks on public property] The *Lakewood* Court identified two risks arising from unbridled licensing schemes: (i) self-censorship in order to obtain a license; and (ii) the difficulty, without standards as guides, of detecting, reviewing, and correcting content-based censorship as applied.

3) **Procedural safeguards.** Flawed licensing schemes may be corrected by promulgating objective standards for administration of the plan. [*See* Cox v. New Hampshire, *supra*] Prior approval of movies was approved in *Freedman v. Maryland*, 380 U.S. 51 (1965), if (i) the standards for denial of a license or permit are narrowly drawn, reasonable, and definite; (ii) the censor promptly seeks an injunction if no permit is to be issued; (iii) the censor has the burden of showing that the film is unprotected speech; and (iv) there is provision for a prompt judicial determination. [*See also* FW/PBS, Inc. v. Dallas, 493 U.S. 215 (1990)—licensing scheme was unconstitutional prior restraint because there was no time limitation for a decision and no provision for prompt judicial review]

   a) **Standing.** Speakers need not seek a permit to sustain a challenge to a law void on its face (*e.g.*, *Lovell* and *Freedman*). However, if the challenge is to the application of a regulation, a permit must be sought before review is requested. [Poulos v. New Hampshire, 345 U.S. 395 (1953)]

   b) **Prior restraint allowed.** In *Kingsley Books, Inc. v. Brown*, 354 U.S. 436 (1957), the Court suggested that prior restraints are not always more harmful to speech than subsequent punishments. Issuance of an injunction halting distribution, promptly followed by a full judicial hearing, protected the *Kingsley* bookseller from prosecution should the books be found obscene. [*See also* Walker v. Birmingham, 388 U.S. 307 (1967)—may not challenge law or injunction if a validly issued injunction is ignored; *and* Carroll v. Princess Anne, 393 U.S. 175 (1968)—injunction unnecessarily issued ex parte is invalid]

c. Injunctions.

1) Defamatory publications--

Near v. Minnesota, 283 U.S. 697 (1931).

Facts. Minnesota (P) enacted a statute that provided for the abatement, as a public nuisance, of "malicious, scandalous, and defamatory" publications. Near (D) published a periodical that criticized law enforcement officers. P brought an action seeking to suppress D's publication. The state courts granted P's request. D appeals.

Issue. May a state provide for prior restraints of defamatory publications?

Held. No. Judgment reversed.

- Permitting public authorities to suppress publication of scandalous matter relating to charges of official dereliction, restrained only by the publisher's ability to satisfy the judge that the charges are true, is the essence of censorship. Liberty of the press under the Constitution has meant, principally although not exclusively, immunity from previous restraints or censorship. The only permissible restraint is the deterrent effect of actions against defamatory publications arising after publication.

Dissent (Butler, Van Devanter, McReynolds, Sutherland, JJ.). The previous restraints precluded by the First Amendment refer to subjection of the press to the arbitrary will of an administrative officer. There is no similarity between such impermissible previous restraint and the decree authorized by this statute to prevent further publication of defamatory articles, and the statute should be upheld.

2) National security--

New York Times Co. v. United States (The Pentagon Papers Case), 403 U.S. 713 (1971).

Facts. The United States (P) sought to enjoin publication by the *New York Times* (D) and *Washington Post* of a classified study known as the Pentagon Papers. All federal courts involved, except the court of appeals in the *New York Times* case, held that P had not met its heavy burden of justification. D appeals the judgment of the court of appeals in its case.

Issue. May the executive branch prevent publication of items which it considers to threaten grave and irreparable injury to the public interest?

Held. No. Judgment reversed.

- The government has failed to meet its heavy burden of showing justification for the enforcement of such a prior restraint.

Concurrence (Black, Douglas, JJ.). The injunctions should have been vacated and the cases dismissed without oral argument because it would be impossible to find that the President has "inherent power" to halt the publication of news by resort to the courts.

Concurrence (Douglas, Black, JJ.). The only possible power possessed by the government to restrict publication by the press of sensitive material arises from its inherent power to wage war successfully. Congress has not declared war, so the government cannot exercise this power.

Concurrence (Brennan, J.). Courts cannot issue temporary stays and restraining orders to accommodate the government's desire to suppress freedom of the press without adequate proof of a direct, inevitable, and immediate serious adverse effect.

Concurrence (Stewart, White, J.). The executive branch has the duty to protect necessary confidentiality through executive regulations. The courts are limited to construing specific regulations and applying specific laws. Since the courts were asked to do neither here, they cannot act.

Concurrence (White, Stewart, JJ.). Some circumstances might justify an injunction as requested, but not these. Congress has relied on criminal sanctions and their deterrent effect to prevent unauthorized disclosures, and the courts should not go beyond the congressional determinations.

Concurrence (Marshall, J.). The Court would violate the concept of separation of powers by using its power to prevent behavior that Congress has specifically declined to prohibit.

Dissent (Burger, C.J.). The Court has not had sufficient time to gather and analyze the facts.

Dissent (Harlan, J., Burger, C.J., Blackmun, J.). Judicial review of executive action in foreign affairs is narrow. The Court should inquire only whether the subject matter is within the president's foreign relations power and whether the head of the department concerned has personally made the determination that disclosure would irreparably impair national security.

Dissent (Blackmun, J.). The case is too important to be handled in such haste and ought to be remanded.

Comment. Distinguishing the *Pentagon Papers* case, a federal district court enjoined a magazine from publishing technical material on hydrogen bomb design, which was available in public documents. In exercising the first instance of prior restraint against a publication, the court cited the government's showing of the likelihood of injury to the nation and the fact that the suppression of the technical portions of the article would not impede the publication in its goal of stimulating public knowledge of nuclear armament and enlightened debate on national policy. [United States v. Progressive, Inc., 467 F. Supp. 990 (W.D. Wis. 1979)]

---

d. **Fair trial and pretrial publicity.** *Nebraska Press Association v. Stuart*, 427 U.S. 539 (1976), involved the criminal trial in a mass murder case. To avoid the dangers that pretrial publicity would present to the fairness of the trial, the judge entered a restrictive order that prohibited the press from reporting certain subjects strongly implicative of the accused. The Court held the pretrial restraint unconstitutional, stating that prior restraints on speech and publication pose the most serious and least tolerable infringement of First Amendment rights. The Court ruled that before any prior restraint is permissible, a court must find a clear and present danger that pretrial publicity would threaten a fair trial, that alternative measures (*e.g.*, jury instructions, sequestration of jurors, change of venue, and careful questioning of jurors) would be inadequate, and that the prior restraint would actually protect the accused.

XIII. RIGHTS ANCILLARY TO FREEDOM OF SPEECH

A. COMPELLED SPEECH: THE RIGHT NOT TO SPEAK

1. **Compelled Individual Speech.** The government may not require citizens to salute the flag or take other actions manifesting assent to a mandated idea.

   a. **Citizen expression.** In *West Virginia State Board of Education v. Barnette*, 319 U.S. 624 (1943), the Court overruled its previous decision in *Minersville School District v. Gobitis*, 310 U.S. 586 (1940), which had sustained another flag salute public school regulation that had been challenged on religious grounds by Jehovah's Witnesses. Characterizing *Barnette* as a freedom of expression, rather than free exercise, action, the Court held that there is no power to make a salute a legal duty, that such a compulsory rite infringes an individual's constitutional liberty, and that under the Bill of Rights, orthodoxy in politics cannot be prescribed. The *Barnette* decision was relied on in *Wooley v. Maynard*, 430 U.S. 705 (1977), in which the Court invalidated a law requiring a religious motto on license plates on the ground that the statute could force an individual to foster an unacceptable ideological viewpoint.

   b. **Compelled disclosure of speaker identity.** In *McIntyre v. Ohio Elections Commission*, 514 U.S. 334 (1995), the Court invalidated an Ohio law that prohibited the distribution of anonymous campaign literature. Margaret McIntyre had distributed leaflets expressing her opposition to a proposed school tax levy. She identified herself on some of the leaflets as "Concerned Parents and Taxpayers" and was fined $100. The Court held that the right to use anonymous literature clearly outweighs any public interest in requiring disclosure of authorship. When a law burdens core political speech, the courts must apply "exacting scrutiny." The Court found that the state's interest in preventing fraud is substantial, but there are other ways to protect that interest, such as simply prohibiting false statements.

2. **Compelled Access for the Speech of Others.** The government may require private parties to provide speech access to private property that shares distinctive public characteristics with traditional public property.

   a. **Compelled rights of reply—contrasting views.**

      1) **Broadcasters.** In *Red Lion Broadcasting Co. v. FCC*, 395 U.S. 367 (1969), the Court upheld the FCC's fairness doctrine, which required broadcast stations to provide free reply time to personal

attacks and political editorials, and to present discussion of public issues with fairness to differing viewpoints. A unanimous Court reasoned that restrictions on the editorial discretion of the broadcasting media would "enhance rather than abridge" freedoms of speech and press. Broadcasting may be more closely regulated than the press because the limited number of frequencies results in the granting of licenses to only a few who apply, thus effectively denying a right to broadcast to all who would so desire. Therefore, those who do receive licenses may be said to be acting as proxies for the entire community and must present views representative of that community. The focal point is the rights of viewers and listeners to receive information of public concern, rather than broadcasters' rights to broadcast only what they want. [*But see* Columbia Broadcasting System, Inc. v. Democratic National Committee, *infra*]

a) **Repeal.** In 1987, the fairness doctrine was repealed because of the rise of competition in the informational services field and after an agency finding that the doctrine chilled broadcasters' First Amendment rights.

2) **Newspapers.** By contrast, the Court in *Miami Herald Publishing Co. v. Tornillo*, 418 U.S. 241 (1974), invalidated a state law requiring newspapers to grant political candidates a right to equal space to reply to criticism of them printed in the paper. Although a responsible press is a desirable goal, it is not constitutionally required. Governmental compulsion to publish that which an editor does not wish to publish is unconstitutional.

b. **Compelled access to private property.**

1) **Shopping centers.** In *PruneYard Shopping Center v. Robins*, 447 U.S. 74 (1980), a shopping center that barred all expressive activity not directly related to its commercial purposes excluded students who attempted to distribute pamphlets and seek petitions against a United Nations resolution. The Court ruled that the center's owner was not denied First Amendment rights by a state constitutional provision permitting free speech on privately owned but publicly available shopping centers. The Court also rejected a Fifth Amendment takings challenge.

2) **Compulsory third-party access for speech.** Pacific Gas and Electric Company ("PG&E") distributed an informational newsletter in its billing envelopes. The Public Utilities Commission ("PUC") determined that the space PG&E had used for the newsletter was the property of ratepayers and ordered that a private advocacy organization, which was typically opposed to PG&E's ratemaking,

be permitted to use this extra space periodically. In *Pacific Gas & Electric Co. v. Public Utilities Commission*, 475 U.S. 1 (1986), the Court held that this violated PG&E's First Amendment rights. The Court found that the compelled access that PUC imposed on PG&E penalized PG&E's expression of a particular point of view and forced PG&E to alter its speech to conform to someone else's agenda. The Court explained that the same concerns in *Tornillo* (*supra*) applied to PG&E. While PG&E did not have the right to freedom from debate, it did have the right to freedom from forced enhancement of its opponent's message. Corporations, like individuals, have the choice of what not to say.

3) **Access to cable stations.** Congress adopted the Cable Television Act of 1992 that required cable operators to carry the signals of local broadcast television stations. The purpose was to counter the concentration of economic power in the cable industry, which Congress found was endangering the availability of free over-the-air broadcast television, especially for those consumers who did not have cable. In *Turner Broadcasting System, Inc. v. FCC*, 512 U.S. 622 (1994) (Turner I), the Court held that these must-carry provisions were not subject to strict scrutiny because the law was content-neutral. Its application to cable owners might affect their editorial discretion, but only based on their channel capacity, not the content of the programming. The must-carry provisions did not force cable operators to alter their own messages, unlike the rules in *Tornillo* and *Pacific Gas & Electric*. Applying intermediate scrutiny, the Court found that the must-carry provision served three important interests unrelated to the suppression of free speech. The four Justices in dissent considered the must-carry rules to be content-based compelled speech. After remand for additional factfinding, the Court affirmed the prior result on the ground that Congress had substantial evidence for making the judgment it did and that the rules were substantially related to the important government interest in competition and diversity in programming. [Turner Broadcasting System, Inc. v. FCC, 520 U.S. 180 (1997) (Turner II)]

4) **Access to a parade.** The Irish-American Gay, Lesbian and Bisexual Group of Boston ("GLIB") was not allowed to participate in the annual St. Patrick's Day parade organized by members of a privately-organized council. GLIB sued under a state law prohibiting any discrimination on the basis of sexual orientation relative to the admission to any place of public accommodation. In *Hurley v. Irish-American Gay, Lesbian and Bisexual Group of Boston, Inc.*, 515 U.S. 557 (1995), the Court held that a state may not require private citizens who organize a parade to include a group imparting a message the organizers do not wish to convey. Pa-

rades are forms of expression and are entitled to First Amendment protection. The protected expression is not limited to banners and songs, but includes the overall activity. Although the council was lenient in admitting a variety of participants, the Court explained that a private speaker does not forfeit constitutional protection by combining various speakers. Newspapers consist of a compilation of numerous writers, and the council's acceptance of a variety of groups was similar. Members of GLIB were not excluded from participating on the same basis as other individuals. The council simply did not want GLIB's message to be part of the parade. The council could not be required to alter the expressive content of their parade; this would violate a fundamental First Amendment principle that the speaker may choose the content of his own message.

B. FREEDOM OF EXPRESSIVE ASSOCIATION

1. Compelled Disclosure of Membership.

a. Emergence of the modern approach--

NAACP v. Alabama, 357 U.S. 449 (1958).

Facts. The Attorney General of Alabama (P) sued the NAACP (D) to enjoin D's activities in the state. P sought large amounts of D's records, including membership lists. D refused to provide the lists, and was fined for contempt. D appeals.

Issue. May a state force production of a private association's membership lists?

Held. No. Judgment reversed.

- P's production order clearly entails the likelihood of a substantial restraint on D's members' right to freedom of association. D's immunity from state scrutiny of its membership lists, being closely related to its members' right of association, is protected by the Fourteenth Amendment. P has shown no controlling justification for its attempt to curb the rights of D's members, and the fine levied against D must fail.

---

b. Background investigation of teachers--

Shelton v. Tucker, 364 U.S. 479 (1960).

Facts. An Arkansas statute required every state teacher to submit a list of all organizations to which he had belonged or contributed in the past five years. Shelton (P), a member of the NAACP, submitted an oath that he was not a member of a subversive group, but refused to submit a list of all groups of which he was a member. P's teaching contract was not renewed, and he challenged the statute. The state courts upheld the state statute; P appeals.

Issue. May a state require all public school teachers to disclose every organizational tie existing over the previous five years?

Held. No. Judgment reversed.

- A state may investigate the competence and fitness of its employed teachers. However, such an investigation must be relevant to a valid state interest, and must not unnecessarily impinge on constitutional freedoms.

- The challenged statute impinges on P's right of free association. It does not provide for confidentiality of disclosed information. It is not limited to disclosure of relevant organizational ties, and therefore discourages associations disfavored by superiors but irrelevant to competence.

Dissent (Frankfurter, Clark, Harlan, Whittaker, JJ.). This is a reasonable requirement, even though there might be less restrictive means of attaining the same purpose.

---

c. **Legislative committee investigation--**

Gibson v. Florida Legislative Committee, 372 U.S. 539 (1963).

Facts. The Florida Legislative Committee (P) ordered Gibson (D), president of the Miami branch of the NAACP, to bring membership and contributors lists to P's hearings on Communist infiltration of the NAACP. D refused to do so, but responded to P's questions based on personal knowledge. D was found guilty of contempt and appeals.

Issue. Must a legislative committee show a close nexus between the information sought and a compelling state interest behind its request before it can force disclosure?

Held. Yes. Judgment reversed.

- Intrusion into First Amendment rights can be justified only where necessary to satisfy a compelling state interest. A legislative committee therefore must show a substantial relation between the information sought and the state interest.

- This case differs from *Barenblatt v. United States*, 360 U.S. 109 (1959), a communist membership case, and others in that here the legislature is requesting the records of a concededly legitimate organization (the NAACP) merely to determine whether persons other than D were members of the NAACP. The government interest in controlling subversion justifies intrusion on the rights of Communist Party members to conceal that membership, but it does not justify automatic forfeiture of the rights of privacy of nonsubversive organizations' members.

Dissent (Harlan, Clark, Stewart, White, JJ.). The Court finds a nonexistent distinction between state investigatory interest in Communist infiltration of organizations and Communist activity by organizations.

---

2. **Compelled Disclosure of Political Campaign Contributions.** In *Buckley v. Valeo*, *infra*, the Court rejected a freedom of association challenge to a federal law requiring political committees and candidates, *inter alia*, to record names of contributors and amounts given. The First Amendment requires strict scrutiny of compelled disclosures, which may be justified only by substantial governmental interests. The Court found that furtherance of voter knowledge, deterrence of corruption, and enforcement of limitations on contributions are sufficiently important governmental interests to outweigh the possibility of infringement of a First Amendment right.

3. **Restrictions on Organizational Activity.**

   a. **Litigation--**

NAACP v. Button, 371 U.S. 415 (1963).

Facts. The NAACP (P) followed a policy of having its lawyers represent persons in cases involving racial discrimination. The staff lawyers received compensation only from P (on a low per-day basis). P encouraged the bringing of such suits. The state of Virginia passed a law that forbade "any agent for an individual or organization to retain a lawyer in connection with an action to which it was not a party and in which it had no pecuniary right or liability." P challenged the constitutionality of the law, and appeals the state court decisions upholding it.

Issue. May states restrict the right of minority groups to associate in order to obtain better legal service?

Held. No. Judgment reversed.

- Although "solicitation" has generally been frowned upon in the legal profession, and the state of Virginia has a legitimate interest in regulating the same, nevertheless, here the law violated the constitutional rights of the NAACP, since the application of a "mere label" was being used to suppress the rights of P to institute litigation on behalf of members of an unpopular minority group.

Dissent (Harlan, Clark, Stewart, JJ.). This is reasonable regulation of conduct. Under P's scheme, attorneys may be unable to maintain undivided allegiance to their true clients when P is paying their fees.

Comments.

- Similarly, in *Brotherhood of Railroad Trainmen v. Virginia*, 377 U.S. 1 (1964), the Court held that the state could not interfere with a union's program by which it set up a system for referring union members to certain attorneys for representation in union-related matters. The Court stated that the right of freedom of expression and association would not permit the state to regulate the conduct of the attorneys in this situation.

- In *United Mine Workers v. Illinois Bar Association*, 389 U.S. 217 (1967), the Court struck down a state ban against a union's employment of a salaried attorney to assist with worker's compensation claims, on the grounds that the ban impaired the associational rights of the union members and was not a necessary protection of the state's interest in the high standards of legal ethics. Later, in *United Transportation Union v. State Bar of Michigan*, 401 U.S. 576 (1971), after emphasizing that collective activity to obtain meaningful access to the courts is a fundamental First Amendment right, the Court also invalidated a state injunction against a union's plan to protect members from excessive fees of incompetent attorneys in FELA actions.

---

b. **Boycotts.** In *NAACP v. Claiborne Hardware Co.*, 458 U.S. 886 (1982), the Court held that a consumer boycott organized to force the white merchants who were being boycotted to make changes in racial practices was essentially political speech and therefore protected from government regulation. This type of boycott was distinguished from labor boycotts organized for economic objectives, which can be prohibited by the government.

4. Denial of Government Benefits Because of Association.

a. **Cold War approach.** In *Konigsberg v. State Bar of California*, 353 U.S. 252 (1957) (Konigsberg I), the Supreme Court found that a bar applicant's refusal to answer questions about his Communist Party membership was a valid reason to deny admission to the bar. A state has an important interest in assuring that lawyers believe in orderly change, which outweighs the possibility that disclosure may inhibit freedom of association.

b. **Loyalty oaths.** In *Cramp v. Board of Public Education*, 368 U.S. 278 (1961), and *Baggett v. Bullett*, 377 U.S. 360 (1964), the Supreme Court overthrew state loyalty oaths that required scienter on the ground that the oaths were too vague in defining what constituted "disloyal activity."

c. **Knowing but guiltless association.** In *Elfbrandt v. Russell*, 384 U.S. 11 (1966), the Court held that a state may not require its employees to make a loyalty oath and may not specify that membership in certain organizations is a per se violation of the oath. The law in *Elfbrandt* applied to membership without the "specific intent" to further the illegal aims of the organization. The Court found that those who join an organization but do not share its unlawful purposes and do not participate in its unlawful activities do not pose the threat sought to be avoided by the legislature. The oath and accompanying statutes rested on the doctrine of guilt by association and could not stand. In *Keyishian v. Board of Regents*, 385 U.S. 589 (1967), the Court again invalidated a loyalty oath requirement for public employment. The Court pointed out that the statute barred all members of listed organizations, without considering whether the membership was knowing or whether the member had specific intent to further the unlawful aims of the organization. The Court ruled that this was overbroad.

d. **Loyalty oath requirement upheld.** In *Cole v. Richardson*, 405 U.S. 676 (1972), the Court synthesized the cases from *Wieman v. Updegraff*, 344 U.S. 183 (1952), to *Keyishian* when it held that an oath required of all state employees "to oppose the overthrow of the government . . . by force, violence, or by an illegal or unconstitutional method" did not violate the First Amendment. The Court noted that the oath did not relate to political beliefs, nor protected speech or association, nor did it reach back to past activities. Rather, the Court read this oath as being like those requiring the taker simply to "support" the Constitution; "to commit themselves to live by the constitutional processes of our system." This oath did not require specific action. Nor was it "void for vagueness"; it provided fair notice because it could be punished only by perjury, which required proof of knowing falsity. Finally, since the oath was valid, a public employee refusing to take it could be discharged without any hearing.

e. **Bar admission.** Admission to the practice of law is not a matter of grace; but it is a right only for those who are qualified by their learning and moral character. Consequently, a state is permitted under the Due Process Clause to exclude anyone from the practice of law for reasons that have a rational connection with fitness or capacity for law practice.

[Schware v. Board of Bar Examiners of New Mexico, 353 U.S. 232 (1957)]

1) **Membership inquiry.** If the inquiry is not confined to "knowing membership," etc., the applicant may not be excluded for his refusal to answer; *i.e.*, the state cannot force an applicant to disclose "mere memberships" or "mere beliefs" as the price for admission to the practice of law. [Baird v. State Bar of Arizona, 401 U.S. 1 (1971)]

a) **Rationale.** "Mere memberships or beliefs" can never, by themselves, be sufficient ground for a state's imposition of criminal punishment or (as here) civil disabilities. No legitimate state interest requires such disclosure, because no rational connection exists between "mere memberships or beliefs" and fitness to practice law.

b) **Applications.** Following this rationale, the Court has overturned a state bar denial of admission to an applicant who refused to list "all organizations to which you have belonged at any time since age 16, or since registering as a law student." [*See In re* Stolar, 401 U.S. 23 (1971)] The same result occurred where denial was based on the applicant's refusal to answer the specific question whether she had ever been a member of the Communist Party (the inquiry not being limited to "knowing membership"). [Baird v. State Bar of Arizona, *supra*]

c) **But compare.** The Court has also stated that bar examiners may ask about Communist affiliations ("knowing" or otherwise) as a preliminary to further inquiry into "the nature of the association"; and may therefore exclude an applicant who refuses to answer if his refusal obstructs the bar examiner's investigation of his qualifications. [Konigsberg v. State Bar of California, 366 U.S. 36 (1961) (Konigsberg II)] However the Court, in *Law Students Civil Rights Research Council v. Wadmond*, 401 U.S. 154 (1971), sustained New York's bar screening process, under which an applicant was first questioned as to whether she had ever belonged to an organization that she knew advocated forceful overthrow of the government, and then, upon receiving an affirmative response, whether the applicant had specific intent to further that goal.

5. Compelled Association: The Right *Not* to Associate.

a. **Compulsory fees.** In *Abood v. Detroit Board of Education*, 431 U.S. 209 (1977), the Court recognized a right not to associate. It held that public school employees who did not belong to a union did not have to pay a service fee to the union if they objected to ideological union expenditures unrelated to collective bargaining. However, the public interest in collective bargaining was greater than the nonunion members' objection to fees for collective bargaining, so they could be required to pay some service fees.

b. **Compulsory inclusion.** In *Roberts v. United States Jaycees*, 468 U.S. 609 (1984), the Court found no infringement on the freedom of association by a state antidiscrimination law requiring an all-male organization to admit women. Although freedom of association includes the right to associate to engage in First Amendment activities and also the right to establish relationships and share ideals and beliefs, the right is not absolute. Infringements may be justified by compelling state interests, unrelated to suppression of ideas, that cannot be achieved by significantly less restrictive means. The law here is content neutral on its face and as applied. [*See also* Board of Directors of Rotary International v. Rotary Club, 481 U.S. 537 (1987)—applying *Roberts*; New York State Club Association v. City of New York, 487 U.S. 1 (1988)—upheld law banning racial, religious, or sex discrimination in large clubs meeting certain criteria]

6. Freedom of Association and Political Party Procedures.

a. **Ballot access.** In *Anderson v. Celebrezze*, 460 U.S. 780 (1983), the Court specifically relied on the First Amendment instead of equal protection to invalidate an early filing deadline that applied to independents but not the nominees of political parties. The Court articulated a balancing test, comparing the restriction's injury to First Amendment rights with the justifications asserted by the state. The *Anderson* Court also made clear that ballot access cases were not to be determined by a single standard, but rather would be decided by weighing the various involved interests on a case-by-case basis. This principle was apparent in *Burdick v. Takushi*, 504 U.S. 428 (1992), in which the Court rejected a First Amendment challenge to Hawaii's ban on write-in voting. The Court noted that all voting restrictions are burdensome to some degrees but if reasonable and nondiscriminatory, strict scrutiny does not apply.

b. **Political party primaries.** First Amendment concerns were also evident in *Tashjian v. Republican Party*, 479 U.S. 208 (1986), where a law requiring party primary voters to be registered members of that party was invalidated because it interfered with associational rights. [*See also* Eu v. San Francisco County Democratic Central Commission, 489 U.S. 214 (1989)—ban on political party endorsements for candidates in partisan elections burdened both speech and associational rights]

C. MONEY AND POLITICAL CAMPAIGNS

1. Contribution and Expenditure Limitations--

Buckley v. Valeo, 424 U.S. 1 (1976).

Facts. Buckley and other candidates and groups (Ps) brought suit against Valeo (D) and other federal officials seeking a declaration that the reporting and disclosure requirements of the Federal Election Campaign Act were unconstitutional. The requirements applied to all political committees and candidates, and involved detailed reporting of contributors and amounts contributed. Ps also challenged the contribution and expenditure limitations, which included the following restrictions:

(i) $1,000 limit on individual and group contributions to a candidate or authorized campaign committee per election;

(ii) $1,000 limit on expenditures relative to a clearly identified candidate;

(iii) Annual ceiling on a candidate's expenditures from personal or family resources; and

(iv) Public financing of presidential campaigns.

The court of appeals upheld the Act in its entirety, and Ps appeal.

Issues.

(i) May Congress impose contribution limitations on federal elections?

(ii) May Congress impose expenditure limitations on federal elections?

(iii) May Congress impose detailed reporting and disclosure requirements on political contribution activity?

(iv) May Congress permit public financing of presidential campaigns?

Held. (i) Yes. (ii) No. (iii) Yes. (iv) Yes. Judgment affirmed in part and reversed in part.

♦ Congress may impose contribution limits.

> The financial limitations imposed on political campaigns cannot be considered regulation of conduct alone, since exercise of free speech depends largely on the ability to finance that speech. This is especially true when the electorate depends on the mass media for so much of its information.
>
> The $1,000 limit on campaign contributions has minimal effect on freedom of association or on the extent of political discussion. On the other

hand, it deals directly with the sources of political corruption, or the appearances thereof, which are the objective of the statute. It does not violate the First Amendment.

- However, Congress may not limit expenditures.

  Even though the expenditure limitations are content-neutral, they impose severe restrictions on freedom of political expression. Equalizing the relative ability of individuals and groups to influence elections is not a sufficient rationale to justify the infringement of First Amendment rights.

  The interest in avoiding the danger of candidate dependence on large contributions, which is asserted as a reason for limiting expenditures, is served by the contribution limits and disclosure requirements. It is not within the government's power to determine that spending to promote one's political views is wasteful, excessive, or unwise.

- The reporting and disclosure requirements satisfy exacting scrutiny.

  The government interest in assuring the free functioning of our national institutions is served by the disclosure requirement. The electorate is provided with relevant information, thereby deterring corruption and facilitating enforcement of contribution limitations.

  Ps claim that the requirements are overbroad as applied to minor parties and independent candidates, but Ps have failed to show any actual harm to these groups. If such harm actually occurs, courts will be available to provide appropriate remedies, but a blanket exemption is unnecessary.

- Public financing of presidential campaigns does not constitute invidious discrimination against minor and new parties in violation of the Fifth Amendment. Even though the scheme provides full funding only for major parties, it assists minor parties and does not limit the ability of minor party candidates to raise funds up to the applicable spending limit.

Concurrence and dissent (Burger, C.J.). It is an improper intrusion on the First Amendment to limit contributions. It is inappropriate to subsidize presidential campaigns.

Concurrence and dissent (White, J.). It is illogical to restrict contributions but permit unlimited expenditures.

Dissent (Marshall, J.). Limits on expenditures of family funds should be valid.

Comments.

- In *California Medical Association v. FEC*, 453 U.S. 182 (1981), the Court upheld provisions of the Act that limit contributions by an unincorporated or incorporated association to a multicandidate political committee. The Court noted that *Buckley* found a candidate's independent expenditures to be constitutionally protected, whereas this case involved speech by someone other than the contributors.

- ♦ The Court invalidated limits on spending by political action committees for presidential candidates who elect to receive public financing. [FEC v. National Conservative PAC, 470 U.S. 480 (1985)]

---

2. **Post-*Buckley* Decisions.**

   a. **Corporations and political campaigns.**

      1) **Political expenditures by corporations.**

         a) **Law invalidated.** In *First National Bank of Boston v. Bellotti*, 435 U.S. 765 (1978), the Court struck down a Massachusetts statute that prohibited certain expenditures by banks and business corporations for the purpose of influencing the vote on referendum proposals, unless the proposals materially affected any of the property, business, or assets of the corporation. First National Bank of Boston wanted to publicize its views in opposition to a state constitutional amendment and challenged the statute. The Court found that First National's proposed speech, an expression of views on an issue of public importance, was at the heart of the First Amendment's protection. The state's interest in promoting individual citizen participation in the electoral process and preventing erosion of confidence in government had not been shown to be adversely affected by First National's proposed speech. Nor was there a risk of corruption. Also, the state asserted an interest in protecting the rights of shareholders whose views differed from those expressed by First National, but the statute was not carefully drawn to deal with this concern.

         b) **Law upheld.** *Bellotti* was distinguished in *FEC v. National Right to Work Committee*, 459 U.S. 197 (1982), when the Court upheld a federal election law prohibiting corporations and labor unions from making contributions or expenditures in connection with federal elections with funds solicited from the public rather than from their members. An organization's associational rights are outweighed by the governmental interest in preventing accumulation of immense war chests as a result of special advantages accompanying the corporate form. However, this corporate restriction is invalid as applied to voluntary political associations that do not present a corruption problem arising from concentrated corporate wealth. [FEC v. Massachusetts Citizens for Life, Inc., 479 U.S. 238 (1986)]

2) **Personal contributions.** A local ordinance limited personal contributions to committees organized to support or oppose local ballot measures. The maximum allowed was $250. The state courts upheld the restriction under *Buckley*. In *Citizens Against Rent Control v. Berkeley*, 454 U.S. 290 (1981), the Court reversed, holding that the restriction violated First Amendment association and speech rights. *Buckley* involved candidate elections; ballot measures present a much lower risk of corruption. [*See also* Mayer v. Grant, 486 U.S. 414 (1988)—law prohibiting payment of persons circulating voter initiative petitions invalid as limitation on fundamental political expression]

3) **Candidates' promises.** Kentucky prohibited candidates from "buying" votes by offering material benefits to voters. One candidate offered to serve at a lower salary. He later retracted the promise when advised it might be illegal. He was elected, but a state court set aside the election because of the illegal promise. In *Brown v. Hartlage*, 456 U.S. 45 (1982), the Court reversed, applying strict scrutiny, because the First Amendment protected such speech and the state has no compelling interest sufficient to overcome such protection.

3. The Constitutionality of the Bipartisan Campaign Reform Act.

a. Restrictions on soft money contributions and issue ads--

McConnell v. Federal Election Commission, 540 U.S. 93 (2003).

Facts. The Bipartisan Campaign Reform Act of 2002 ("BCRA"), also known as the McCain-Feingold law, restricted the use of soft money and issue ads. It amended the Federal Election Campaign Act of 1971 ("FECA"), which had imposed limitations only on "hard money" contributions, or money used to influence an election for federal office. "Soft money," or money used for state or local elections and for issue ads, was unregulated under FECA. Title I of BCRA (the new section 323(a) of FECA) prohibited national party committees from soliciting, receiving, directing or spending any soft money. Section 323(b) prevented state and local party committees from using soft money for activities that affect federal elections. Section 323(d) prohibited political parties from donating funds to tax exempt organizations such as the section 527 groups that are organized for the express purpose of engaging in partisan political activity. Section 323(f) imposed restrictions on candidates' use of soft money. Title II imposed restrictions on corporations and labor unions to prevent them from funding electioneering communications, defined as political broadcasts that refer to a clearly identified federal candidate that are made within 60 days before an election. Senator McConnell and others (Ps) challenged the law by suing the Federal Election Commission (D). The district court upheld part of the law and found some parts unconstitutional. Ps appeal.

Issue. May Congress limit the use of soft money contributions and impose detailed restrictions on how organizations can influence elections?

Held. Yes. Judgment affirmed in part and reversed in part.

- The Court has previously held that a contribution limit may impose significant interference with the right of association so long as it is closely drawn to match a sufficiently important interest. The Court must defer to Congress's ability to weigh competing constitutional interests in an area in which it enjoys particular expertise.

- The FECA limits have a marginal impact on political speech. They limit the source and individual amount of donations, but they do not limit the total amount of money that the parties can spend.

- The rationale behind the contribution restrictions in section 323(a) is that contributions to a candidate's party to aid the candidate's campaign threaten to create a sense of obligation. Large soft money donations have a corrupting influence. For example, special interests influence the congressional calendar that determines what legislation gets voted on. The six national party committees have menus of opportunities for access to would-be soft-money donors, with more access available in return for higher contributions. The best means to prevent these abuses is to identify and remove the temptation, so section 323(a) is not unconstitutional.

- Section 323(b)'s limits on state committees is designed to prevent wholesale evasion of section 323(a). Congress determined that without this provision, soft-money contributors would simply contribute to the state parties, which would create the same sense of obligation on the part of candidates as would contributions to the national parties. The Court must defer to Congress in this area, and the provisions are closely drawn to match the important governmental interests Congress has identified.

- Section 323(d) is not unconstitutional when narrowly construed to ban only donations not raised in compliance with FECA. Without this restriction, the various party committees would have an incentive to use their fundraising system to benefit like-minded tax-exempt organizations that would benefit their candidates, bringing with it all of the corrupting influences Congress was concerned about. This is basically an anti-circumvention measure.

- Section 323(f) prevents candidates from spending soft money on advertising that refers to a clearly identified federal candidate, whether pro or con. It limits contributions, but not expenditures. This is a narrow focus on the soft-money donations that have the greatest potential for corruption, and is a permissible means for addressing the problems that Congress has identified.

- ♦ Title II's restrictions on funding by corporations and labor unions has been established previously, and these institutions are able to engage in express advocacy by forming separate segregated funds to pay for it. Organizations can still fund electioneering communications with PAC money, so there is no complete ban on expression. The regulation of this speech is constitutional.

- ♦ Section 213, however, prohibits political parties in certain circumstances from using specific words. There is no meaningful governmental interest in requiring parties to avoid the use of such magic words, and this portion of the statute is invalid.

Dissent (Rehnquist, C.J., Scalia, Kennedy, JJ.), with respect to Titles I and V. The issue under Title I is not whether Congress can permissibly regulate campaign contributions to candidates or attempt to eliminate corruption. Title I is regulation of much speech that has no plausible connection to either candidate contributions or corruption. It regulates all donations to national political committees, regardless of how the funds are used. As such, Title I is overinclusive. The Court should only permit regulation of financing that is closely linked to corruption or the appearance of corruption. In effect, the Court has eliminated the "closely drawn" tailoring requirement and meaningful judicial review.

Dissent (Scalia, J.) with respect to Titles I and V. *Buckley* was wrongly decided. Today the Court, which sternly disapproves of restrictions on pornography, approves of a law that cuts to the heart of the First Amendment: the right to criticize the government. BCRA basically prohibits the criticism of Members of Congress by those entities most capable of criticizing effectively: the national political parties and corporations. Even though it also prohibits criticism of those candidates challenging Members of Congress, such even-handedness is not fairness. It favors incumbents, who typically raise about three times as much "hard money" as challengers. Regulation of money used for disseminating speech is equivalent to regulating the speech itself.

Dissent (Thomas, Scalia, JJ.) with respect to Titles I and V. Besides continuing the errors of *Buckley*, the Court now expands the anti-circumvention rationale beyond reason. The Court should require a showing of why bribery laws are insufficient to address the concerns asserted by Congress. The Court also continues to decrease the level of scrutiny applied to restrictions on core political speech.

Dissent (Kennedy, J., Rehnquist, C.J., Scalia, Thomas, JJ.) with respect to Titles I and II. The citizens have the right to judge for themselves the most effective means for expressing political views, and to decide for themselves whom to believe. BCRA is the codification of an assumption that the mainstream media alone can protect freedom of speech, and is an effort by Congress to make sure that civic discourse takes place only through the modes of its own choosing. The Court has moved beyond the anti-corruption rationale of *Buckley* to allow regulation of any conduct that wins goodwill from or influences a Member of Congress. Access, in itself, is not corruption. The new regulations impose far greater burdens on associational rights than do regulations that merely cap the amount of money a person can contribute to a political candidate or committee.

Comment. The Court's opinion was actually delivered by four separate Justices. Justices Stevens and O'Connor delivered the opinion on BCRA Titles I and II; Chief Justice Rehnquist delivered the opinion regarding Titles III and IV; and Justice Breyer delivered the opinion on Title V.

---

b. Pre-election issue advocacy--

Federal Election Commission v. Wisconsin Right to Life, 127 S. Ct. 2652 (2007).

Facts. Section 203 of the Bipartisan Campaign Reform Act of 2002 ("BCRA") makes it illegal for any corporation to broadcast, shortly before an election, any communication that names a federal candidate for elected office and is targeted to the electorate. In *McConnell*, *supra*, the court upheld section 203 against a facial challenge as long as the forbidden speech was express campaign speech or its functional equivalent. Wisconsin Right to Life (P) is a 501(c) nonprofit advocacy organization. P planned to run broadcast ads during the election blackout period to encourage voters to call Senator Feingold to protest the filibuster of judicial nominees. P filed suit against the Federal Election Commission (D), seeking declaratory relief that would permit the running of these ads. The Supreme Court granted certiorari.

Issue. May the BCRA be applied to prohibit issue advocacy that mentions a candidate for federal office but is not an appeal to vote for or against a specific candidate?

Held. No. Judgment affirmed.

- BCRA section 203 is subject to strict scrutiny because it burdens political speech. Although BCRA survived a facial challenge in *McConnell*, it is still subject to as-applied challenges.

- The test for an as-applied challenge does not depend on the speaker's intent. An intent-based test would chill political speech and would offer no security for free discussion. The proper standard must be objective. It must focus on the substance of the communication and must give the benefit of any doubt to protecting rather than stifling speech.

- An ad is the functional equivalent of express advocacy only if it is susceptible of no reasonable interpretation other than as an appeal to vote for or against a specific candidate. Under this test, P's ads are not the functional equivalent of express advocacy. They focus on a legislative issue (the filibuster), take a position on the issue, exhort the public to adopt that position, and urge the public to contact public officials regarding the issue. They do not mention an election, candidacy, political party, or challenger. They also do not take a position on a candidate's character, qualifications, or fitness for office.

- Because P's ads are not the functional equivalent of express advocacy, section 203 may be applied to P's ads only if it is narrowly tailored to further a compelling interest. *McConnell* assumed that the governmental interest in preventing corruption in election campaigns justified regulation of express advocacy, and then extended this interest to ads that were the functional equivalent of express advocacy. But there is no basis for further extending this interest to ads that are not the functional equivalent of express advocacy.

Concurrence (Alito, J.). Section 203, as applied, cannot ban any advertising that may reasonably be interpreted as anything other than an appeal to vote for or against a candidate. Because section 203 is unconstitutional as applied to P's ads, we need not decide today whether section 203 is unconstitutional on its face. However, if the implementation of the as-applied standard chills political speech, in a future case we may need to reconsider the facial validity of section 203.

Concurrence (Scalia, Kennedy, Thomas, JJ.). *Austin v. Michigan Chamber of Commerce*, 494 U.S. 652 (1990), was wrongly decided, but at least it was limited to express advocacy. Section 203 bans political advocacy that is indistinguishable from previously protected speech. *McConnell* should be overruled. BCRA has concentrated more political power into the hands of the country's wealthiest individuals and their 527 organizations, which are unregulated by section 203.

Dissent (Souter, Stevens, Ginsburg, Breyer, JJ.). The Court has effectively overruled *McConnell*. There is a long tradition of campaign finance reform that responds to documented threats to electoral integrity. P is a nonprofit corporation funded in large part by other corporations. P clearly wanted Senator Feingold to lose the election. Its ads were run after the Senate recessed and did not resume after the election. Voters would have known that P's ads were intended to encourage voters to vote against Feingold. The ads fall within the prohibition of section 203.

D. FREEDOM OF THE PRESS

1. **Introduction.** Although the First Amendment separately mentions freedom of the press, the Court has not recognized any special right for the press additional to the general freedom of speech. Yet the institutional press often faces problems different from those faced by citizens in general, which has prompted some claims that special protection is appropriate.

a. **No special status.** In considering the exact constitutional protection of the press in *First National Bank of Boston v. Bellotti*, *supra*, an election expenditure case, the Court stated that the Press Clause did not confer a special status or institutional privilege on a limited group, and that there was no difference in the First Amendment freedom to disseminate ideas through the newspaper or through those who gave lectures that encourage publication and wide dissemination.

2. **Press Access to Government Information.**

a. **Press access to jails.** Prison inmates can be prohibited from being interviewed by news media as long as alternative means of communication are available (mail, visitors). There is no "freedom of the press" to interview prisoners. [*See* Pell v. Procunier, 417 U.S. 817 (1974) and Saxbe v. Washington Post Co., 417 U.S. 843 (1974)] However, if the government voluntarily grants such access, the public and the press must be treated equally. Where limitations that might be reasonable as to individual members of the public would impede effective reporting (*e.g.*, prohibition of cameras), such limitations may not—consistent with reasonable prison rules—be used to hamper effective media presentation of what is seen by individual visitors. [*See* Houchins v. KQED, Inc., 438 U.S. 1 (1978)]

b. **Press access to judicial proceedings.**

1) **Courtroom proceedings.** In *Gannett Co. v. DePasquale*, 443 U.S. 368 (1979), the Court held that neither the public nor the press has an enforceable right of access to a pretrial suppression hearing in a murder case when the parties had agreed to closure. However, in *Richmond Newspapers, Inc. v. Virginia*, 448 U.S. 555 (1980), the Court held that, absent an overriding interest articulated in the findings, the right of the public and the press to attend criminal trials is guaranteed by the Constitution. The Court noted that throughout the evolution of the trial procedure, the trial has been open to all who cared to observe. Although the Constitution contains no explicit provisions protecting the public from exclusion, the First Amendment protections of freedom of speech and press assure freedom of communication on matters relating to the functioning of government. The manner in which trials are conducted is of significant concern and importance to the public. Other constitutional rights, not explicitly established, have been recognized as implied. The Court ruled that the public interest in judicial functions and in freedom of speech requires open trials. Also, the Court found no overriding interest articulated in the findings in the *Richmond Newspapers* case.

2) **Mandatory closure for minor victims not permissible.** The Court in *Globe Newspaper Co. v. Superior Court*, 457 U.S. 596 (1982), held that a state may not require judges to exclude the press and the public from all victim testimony about certain sexual offenses. Instead, judges must be given discretion to exclude the press and public from testimony by minor victims.

3) **Voir dire examination.** The Court applied the standard of *Richmond Newspapers* in *Press-Enterprise Co. v. Superior Court*, 464 U.S. 501 (1984), a challenge to a closure order to voir dire examination in a criminal trial for the rape and murder of a teenage girl. Although the Court held that the public did not have an absolute right to access of this part of the trial, it invalidated the trial court's order because the court had failed to consider alternatives to closure to protect the privacy of the prospective jurors.

4) **Preliminary hearing.** *Richmond Newspapers* was extended even further in *Press-Enterprise Co. v. Superior Court*, 478 U.S. 1 (1986), which held that newspapers had a right of access to preliminary hearing transcripts in criminal cases. In response to the contentions of all parties, including the judge, that pretrial publicity would hinder the defendant's right to a fair trial, the Court stated that opening the process to neutral observers is an important method of assuring a fair trial.

5) **Punishment for publication.** In *Landmark Communications, Inc. v. Virginia*, 435 U.S. 829 (1978), the Court reversed a publisher's conviction under state law for printing an accurate report of a pending inquiry of a state judge. Operation of judicial inquiry systems is a matter of public interest even though the state has made it confidential for reasons of efficiency, protection of judiciary reputation, and maintenance of integrity of the courts. Injury to official reputation is not sufficient to repress otherwise free speech.

   a) **Clear and present danger.** The *Landmark* Court relied heavily on a line of cases beginning with *Bridges v. California*, 315 U.S. 252 (1941), which held that publications (or speech) regarding pending proceedings are not punishable unless they constitute a clear and present danger that justice would be obstructed. [*See also* Pennekamp v. Florida, 328 U.S. 331 (1946); Craig v. Harney, 331 U.S. 367 (1947); Wood v. Georgia, 370 U.S. 375 (1962)]

3. **Testimonial Privilege--**

Branzburg v. Hayes, 408 U.S. 665 (1972).

Facts. Branzburg (D), a reporter, observed illegal drug transactions and wrote about them in a news article. After being subpoenaed to appear before a grand jury, he sought prohibition and mandamus to avoid having to reveal his confidential information, but the state courts denied his petition. D appeals. (Other cases involving two similarly situated reporters were joined for decision by the Court.)

Issue. Does the First Amendment grant a special testimonial privilege to reporters, protecting them from being forced to divulge confidential information to a grand jury's investigation?

Held. No. Judgment affirmed.

- ♦ D claims that forcing reporters to reveal confidences to a grand jury will deter other confidential sources of information, thus curtailing the free flow of information protected by the First Amendment. However, journalists have no constitutional right of access to several types of events (grand jury proceedings, meetings of private organizations and of official bodies gathered in executive session, etc.). Although these exclusions tend to hamper news gathering, they are not unconstitutional.

- ♦ All citizens have an obligation to respond to grand jury subpoenas and to answer questions relevant to crime investigation. The only testimonial privilege for unofficial witnesses is in the Fifth Amendment; there is no necessity to create a special privilege for journalists based on the First Amendment. The public interest in pursuing and prosecuting those crimes reported to the press by informants and thus deterring future commission of those crimes is not outweighed by the public interest in possible future news about crime from undisclosed, unverified sources.

- ♦ A judicially created journalist's privilege would necessarily involve significant practical and conceptual problems in its administration. However, Congress and the state legislatures are not precluded from fashioning whatever standards and rules they might deem proper if they choose to create a statutory journalist's privilege.

Concurrence (Powell, J.). Journalists are not without remedy in the face of a bad faith investigation. Motions to quash and appropriate protective orders are available where the requested testimony is not within the legitimate hold of law enforcement.

Dissent (Stewart, Brennan, Marshall, JJ.). The Court undermines the independence of the press by inviting authorities to annex the journalistic profession as an investigative arm of government. Exercise of the power to compel disclosure will lead to "self-censorship" and, as a consequence, significantly impair the free flow of information to the public. To force disclosure, the government must show (i) probable cause that the journalist has information clearly relevant to a specific probable violation of law, (ii) that there is no less obtrusive means of obtaining the information, and (iii) a compelling and overriding interest in the information.

Dissent (Douglas, J.). Journalists have an absolute privilege against appearing before a grand jury, unless personally implicated in a crime, in which case the Fifth Amendment immunity applies.

Comment. The Court also rejected a claim by the press for special protection against a newsroom search in *Zurcher v. Stanford Daily*, 436 U.S. 547 (1978). Protection under the Fourth Amendment (unreasonable searches) was considered adequate.

---

4. Special Tax Treatment for the Press--

Minneapolis Star & Tribune Co. v. Minnesota Commissioner of Revenue, 460 U.S. 575 (1983).

Facts. Minnesota imposed a general sales tax and a related use tax (for items on which no sales tax had been paid). Publications were exempt from these taxes until 1971, when the state imposed a use tax on the cost of paper and ink products consumed in producing a publication. Three years later, the state exempted the first $100,000 of paper and ink used. As a result, the Minneapolis Star & Tribune Co. (P), one of 11 newspapers (out of 388 in the state) which had to pay a use tax, paid nearly two-thirds of all the use tax collected. P sued the Minnesota Commissioner of Revenue (D) for a refund. The state courts upheld the tax and P appeals.

Issue. May the states single out the press for special tax treatment?

Held. No. Judgment reversed.

- Other than the structure of the tax itself, there is no indication that the state imposed the tax with an impermissible or censorial motive. This case therefore differs from *Grosjean v. American Press Co.*, 297 U.S. 233 (1936), in which a publishing tax was held invalid because of improper government motive.

- Differential taxation of the press, unrelated to any special characteristic that requires such treatment, is unconstitutional. Such treatment suggests suppression of expression, a presumptively unconstitutional goal. In the absence of a compelling counterbalancing interest, differential taxation may not be allowed.

- D has no adequate justification for the tax. Even though the tax burden may be lighter than it would be under general application of the regular sales tax, differential treatment of any kind opens the door for more burdensome treatment.

- The tax also targets a small group of large newspapers, presenting an impermissible potential for abuse.

Dissent (Rehnquist, J.). This tax favors newspapers. It does not abridge the freedom of the press. D's scheme is rational because the large volume of inexpensive items involved (newspapers) makes the regular sales tax impractical.

Comments.

- In *Arkansas Writers' Project, Inc. v. Ragland*, 481 U.S. 221 (1987), the Court held that a state could not exempt from taxation newspapers and magazines that fell within the category of "religious, professional, trade, or sports journals." A magazine's tax status cannot depend on its content. However, it is permissible for a generally applicable tax to place different burdens on certain types of the media if the differences are not content-based and do not penalize particular speakers or particular ideas. [Leathers v. Medlock, 499 U.S. 439 (1991)—general sales tax exempted all media except cable TV; *see also* Turner II, *supra*]

- Note that laws of general applicability do not offend the First Amendment merely because enforcement against the press would incidentally affect its ability to gather and report news. [Cohen v. Cowles Media Co., 501 U.S. 663 (1991)—damages upheld against newspaper that breached its promise of confidentiality to a source]

---

5. **Regulation of Broadcast Media.**

   a. **Limited right of access.** For a discussion of the fairness doctrine, *see* Red Lion Broadcasting Co. v. FCC, *supra*. Note that the fairness doctrine was upheld in 1987.

   b. **No right to editorial advertisements.** In *Columbia Broadcasting System, Inc. v. Democratic National Committee*, 412 U.S. 94 (1973), the Court held that a broadcaster may refuse, as a general policy, to sell broadcast time to responsible parties for comment on public issues. The Court noted that in broadcasting, a system of self-appointed editorial commentators would require FCC determination of access on a case-by-case basis. This is less desirable than the present system of "public trustee" broadcasting. Thus, no broad right of access may be inferred from the *Red Lion* opinion.

   c. **Standard of review.** The standard of review in broadcasting cases was set forth in *FCC v. League of Women Voters*, *supra*. Regulation of the content of broadcasting will be sustained only when the restriction is narrowly tailored to further a substantial governmental interest, such as ensuring adequate and balanced coverage of public issues. Special features of broadcasting permit applying a standard lower than strict scrutiny.

d. **The Internet.** The rapid expansion of the Internet has presently many issues regarding free speech versus the proper extent of government regulation, *e.g.*, pornography, privacy. The first major test of government regulation occurred in *Reno v. American Civil Liberties Union*, *supra*, in which a federal law making it a crime to use any interactive computer service to send indecent or patently offensive messages to minors was invalidated because it effectively constituted a total ban on that content.

XIV. THE RELIGION CLAUSES: FREE EXERCISE AND ESTABLISHMENT

A. INTRODUCTION

The First Amendment provides that "Congress shall make no law respecting an establishment of religion or prohibiting the free exercise thereof." The Free Exercise Clause forbids Congress from putting restraints on the practice of religion other than reasonable limits as to time, place, and manner. The Establishment Clause "requires the state to be neutral in its relations with groups of religious believers and nonbelievers." The Fourteenth Amendment protects an individual from state infringement of his religious rights. In *United States v. Ballard*, 322 U.S. 78 (1944), the Court held that the First Amendment prohibits the submission to a jury of the truth of a party's religious beliefs. An influential review of the history of the religion clauses is found in *Everson v. Board of Education, infra*.

B. THE FREE EXERCISE OF RELIGION

The Free Exercise Clause absolutely prohibits any infringement on the freedom to believe. However, action (or inaction) undertaken because of religious beliefs is not absolutely protected, and may be regulated or prohibited by government if there is an important or compelling state interest. Generally, the clause protects against interference with the dissemination of religious beliefs as such, interference with the observance of religious practices, or discriminatory interference that favors one religion over another.

1. Laws Discriminating Against Religion.

a. **Introduction.** The government clearly cannot outlaw or compel belief in a particular religious faith. For example, a state may not require all public officials to declare their belief in the existence of God. [Torcaso v. Watkins, 367 U.S. 488 (1961)] In *McDaniel v. Paty*, 435 U.S. 618 (1978), the Court overturned a state constitutional provision that prohibited ministers from serving as state legislators. The Court noted that experience had shown that clergymen were not less faithful to their oaths of civil office than unordained legislators, and that, applying a balancing test, the restriction violated the Free Exercise Clause.

b. **Laws aimed at a particular religion--**

Church of the Lukumi Babalu Aye v. City of Hialeah, 508 U.S. 520 (1993).

Facts. The Church of the Lukumi Babalu Aye (P) announced plans to open a church in the city of Hialeah (D). P's religion involved animal sacrifice. D adopted a resolution that noted the concern by residents about certain religions, and subsequently adopted three ordinances that effectively prohibited religious animal sacrifice. P challenged the ordinances. The lower courts upheld the ordinances.

Issue. May a government prohibit certain religious practices if it does not restrict other conduct producing other harm of the same sort?

Held. No. Judgment reversed.

- The record demonstrates that the suppression of P's animal sacrifices was the object of the ordinances. D's ordinances do not prohibit animal killing generally, but only those killings that are for religious reasons. It thereby singles out religious practice for discriminatory treatment.

- A law burdening religious practice that is neither neutral nor of general application must survive the most rigorous of scrutiny. Even if D's interests had been compelling, the ordinances are overbroad or underinclusive. They prohibit only religiously motivated conduct, while leaving untouched the same conduct motivated by other reasons.

Concurrence (Scalia, J., Rehnquist, C.J.). The Court should not consider the subjective motivation of the lawmakers. If they had intended to prohibit P's religion, but failed to do so, the ordinances would not be invalid; alternatively, if these ordinances had been adopted out of a legitimate motive, they would still be invalid because of their effect on P.

---

c. Excluding the study of religion from public scholarships--

---

Locke v. Davey, 540 U.S. 712 (2004).

Facts. Davey (P) received a Promise Scholarship under a program funded by the state of Washington. Recipients were prohibited from using the scholarship at an institution where they would pursue a degree in devotional theology. P wanted to attend a private Christian college to become a church pastor. When P learned he could not use his scholarship to pursue his desired degree, he sued Locke (D), the Governor of Washington, for damages and injunctive relief. The district court granted D summary judgment. The Ninth Circuit reversed on the ground that D had singled out religion for unfavorable treatment, contrary to *Lukumi*. The Supreme Court granted certiorari.

Issue. May a state prohibit recipients of state-financed scholarships from using the money to pursue a degree in devotional theology?

Held. Yes. Judgment reversed.

- ♦ States may take actions that are permitted by the Establishment Clause but not required by the Free Exercise Clause. In this case, D could have permitted Promise Scholars to pursue a degree in devotional theology without violating the Establishment Clause.

- ♦ P claims that under *Lukumi*, D's program is presumptively unconstitutional because it is not facially neutral with respect to religion. But *Lukumi* involved sanctions on a type of religious service or rite, whereas D's scholarship program merely chooses not to fund a distinct category of instruction.

- ♦ Training someone to become a minister is an essentially religious endeavor and is distinct from other academic pursuits. D has a substantial interest in not establishing religion. States even included provisions in their constitutions to exclude the ministry from receiving state funding. D's scholarship program does allow attendance at religious schools and covers theology courses; it merely denies funding for vocational religious instruction. The difference between the two religion clauses is illustrated by this case.

Dissent (Scalia, Thomas, JJ.). D's exclusion of religion from a public benefit generally available violates the Free Exercise Clause as much as would a special tax on vocational religious instruction. No field of study but religion is singled out for disfavor. This is unlike a situation where a state would single out clergy to receive special benefits. D acted purely from a philosophical preference, and D's rationale could be extended to deny priests and nuns other generally available public benefits, including health benefits.

---

2. Neutral Laws Adversely Affecting Religion.

a. **Introduction.** The belief-action distinction arose in *Reynolds v. United States*, 98 U.S. 145 (1878), which upheld a law against bigamy aimed at stopping the practice of polygamy by Mormons. The Mormons practiced polygamy as a religious belief; the Court held that because polygamy was traditionally condemned, the practice could be outlawed. In *Cantwell v. Connecticut*, 310 U.S. 296 (1940), an action involving fund solicitation by a Jehovah's Witness, the Court modified the *Reynolds* ruling that religious conduct was outside the protection of the First Amendment. The Court found that the freedom to act, under the Free Exercise Clause, although not absolute like the freedom to believe, must be regulated without undue infringement of the freedom to believe. In *Braunfeld v. Brown*, 366 U.S. 599 (1961), the Court held that Sunday closing laws are constitutional, even if they make the practice of certain beliefs (such as those whose Sabbath is Saturday) more difficult.

b. ***Sherbert* approach to religious exemptions--**

Sherbert v. Verner, 374 U.S. 398 (1963).

Facts. South Carolina (through Verner (D)) denied unemployment compensation benefits to workers who failed to accept employment when offered, without good cause. Sherbert (P) was denied benefits because she failed to accept a job that required Saturday work. Her basis for refusal was her membership in the Seventh-Day Adventist Church, which recognized Saturday as the Sabbath day. The state courts upheld the denial of benefits; P appeals.

Issue. May a state deny benefits to otherwise eligible recipients whose failure to meet all the requirements is based on a religious belief?

Held. No. Judgment reversed.

- Conditioning the availability of benefits upon P's willingness to violate a cardinal principle of her religious faith effectively penalizes the free exercise of her constitutional liberties, and can only be justified by a compelling state interest.
- The only state interest lies in discouraging spurious claims, but D has failed to show that this possibility is significant or that no alternative, less damaging regulation exists.
- The result here reflects merely the governmental obligation of neutrality in the face of religious differences and does not promote or favor one religion over the other.

Concurrence (Stewart, J.). The Establishment Clause as previously construed by this Court requires denial of P's claim; otherwise the government would be establishing P's religion by granting her benefits because of her beliefs, while others, not of P's faith, are denied benefits. The decision proves that the Court has incorrectly construed that clause in prior cases. Additionally, we should specifically overrule *Braunfeld* here.

Dissent (Harlan, White, JJ.). The Court actually overrules *Braunfeld*, since the secular purpose of the statute here is even clearer than the one in that case. The Court goes too far in holding that a state must furnish unemployment benefits to one who is unavailable for work whenever the unavailability arises from the exercise of religious convictions.

c. **Compulsory education.** In *Wisconsin v. Yoder*, 406 U.S. 205 (1972), the Court ruled that a state's interest in universal education must be strictly scrutinized when it impinges on fundamental rights and interests, such as the right of free exercise. Yoder, an Amish parent, had refused to send his 15-year-old daughter to school beyond eighth grade, despite a Wisconsin law requiring attendance until age 16. The Amish claim that further education would violate their religious beliefs because the values taught in public high schools contrast with the Amish values and way of life. After Yoder was convicted and fined $5.00, his conviction was reversed by the Wisconsin Supreme Court, and the United States Supreme Court affirmed the reversal. The Court explained that the Amish way of life is an essential part of their religious beliefs and practices. Elementary education, given locally, did not subject Yoder's daughter to adverse influences, and was not challenged. However, it was adequately shown that secondary education would tend to severely infringe on the religious beliefs of the Amish. The Court reasoned that the state's interest in assuring education is substantially achieved in the elementary grades. The Amish children continue their education through parent-supervised agricultural vocational training and are thus fully prepared for responsibility. The Court found that the state's interest in requiring the one or two extra years of education was minimal compared with the religious interests of the Amish.

d. **Other denials of free exercise exemption claims between *Sherbert* and *Smith*.** An employer may be required to pay Social Security on his employees' wages despite objection based on religious belief. [United States v. Lee, 455 U.S. 252 (1982)] The IRS may deny tax-exempt status to religious schools that practice racial discrimination. [Bob Jones University v. United States, 461 U.S. 574 (1983)] Abandoning heightened scrutiny, the Court adopted a deferential approach in ruling valid a military regulation regarding uniform dress requirements, under which an Orthodox Jew was denied an exemption to wear a yarmulke while on duty at a military hospital. [Goldman v. Weinberger, 475 U.S. 503 (1986)] Similarly, deference was accorded to prison regulations relating to time and places of work that had the effect of preventing Muslims from attending a Friday midday service. [O'Lone v. Estate of Shabazz, 482 U.S. 342 (1987)] In *Bowen v. Roy*, 476 U.S. 693 (1986), the Court upheld a requirement that recipients of welfare benefits have social security numbers. And a challenge to a government road being built in a national forest area traditionally used by several Native American tribes for religious rituals was rejected in *Lyng v. Northwest Indian Cemetery Protective Association*, 485 U.S. 439 (1988).

e. ***Smith* approach to religious exemptions--**

Employment Division, Department of Human Resources v. Smith, 494 U.S. 872 (1990).

Facts. Oregon made it a crime to use peyote. Smith (P) was dismissed from his job for using peyote as part of his religious ritual as a member of the Native American Church. P was denied unemployment benefits because his dismissal was due to misconduct. P sued the Employment Division, Department of Human Resources (D), claiming that his use of peyote was inspired by religion and therefore was protected under the Free Exercise Clause. The Oregon Supreme Court reversed, holding that the criminal sanction was unconstitutional as applied to the religious use of peyote, and ruled that P was entitled to unemployment benefits. The Supreme Court granted certiorari.

Issue. May a state make criminal certain conduct that is part of a religious organization's ritual?

Held. Yes. Judgment reversed.

- P relies on *Sherbert*, which held that a state could not condition the availability of unemployment insurance on an applicant's willingness to forgo conduct required by her religion. In that case, however, the conduct was not prohibited by law; in this case, peyote use was prohibited by law.

- The states cannot ban acts or abstentions only when they are engaged in for religious reasons, or only because of the religious belief they display, because this would constitute a prohibition on the free exercise of religion. This does not mean that a religious motivation for illegal conduct exempts the actor from the law. If prohibiting the exercise of religion is merely an incidental effect of a generally applicable and otherwise valid law, the First Amendment is not implicated.

- In some cases, such as *Wisconsin v. Yoder*, the First Amendment may prevent application of a neutral, generally applicable law to religiously motivated action, but these cases involve the Free Exercise Clause in connection with other constitutional protections, such as parents' right to direct the education of their children.

- P argues that the *Sherbert* test should be applied, but this test has never invalidated governmental action except the denial of unemployment compensation, and should not be extended beyond that field to require exemptions from a generally applicable criminal law. In the unemployment cases, the test is applied to prevent a state from refusing to extend a system of individual exemptions to religious hardship cases.

- If the compelling interest requirement were applied to religion cases such as this, many laws would not satisfy the test, and the result would approach anarchy, particularly in a society such as ours that contains a diversity of religious beliefs. This alternative would raise a presumption of invalidity, as applied to the religious objector, of every regulation of conduct that does not protect an interest of the highest order. The states are free, as many have, to exempt from their drug laws the use of peyote in sacramental services, but the states are not constitutionally required to do so.

Concurrence in part (O'Connor, Brennan, Marshall, Blackmun, JJ.). A law that prohibits religiously motivated conduct implicates First Amendment concerns, even if it is generally applicable. The First Amendment does not distinguish between laws that are generally applicable and laws that target particular religious practices; it applies to generally applicable laws that have the effect of significantly burdening a religious practice. The balance between the First Amendment and the government's legitimate interest in regulating conduct is struck by applying the compelling interest test. To be sustained, a law that burdens the free exercise of religion must either be essential to accomplish an overriding governmental interest or represent the least restrictive means of achieving some compelling state interest. In this case, the prohibition on use of peyote satisfies the compelling state interest test.

Dissent (Blackmun, Brennan, Marshall, JJ.). The state's broad interest in fighting the war on drugs is not the interest involved in this case; the interest is the state's refusal to make an exception for the religious, ceremonial use of peyote. There is no evidence that the religious use of peyote ever harmed anyone, and 23 other states have adopted exemptions for the religious use of peyote. The assertion that requiring the state to make an exemption in this case would open the government to anarchy is speculative; such a danger is addressed through the compelling interest test.

C. THE ESTABLISHMENT CLAUSE

1. **Introduction.** There are three basic approaches to the Establishment Clause.

   a. **No-aid theory.** This view requires the government to do nothing that involves governmental support of religion, or which is favorable to the cultivation of religious interests. It leaves open the problem of the constitutionality of legislation with incidental impact on religion.

   b. **Neutrality theory.** This view requires the government to be neutral with respect to religious matters, doing nothing to either favor or hinder religion. This combines the no-aid test with a no-hinder test.

   c. **Balancing test.** This view assumes that it is impossible for the government to preclude all aid to religion, or to observe absolute neutrality. Governmental action must take into account the free exercise guarantee, and in some situations, the government must, and in others may, accommodate its policies and laws to further religious freedom. This is the most prevalent view.

2. ***Lemon* Test.** As applied to schools, the freedom of religion guarantee means that the state may not enact laws that either further the religious training or doctrines of any sect, or prevent any sect from carrying out its own religious training programs. The court has established a three-part test for determin-

ing the validity of statutes granting financial aid to church-related schools. [*See* Lemon v. Kurtzman, 403 U.S. 602 (1971)] To be upheld under the Establishment Clause, the law in question must:

a. Reflect a clearly secular purpose;

b. Have a primary effect that neither advances nor inhibits religion; and

c. Avoid excessive government entanglement with religion.

3. Establishing Official Beliefs.

a. Released time programs in public schools--

Zorach v. Clauson, 343 U.S. 306 (1952).

Facts. New York City established a "released time" program pursuant to which students whose parents so requested were permitted to leave the school grounds for religious instruction. Zorach and other parents whose children attended the New York public schools (Ps) challenged the program. The lower courts upheld it; Ps appeal.

Issue. May a state grant willing students permission to leave public school grounds during school hours to receive religious instruction elsewhere?

Held. Yes. Judgment affirmed.

- There is no evidence of coercion on the part of school officials. Only those students whose parents requested their release were permitted to participate.
- Although the First Amendment requires a separation of church and state, that separation is not absolute but well defined. Otherwise there would be hostility between the two, and religious groups would be unable to benefit from such basic services as fire and police protection.
- Clearly, students may be released from school to attend religious holidays or observances. This release time program is not different in character.
- Religion is an integral part of our society, and although the state may not coerce religious observance, it may make provision for those citizens desiring to retreat to a religious sanctuary for worship or instruction.

Dissent (Black, J.). The state, by manipulating its compulsory education laws to help religious sects get pupils, has combined church and state.

Dissent (Jackson, J.). The wall between church and state is now warped and twisted. Now the public schools act as temporary jails for students who do not attend religious school during the release time.

Comment. The Court distinguished this case from *McCollum v. Board of Education*, 333 U.S. 203 (1948), which invalidated a program permitting religious instructors to hold their classes in the public school classrooms.

---

b. **School prayer.** In *Engel v. Vitale*, 370 U.S. 421 (1962), the Court held that a state law that required daily recitation of a state-composed, nondenominational prayer in public schools violated the Establishment Clause. The Court has also held that selection and reading of verses from the Bible and daily recitation of the Lord's Prayer are religious activities and cannot be part of the curricular activities of public schools. [*See* School District of Abington Township v. Schempp, 374 U.S. 203 (1963)] The Court has also held that establishing a moment of silence for "meditation or voluntary prayer" demonstrated an unconstitutional attempt to encourage prayer in public schools. [Wallace v. Jaffree, 472 U.S. 38 (1985)]

c. **Prayer at graduation ceremonies--**

Lee v. Weisman, 505 U.S. 577 (1992).

Facts. Lee (D), the principal of a middle school, invited a rabbi to deliver prayers at a graduation exercise. He gave the rabbi a pamphlet containing guidelines that recommended public prayers be composed with "inclusiveness and sensitivity," and advised the rabbi that the prayers should be nonsectarian. Weisman (P), one of the students, objected to the prayers being part of the graduation ceremonies. The rabbi offered the prayers, which were nondenominational but did refer to and acknowledge God. P sued to enjoin school officials from inviting clergy members to deliver prayers at future graduations. The district court held that D's inclusion of prayers violated the Establishment Clause and granted the injunction because it violated the second *Lemon* test; *i.e.*, it did not have a primary effect that neither advances nor inhibits religion. The court of appeals affirmed. The Supreme Court granted certiorari.

Issue. May a public school invite members of the clergy to offer prayers at graduation ceremonies?

Held. No. Judgment affirmed.

- At a minimum, the Constitution guarantees that government may not coerce anyone to support or participate in religion or its exercise. In this case, D as a public official directed the performance of a formal religious exercise at a graduation ceremony for a public secondary school. Although attendance is not a condition for receipt of the diploma, students' attendance and participation is in a fair and real sense obligatory, even for students who object to the religious exercise. Including the prayer thus violated the Constitution.

- The government did not only decide to include a prayer and choose the clergyman, but D advised the rabbi about the content of the prayer. This means that D directed and controlled the content of the prayer. But the Establishment Clause does not allow the government to compose official prayers to be recited as part of a religious program carried on by the government. The fact that D acted in good faith does not make its participation in the content of the prayer permissible.

- Religious beliefs and religious expression are too precious to be either proscribed or prescribed by the government. The government cannot choose to compose a nonsectarian prayer, even if it were possible to devise one that would be acceptable to members of all faiths.

- The First Amendment protects speech and religion differently. Speech is protected by insuring its full expression even when the government participates, since some of the most important speech is directed at the government, but in religious debate or expression, the government is not a prime participant. The Free Exercise Clause is similar to the Free Speech Clause, but the Establishment Clause prevents the government from intervening in religious affairs, a prohibition with no counterpart in the speech provisions.

- Prayer exercises in public schools carry a particular risk of indirect coercion, particularly in the elementary and secondary public schools. Even at the graduation ceremony, there is pressure to stand and remain silent during the prayer, signifying a degree of adherence or assent. The government may not exact religious conformity from a student as the price of attending her own school graduation.

Concurrence (Blackmun, Stevens, O'Connor, JJ.). Under the Establishment Clause, the government may neither promote nor affiliate itself with any religious doctrine or organization, nor intrude into the internal affairs of any religious institution. In *Engel v. Vitale* (*supra*), the Court held for the first time that a prayer selected by school officials could not be recited in a public school, even though it was "denominationally neutral." In *School District of Abington Township v. Schempp* (*supra*), the Court held unconstitutional a public school's opening exercises that consisted of a reading from the Bible or a recitation of the Lord's Prayer. The prayers offered at the graduation ceremonies in this case are likewise prohibited by the Constitution. Even if no one is forced to participate, mixing government and religion threatens free government because it conveys a message of exclusion to all who do not adhere to the favored belief.

Concurrence (Souter, Stevens, O'Connor, JJ.). The Establishment Clause is just as applicable to governmental acts favoring religion generally as it is to acts favoring one religion over others. In *Wallace v. Jaffree* (*supra*), a moment-of-silence statute was invalidated, even though it did not encourage students to pray to any particular deity, because it was intended to return voluntary prayer to public schools. In fact, the framers of the Bill of Rights deleted references to "a religion," and "a national religion" in favor of a prohibition on state support to "religion" in general. At any rate, the courts are not in a position to determine what, if any, practices are ecumenical enough to satisfy the Establishment Clause. And it is not necessary to show coercion to prove a violation of the Establishment Clause. While the government must remain neutral in religious matters, nothing prevents it from ever taking religion into account by accommodating the free exercise of religion. But such accommodation must lift a discernible burden on free exercise. Students at P's school who see spiritual significance in their graduation are not burdened by excluding prayer; they may simply conduct their own private-sponsored exercises accompanied by like-minded students.

Dissent (Scalia, J., Rehnquist, C.J., White, Thomas, JJ.). The meaning of the Establishment Clause must be determined by reference to historical practices and understandings. Yet the majority ignores history in its holding. The tradition of invocations and benedictions at graduation ceremonies is as old as the ceremonies themselves. Even the Declaration of Independence appeals to "the Supreme Judge of the world," and relies on the "protection of divine Providence." Presidents, beginning with George Washington, have included prayer in their official acts. The Court's test of psychological coercion is boundless and boundlessly manipulable, and is based on facts that are not true in any relevant sense. Even if students were coerced to stand, which they were not, such an act does not establish a "participation" in a religious exercise, any more than standing for the Pledge of Allegiance moments earlier constituted coerced approval of the political message it contains. The Establishment Clause was aimed at coercion of religious orthodoxy and financial support by force of law and threat of penalty, but P in this case faced no threat of penalty or discipline. This situation is entirely different from daily prayers in classroom settings where parents are not present, which could raise concerns about state interference with the liberty of parents to direct the religious upbringing of their children. The Constitution must have deep foundations in the historic practices of our people, not the changeable philosophical predilections of the Justices of the Court.

---

d. **Prayer at school functions.** In *Santa Fe Independent School District v. Doe*, 530 U.S. 290 (2000), the Court held that a public school district may not allow student-led, student-initiated prayer at high school football games. The school district had adopted a policy that authorized two student elections, the first to determine whether "invocations" should be delivered at games, and the second to select the spokesperson to deliver them. The Court explained that by subjecting the issue of prayer to a majoritarian vote, the district established a governmental mechanism that turned the public school into a forum for religious debate and empowered the majority of students to subject students of minority views to constitutionally improper messages. The school district claimed that

Lee, *supra*, did not apply because the district's policy resulted in messages that were private student speech, not public speech. However, the Court found that the delivery of a message such as the invocation in this case—on school property, at school-sponsored events, over the school's public address system, by a speaker representing the student body, under the supervision of school faculty, and pursuant to a school policy that explicitly and implicitly encourages public prayer—was not properly characterized as "private" speech. Also, the Court pointed out that while attendance at a football game may be voluntary for many students, for others, such as cheerleaders, band members, and team members, it may be part of their class requirements. And there is also great social pressure on students to attend. The Court declared that students cannot be forced to decide whether to attend or risk facing a personally offensive religious ritual.

e. **Religious curriculum generally.** In *Stone v. Graham*, 449 U.S. 39 (1980), the Court held that a law requiring the posting of copies of the Ten Commandments from the Bible in public schoolrooms clearly had no secular legislative purpose, even though the law required a statement on the copies explaining a secular application of the Commandments as the basis of the common law. In *Epperson v. Arkansas*, 383 U.S. 97 (1968), the Court held that a statute making it unlawful to teach evolution in state-supported schools violated the Establishment Clause, because the clear purpose of the law was religious.

f. **Requirement to teach creationism--**

Edwards v. Aguillard, 482 U.S. 578 (1987).

Facts. Louisiana enacted a law requiring "balanced treatment" of the theories of creation and evolution if the subject of the origin of man, life, the Earth, or the universe was dealt with in public schools. Neither theory could be taught without the other, although neither had to be taught, and both were statutorily defined as science. The lower courts held that the law was unconstitutional because the theory of creation is a religious belief. The Supreme Court granted certiorari.

Issue. May a state require its public schools to teach creation science if they teach evolution?

Held. No. Judgment affirmed.

- The first requirement under *Lemon* is that a statute must have been adopted with a secular purpose. The legislature here purportedly adopted this statute to protect academic freedom, but the public school teachers were not prohibited from teaching any particular scientific theory before the statute was adopted anyway. The legislative history indicates the statute was intended to eliminate the teaching of evolution, and the statute protects creationism and its proponents without protecting evolutionists.

- ♦ There is a well-known antagonism between the teachings of certain religions and the teaching of evolution. The clear purpose of the statute was to advance the religious viewpoint by restructuring the science curriculum. This does not mean that a variety of scientific theories may not be taught, but only that this act violated the Establishment Clause because it was intended to endorse a particular religious doctrine.

Concurrence (Powell, O'Connor, JJ.). The Establishment Clause only prohibits the use of religious teachings in public schools when the purpose of their use is to advance a particular religious belief, not when the purpose is a better understanding of culture, history, and so forth.

Dissent (Scalia, J., Rehnquist, C.J.). So long as there was a genuine secular purpose, the act should not be invalidated. The secular purpose set forth in the act should not be dismissed. In addition, the *Lemon* test is not based on the language of the Establishment Clause and leads to unpredictable decisions. The purpose test should be abandoned.

---

g. **Religious activity and secular law.**

1) **Sunday closing law.** While originally Sunday closing laws were motivated by religious forces, the Court has held that the laws have lost their religious flavor. The Court also recognized a secular state interest in promoting a uniform day of rest. The fact that the effect was the same as if the law were motivated by religious reasons is irrelevant. Thus, in *McGowan v. Maryland*, 366 U.S. 420 (1961), the Court upheld a Sunday closing law, reasoning that the appellants suffered only economic damage, and suffered no infringement of their religious liberties.

2) **Legislative prayer.** State legislatures may open legislative days with a prayer by a state-employed chaplain. [Marsh v. Chambers, 463 U.S. 783 (1983)]

4. **Public Displays of Religious Symbols Outside the Schools.**

a. **Government sponsorship of Christmas display--**

Lynch v. Donnelly, 465 U.S. 668 (1984).

Facts. The city of Pawtucket, Rhode Island, annually erected a Christmas display that included Santa Claus and related figures, colored lights, and a creche, or nativity scene, containing the Infant Jesus, Mary, Joseph, and other traditional figures. Donnelly and other citizens (Ps) brought suit in federal court against Lynch and other city officials (Ds) to have the creche removed. The district court enjoined Ds from including the creche in the display and the court of appeals affirmed. The Supreme Court granted certiorari.

Issue. May a city include a nativity scene in its annual Christmas display?

Held. Yes. Judgment reversed.

- The First Amendment is intended to prevent the intrusion of either the church or the state upon the other, but total separation is not possible. Some relationship between the two must exist. The Constitution requires accommodation of all religions.

- The same week that Congress approved the Establishment Clause as part of the Bill of Rights, it provided for itself paid chaplains. The role of religion in American life has been officially acknowledged in numerous ways. For example, the government subsidizes holidays with religious significance, such as Christmas and Thanksgiving, by giving its employees paid time off.

- Under *Lemon*, the display of the creche has a valid secular purpose—to celebrate the holiday and to depict the origins of that holiday. Its inclusion in Ds' display has less effect on advancing religion than do other types of government accommodation of religion, including providing textbooks to religion-sponsored schools and tax exemptions for church properties. Nor does the minimal cost cause excessive entanglement between religion and government.

Concurrence (O'Connor, J.). The Establishment Clause prohibits government from making adherence to a religion relevant to a person's standing in the political community. Excessive entanglement with religious institutions and government endorsement or disapproval of religion violates this principle. Ds' creche display falls within neither category of government activity.

Dissent (Brennan, Marshall, Blackmun, Stevens, JJ.). Ds' display constitutes an impermissible governmental endorsement of a particular faith. The display does not satisfy the *Lemon* test. It excludes non-Christians on religious grounds. Christmas has both secular and religious aspects, and the government should not emphasize the religious aspects. The inclusion of a creche serves no secular purpose that could not be achieved absent the creche.

Dissent (Blackmun, Stevens, JJ.). The Court abandons precedent with its holding. Furthermore, the holding encourages misuse of a sacred religious message.

Comment. In an attempt to further refine its approach, the Court prohibited a free-standing nativity scene at a county courthouse, but permitted a display that included a

Jewish Chanukah menorah with a Christmas tree and a sign celebrating liberty. The focus was on whether the display "endorsed" religion. [*See* Allegheny County v. Greater Pittsburgh ACLU, *infra*]

b. **Limitations on religious displays on government property.** In *Allegheny County v. ACLU,* 492 U.S. 573 (1989), the Court held that a county could not allow a crèche, standing alone, in the county courthouse. The Court applied a "no endorsement" analysis and found that the display of the crèche could give the appearance that the government was promoting or affiliating with a religious doctrine or organization.

c. **Unattended religious symbol on public forum.** In *Capitol Square Review & Advisory Board v. Pinette*, 515 U.S. 753 (1995), the Court allowed the Ku Klux Klan to erect a cross on a public square where other unattended displays had been permitted, including a state-sponsored lighted tree during Christmas and a privately-sponsored menorah during Chanukah. The Court held that the state did not sponsor the expression, which was made on government property open to the public for speech. A plurality held that there was no endorsement of religion, but three Justices believed there could be an endorsement where the government operates a public forum.

d. **Purpose of Ten Commandments display--**

McCreary County v. ACLU of Kentucky, 545 U.S. 844 (2005).

Facts. McCreary County and Pulaski County (Ds) installed framed copies of the Ten Commandments, taken from the King James version of the Bible, in their county courthouses. The ACLU of Kentucky sued Ds to enjoin the displays. Ds adopted resolutions stating that the Ten Commandments were the precedent legal code upon which the codes of Kentucky were founded. The district court ordered the displays to be removed. Ds then installed displays that contained the Ten Commandments along with the Magna Carta, Declaration of Independence, and other historic documents. The district court extended its injunction to this display. The Supreme Court granted certiorari.

Issue. May the government display the Ten Commandments as part of a display of historic documents if its purpose is to advance religion?

Held. No. Judgment affirmed.

♦ When the government acts with the predominant purpose of advancing religion, it violates the central Establishment Clause value of official religious neutrality. Ds assert that the purpose test of *Lemon*, *supra*, should be abandoned, or at least not applied in this case. Ds argue that, because true purpose is unknowable, the purpose test allows courts to act selectively and unpredictably in picking out evidence of subjective intent. But in an Establishment Clause analysis, the courts evaluate official objectives based on readily discoverable facts.

- ♦ In the first display in this case, as in the display rejected in *Stone v. Graham*, *supra*, the text of the Commandments was not part of a secular display. *Stone* stressed the importance of integrating the Commandments into a secular scheme to avoid an otherwise clearly religious message.

- ♦ Each D authorized a second display, which was accompanied by religious references, showed that Ds were posting the Commandments because of their sectarian content, and included the resolution's claim about the embodiment of ethics in Christ, disclosing an impermissible purpose.

- ♦ When Ds put up their third displays, the "Foundations of American Law and Government" exhibit, Ds placed the Commandments along with other documents they considered significant in the historical foundation of American government. However Ds did not repeal nor repudiate the resolutions of the former displays. In fact, the third displays quoted more of the Commandment's purely religious language than the first two displays had done.

- ♦ We do not hold that a sacred text can never be integrated constitutionally into a governmental display on the subject of law or American history. But purpose must be taken seriously under the Establishment Clause and must be understood in light of context.

- ♦ The framers' views on the Establishment Clause were varied, and there was no common understanding about the limits of the Establishment Clause. But the divisiveness of religion in public life is clear. The government must stay neutral on religious belief.

Concurrence (O'Connor, J.). The history of Ds' displays demonstrates that the purpose was religious. The framers knew that line-drawing between religions is an enterprise that, once begun, has no logical stopping point. The Religions Clauses protect adherents of all religions, as well as those who believe in no religion at all.

Dissent (Scalia, J., Rehnquist, C.J., Thomas, Kennedy, JJ.). Our nation has a long tradition of recognizing God. Even the day after Congress proposed the First Amendment, Congress asked the President to proclaim a day of thanksgiving and prayer, acknowledging the many favors of God. Hence, government can favor religion over irreligion, as the First Amendment itself does by giving religion, and no other manner of belief, special constitutional protection. The *Lemon* test has been manipulated to fit whatever result the Court has aimed to achieve. Today the Court sets forth an "objective observer" test of intent, so that even with proof that a government did not have the purpose of advancing religion, its actions could be held unconstitutional. The Court holds that a secular purpose must predominate over any purpose to advance religion. Even under the Court's *Lemon*-based premises, Ds displays were constitutional because the Ten Commandments were put in context as part of a larger display that showed their unique contribution to the development of the legal system.

---

e. Monument of Ten Commandments with secular purpose--

Van Orden v. Perry, 545 U.S. 677 (2005).

Facts. The grounds of the Texas State Capitol contained 17 monuments and 21 historical markers, including a six-feet high monolith inscribed with the text of the Ten Commandments. The monument was provided by the Fraternal Order of Eagles, a private, civic organization. Van Orden (P) sued state officials, seeking a declaration that the monument's placement on these grounds violated the First Amendment. The district court entered judgment for the state, and the court of appeals affirmed. The Supreme Court granted certiorari.

Issue. May a state include a monument inscribed with the Ten Commandments on the grounds of its state capitol along with numerous other monuments and markers commemorating the people, ideals, and events related to the state?

Held. Yes. Judgment affirmed.

- Our institutions presuppose a Supreme Being, but they cannot press religious observances upon their citizens. Government can look to the past and acknowledge our nation's heritage and also look to the present and demand a separation of church and state. We should not demonstrate hostility toward religion by ignoring our religious heritage.

- The *Lemon* test does not help decide a challenge to a passive monument such as the one in this case. The monolith acknowledges the role played by the Ten Commandments in our nation's heritage. There are similar displays inside the courtroom of the Supreme Court and many other places. Moses was a lawgiver as well as a religious leader. In this context, the monolith also has dual significance and does not violate the Establishment Clause.

Concurrence (Scalia, J.). There is nothing unconstitutional about a state favoring religion generally, such as by honoring God through public prayer and acknowledgment or venerating the Ten Commandments in a nonproselytizing manner.

Concurrence (Thomas, J.). The Establishment Clause should not be applied to restrain the states. Even if it is, it should only apply to an actual "establishment" in the sense that it would prohibit legal coercion. Texas does not compel P to do anything.

Concurrence (Breyer, J.). This is a borderline case that turns on the context of the display. The placement of this monument suggests that the state intended the nonreligious aspects of the tablets' message to predominate.

Dissent (Stevens, Ginsburg, JJ.). The sole function of this monument is to display one version of the Ten Commandments. It is not a work of art and does not refer to any event in the state's history. It only communicates the message of the Ten Commandments and transmits the message that the state endorses the divine code of the Judeo-Christian God. The speeches of the founders reflect the personal views of the speakers, not the official policy of the government. They should not be relied on.

Dissent (O'Connor, J.). My concurrence in *McCreary County* also applies here.

Dissent (Souter, Stevens, Ginsburg, JJ.). The display in this case is obviously religious and is unlike neutral displays where Moses is placed in the framework of a lawgiver. There is no common denominator among the displays on the Texas grounds; each memorial stands on its own terms. The message of this monument is that God is the source of Jewish and Christian morality.

---

5. Public Financial Aid to Religious Institutions.

a. *Everson* approach--

Everson v. Board of Education, 330 U.S. 1 (1947).

Facts. A local New Jersey Board of Education (D) authorized reimbursement to parents of the costs of using the public transportation system to send their children to school, whether public or parochial. Everson (P) challenged the scheme as an unconstitutional exercise of state power in support of church schools. P appeals adverse lower court decisions.

Issue. May a state use public funds to assist student transportation to parochial as well as public schools?

Held. Yes. Judgment affirmed.

- ♦ The Establishment Clause was intended to erect a wall between church and state. It does not prohibit a state from extending its general benefits to all its citizens without regard to their religious belief. Reimbursement of transportation is intended solely to help children arrive safely at school, regardless of their religion. It does not support any schools, parochial or public.

- ♦ To invalidate D's system would handicap religion, which is no more permissible than favoring religion.

Dissent (Jackson, Frankfurter, JJ.). The Court's rationale contradicts its conclusion.

Dissent (Rutledge, Frankfurter, Jackson, Burton, JJ.). The Court should be as strict to prohibit use of public funds to aid religious schools as P is to prevent introduction of religious education into public schools.

---

b. Aid to parochial education.

1) Tax deduction for tuition permitted--

Mueller v. Allen, 463 U.S. 388 (1983).

Facts. Minnesota allowed state income taxpayers to deduct the costs of their children's tuition, physical education clothing, supplies, and other items. The deduction applied regardless of whether the school was public or private. Most private schools in the state were sectarian. Allen (P) challenged the statute under the Establishment Clause. The state courts upheld the deduction. The Supreme Court granted certiorari.

Issue. May a state permit parents to deduct from their income tax the cost of their children's education, including tuition paid to private sectarian schools?

Held. Yes. Judgment affirmed.

- The deduction is limited to actual expenses incurred for the tuition, textbooks, and transportation of dependents attending elementary or secondary schools. The validity of the deduction depends on application of the three-part *Lemon* test.
- The tax deduction has a secular purpose because it promotes education in all types of schools. The statute does not have the primary effect of advancing the sectarian aims of nonpublic schools because it is part of a broader scheme of tax deductions, it is available to all parents, and whatever aid it provides to parochial schools is available only through the decisions of individual parents. Thus there is no imprimatur of state approval. Finally, the statute does not excessively entangle the state in religion, because the only state involvement is the determination as to which textbooks qualify for a deduction (the cost of religious books is not deductible).
- Because the three-part test is satisfied, the deduction does not violate the Establishment Clause.

Dissent (Marshall, Brennan, Blackmun, Stevens, JJ.). The Establishment Clause prohibits state subsidies to sectarian schools, including deductions for tuition payments.

Aid to sectarian schools must be restricted so it is not used to further the religious mission of those schools. This tax deduction scheme is not so restricted, so it is unconstitutional.

---

2) **Remedial, guidance, and job counseling services.** A neutral government program for "auxiliary services" to ***all*** disadvantaged children—***including those students attending parochial schools*** —with public school personnel providing such things as remedial instruction and guidance counseling, is valid. The presence of public employees in parochial schools does not automatically mean that they will inculcate religion or constitute a symbolic union between religion and government. [Agostini v. Felton, *infra*, *overruling* Aguilar v. Felton, 473 U.S. 402 (1985)] *Agostini* also called into question the continued validity of one aspect of *Aguilar's* companion case, *Grand Rapids School District v. Ball*, 473 U.S. 373 (1985), which invalidated a "Shared Time" program similar to the one in *Aguilar*. Still intact is the other part of *Grand Rapids*, invalidating a program paying a portion of private school ***teachers' salaries*** (for their secular classes), since the primary effect would be to advance religion, and a system to ensure that the money/teachers not be used for religious purposes would involve excessive entanglements.

3) **Higher education.** The Court tends to find the three-part *Lemon* test satisfied more often in cases involving higher education than in those involving elementary and secondary schools. In *Tilton v. Richardson*, 403 U.S. 672 (1971), the Court permitted federal grants to finance construction at church-related colleges under certain conditions. *Tilton* was extended further in *Roemer v. Maryland Public Works Board*, 426 U.S. 736 (1976), with approval of annual, noncategorical grants to eligible private colleges, restricted only in that the funds not be used for sectarian purposes.

c. **Assimilation.**

1) **Use of state university's facilities.** The three-part test of *Lemon* was successfully used in *Widmar v. Vincent*, 454 U.S. 263 (1981), to invalidate a state university's ban against religious groups using its buildings. The university opened its facilities to student groups in general, except religious groups. The Court held that this violated the First Amendment rights of the religious groups; a fully open-forum policy could satisfy the three-part Establishment Clause test because it would have a secular purpose, avoid entanglement, and would not have a primary effect of advancing re-

ligion. [*See also* Walz v. Tax Commission, 397 U.S. 664 (1970)—state tax exemption for religious, educational, or charitable purposes is valid]

2) **Other educational grants.** In *Bowen v. Kendrick*, 487 U.S. 589 (1988), the Court rejected a facial challenge to federal grants to public and nonpublic organizations, including those with religious affiliation, for counseling services regarding adolescent sexual activity and pregnancy. The law had a secular purpose and did not involve excessive government entanglement with religion. Any effect of advancing religion was incidental and remote. However, the case was remanded for factfinding regarding the law as applied. Similarly, vocation rehabilitation aid to a visually handicapped student who attended a sectarian school in order to become a pastor [Witters v. Washington Department of Services for the Blind, 474 U.S. 481 (1986)] and provision of a publicly funded sign language interpreter to a deaf student in a parochial school [Zobrest v. Catalina Foothills School District, 509 U.S. 1 (1993)] were not violative of the Establishment Clause.

3) **Printing costs of student publication.** In *Rosenberger v. Rector and Visitors of University of Virginia*, *supra*, the Court pointed out that it does not violate the Establishment Clause if a public university grants access to its facilities on a religion neutral basis to student groups that use meeting rooms for sectarian activities, along with some devotional exercises, even where the upkeep of those facilities is paid from a student activity fund to which students are required to contribute. The Court reasoned that a public university may also give student groups access to the university's computer facility, including the use of the printers, on a religion neutral basis. The Court found no difference in logic or constitutional significance between a school using its funds to operate a facility to which students have access and a school paying a third-party contractor to operate the facility on its behalf. Thus, the Court held that a public university may not deny reimbursement to a student newspaper solely on the ground that the newspaper expresses a religious viewpoint.

4) **Remedial instruction in parochial schools.** In *Agostini v. Felton*, 521 U.S. 203 (1997), the Court held that a federally funded program providing supplemental, remedial instruction to disadvantaged children on a neutral basis is not invalid when such instruction is given on the premises of sectarian schools. The Court noted that earlier cases were based on the assumption that the mere placement of public employees on parochial school grounds inevitably resulted in impermissible state-sponsored indoctrination or a sym-

bolic union between government and religion. This assumption had already been abandoned when *Agostini* was decided.

5) **Publicly funded educational materials.** *Mitchell v. Helms*, 530 U.S. 793 (2000), involved a program that provided publicly funded educational materials, such as computers, to public and private schools, including parochial schools. In upholding the program, the Court explained that any indoctrination that occurred at the school could not reasonably be attributed to governmental action. To determine whether indoctrination was attributable to the government, the Court applied the neutrality principle—aid that is offered to a broad range of groups or persons without regard to their religion is permitted.

6) **Publicly financed school choice--**

Zelman v. Simmons-Harris, 536 U.S. 639 (2002).

Facts. The state of Ohio adopted a pilot program that gave financial assistance to families living in any Ohio school district that was under a federal court order to be supervised by the state education superintendent, Zelman (D). The Cleveland City School District, which included 75,000 children, was the only district in that category. The children in the Cleveland district were mostly from low-income and minority families. The pilot program provided tuition aid for students to attend a participating public or private school chosen by their parents instead of the one they would otherwise be assigned to. Any private school, religious or nonreligious, could participate in the program, but the school had to agree not to discriminate on the basis of race, religion or ethnic background. Forty-six of the fifty-six participating private schools had a religious affiliation, and 96% of the students who participated in the program attended the religious schools. Simmons-Harris and other taxpayers (Ps) sought an injunction against the program. The district court granted Ps summary judgment. The Court of Appeals affirmed. The Supreme Court granted certiorari.

Issue. May a state provide tuition vouchers that enable students who would otherwise attend public schools to attend private religious schools?

Held. Yes. Judgment reversed.

♦ The state had a valid secular purpose for adopting the program—to provide educational assistance to poor children in a demonstrably failing public school system. The program would violate the Establishment Clause only if it has the forbidden "effect" of advancing or inhibiting religion.

♦ There is a clear distinction between government programs that provide aid directly to religious schools and programs that allow, through the exercise of true private choice, for government aid going to religious schools. In *Mueller*, *Witters*, and *Zobrest*, the Court has upheld neutral government programs that provided aid directly to individuals who, through their own choice, directed the aid to religious schools.

- Funding programs based on choice might lead to the incidental advancement of a religious message, but that advancement is attributable to the individual recipient who makes the choice, not to the government. Ohio's program does not give rise to any reasonable inference that the government is endorsing religious schools in general.

- The program in this case actually gives more aid to participating public schools than it gives to private schools. Families who send their children to private schools must co-pay a portion of the school's tuition.

- The dissent notes that 96% of the children in private schools are enrolled in religious schools, but when all children enrolled in nontraditional schools are counted, that percentage drops to 20%. The program is neutral with respect to religion.

Concurrence (O'Connor, J.). The Court's decision today follows precedent. Although a significant portion of the funds appropriated for the program reach religious schools with no restriction on the use of the funds, the total amount of $8.2 million that flows to religious schools in one year is small compared with the amount provided to religious institutions at all levels of government through tax credits and exemptions and other public benefit programs. The main point is that the parents are free to have their children attend either nonreligious or religious private schools.

Concurrence (Thomas, J.). Ohio's program is a response to an educational emergency that deprived the inner-city children of the opportunity for a good education. The Fourteenth Amendment was adopted to guarantee individual liberty and should not be used to prohibit the exercise of educational choice.

Dissent (Souter, Stevens, Ginsburg, Breyer, JJ.). Ohio's program allows the government to pay tuition at private religious schools to support the schools' religious missions. In *Everson*, the Court held that no tax may be levied to support any religious activities or institutions. Ohio's program allows tax money to be used to teach religious doctrines in these schools. The Court is ignoring *Everson*. The fact that over 96% of the students attending private schools are in religious schools, and that most families did not choose the schools because of the religion taught there, demonstrate that the problem is a lack of sufficient nonreligious schools. Parents' choices are actually restricted to choosing which religious school to send their children to.

---

6. Accommodation of Religion.

a. **Accommodation and delegation.** Government cannot delegate its power to veto applications for liquor licenses to establishments within 500 feet of a church (or school) because such action fails the advancing religion and excessive entanglement prongs of the *Lemon* test. [Larkin v. Grendel's Den, Inc., 459 U.S. 116 (1982)]

b. **Cannot require Sabbath recognition.** A statute requiring employers to provide one day a week off for an employee's Sabbath impermissibly advances the religious practices of certain groups. [Estate of Thornton v. Caldor, 472 U.S. 703 (1985)]

c. **Employment discrimination permitted.** In *Corporation of Presiding Bishop v. Amos*, 483 U.S. 327 (1987), Congress provided that an antidiscrimination provision of Title VII does not apply to religious corporations in the employment of persons of a particular religion to perform work in connection with carrying on the corporation's activities. The Court found that the exemption was in no way questionable under *Lemon*.

d. **Sales tax exemption.** In *Texas Monthly v. Bullock*, 489 U.S. 1 (1989), the Court held that a statute exempting religious publications from a state sales tax was unconstitutional. The exemption had insufficient breadth of coverage; it did not apply to nonreligious publications that contributed to the community's cultural, intellectual, and moral betterment. Hence, it constituted an unjustifiable award of assistance to religious organizations and conveyed a message of endorsement. The dissent argued that breadth of coverage was not relevant unless the state asserted purely secular grounds for the exemption. When religion was singled out, particularly for an exemption from a tax that could be construed as an unconstitutional burden on religion, the exemption should be construed as an accommodation.

e. **Equal access for students.** Three years after *Widmar v. Vincent*, *supra*, the right of equal access for secondary students to meet for religious purposes on school premises during non-school hours was ruled valid. Access was accorded to both secular and religious speech. [Board of Education v. Mergens, 496 U.S. 226 (1990)]

f. **Religious gerrymandering.** *Board of Education of Kiryas Joel v. Grumet*, 512 U.S. 687 (1994), involved the creation of a separate public school district to accommodate a religious community. The practitioners of a strict form of Judaism, Satmar Hasidim, sought to avoid assimilation into the modern world and educated their children in private religious schools. These schools did not provide any distinctive services to handicapped children. Such services were provided by the public school district that included the Satmar village, until the Court decided in *Aguilar v. Felton* (*supra*) that such arrangements were unconstitutional. In *Grumet*, the Court ruled that, by creating the separate school district, the state had delegated civic power to the district's voters, instead of specifically to religious authorities or only to adherents of a particular religion. But in the context of this case, the recipients of governmental authority were in effect determined by reference to doctrinal adherence. The Court held that a state may not create a separate school district having boundaries that are determined by the boundaries of a village inhabited exclusively by a distinct religious group.

TABLE OF CASES

(Page numbers of briefed cases in bold)

NOTES

NOTES

NOTES

NOTES

NOTES

NOTES